THE F.
OF THE CHURCH

A NEW TRANSLATION

VOLUME 9

THE FATHERS
OF THE CHURCH

A NEW TRANSLATION

SAINT BASIL

ASCETICAL WORKS

Translated by
SISTER M. MONICA WAGNER, C. S. C.

The Catholic University of America Press
Washington 17, D. C.
1962

INTRODUCTION

WHATEVER MAY HAVE BEEN the factors responsible for the marked ebullience of the ascetical movement in the Church during the fourth century, the impulse to withdraw from society and enter a life of rigorous austerity in deserts or mountain fastnesses was widely experienced and it constitutes a dominant spiritual phenomenon of the age. An incident casually introduced by St. Augustine in the eighth book of his *Confessions* illustrates the far-reaching and impetuous force of this ascetical urge. During a conversation in Milan with Augustine and Alypius, Ponticianus, a fellow African and an imperial court official, recalls the marvels of the life of St. Anthony of Egypt and his followers. Amazed to find his hosts quite unacquainted with the history of so renowned a personage and ignorant as well of the fact that a populous monastery under the care of Bishop Ambrose was established just outside Milan, Ponticianus enlarges upon his theme to relate an instance of a sudden call to the monastic life which had been experienced by two of his colleagues. Upon merely reading the life of St. Anthony which they had come upon by chance during an afternoon's stroll, both men were so profoundly affected and so transformed inwardly that they determined to embrace then and there the monastic life, without even a final return to the imperial palace. Both, as it happened, were betrothed and their fiancées, upon hearing of their resolve, also consecrated their lives to God.

Such was the environmental context in which providentially appeared and matured the masterful spirit of St. Basil the Great. His family background and his own inborn tendencies were, besides, admirably suited to the spirit of his age. Among the nine surviving children born to the staunchly Christian and socially prominent Basil (father of the saint) and Emmelia, there were three bishops, a monk, and a nun, Macrina, the eldest of the five daughters who became one of the most remarkable women of the fourth century. In her later years Emmelia, herself eminently holy, yielded to the persuasion of Macrina and gave up the comforts and privileges of her rank to live in a manner similar to that of her maids. Subsequently, when the family property has been divided among the children the widowed Emmelia, Macrina, the youngest son, Peter, the family servants, and a number of other highborn women of Cappadocia and Pontus took up a retired life under a strict monastic regime in the ancestral home on the banks of the Iris opposite St. Basil's Pontic retreat.

On this family estate at Annesi near Neo-Caesarea, St. Basil had received his first instruction in religion from his paternal grandmother, Macrina. Earlier, Macrina had been a disciple of St. Gregory Thaumaturgos and a fugitive with her husband, a wealthy landholder and a devout Christian, from the persecution of Maximian. To his father, a prominent member of the bar in Caesarea and also a teacher of rhetoric, Basil owed his introduction to liberal studies and to that broad culture which later distinguished him. His subsequent training in Caesarea, the literary as well as the civil capital of Central Asia Minor, won him a local reputation for excellence in rhetoric and philosophy. More advanced study followed at Constantinople and finally at Athens, now only a little provincial city but an intellectual and academic metropolis.

During his sojourn in Athens, St. Basil and his famous inseparable friend, St. Gregory of Nazianzus, had often planned the monastic retreat which they promised each other one day to share. In 358, this dream was realized in the forest solitude on the banks of the Iris, where Basil and Gregory collaborated over the *Philocalia,* a compilation of selected excerpts from Origen, and also in the drawing up of some monastic rules. Between the close of his university career in Athens in about 355 and his first retirement to the hermitage on the Iris, Basil had enjoyed a short but brilliant career as a teacher of rhetoric in Neo-Caesarea. His instinctive yearning for the monastic life, however, supported by the urging of his sister, Macrina, who feared (and with some reason according to St. Gregory of Nyssa) the effect of worldly success upon her gifted brother, led him to renounce his professional career and, after receiving Baptism, to dedicate himself thenceforward to God. In Epistle 223, we have Saint Basil's own account of his 'conversion':[1]

'Having lavished much time on the vanity and having consumed almost all my youth in the futility, which were mine while I occupied myself with the acquirement of the precepts of that wisdom made foolish by God, when one day arising as from a deep sleep I looked out upon the marvelous light of the truth of the Gospel, and beheld the uselessness of the wisdom "of the princes of this world that come to nought," bemoaning much my piteous life, I prayed that there be given me a guidance to the introduction to the teachings of religion. And before all things my care was to make some amendment in my character, which had for a long time been perverted by association with the wicked. And accordingly, having read the Gospel and having perceived therein that the greatest incentive to perfection is the selling of one's goods and the sharing of them with the needy of the brethren, and the being entirely without thought of this life, and that the soul should

---

1 The following excerpt is from the translation by Roy J. Deferrari, *Saint Basil, The Letters* III (Loeb Classical Library, London and New York 1930).

have no sympathetic concern with the things of this world, I prayed that I might find some one of the brethren who had taken this way of life, so as to traverse with him this life's brief flood.

'And indeed I found many men in Alexandria and many throughout the rest of Egypt, and others in Palestine and in Coele-Syria and Mesopotamia, at whose continence in living I marvelled, and I marvelled at their steadfastness in sufferings, I was amazed at their vigour in prayers, at how they gained the mastery over sleep, being bowed down by no necessity of nature, ever preserving exalted and unshackled the purpose of their soul, in hunger and thirst, in cold and nakedness, not concerning themselves with the body, nor deigning to waste a thought upon it; but as if passing their lives in alien flesh, they showed in deed what it is to sojourn here below, and what to have citizenship in heaven. Having marvelled at all this and deeming the lives of these men blessed, because by deed they show that they bear about in their body the mortification of Jesus, I prayed that I myself also, in so far as was attainable by me, might be an emulator of these men.'

St. Basil's journey in search of a guide in the way of the monastic life took him to Egypt as an obvious main objective. Here the Christian Church was eminent both for orthodoxy and asceticism and here also was to be found the cradle of Christian eremetical or semi-eremetical life in its two lines of development: the Antonian and Pachomian systems. The first originated in the life and example of the Coptic solitary, St. Anthony, who, in spite of himself, attracted numerous disciples. Colonies of such hermits spread throughout Egypt and the East, but even the largest settlements remained essentially eremetical. The system of Pachomius, a younger contemporary of Anthony, while it also involved an element of voluntary, individual effort, especially as regards personal interior life, in its external framework it represents the earliest systematic effort toward a corporate and stable monasticism. Pachomian coenobitism, considerably corrected and modified, was the model of the monastic system propagated by St. Basil. After something over a year spent in Eastern travel, Basil returned home to take up his own life of ascetical rigor in his Pontic solitude. Here he would realize his monastic ideals in a daily round of prayer, study, and agricultural labors. The disciples who flocked to Basil when he had settled in his retreat had not been directly inspired by his personal influence, however, although his prestige undoubtedly gave exceptional persuasiveness to his example. Monasteries had already been established in Pontus as well as in Roman Armenia and Paphlagonia by Eustathius of Sebaste, who was St. Basil's master in the ascetical life and his intimate friend until a breach on doctrinal grounds permanently ruptured the intimacy. Precisely how much Basil owed to his predecessor in the development of his monastic ideals is difficult to assess, but it is undeniable that his influence was of capital importance in the formation of St. Basil's ascetical doctrine and even in the practical organization of his monasteries. It was probably at the advice of Eustathius that he undertook his extensive Eastern travels and at his return he placed himself under the direction of the Bishop of Sebaste.

Perhaps it may safely be asserted that the creation of true coenobitical monachism, receptive of both sexes and all classes, was substantially the work of St. Basil. Such features as the common house, the common table, prayer in common, all of which became constant and permanent in Western monasticism, may be considered original with him in the sense that he regulated and systematized these elements. The Antonian colony and the Pachomian coeobium became under Basil's system a true society. Original also is the note of moderation, deriving, perhaps, from St. Basil's Greek sense of proportion, which marks his development and modification of the Pachomian regime. He prescribes monasteries of moderate size in contrast to the sprawling Pachomian aggregates. He insists upon a reasonable standard of corporal austerity, outlawing thus the spectacular rivalries in ascetical rigor which characterized Egyptian asceticism. Private fasts might not be undertaken by his monks without the superior's permission, on the principle that self-will is quite as likely to find expression in this matter as in any other. But, although corporal mortifications are controlled by explicit prescription, the Rule of St. Basil is uncompromisingly stringent as compared, for instance, with that of Pachomius in the matter of monastic detachment. The renunciation of relatives and the leading of the common life so dominated the entire existence of the early Basilian monk that it constituted in itself no mean penitential exercise. A new strictness was also attached by St. Basil to the obligations assumed by the monk or nun. With him, as Clarke has shown, the monastic profession involved a permanent and irrevocable vow. Even as regards bodily austerities, St. Basil's references to pallor and leanness as proper attributes of the Christian monk warn us against interpreting the moderation counseled by him according to Western contemporary standards. There is, furthermore, a marked strain of Stoic rigorism in St. Basil's insistence upon the extreme gravity of sin to the extent that he does not recognize degrees of heinousness—all sin is equally serious—and also in his stern demand for the renunciation of all fleshly pleasures. On the other hand, while St. Basil strongly insists upon obedience 'even unto death,' the superior does not have absolute power; but his acts are subject to certain limitations and he may and should be admonished when necessary by a select group of elder brethren. Obedience, moreover, is not only a matter of compliance with formal precepts but an ideal inspiring all of life both physical and spiritual, affecting the interior of the soul as well as imposing certain external checks.

Sanctity, furthermore, according to St. Basil's view, is social in character. Love of God and neighbor find full expression only in community life where all cooperate in their efforts toward perfection. For instance, spiritual direction is insisted upon as an obligation. The social ideal of St. Basil is further illustrated by his minute prescriptions as to regular hours for common prayer, as to the quantity and quality of food and clothing and numerous other details regarding life and conduct. This enthusiasm for the principle of the common life rests upon his conviction that a life of seclusion from one's fellow men offers no scope for the practice of humility and obedience and is plainly opposed to the law of charity. Further, he declared that life in common followed the apostolic precedent and illustrated that corporate fellowship which St. Paul represents under the figure of the body and its members. The Scriptures, it must be added, are the firm basis of Basil's entire monastic doctrine. He continually adduces Scriptural support for his ascetical teachings and their application.

Because of the paramount obligation of charity toward one's fellow man, Basilian coenobia are established in towns instead of in desert wastes. The monks dwell in the midst of their secular brethren so as by their conduct to provide them with a model for true Christian living. The external works of the monastic life are to be undertaken not only as corporal discipline but from the love of neighbor, that his needs may be provided for; yet the tasks undertaken must not be of the sort that would interfere with or distract from the ordered tranquility of the monastic life. Labor in Basil's view is essential and obligatory and must be, above all, unselfish. As for prayer, even the true Christian—and most especially the monk —is insistently urged to pray so constantly and continuously that prayer will become a spontaneous habit of mind.

But works of philanthropy, no more than the life in common, were to be regarded as an end in themselves. All acts of benevolence toward fellow men, as well as the entire mechanism of monastic discipline—work, silence, mortification—had one end in view to which all these were to be duly subordinated as means. This end was union with God. Self-renunciation as practically achieved through a life of physical and mental discipline in a monastic community and works of active charity toward fellow men are inevitable corollaries to the love of God. The systematic formulation of this great conception which is the guiding principle of modern Western coenobitism is the essential contribution of St. Basil of Caesarea. Thus, St. Basil has become, in the words of Theodoret of Cyrus, 'the light not only of Cappadocia but of the whole world.' St. Benedict, the 'Father of Western Monasticism,' knew and used the Rule of St. Basil in the Latin translation of Rufinus and, apart from certain borrowings from Cassian in matters of detail, depends more heavily upon St. Basil than upon any other monastic legislator. To this day, moreover, the fundamental concept of Greek and Slavonic monasticism continues to be the conception of St. Basil. His single name and personality has welded all Eastern monastic communities together under the common title, 'Basilian,' even though it must be admitted that the monastic traditions established by the Bishop of Caesarea are preserved in the East mainly in their external framework.

WRITINGS
OF
SAINT BASIL

VOLUME 1

CONTENTS

PREFATORY NOTE

Of the ascetical works traditionally ascribed to Saint Basil of Caesarea, this volume contains a translation of the following:

Three short treatises, seemingly addressed to ascetics, comprising exhortations to the monastic life and ascetical recommendations and prescriptions on certain matters of behavior in community life. Two additional tracts, placed after the *Morals,* are of similar content, with greater emphasis on detail.

The *Morals* or *Ethics,* with its double prologue, the treatise, *On the Judgment of God* and *Concerning Faith.* The *Morals* consists of eighty precepts or rules, some with subdivisions, based upon the teachings of the Gospel. In general, the work appears to be directed to the Christian laity, but particular sections are concerned with the duties and needs of monks and of clergy living in the world.

The *Long Rules,* with its preface. The fifty-five chapters or instructions of the *Long Rules,* mostly in the form of questions and answers, deal with specifically monastic problems.

Concerning Baptism. Although they do not form a part of the *Ascetica* proper, the two books, *Concerning Baptism,* have been added because of their moral and ascetical content. Similarly, selected homilies on ethico-ascetical themes attributed to St. Basil are included.

The Migne reprint of the Benedictine edition was used as the text and the Scriptural passages follow the Douay-Rheims translation.

SELECT BIBLIOGRAPHY

Texts:

Amand, Dom David, *L'Ascèse Monastique de Saint Basile, Essai Historique* (Maredsous 1949).

Bardy, Gustave, 'Basile (Saint), évêque de Césarée de Cappadoce,' *Dictionnaire de spiritualité ascétique et mystique* (Paris 1937), 1:1273-1283; 2:1276-1283.

Clarke, W. K. Lowther, *St. Basil the Great. A Study in Monasticism* (Cambridge, Eng. 1913).

Humbertclaude, Pierre, *La Doctrine Ascétique de Saint Basile de Césarée* (Paris 1932).

Morison, E. F., *St. Basil and His Rule. A Study in Early Monasticism* (Oxford 1912).

Murphy, Sister Margaret Gertrude, *St. Basil and Monasticism* (Washington 1930).

SAINT BASIL
ASCETICAL WORKS

Translated

by

SISTER M. MONICA WAGNER, C. S. C.
Dunbarton College of the Holy Cross

AN INTRODUCTION TO THE ASCETICAL LIFE

NOBLE ARE THE ORDINANCES decreed by a king for his ordinary subjects, but nobler and more regal are the commands he addresses to his soldiers. As if military orders are being proclaimed, therefore, let that man give ear who desires what is of great and celestial worth, who wishes to be ever Christ's comrade in battle, who heeds that mighty word: 'If any man minister to me, let him follow me; and where I am, there also shall my minister be.'[1] Where is Christ, the King? In heaven, to be sure. Thither it behooves you, soldier [of Christ], to direct your course. Forget all earthly delights. A soldier does not build a house; he does not aspire to the possession of lands; he does not concern himself with devious, coin-purveying trade. 'No man, being a soldier to God, entangleth himself with secular businesses; that he may please him to whom he hath engaged himself.'[2] The soldier enjoys a sustenance provided by the king; he need not furnish his own, nor vex himself in this regard. By royal edict, a home lies open to him wherever there are subjects of the king. He is not required to toil at building a house. On the open road is his tent and he takes his food as necessity demands; water is his drink, and his slumber such as nature provides. Many are his marches and vigils; his endurance of heat and cold, engagements with the foe, the worst and greatest of perils; often, perchance, death itself—but a glorious death followed by rewards and a king's gifts. His life is

---

1 John 12.26.
2 2 Tim. 2.4.

9

toilsome in war; in peace it is joyous. The prize of valor, the crown awarded to him who has lived nobly in righteousness, is to be endowed with sovereignty, to be called the King's friend, to stand at His side, to receive His salutation, to accept honors from the King's own hand, to be eminent among the King's people, and to play the mediator for his friends without the court in whatever they desire.

Come, then, soldier of Christ, with the aid of these ordinary parallels drawn from human considerations conceive the desire of everlasting goods. Set before yourself a life without house, homeland, or possessions. Be free and at liberty from all worldly cares, lest desire of a wife or anxiety for a child fetter you. In the celestial warfare this cannot be, 'For the weapons of our warfare are not carnal, but mighty to God.'[3] Bodily nature does not exercise dominion over you, nor does it constrain you against your will; it does not make you slave instead of free. Desire not to leave behind you progeny upon the earth, but to lead them to heaven; nor to cleave to fleshly unions, but to strive after spiritual ones—to exercise power over souls and beget sons in the spirit. Follow the Heavenly Bridegroom; withstand the onset of invisible foes; wage war against principalities and powers,[4] driving them out first from your own soul that they may have no part with you and, thereafter, out of those who fly to you and, seeking the protection of your counsel, cast themselves at your feet as their leader and champion. Repudiate those disputes which are opposed to the faith of Christ. Fight with the word of piety against the impious and wicked counsel; 'destroying counsels,' as the Apostle says, 'and every height that exalteth itself against the knowledge of God.'[5] Place your trust, most

3 2 Cor. 10.4.
4 Eph. 6.12.
5 2 Cor. 10.4-5.

of all, in the arm of the great King, the mere beholding of which makes His enemies fear and tremble. But whenever He wills that you also become holy through the endurance of perils and wishes to pit His own forces against the foe, then, in every struggle let your arms be invincible, your soul undaunted by danger, and with ready will change your abode from land to land and from sea to sea. 'And when they shall persecute you, flee from city to city,' says the Evangelist.[6] When you are summoned to court and must stand, perforce, before the magistrates or be a victim of popular attack; when you are forced to behold the dread visage of the executioner and hear his harsh voice, or endure the cruel sight of instruments of torment, or be tried by torture—fight even to the death. Be not faint-hearted in the face of all these sufferings. Keep before your eyes Him who for your sake was afflicted by them, knowing that for the sake of Christ you also must be tried therein, and you will be victorious over them; for you follow a King who is a victor, and who wishes you to share in His victory. Moreover, not even if you die have you been conquered—nay, then, in truth, have you won the perfect victory, inasmuch as you have preserved unto your own self and even to the end the truth which remains ever unchanged and you have maintained an intrepid boldness in speaking on behalf of the truth.

From death you shall pass to everlasting life, from ignominy in men's sight to glory with God, and from the adversities and chastisements of this world to eternal peace with the angels. Earth did not accept you as a citizen, but heaven will welcome you. The world persecuted you, but the angels will bear you aloft to the presence of Christ. You will even be called friend by Him and will hear the longed-for word

---

6 Matt. 10.23.

of commendation: 'Well done, good and faithful servant, brave soldier and imitator of the Lord, follower of the King, I shall reward you with My own gifts and I shall pay heed to your words even as you did to Mine.' You will ask the salvation of your brethren still laboring under tribulation and you will receive from the King for your comrades in the faith and in holy charity a share in His blessings. You will join in the never-ending dance and wear your crown in the sight of the angels, ruling under the King over His creatures and living blessedly in the company of the blessed. But if He wish to leave you still on earth after your conflicts in order to wage other and more diversified kinds of warfare and rescue many from contests with visible and invisible foes, great will be your glory even upon earth; you will be held in honor by your friends who will have found in you a defender, a friend in need, and an able spokesman. They will cherish you as a brave soldier; they will honor you as a noble champion; they will salute you as a friend and welcome you with joy as an angel of God and, according to Paul, as Christ Jesus.[7] Such, then, are the similitudes of the spiritual warfare. But our discourse is not addressed to men only; for members of the female sex are not rejected because of physical weakness, but, chosen for the army of Christ by reason of their virility of spirit, they also battle on the side of Christ and fight no less valiantly than men. Some even win a greater renown. Of the number of these are they who compose the virgin throng. Of these are they who are pre-eminent in the combat for the confession of the faith and in the triumphs of martyrdom. Indeed, women as well as men followed after the Lord during His life on earth and both sexes ministered to our Saviour. Since this is the glorious recompense laid up for the army of

Women are in the Army of Christ

7 Gal. 4.14.

Christ, the fathers of sons and the mothers of daughters should be filled with longing for it. Let them, in their desire to have worthy envoys and spokesmen with Christ, bring before Him their offspring, rejoicing in the everlasting hopes which their children will share in with themselves. And let us not become faint-hearted in our concern for our children nor grow fearful if they suffer tribulation, but let us be happy that they will be glorified. Let us offer to the Lord the gifts received from Him, so that we may be partners with our children in glory, going before Him together with them and standing with them in His presence. Certainly, to those who show an alacrity such as this and who nobly contend for the victory, the words of the Psalmist may be appropriately applied: 'Blessed be you of the Lord, who made heaven and earth.'[8] And the prayer of Moses will be offered for them: 'Bless, O Lord, their works, strike the brow of their enemies.'[9] Fight manfully, then, like good soldiers and run nobly your race for the everlasting crown[10] in Christ Jesus, our Lord, to whom be glory for ever. Amen.

---

8 Ps. 113.15.
9 Deut. 33.11.
10 1 Cor. 9.24,25.

AN ASCETICAL DISCOURSE AND EXHORTATION ON THE RENUNCIATION OF THE WORLD AND SPIRITUAL PERFECTION

'COME TO ME, all you that labor and are burdened and I will refresh you,'[1] says the Divine Voice, signifying either earthly or heavenly refreshment. In either case, He calls us to Himself, inviting us, on the one hand, to cast off the burden of riches by distributing to the poor, and, on the other, to make haste to embrace the cross-bearing life of the monks by ridding ourselves through confession and good works of the load of sins contracted by our use of worldly goods. How truly admirable and happy, then, is he who has chosen to heed Christ and hastens to take up the life of lowliness and recollection! But, I beseech you, let no man do this thoughtlessly nor promise himself an easy existence and salvation without a struggle. He should, rather, undergo rigorous preliminary discipline with a view to proving his fitness to endure tribulations both of body and soul, lest, exposing himself to unforeseen stratagems, he be unable to resist the assaults against him and find himself in full retreat to his starting point, a victim of disgrace and ridicule. Moreover, in returning to the world with a judgment of condemnation on his soul, he becomes a scandal to many, creating in the minds of all suspicions that the life in Christ is an impossibility—and of the perils of such an eventuality all you are aware who read the Gospels in which the Divine Voice says: 'It were

---

1 Matt. 11.28.

15

better for him that a mill-stone should be hanged about his
neck and that he be cast into the sea than that he scandalize
one of these little ones.'[2] For not only will he be liable to condemnation as a deserter, but he will be responsible also for
the ruin of those who are undone by his defection, even if
he pretend to convince himself by foolish arguments that he
will propitiate the Divinity by a life of good works in the
world—an impossibility for him. If he is not strong enough
to bear the blows of his adversary in a state of life where occasions of sin are remote because of greater retirement, how
will he be able to perform any virtuous actions in a state which
is openly exposed to evil and in which he is his own master?
Even assuming that he direct his personal life properly, he will
not escape the reproach of abandoning Christ any more than
did those disciples mentioned in the Gospel, concerning whom
the inspired writer says: 'Many of the disciples went back,
and walked no more with Jesus, saying, "His saying is hard,
and who can hear it?" '[3] For this reason, also, the benevolent
God, solicitous for our salvation, ordained two states of life
for men—marriage and virginity—that he who is not able to
endure the hardships of virginity might have recourse to the
married state, realizing, however, that he will be required to
give an account of his sobriety and holiness and of his resemblance to the saints who passed their lives in the married state
and in the rearing of children. Such a one was Abraham in
the Old Testament, who, in sacrificing his only son without
showing grief, gained great glory by thus preferring God
before all. Moreover, he kept the doors of his tent open and
ready to receive those who were in quest of hospitality,[4] for
he had not heard the counsel, 'Sell what thou hast and give

---

2 Matt. 18.6.
3 John 6.67,61.
4 Gen 18.1,2.

to the poor.'[5] Job, also, and a host of others—David and Samuel, for instance—bore even greater testimony. In the New Testament, Peter is an example and also the other Apostles. Every man, indeed, will be asked for the fruits of his love of God and neighbor and he will pay the penalty for his violation of these as well as of all the commandments, as the Lord declares in the Gospel, saying: 'He that loveth father or mother more than me is not worthy of me'[6] and 'Whoever does not hate his father and mother and wife and children, yea, and his own life, also, he cannot be my disciple.'[7]

Does it not seem to you, then, that the Gospel applies to married persons also? Surely, it has been made clear that obedience to the Gospel is required of all of us, both married and celibate. The man who enters the married state may well be satisfied in obtaining pardon for his incontinency and desire of a wife and marital existence, but the rest of these precepts are obligatory for all alike and are fraught with peril for transgressors. Christ, when He preached the commands of His Father, was speaking to persons living in the world; He clearly testified this by His answer on one occasion when He was privately questioned by His disciples: 'And what I say to you, I say to all.'[8] Do not relax your efforts, therefore, you who have chosen the companionship of a wife, as if you were at liberty to embrace worldliness. Indeed, you have need of greater labors and vigilance for the gaining of your salvation, inasmuch as you have elected to dwell in the midst of the toils and in the very stronghold of rebellious powers, and night and day all your senses are impelled toward desire of the allurements to sin which are before your eyes.

5 Matt. 19.21.
6 Matt. 10.37.
7 Luke 14.26.
8 Mark 13.37.

Be assured, then, that you will not escape doing battle with the Renegade nor will you gain the victory over him without much striving to observe the evangelical doctrines. How will you, stationed in the very thick of the battle, be able to win the contest against the Enemy? That he wanders over all the earth under heaven and ranges about like a mad dog seeking whom he may devour,[9] we learn from the history of Job. If, then, you refuse battle with your Antagonist, betake yourself to another world where he is not; then, avoidance of conflict with him will be possible for you, as well as relaxation without peril to evangelical doctrines. But, if this cannot be, make haste to learn how to fight with him, taking instruction from the Scriptures in the art of conflict, that you may not be defeated through your ignorance and consigned to everlasting fire.

These counsels should be given casually, as it were, to persons living in the married state who are not dangerously negligent in observing Christ's precepts. But, you who aspire to become a lover of the celestial polity, an active participant in the angelical life, and a fellow soldier of Christ's holy disciples, brace yourself for the endurance of tribulations and manfully betake yourself to the company of the monks. Even in the beginning of your renunciation of the world show yourself a man, and, that you may not be dragged down by attachments to your blood relatives, strengthen yourself by exchanging mortal for immortal aspirations. Furthermore, when you make renouncement of the goods you possess, be adamant in your resolve, convinced that you are merely dispatching these goods to heaven in advance; for, although you are hiding them in the bosom of the lowly, you will find them again with God, greatly increased. Moreover, be not

9 1 Pet. 5.8.

cast down at having divested yourself of friends and relatives.
since you are thereby united with Christ who was crucified
for you; and what greater proof of love could be conceived
of than this?[10] And when, with God's help, you will have
gained victory over your Enemy in this first onset, do not be
careless of yourself as if you were a useless vessel—for, indeed, by the renouncement of earthly goods you have won
honor with Christ—but with much care and forethought set
about finding a man skilled in guiding those who are making
their way toward God who will be an unerring director of
your life. He should be adorned with virtues, bearing witness
by his own works to his love for God, conversant with the
Holy Scripture, recollected, free from avarice, a good, quiet
man, tranquil, pleasing to God, a lover of the poor, mild, forgiving, laboring hard for the spiritual advancement of his
clients, without vainglory or arrogance, impervious to flattery, not given to vacillation, and preferring God to all things
else. If you should find such a one, surrender yourself to him,
completely renouncing and casting aside your own will, that
you may be found a clean vessel, preserving unto your praise
and glory the good qualities deposited in you. For, if you
suffer any of your former vices to remain within you, those
virtues that were placed in you will become contaminated and
you will be cast out like a vessel unfit for use.

And now we shall consider the second contest against the
Enemy of our salvation. Good masters teach good doctrine,
but that taught by evil masters is wholly evil. Whenever,
therefore, our wicked Adversary is not able to prevail upon
us to remain amid the tumult and perdition of the world, he
endeavors to persuade us not to devote ourselves to a life of
discipline or surrender ourselves to a man who will place all

10 John 15.13.

our sins before our eyes and correct them. On the contrary, he urges us toward one who is bent on popularity and who puts a favorable light on his own vices under the pretext of indulgence to his associates, so that, when he has thus imperceptibly increased our vices a thousandfold, he may cause us to be fettered by chains of sin we ourselves have forged. But, if you place yourself in the hands of a man rich in virtue, you will become the heir of the good qualities he possesses and you will be supremely blessed with God and men. On the other hand, if, to spare the body, you seek a master who will condescend or, rather, degrade himself to the level of your vices, all in vain did you endure the struggle of renunciation, since you have surrendered yourself to a life of gratifying your passions by choosing a blind guide who will lead you into the pit; 'for if the blind lead the blind, both fall into the pit.'[11] 'It is enough for the disciple that he be as his master.'[12] This is the voice of God and it shall not be falsified.[13] You must live in accordance with the rules of the contest; if you do not, you will not be crowned, as the Apostle says: 'He also that striveth for the mastery is not crowned except he strive lawfully.'[14]

If, then, with the grace of God, you find a teacher of good works (for if you really seek, you will find[15]) keep a watch over yourself so as to do nothing against his will; for whatever is done without his consent is, as it were, a piece of thievery and a sacrilege leading not to your profit but to your ruin, however good it may seem to you. For, if it be good, why is it done secretly and not in the open? Challenge your reason which, by specious assurances, is contriving, to make a robber of you; by misrepresenting the good, it disposes you to evil.

---

11 Matt. 15.14.
12 Matt. 10.25.
13 Matt. 24.35.
14 2 Tim. 2.5.
15 Matt. 7.7.

Do not undertake to chant as an expert would the incantations pronounced over persons who have been bitten by serpents, inexperienced as you are in the art of weaving spells, lest, perhaps, having attracted the reptiles and being caught fast in their coils, you become powerless to resist them and they destroy you mercilessly. Do not rely upon noble birth in a fleshly sense or seek worldly fame, 'for the sensual man perceiveth not the things that are of the Spirit.'[16] Do not attempt to undermine true and established custom, thereby becoming, through your own laxity, a stumbling block to those who are themselves striving for the mastery. Do not accumulate a heavy burden of sins for yourself by having too soft a bed or by the style of your garments, or shoes, or any other part of your dress; by variety in food, or a table too richly appointed for your stage of self-renunciation, by the way you stand or sit, or by being too negligent or too fastidious with regard to manual labor. All these things bring harmful results not only if they already exist in your life, but even if they are objects of your desire. Indeed, unless you quickly recognize them as a diabolical snare and root them out of your heart, they will lead you to defection from the life in Christ. On the contrary, having the inner conviction that you are the most ignominious of men and the worst of sinners, a stranger and a vagrant, received out of compassion by those who renounced the world before you, strive eagerly to be the last of all and the servant of all. This latter course, not the former, will bring you honor and true glory. With your ears opened to give heed and your hands ready to execute the command you have heard, let your tongue be silent and keep your heart under custody. Be slow and dull for idle talk, but knowing and wise in hearkening to the saving words of the

16 1 Cor. 2.14.

Holy Scriptures. Let the hearing of worldly tales be to you as a bitter taste in your mouth, but the discourse of holy men as a honeycomb.[17] Be eager to imitate men of disciplined habits and do not wait to be taught each thing. Strive to attain to the greater virtues, but do not neglect the lesser ones. Do not make light of a fall even if it be the most venial of faults; rather, be quick to repair it by repentance, although many others may commit a large number of faults, slight and grievous, and remain unrepentant. Judge not the sins of others, for they have a just Judge 'who will render to every man according to his works';[18] but be master of what is your own and lighten your own burden insofar as you have the power, for he who increases his own burden will also carry it. In repentance is salvation, but folly[19] is the death of repentance.

Hide yourself from the frivolous, but appear before God as often as possible. To avoid dissipation of the heart, refrain as much as you can from going abroad at all. Have you deserted your cell? Then you have left continency behind you; you have lowered your gaze toward the world; you have fallen in with a harlot who, charming your ears with her provocative words, your eyes with the beauty of her countenance, and your appetite with dainty viands, will draw you to herself as with a hook. Then, when you are clasped in a mutual embrace, she will weaken the firmness of your desire for continency and after thus drawing you away little by little from the life of virtue she will be the cause of your utter ruin. Even if by some means and with God's help you are enabled to escape the snares of this harlot, you will return to your cell, indeed; yet not as the same person, but as one enervated,

17 Prov. 16.24.   *Temptations drag down*
18 Rom. 2.6.
19 *anoia* for *agnoia?* Cf. *PG.* 31.636 n. 90.

sickened, and peevishly disinclined to all virtuous action—and only after a long period of time will you be able to return to your own proper dispositions. Your longing after the other state of life will cause you anguish of mind, and only at the cost of much distress will you be enabled to concede the prize of victory to your soul. If, then, it should happen that circumstances force you to leave your cell and go abroad, arm yourself with the breastplate of the fear of God, clasp in your hand the love of Christ, and repulse with all continency the attacks of sensual pleasure. As soon as your business is completed, take your departure without delay and return on swift wing like a guileless dove going back to the ark which sent you forth,[20] bearing the mercies of Christ on your lips, thus silencing interior protests and persuading yourself that saving tranquility cannot be secured in any other place.

If you are youthful in body or mind, fly from intimate association with comrades of your own age and run away from them as from fire. The Enemy has, indeed, set many aflame through such means and consigned them to the eternal fire, casting them down into that loathsome pit of the five cities[21] on the pretext of spiritual love. Even those who have come safely through every wind and tempest on the sea and are safe in port he has sent down into the deep, together with the ship and crew. At meals take a seat far away from your young brother; in lying down to rest, let not your garments be neighbor to his; rather, have an elderly brother lying between you. When a young brother converses with you or is opposite you in choir, make your response with your head bowed lest, perchance, by gazing fixedly into his face, the seed of desire be implanted in you by the wicked Sower and you reap sheaves

20 Gen. 8.9.
21 Gen. 10.19; Deut. 29.23.

of corruption and ruin. At home or in a place where there is no witness of your actions, be not found in his company under the pretext of meditation on the Divine Words or for any other excuse, even the most urgent need; nothing is of greater urgency than the soul for whom Christ died. Do not believe the crafty argument which suggests to you that this is a quite harmless thing to do, but be fully convinced, by the oft-repeated experience of those who have fallen and have clearly demonstrated it to be so, that it is of itself an offensive act.

Believe these words of mine which proceed from the fraternal charity of my heart. Have recourse to older men who make themselves difficult of access and in no way harm the young by their charm of countenance, but animate them to virtuous deeds by sayings from Proverbs. 'With all watchfulness, keep thy heart';[22] for, like golden treasure, it is the object of the constant vigilance of thieves, night and day, and in an unguarded moment it is stolen without your being aware of it. See that the Adversary does not seduce you into the sin of our first parent and cast you with all speed out of the paradise of delight. He who lured Adam from the life in paradise by causing him to steal food[23] and expected to catch even Jesus off His guard[24] will be far bolder in preparing as a drink for you this first cause of evil, knowing that it is a strong poison. The vice of gluttony is wont to display its proper force not with regard to a great quantity of food, but in the appetite for a little taste. If, therefore, desire of some bit of food succeed in making you subject to the vice of gluttony, he will give you up to destruction without further ado. For, as the nature of water that is channeled along

---

22 Prov. 4.23.
23 Gen. 3.1-6.
24 Matt. 4.3.

many furrows causes it to make verdant the whole area around the furrows, so also the vice of gluttony, if it issue from your heart, irrigates all your senses, raising a forest of evils within you and making your soul a lair of wild beasts. I have seen many who were slaves to vice restored to health, but I have not seen this happen in the case of even one person who was given to nibbling in secret or gluttonous. Either they abandon the life of continency and are destroyed by the world, or they attempt to remain undetected among the continent and fight in league with the Devil by leading a luxurious life. They are liars, profane, perjurors, quarrelsome, pugnacious, noisy, given to disavowing their gluttony, mean, effeminate, querulous, prying, lovers of darkness, and deliberately hostile to every virtuous mode of life; in their efforts to cover up the vice of gluttony they are caught in a swarm of evils. In appearance, indeed, they seem to be among the number of the saved, but by their conduct they are included with the reprobate.

This vice of gluttony delivered Adam up to death; by the pleasure of the appetite consummate evil was brought into the world. Through it Noah was mocked,[25] Cham was cursed,[26] Esau was deprived of his birthright and married into a Canaanite family.[27] Lot became both his own son-in-law and father-in-law, by marrying his own daughters; the father was husband, and the grandfather, father—thus making a double mockery of the laws of nature.[28] Gluttony, also, made the people of Israel worshipers of idols and strewed the desert with their bodies.[29] Gluttony caused a certain

25 Gen. 9.21..
26 Gen. 9.25.
27 Gen. 25.33; 36.2.
28 Gen. 19.35.
29 Num. 14.29ff.

Prophet, sent by God to upbraid an impious king, to become
the prey of a wild beast, and him upon whom King Jereboam
with all his royal might could not wreak vengeance was taken
captive by his treacherous appetite and fell victim to a miserable death.[30] Daniel, however, the man of desires, having
gained the mastery over his appetite,[31] had complete dominion
over the kingdom of the Chaldeans—he overthrew their idols,
destroyed the dragon, tamed the lions, heralded the Incarnation, and interpreted hidden mysteries.[32] The three holy
youths who showed themselves superior to the pleasures of
the appetite scorned a king's wrath and braved with intrepid
courage the horrors of that fiery furnace which King Nabuch-
odonoser had ordered to be lighted.[33] They proved the gold-
en statue worshiped as a god to be of no avail and, taking
as spoils the idol erected by Satan[34] and standing for so long
a time as an outrage to the glory of God, they brought it as
an offering to their own Lord. At their instigation, too, that
most wicked king himself and the whole army drawn up
against God came to sing His praises, together with all creation. To sum it all up, if you gain the mastery over your
appetite, you will dwell in paradise; if you do not, you will
die the death.

Be a safe treasure house of virtue and keep as its key the
tongue of your spiritual father. Let this open your mouth for
the taking of bread and let this also close it. Do not admit the
Serpent as your counselor, since he desires to take you captive in return for his good advice. Be on your guard against
the sin of eating in secret, even to tasting with the tip of the

---

30 1 Kings 13.24.
31 Dan. 10.3.
32 Dan. 5,9,14.
33 Dan. 3.12ff.
34 *Kataskeuastheisan upo tou Satana* for *kataschetheisan upo tou Satana?*
   Cf. *PG* 31.641 n. 11.

tongue; for, if he will succeed in defeating you in a small matter, he has already overthrown you in the combat and holds you bound with his chains. Do not give ear to every babbler, nor a response to every trifler in conversations which do not comport with the ascetical life. Be attentive to worthy teachings and, by meditating on these, keep a strict watch over your heart. Refrain from listening to worldly tales, that you may not in any way stain your soul with the spattering of mud. Be not anxious to hear the sayings of others nor to thrust yourself into others' conversations, so that you may not make yourself an object of ridicule and cause these others to commit slander. Be not inquisitive nor desirous of seeing everything, so as not to have in your mind the poisonous discharge of vice. Use your eyes to the purpose, use your ears to the purpose, speak to the purpose, answer to the purpose. In the presence of a senior, be not eager to take your seat; if you are so bidden, do not sit beside him, but look carefully about and try to find a lower place, that God may glorify you because of your humility. When you are questioned, answer in a fitting and modest tone; when you are not addressed, remain silent. If another is being questioned, hold your tongue, lest, under the stress of emotional impulse your tongue run away with you and, by offending one who is practicing a strict ascetical life, cast you into the fetters of reproach. When you sit, do not cross your legs, for this is a sign of a wandering attention and an absent mind. In conversing with an inferior or upon being asked something by him do not answer thoughtlessly, holding your brother in contempt and thus insulting God; for, 'he that despiseth the poor, reproacheth his Maker' says the Book of Proverbs.[35] In affirmation of your love of neighbor, preface your discourse with

---

35 Prov. 17.5.

words of comfort or exhortation. Let such words also find a place in the middle and at the end, and let your countenance be bright and cheerful withal, that you may give joy to him who speaks with you. Rejoice in every success achieved by your neighbor and glorify God, for his triumphs are yours as your also are his. Shun the first seats at table and the first chairs at assemblies, but strive to sit in the last place, that it may be said to you: 'Friend, go up higher.'[36] At table let not your left hand usurp the function of the right in disorderly fashion; rather, let it lie at rest, or, if it must be active, let it assist the right. Whenever you are summoned to prayer, let your voice respond and remain at an exercise of rule until the prayers are finished, regarding failure in this respect as a great loss. When you take food to nourish your body, you can scarcely be induced to leave the table before you have fully satisfied your need and, except for an urgent reason, you will not readily do so. How much more eagerly ought you to linger over spiritual nourishment and strengthen your soul with prayer; for the soul is as far superior to the body as heaven is above the earth and heavenly things above those of earth.

The soul is an image of heaven because the Lord dwells within it, but the flesh is of earth, wherein live mortal men and irrational beasts. Regulate the needs of your body, therefore, in conformity with the hours of prayer and be prepared to dismiss arguments which would draw you away from observance of the rule; for it is the way of the devils to urge us to be absent during the time of prayer on the pretext of a seemingly worthy reason, so that they may plausibly draw us away from saving prayer. Do not make excuses, saying, 'Alas, my head! Alas, my stomach!' alleging invisible proofs of non-existent pain and relaxing the rigor of the vigil for the sake

36 Luke 14.10.

of taking rest. Rather, be constant in secret prayer which God beholds in secret and will repay you for openly.[37] Hoard the accruing gains of the most perfect way of life, that in the day of need you may discover hidden wealth. When it is your turn to serve, add to your physical labor a word of exhortation and comfort for love of those whom you serve, that your ministry, seasoned thus with salt,[38] may be acceptable. Do not allow another to do the work that is rightly yours, so that the reward as well may not be taken from you and given to another and he be enriched with your wealth while you are put to shame. Perform the duties of your ministry decently and with care as if you were serving Christ, for, 'Cursed,' says the Prophet, 'be every man that doth the work of the Lord negligently.'[39] Fear, as if the eye of the Lord were upon you, the perversity which arises from fastidiousness and contempt, even though the task in hand seem to you a menial one. The work of the ministry is an exalted work and leads to the kingdom of heaven. It is a dragnet of the virtues, comprising within itself all the commandments of God. It contains, first of all, the virtue of virtues, humility, which brings with itself a host of blessings; secondly, there is that saying of the Lord: 'I was hungry and you gave me to eat; I was thirsty and you gave me to drink; stranger and weak and in prison and you ministered to me.[40] There is, furthermore, a special merit in performing the owed service in a humble spirit without arrogance or irritation and murmuring. Be a zealous follower of those who lead upright lives and inscribe their deeds upon your heart. Pray to be among the few, for the good is rare; wherefore, few, also, are they who enter into the kingdom of

37 Matt. 6.18.
38 Col. 4.6.
39 Jer. 48.10.
40 Matt. 25.35,36.

heaven. Do not think that all who live in a cell are saved, the bad as well as the good, for this is not true. Many, indeed, take up the life of virtue, but few bear its yoke. The kingdom of heaven is the prize of the violent and the violent bear it away—these are the words of the Gospel.[41] By 'violence' is meant the affliction of the body which the disciples of Christ voluntarily undergo in the denial of their own will, in the refusal of respite to the body, and in the observance of Christ's precepts. If, then, you wish to bear away the kingdom of God, become a man of violence; bow your neck to the yoke of Christ's service.[42] Bind the strap of the yoke tightly about your throat. Let it pinch your neck. Rub it thin by labor in acquiring virtues, in fasting, in vigils, in obedience, in silence, in psalmody, in prayer, in tears, in manual labor, in bearing all the tribulations which befall you at the hands of men and demons.

Let not presumptuous thoughts induce you, as time goes on, to abate your labors, so that you may not be caught destitute of virtue, perhaps at the very moment of your departure, and be kept outside the gates of the kingdom. Let not the rank of cleric elate you but let it, rather, make you humble, for advancement in the spirit is advancement in humility; defection and disgrace are born of haughtiness. The nearer you approach the higher ranks of sacred orders, the more you should abase yourself, recalling with fear the example of the sons of Aaron.[43] Knowledge of holy living is knowledge of meekness and humility. Humility is the imitation of Christ; highmindedness and boldness and shamelessness, the imitation of the Devil. Become an imitator of Christ, not of Anti-Christ; of God and not of the adversary of God; of the Mas-

---

41 Matt. 11.12.
42 Matt. 11.30.
43 Lev. 10.

ter, not the fugitive slave; of the merciful One, not the merciless; of the lover, not the enemy, of mankind; of the inmates of the bridal chamber, not the inhabitants of darkness. Be not eager to wield authority over the community, that you may not place upon your own neck others' burdens of sin. Examine the actions of each day, compare them with those of the previous day and press on toward improvement. Advance in virtue, that you may become a companion of the angels. Spend your time in retirement, not for days nor months, but throughout many years, praising your Lord in song, night and day, in imitation of the Cherubim. If thus you begin and thus make an end, traveling the straight road for the short time of your probation, you will, by the grace of God, enter into paradise with the lamp of your soul brilliantly alight, to rejoice with Christ for ever and ever. Amen.

A DISCOURSE ON ASCETICAL DISCIPLINE

How the monk should be equipped

FIRST AND FOREMOST, the monk should own nothing in this world, but he should have as his possessions solitude of the body, modesty of bearing, a modulated tone of voice, and a well-ordered manner of speech. He should be without anxiety as to his food and drink, and should eat in silence. In the presence of his superiors, he should hold his tongue; before those wiser than he, he should hearken to their words. He should have love for his equals, give charitable counsel to his inferiors, and keep aloof from the wicked, the carnal, and the officious. He ought to think much but speak little, be not forward in speech nor given to useless discoursing, not easily moved to laughter, respectful in bearing, keeping his eyes cast down and his spirit uplifted, not answering contradiction with contradiction, docile. He should work with his hands, be ever mindful of his last end, joyful in hope, patient in adversity, unceasingly prayerful, giving thanks in all things, humble toward everyone, hating pride, sober and watchful to keep his heart from evil thoughts. He ought to heap up treasure in heaven[1] by observing the commandments, examining himself as to his daily thoughts and actions, not entangling himself in the occupations and superfluities of the world.[2] It ill befits him to concern himself about those who lead careless lives;

1 Luke 12.33.
2 2 Tim. 2.4.

33

he should emulate the life of the holy fathers, rejoicing with those who are successful in the practice of virtue and not envying them. He must sympathize with the suffering and weep with them,[3] sorrowing deeply for these, but not on any account should he condemn them, nor upbraid him who has renounced his sin, nor ever justify himself. He should, above all, confess before God and men that he is a sinner. It is his duty, moreover, to admonish the undisciplined, encourage the faint-hearted, minister to the sick, wash the feet of the saints,[4] and be mindful of the duties of hospitality and fraternal charity. He must preserve peace with the members of the household of the faith, shun the heretic, read the canonical Scriptures, but have nothing at all to do with apocryphal books. It befits him not to dispute about Father and Son and Holy Spirit, but he should freely confess in thought and word the uncreated and consubstantial Trinity and say to them who put this matter to question that we ought to be baptized according to the tradition we have received, and hold the belief in which we have been baptized, and worship according as we have believed. He should spend his time in good words and deeds, swear not at all, nor lend money for interest, nor sell grain and wine and oil for profit. He must refrain from reveling and drunkenness and have nothing to do with secular concerns, converse without deceit, speak no word against anyone, and neither gossip nor take pleasure in listening to gossip. He should not be quick to trust evil report of anyone, nor be mastered by ill temper nor overcome by despondency. He ought not become angry with his neighbor without cause, nor nurse wrath against anyone, nor return evil for evil. It behooves him to be reviled rather than to revile,

---

3 Rom. 12.15.
4 1 Tim. 5.10.

to be struck rather than to strike, to be wronged rather than to do wrong, to be despoiled rather than to despoil.

Before all else, also, the monk must abstain from the society of women and from wine-bibbing because wine and women will cause even the wise to fall away.[5] He must not grow weary in observing the precepts of the Lord to the best of his ability, but he should await reward and praise from Him, continuing in his desire for the enjoyment of everlasting life, keeping ever before his eyes the words of David, and saying: 'I set the Lord always in my sight; for he is at my right hand, that I be not moved.'[6] Moreover, he should love God as a son, with his whole heart and strength and mind and with all the power that is in him;[7] but as a servant he should reverence, fear, and obey Him and work out his salvation in fear and trembling,[8] fervent in spirit,[9] girt about with the full armor of the Holy Spirit. He must run not as without a purpose and fight not as beating the air,[10] overthrowing his adversary in weakness of body and poverty of spirit, doing all things commanded him, and confessing that he is an unprofitable servant.[11] He should give thanks to God, aweful, glorious, and holy, and do nothing in a spirit of contention and vainglory[12] but for God's sake and to please Him; 'for God hath scattered the bones of them that please men.'[13] He ought never to glorify himself nor speak in his own praise, nor take pleasure in hearing praise from another; but serve in all things secretly, not acting with a view to display before men, but

---

5 Eccli. 19.2.
6 Ps. 15.8.
7 Luke 10.27.
8 Phil. 2.12.
9 Rom. 12.11.
10 1 Cor. 9.26.
11 Luke 17.10.
12 Phil. 2.3.
13 Ps. 52.6.

seeking praise from God alone and meditating on His coming, glorious and terrible, as well as upon his own passing out of this world, upon the good things laid up for the just and also on the fire prepared for the Devil and his angels.[14] But, over and above all this, he must be mindful of the words of the Apostle: 'For the sufferings of this time are not worthy to be compared with the glory to come that shall be revealed in us';[15] and in anticipation proclaim with David that, for those keeping the commandments, there is a great reward,[16] munificent recompense, and crowns of justice, everlasting dwellings, life without end, joy unspeakable, an imperishable mansion with the Father and the Son and the Holy Spirit who is true God in heaven, manifestation face to face, dances in company with angels, Fathers, Patriarchs, Prophets, Apostles, Martyrs, Confessors, and with all those who have been well-pleasing to God from all eternity. Among these let us eagerly strive to be numbered, by the grace of our Lord Jesus Christ, to whom be power and glory for ever and ever. Amen.

---

14 Matt. 25.41.
15 Rom. 8.18.
16 Ps. 18.12.

PREFACE ON THE JUDGMENT OF GOD

LIBERATED FROM THE ERROR of pagan tradition through the benevolence and loving kindness of the good God, with the grace of our Lord Jesus Christ, and by the operation of the Holy Spirit, I was reared from the very beginning by Christian parents. From them I learned even in babyhood the Holy Scriptures which led me to a knowledge of the truth. When I grew to manhood, I traveled about frequently and, in the natural course of things, I engaged in a great many worldly affairs. Here I observed that the most harmonious relations existed among those trained in the pursuit of each of the arts and sciences; while in the Church of God alone, for which Christ died and upon which He poured out in abundance the Holy Spirit, I noticed that many disagree violently with one another and also in their understanding of the Holy Scriptures. Most alarming of all is the fact that I found the very leaders of the Church themselves at such variance with one another in thought and opinion, showing so much opposition to the commands of our Lord Jesus Christ, and so mercilessly rending asunder the Church of God and cruelly confounding His flock that, in our day, with the rise of the Anomoeans, there is fulfilled in them as never before the prophecy, 'Of your own selves shall arise men speaking perverse things, to draw away disciples after them.'[1]

Witnessing such disorders as these and perplexed as to what the cause and source of such evil might be, I at first

---

1 Acts 20.30.

was in a state, as it were, of thick darkness and, as if on a balance, I veered now this way. now that—attracted now to one man, now to another, under the influence of protracted association with these persons, and then thrust in the other direction, as I bethought myself of the validity of the Holy Scriptures. After a long time spent in this state of indecision and while I was still busily searching for the cause I have mentioned, there came to my mind the Book of Judges which tells how each man did what was right in his own eyes and gives the reason for this in the words: 'In those days there was no king in Israel.'[2] With these words in mind, then, I applied also to the present circumstances that explanation which, incredible and frightening as it may be, is quite truly pertinent when it is understood; for never before has there arisen such discord and quarreling as now among the members of the Church in consequence of their turning away from the one, great, and true God, only King of the universe. Each man, indeed, abandons the teachings of our Lord Jesus Christ and arrogates to himself authority in dealing with certain questions, making his own private rules, and preferring to exercise leadership in opposition to the Lord to being led by the Lord. Reflecting upon this and aghast at the magnitude of the impiety, I pursued my investigation further and became convinced that the aforesaid cause was no less the true source also of secular difficulties. I noticed that as long as the common obedience of the others to some one leader was maintained, all was discipline and harmony in the whole group; but that division and discord and a rivalry of leaders besides proceeded from a lack of leadership. Moreover, I once had observed how even a swarm of bees, in accordance with a law of nature, lives under military discipline and obeys its own king

---

2 Judges 21.24.

with orderly precision. Many such instances have I witnessed and many others I have heard of, and persons who make profession of such matters know many more still, so that they can vouch for the truth of what I have said. Now, if good order with its attendant harmony is characteristic of those who look to one source of authority and are subject to one king, then universal disorder and disharmony are a sign that leadership is wanting. By the same token, if we discover in our midst such lack of accord as I have mentioned, both with regard to one another and with respect to the Lord's commands, it would be an indictment either of our rejection of the true king, according to the Scriptural saying: 'only that he who now holdeth, do hold, until he be taken out of the way,'[3] or of denial of Him according to the Psalmist: 'The fool hath said in his heart: There is no God.'[4] And as a kind of token or proof of this, there follow the words: 'They are corrupt and are become abominable in their ways.'[5]

Herein, therefore, the Scripture has represented the manifest evil as a sign of the evil lurking hidden in the soul. But the blessed Apostle Paul, employing a more vigorous method of converting the reprobate in heart[6] to a fear of the judgments of God, lays down the following penalty to be inflicted upon those who are negligent in acquiring true knowledge of God. What are his words? 'And as they liked not to have God in their knowledge, God delivered them up to a reprobate sense to do those things which are not convenient, being filled with all iniquity, malice, avarice, wickedness, full of envy,'[7] and so on. And this, I think, the Apostle says with reference

---

3 2 Thess. 2.7.
4 Ps. 13.1.
5 Ibid.
6 Or, 'those not reprobate in heart' (tous me apololekotas). Cf. PG 31.656 n. 52.
7 Rom. 1.28,29.

to the judgment, not speaking of himself (for he had Christ speaking within him[8]) but guided by the voice of Him who said that He spoke to the crowd in parables that they might not understand the divine mysteries of the Gospel,[9] since they had first shut their eyes and had been dull of hearing with their ears and their foolish heart had become gross.[10] Because they had previously and of their own volition become blinded by darkening the eye of their soul, they therefore would suffer as punishment that their blindness should persist with regard to higher things; and David, fearing this affliction, said: 'Enlighten my eyes that I never sleep in death.'[11] From this and similar evidence I concluded that, in general, as a result of not knowing God, the wickedness of vice produces a reprobate understanding and, in particular, that the disagreement in the world comes from the fact that we have rendered ourselves unworthy of the Lord's leadership. But, if I should apply myself to an inquiry into such behavior, I should be unable to assess the full extent of its obtuseness, or irrationality, or madness, or—what word I should use I know not, because of the enormity of the evil. If even among the very brutes we find mutual harmony preserved by reason of their obedience to a leader, what ought we to say of the great disharmony existing among ourselves and of our insubordination to the Lord's commands? Must we not think that all these models are proposed to us now by the good God for our instruction and conversion, but that in the great and dreadful day of judgment they will be brought forward by Him unto the shame and condemnation of those who have not profited by the instruction? Already, to be sure, He has said and He

---

8 2 Cor. 13.3.
9 Matt. 13.13.
10 Matt. 13.15.
11 Ps. 12.4.

ever keeps saying: 'The ox knoweth his owner, and the ass his master's crib; but Israel hath not known me and my people hath not understood,'[12] and many other utterances of this kind are to be found. Consider, further, these words of the Apostle: 'And if one member suffer anything, all the members suffer with it; or if one member glory, all the members rejoice with it';[13] likewise, that saying: 'that there might be no schism in the body, but the members might be mutually careful one for another'[14]—that is to say, being animated by one soul dwelling therein. Wherefore is it so ordained? In my opinion, so that this conformity and harmony may exist in a pre-eminent degree in the Church of God to which are addressed the words: 'Now you are the body of Christ and members of member'[15]—that is, the one and only true Head which is Christ exercises dominion over and unites the members, each with the other, unto harmonious accord. With those among whom harmony is not secured, however, the bond of peace is not preserved, mildness of spirit is not maintained, but there dissension, strife and rivalry are found. It would be a great piece of audacity to call such persons 'members of Christ' or to say that they are ruled by Him; but it would be the expression of an honest mind to say openly that the wisdom of the flesh is master there and wields a royal sovereignty, according to the words of the Apostle who says definitively: 'To whom you yield yourselves servants to obey, his servants you are whom you obey,'[16] and he clearly enumerates the characteristics of this wisdom when he says: 'For

12 Isa. 1.3.
13 1 Cor. 12.26.
14 1 Cor. 12.25.
15 1 Cor. 12.27.
16 Rom. 6.16.

whereas there is among you envying and contention and seditions are you not carnal?'[17] At the same time he teaches emphatically the grievous result to which these vices lead and their incompatibility with holiness in these words: 'The wisdom of the flesh is an enemy to God; for it is not subject to the law of God, neither can it be';[18] wherefore, the Lord says: 'No man can serve two masters.'[19]

The Only-begotten Son of God, our Lord and God, Jesus Christ, by whom all things were made, also cries out: 'I came down from heaven, not to do my own will but the will of him that sent me, the Father,'[20] and 'I do nothing of myself,'[21] and 'I have received a commandment what I should say and what I should speak.'[22] Likewise, when the Holy Spirit dispenses His great and wonderful gifts, bringing to pass all things in all, He says nothing of Himself; but whatever He hears from the Lord, this He speaks.[23] Is there not a far greater obligation, then, upon the whole Church of God to be zealous in maintaining the unity of the Spirit in the bond of peace,[24] fulfilling those words in the Acts: 'The multitude of believers had but one heart and one soul.'[25] That is, no individual put forward his own will, but all together in the one Holy Spirit were seeking the will of their one Lord Jesus Christ, who said: 'I came down from heaven not to do my will but the will of Him that sent me, the Father,' to whom He says: 'Not for them only do I pray, but for them also who through

17 1 Cor. 3.3.
18 Rom. 8.7.
19 Matt. 6.24.
20 John 6.38.
21 John 8.28.
22 John 12.49.
23 John 16.13.
24 Eph. 4.3.
25 Acts 4.32.

their word shall believe in me, that they all may be one.'[26] In the light of these and many more sayings which I pass over in silence, it is so obviously and undeniably essential for unity to be fully realized in the whole Church at once, according to the will of Christ in the Holy Spirit, and, on the other hand, disobedience to God through mutual discord is so dangerous and fatal ('for,' says the Evangelist, 'he that believeth not the Son shall not see life, but the wrath of God abideth on him'[27]), that I thought the following inference could be drawn: Whatever sins a man is able to gain pardon for from God, or whatever be their number or their gravity, he is, in any case, liable to condemnation for contumacy. Accordingly, I find, in taking up the Holy Scripture, that in the Old and New Testament contumacy toward God is clearly condemned, not in consideration of the number or heinousness of transgressions, but in terms of a single violation of any precept whatsoever, and, further, that the judgment of God covers all forms of disobedience. In the Old Testament, I read of the frightful end of Achar[28] and the account of the man who gathered wood on the Sabbath day.[29] Neither of these men was guilty of any other offense against God nor had they wronged a man in any way, small or great; but the one, merely for his first gathering of wood paid the inescapable penalty and did not have an opportunity to make amends, for, by the command of God, he was forthwith stoned by all his people. The other, only because he had pilfered some part of the sacrificial offerings, even though these had not yet been brought into the synagogue nor had been received by those who perform this function, was the cause not only of his

---

26 John 17.20,21.
27 John 3.36.
28 Jos. 7.19-26.
29 Num. 15.32-36.

own destruction but of that also of his wife and children and of his house and personal possessions besides. Moreover, the evil consequences of his sin would presently have spread like fire over his nation—and this, too, although the people did not know what had occurred and had not excused the sinner— unless his people, sensing the anger of God from the destruction of the men who were slain, had promptly been struck with fear, and unless Josue, son of Nun, sprinkling himself with dust, had prostrated himself together with the ancients, and unless the culprit, discovered thus by lot, had paid the penalty mentioned above.

Perhaps someone will raise the objection that these men might plausibly be suspected of other sins for which they were overtaken by these punishments, yet the Holy Scripture made mention of these sins alone as very serious and worthy of death. And if anyone were so exceedingly audacious as to make additions or deletions in the Scriptural account, he would surely not accuse Mary, the sister of Moses, of having committed numerous sins—her, whose virtue is well-known, I think, to all the faithful. Although she merely said something about Moses by the way of blame—and it was the truth ('for,' she said, 'he has taken unto himself an Ethiopian woman'[30]) —she was visited with the wrath of God to such an extent that the penalty was not revoked even at the intercession of Moses himself. Furthermore, Moses also, the servant of God, the great patriarch who was deemed worthy by God of so much and such high honor and was repeatedly commended by God's own testimony, so that it was said to him: 'I know thee by name and thou has found favor in my sight'[31]—even Moses I behold in the waters of contradiction for no other reason

30 Num. 12.1.
31 Exod. 33.12.

than that he merely had said to his people who were murmuring because there was no water, 'Can we bring you forth water out of this rock?'[32] For this alone he straightway received the threat that he should not enter into the land of promise, which was at that time the chief of all the promises made to the Jews. When I behold this man asking and not obtaining pardon, when I see him not deemed worthy of forgiveness because of those few words, even in consideration of so many righteous deeds, verily do I discern, in the words of the Apostle, 'the severity of God';[33] verily am I persuaded that these words are true: 'If the just man shall scarcely be saved, where shall the ungodly and the sinner appear?'[34] And why do I select these warnings as impressive? For, when I hear that dread sentence of God which is pronounced against him who transgresses through ignorance even one commandment, I know not how to fear sufficiently the greatness of His wrath. It is written: 'If any one sin through ignorance and do one of all those things which by the law of the Lord are forbidden, and being guilty of sin, understand his iniquity, he shall offer of the flocks a ram without blemish to the priest, according to the measure and estimation of the sin; and the priest shall pray for him because he did it ignorantly and it shall be forgiven him; because by mistake he trespassed against the Lord.'[35] But, if the judgment of sins committed in ignorance be so severe and sacrifice is necessary for expiation, to which fact the just Job also bears witness in offering sacrifice on behalf of his sons,[36] what should be said about those who knowingly commit sin or who by their silence acquiesce in the sinful deeds of others? So as not to seem to be drawing

---

32 Num. 20.10.
33 Rom. 11.22.
34 1 Pet. 4.18.
35 Lev. 5.17-19.
36 Job 1.5.

conclusions as to God's displeasure in their regard from conjectures alone, we must again call to mind the Holy Scripture itself, which can satisfy the present purpose by showing in one historical instance only the doom pronounced upon such men. 'Now the sons of Heli, the priest,' says the Scripture, 'are sons of worthlessness.'[37] Because their father did not chastise them with enough severity for being such, he moved the forbearance of God to wrath so great that foreign peoples rose up against them and slew those sons of his in war in one day. His entire nation, furthermore, was vanquished and a considerable number of his people fell. Now, this happened even with the ark of the holy covenant of God nearby—an unheard of thing—so that the ark, which it was not lawful at any time for the Israelites or even for all their priests themselves to touch and which was kept in a special place, was carried hither and yon by impious hands and was put in the shrines of idols instead of the holy temples. Under such circumstances one can readily conjecture the amount of laughter and mockery that were inflicted upon the very Name of God by these foreigners. Add to this, also, that Heli himself is recorded to have met a most pitiable end after hearing the threat that his seed would be removed from the sacerdotal dignity; and so it happened.

Such, then, were the disasters which befell that nation. Such griefs did the father suffer because of the iniquity of his sons, even though no accusation was ever made against his personal life. Moreover, he did not bear with those sons of his in silence, but he earnestly exhorted them not to persist longer in those same wicked deeds, saying: 'Do not so, my sons; for it is no good report that I hear of you.'[38] And to stress the enormity of their sin, he confronted them with an

---

37 1 Sam. 2.12.
38 1 Sam. 2.24.

alarming view of their perilous state. 'If one man shall sin against another,' he said, 'they will pray for him to the Lord; but if a man shall sin against God, who shall pray for him?'[39] Yet, as I said, because he did not exercise a suitable rigor of zeal in their regard, the disaster recounted above took place. And so I find throughout the Old Testament a great many instances of this kind illustrating the condemnation of all disobedience. Again, when I consult the New Testament, I find that our Lord Jesus Christ does not absolve from punishment even sins committed in ignorance, although he attaches a harsher threat to deliberate sins, in the words: 'And that servant who knew the will of his Lord and prepared not himself and did not according to his will, shall be beaten with many stripes. But he that knew not, and did things worthy of stripes, shall be beaten with few stripes.'[40] When I hear such an utterance as this from the lips of the Only-begotten Son of God, and when I consider the indignation of the Holy Apostles against sinners, and when I observe that the sufferings of those who have transgressed in even one particular are of a no less serious nature, but rather more so, than those cited from the Old Testament, I well comprehend the severity of the judgment; for our Lord says: 'unto whomsoever much is given, of him much shall be required.'[41] Consider, also, the blessed Paul, who says, showing at the same time the dignity of his calling and his indignation at all sin: 'For the weapons of our warfare are not carnal, but mighty to God unto the pulling down of fortifications, destroying counsels, and every height that exalteth itself against the knowledge of God, and bringing into captivity every understanding unto the obedience of Christ,' and not only this, but: 'and having in readiness to

39 1 Sam. 2.25.
40 Luke 12.47,48.
41 Luke 12.48.

revenge all disobedience.'[42] Here, also, one who examines each word minutely can gain a very accurate knowledge of the meaning of the Holy Scripture, so that there is no excuse for any of us being led astray into the snare of sin by an erroneous belief that some sins are punished, while others may be committed with impunity. For, what says the Apostle? —'destroying counsels and every height that exalteth itself against the knowledge of God'; so that every sin, because it is an expression of contempt for the divine law, is called a 'height that exalteth itself against the knowledge of God.' This truth, furthermore, is made still more evident in the Book of Numbers. After God had enumerated the involuntary sins and had appointed the sacrifices to be offered in expiation of them, He willed to make other legislation for His people with regard to voluntary sins and He begins as follows: 'But the soul that doth anything with the hand of pride'—He calls the audacity of those who commit voluntary sins 'the hand of pride'; and this the Apostle speaks of as a 'height that exalteth itself against the knowledge of God'—He says, therefore: 'The soul that doth anything with the hand of pride, whether he be born in the land or a stranger, he is rebellious against the Lord and his soul shall be cut off from among his people; for he hath contemned the word of the Lord and made void his precepts; therefore shall he be destroyed and shall bear his iniquity.'[43]

Here it should be observed that, unless the life of the sinner had been destroyed, his sin would not have rested upon himself alone, but also upon those who did not display a righteous indignation toward him. And such an eventuality is on record in many places and actually occurred many times. Further, so that from lesser examples we may learn caution in more

---

42 2 Cor. 10.4-6.
43 Num. 15.30,31.

important matters, let us note well what great wrath is brought to bear in the Book of Deuteronomy upon those who are disobedient to a priest or a judge. The passage reads as follows: 'But he that will be proud and refuse to obey the priest who ministereth at that time in the name of the Lord thy God or the judge whoever he may be in those days, that man shall die and thou shalt take away the evil from Israel. And all the people hearing it shall fear and shall no longer commit impious deeds.'[44] Here it is well to note how one already duly impressed would be struck with still greater awe by these words. Then, too, the Apostle says: 'and bringing into captivity every understanding unto the obedience of Christ'; 'every understanding,' not this one or that one. 'And having in readiness to revenge'[45]—here again, not this or that particular act, but 'all disobedience.'

A very wicked convention, however, leads us astray and a perverted human tradition is the source of great evil for us; I mean that tradition according to which some sins are denounced and others are viewed indifferently. Crimes like homicide and adultery are the object of a violent but feigned indignation, while others, such as anger or reviling or drunkenness or avarice, are not considered deserving of even a simple rebuke. Yet, regarding all these transgressions, Paul, speaking in Christ, also expressed in another place the view noted above, saying: 'they who do such things are worthy of death.'[46] And certainly, where every height that exalteth itself against the knowledge of God is destroyed, and every understanding is brought into captivity unto the obedience of Christ, and every disobedience receives condign punishment, there, nothing is left undestroyed, nothing remitted without

44 Deut. 17.12,13.
45 2 Cor. 10.5,6.
46 Rom. 1.32.

penalty, nothing is exempt from the obedience of Christ. Moreover, the Apostle has shown also that all forms of disobedience
have a common feature in that they all represent the very
greatest impiety. He says: 'Thou that makest thy boast of
the law, by transgression of the law dishonorest God.'[47] Are
these mere words and are they not to have effect? Consider
further: The man in Corinth who had his father's wife, although he was charged with no other crime except this, was
not only himself delivered over to Satan for the destruction
of his flesh until he made amends for his sin by fruits worthy
of penance,[48] but Paul includes the whole Church likewise in
his reproaches, since it did not exact vengeance for the crime
of this man: 'What will you? Shall I come to you with a
rod?'[49] And a little further on: 'And you are puffed up; and
have not rather mourned, that he might be taken away from
you, that hath done this deed.'[50] Furthermore, there is the
case of Ananias who is mentioned in the Acts.[51] What other
transgression is he found guilty of except that of disobedience?
How, then, does he seem to deserve such vehement wrath?
Having sold his own property, he brought the money and
laid it at the feet of the Apostles; but, because he kept back
a part of the price of the land, he, simultaneously with his
wife, was given the death sentence and he was not deemed
worthy to learn of any terms of penance for his sin nor did
he even obtain an opportunity for remorse nor time to do
penance. And the exactor of a punishment so severe, the
executor of the mighty wrath of God upon the sinner, is St.
Peter—he who was preferred above all the disciples, he who
alone was distinguished above the others by the testimony [of

---

47 Rom. 2.23.
48 1 Cor. 5.1-5; Luke 3.8.
49 1 Cor. 4.21.
50 1 Cor. 5.2.
51 Acts 5.1-11.

Christ] and, in being called blessed by Him, he who was entrusted with the keys of the kingdom of heaven.[52] Will he quail, think you, before any harsh action whatsoever when fear and trembling before the judgment of God is in question, especially when he recalls the words of the Lord: 'If I wash thee not, thou shalt have no part with me'?[53] And these words were said to him even though he had committed no sin nor showed any sign of contempt, but, rather, had offered supererogatory honor to his Lord and manifested a piety befitting a servant and disciple. Upon beholding his own and all men's God and Lord and King, Master and Teacher and Saviour, and all things else as well, in the guise of a servant, girded with a towel and desirous of washing his feet, immediately, as if realizing his own unworthiness and awe-struck by the dignity of Him who was approaching, he cried out: 'Lord, dost thou wash my feet?'[54] and again: 'Thou shalt never wash my feet!'[55] Thereupon, he was threatened so severely that unless, by again recognizing the truth of the Lord's words, he had not avoided an act of disobedience by retracting his refusal, none of his previous merits would have sufficed for excusing his present act of contumacy — neither his own righteous deeds, nor the testimonies of the Lord proclaiming him blessed, nor His gifts and promises, nor the revelation itself from God the Father concerning His great satisfaction in His Only-begotten Son.[56]

But, if I should wish to enumerate all the examples which I find in the Old and New Testaments, time would perhaps fail me in the recounting of them. As soon as I come to the words of our Lord Jesus Christ in the Gospel, however, the

---

52 Matt. 16.17-19.
53 John 13.8.
54 John 13.6.
55 John 13.8.
56 Matt. 17.5.

words of Him who is to judge the living and the dead, words which to the faithful are more worthy of credence than any other historical account or argument, great and compelling is the insistence (if I may so speak) which I note in them all regarding obedience to God in all things. I observe that absolutely no pardon respecting any precept whatsoever is extended to those who do not repent of their disobedience. And, surely, no one would have the temerity to offer some other testimony or even so much as think of doing so in the face of of pronouncements so bald and clear and absolute. 'Heaven and earth shall pass,' He says, 'but my words shall not pass.'[57] Here there is no distinction, there is no discrimination; no exception is made anywhere. He does not say: 'these words' or 'those words,' but 'my words'—all alike, that is, 'shall not pass'; for it is written: 'The Lord is faithful in all his words,'[58] whether in forbidding or enjoining something, whether promising or threatening, or whether with regard to doing acts that are forbidden or omitting acts that are commanded. That the omission of good deeds is condemned, as well as the commission of sinful acts, the aforementioned verdict in Peter's case suffices for illustration and full proof to a soul who has not entirely succumbed to the disease of incredulity. He who had done nothing forbidden nor, indeed, had omitted the fulfillment of any command, whereby the guilty one becomes liable to the charge of negligence or contempt, but merely showed a reverential hesitation to accept ministration and honor from his Master, was the object of a threat which would inevitably have been realized, unless, as I said above, Peter had forestalled his Lord's wrath by swift and vigorous amendment. Indeed, our good and compassionate God was pleased to be long-suffering toward us

57 Matt. 24.35.
58 Ps. 144.13.

and to illustrate repeatedly and by many examples the same truth, so that, by reason of their great number and continuous succession, the soul, deeply stirred and overwhelmed, might be able at length, although with difficulty still, to renounce its inveterate habit of sin.

For the present purpose, therefore, it is necessary merely to mention those who are to stand at the left hand of our Lord Jesus Christ on the great and terrible day of judgment; those to whom He who has received from the Father all power of judgment,[59] who comes to bring to light the hidden things of darkness and make manifest the counsels of the heart,[60] will say: 'Depart from me, you cursed, into everlasting fire which was prepared for the devil and his angels.'[61] Moreover, He adds the reason, not saying: 'because you have committed murder or fornication' or 'because you have lied or wronged anyone or performed any other forbidden act, even the most venial,' but—what is it that He says?—'because you were negligent in good works'; 'For I was hungry and you gave me not to eat; I was thirsty and you gave me not to drink; I was a stranger and you did not take me in; naked and you covered me not; sick and in prison and you did not visit me.'[62] Such words as these I came upon in the Holy Scriptures by the grace of the good God 'who will have all men to be saved and to come to the knowledge of the truth'[63] and who teaches this knowledge to men.

Thus did I recognize the dread source of the great discord among the majority of mankind, both as regards one another and respecting the commands of our Lord Jesus Christ. Here-

---

59 John 5.22.
60 1 Cor. 4.5.
61 Matt. 25.41.
62 Matt. 25.42,43.
63 1 Tim. 2.4.

in was I instructed as to the terrible doom imposed for such transgression of the law. Hereby I learned to denounce in equal measure every form of disobedience to every one of God's decrees and noted that frightful condemnation of those not guilty of sin, yet having a part in the wrath through not showing a righteous zeal toward the sinners, even though the former were often not even aware of the fault committed. Consequently, I have deemed it my duty, insofar as I am able and with the aid of the prayers of all, even though the hour is late (because I ever await those who have undertaken the same contest for holiness and I do not trust in myself alone) to bring forward as a reminder, now, at least, and perhaps not inopportunely, to those engaged in the combat of the devout life, the passages I have culled from the Holy Scriptures regarding what is displeasing to God and with what He is well pleased.

That we may be justified by the grace of our Lord Jesus Christ and by the guidance of the Holy Spirit, let us repudiate the customary actions of our own wills and the observance of human traditions. Let us, on the other hand, go forward by means of the Gospel of the Blessed God, Jesus Christ, our Lord. Having lived during this present life in a manner acceptable to Him, by a rigorous avoidance of all that is forbidden and a zealous observance of whatever is commended, may we be able in the future age of immortality to escape the wrath to come upon the sons of contumacy and be found worthy of obtaining eternal life and the heavenly kingdom which has been promised by our Lord Jesus Christ 'to such as keep his covenant and are mindful of his commandments to do them.'[64] Moreover, remembering the words of the Apostle, 'in Christ Jesus neither circumcision availeth any-

---

64 Ps. 102.18.

thing nor uncircumcision, but faith that worketh by charity,[65] I regarded it as at once appropriate and necessary to set forth first the sound faith and sacred doctrine respecting the Father and Son and Holy Ghost, and then add the Morals.

---

65 Gal. 5.6.

CONCERNING FAITH

HEN, BY THE GRACE OF GOD, I learned of your piety's command, worthy as it is of the love you bear God in Christ, whereby you sought from us a written profession of our holy faith, I hesitated at first as to my answer, sensible as I am of my own lowliness and weakness. But when I recalled the words of the Apostle, 'supporting one another in charity,'[1] and, again, 'For with the heart we believe unto justice; but with the mouth confession is made unto salvation,'[2] I considered it a very hazardous act to deny your request and not to make that salutary profession. Moreover, I placed my confidence in God through Christ as it is written: 'Not that we are sufficient to think anything of ourselves as of ourselves; but our sufficiency is from God,'[3] who rendered the men of apostolic days, and now us, at your instigation, sufficient to become ministers of the New Testament, 'not in the letter but in the spirit.'[4] At any rate, you yourselves know that a faithful minister must preserve unadulterated and unalloyed whatever has been entrusted to him by his good master for dispensation to his fellow servants.[5] Consequently, I also am obliged in the common interest to place before you, in accordance with God's good pleasure, what I have learned from the Holy Scriptures. For the Lord Himself, in whom

1 Eph. 4.2.
2 Rom. 10.10.
3 2 Cor. 3.5.
4 2 Cor. 3.6.
5 Luke 12.42.

the Father was well pleased,[6] 'in whom are hid all the treas-
uresures of wisdom and knowledge,'[7] said, having received
from the Father all power and all judgment:[8] 'he gave me
commandment what I should say and what I should speak'[9]
and again: 'The things, therefore, that I speak, even as the
Father said unto me, so do I speak.'[10] If, likewise, the Holy
Spirit does not speak of Himself, but whatsoever He hears
from Him, these things He speaks,[11] how much more pious
and safe it is for us to think and act thus in the Name of
our Lord Jesus Christ.

Now, while I was compelled to fight the heresies that arose
from time to time, I thought it appropriate to the specific
nature of the impiety sown by the Devil that I should check
or confute if I could the blasphemies which were brought
forward [by the opposing side]—and in this I was imitating
the example of my predecessors—by arguments gleaned from
various sources as the need of those weak in faith required;
and in many cases these were not written down, yet were
not out of harmony with sound Scriptural teaching. In fact,
the Apostle often was not above using even pagan utterances
which were congruent with his special purpose.[12] In this
present case, however, I have regarded it as befitting our
joint intent, yours and mine, to obey in the simplicity of a
sound faith that injunction of yours springing from your love
in Christ and to declare what I have learned from the Holy
Scripture, making a sparing use of titles and words which
are not found literally in Holy Writ, even though they pre-

---

6 Mark 1.11; Luke 3.22.
7 Col. 2.3.
8 Matt. 28.18; John 5.22.
9 John 12.49.
10 John 12.50.
11 John 16.13.
12 Acts 17.28.

serve the sense of the Scripture. In addition, I shall wholly avoid as alien and foreign to our holy faith everything which introduces an unusual sense as well as an unfamiliar text, and also whatever is not found in the teaching of the saints. Now, then, faith is a whole-hearted assent to aural doctrine with full conviction of the truth of what is publicly taught by the grace of God. This faith Abraham had, as is testified in the words: 'he staggered not by distrust; but was strengthened in faith, giving glory to God; most fully knowing that whatsoever he has promised he is able also to perform.'[13] But, if 'the Lord is faithful in all his words'[14] and 'All his commandments are faithful, confirmed for ever and ever, made in truth and equity,'[15] to delete anything that is written down or to interpolate anything not written amounts to open defection from the faith and makes the offender liable to a charge of contempt. For our Lord Jesus Christ says: 'My sheep hear my voice,'[16] and, before this, He had said: 'But a stranger they follow not but fly from him because they know not the voice of strangers.'[17] And the Apostle, using a human parallel, more strongly forbids adding to or removing anything from Holy Writ in the following words: 'yet a man's testament if it be confirmed, no man despiseth nor addeth to it.'[18]

So, then, we have determined in this way to avoid now and always every utterance and sentiment not found in the Lord's teaching, since the purpose at hand, yours and mine, is, as I said before, widely different from that of those disputes by which we were induced on other occasions to write or speak

---

13 Rom. 4.20,21.
14 Ps. 144.13.
15 Ps. 110.8.
16 John 10.27.
17 John 10.5.
18 Gal. 3.15.

otherwise. Whereas the object of my zeal then was the refutation of heresy and the foiling of the Devil's wiles, now the task at hand is simple exposition and profession of a sound faith; wherefore the type of discourse which I formerly employed is not appropriate for me now. As a man would not take in hand the same implements for waging war as he does for working his farm (for the tools of those who labor for their livelihood in sweet security differ from the full accoutrement of those drawn up for battle), so he who delivers an exhortation on sound doctrine would not say the same things as he who is engaged in putting his adversaries to rout. The speech which refutes and that which exhorts represent different genres. The simplicity of those making a tranquil profession of piety is one thing and the sweating toil of those resisting the attacks of a so-called system of knowledge is something quite different. Consequently, I, also, organizing my discourses in this judicious fashion, will employ in every instance methods which are pertinent to the safeguarding or the deepening of faith—now, by vigorously opposing those who attempt to destroy it by the craft of the Devil; again, by expounding the faith in a more straightforward and informal manner to such as desire to be strengthened therein; and in this I am at one with the words of the Apostle: 'that you may know how you ought to answer every man.'[19]

But, before I take up the matter itself of the profession of faith, the following warning should be given: It is impossible to express in one word or one concept, or to grasp with the mind at all, the majesty and glory of God, which is unutterable and incomprehensible, and the Holy Scripture, although for the most part employing words in current use, speaks obscurely 'as through a glass'[20] even to the clean of heart.[21] The

---

19 Col. 4.6.
20 1 Cor. 13.12.
21 Matt. 5.8.

beholding face to face and the perfect knowledge[22] have been promised to those who are accounted worthy in the life to come. But now, even if a man be a Paul or a Peter, even though he truly sees what he sees and is not misled nor deceived by his imagination, yet he sees through a glass and in a dark manner, and he looks forward with great joy to perfect knowledge in the future of that which he receives now in part with thanksgiving.[23] This the Apostle Paul confirms by the implication in the following words: 'When I was a child'—that is, fresh from committing to memory the first elements of the divine oracles—'I spoke as a child, I understood as a child, I thought as a child. But now that I have become a man'—that is, and am hastening to attain to the measure of the age of the fullness of Christ[24]—'I have put away the things of a child'[25]—that is, I have arrived at such an advanced stage and achieved such proficiency in the understanding of the Holy Scripture that full knowledge according to the Jewish religion seems like the stirrings of a childish mind, while the knowledge gained through the Gospel appears wholly suitable to one who has now reached perfect manhood. And so, in comparison with the knowledge which will be revealed to the deserving in the life to come, that in our knowledge which now seems perfect is a dim and fragmentary thing; so much so that it falls shorter of the clarity we look for in the age to come than the gazing through the glass—and darkly besides—falls short of the beholding face to face. To this fact blessed Peter and John and the other disciples of the Lord also are witnesses. Although in this life they made ever greater progress and advancement, yet they were given the assurance that this proficiency would be far

---

22 1 Cor. 13.12.
23 1 Cor. 13.10.
24 Eph. 4.13.
25 1 Cor. 13.11.

surpassed by the knowledge which was reserved for them in the life to come. Even they, after proving themselves worthy of the Lord's choice, of living in His company, of being His Apostles, of receiving spiritual favors, and after hearing Him say to them: 'To you it is given to know the mysteries of the kingdom of heaven'[26]—after attaining to knowledge as profound as this and to the revelation of secrets withheld from the crowd, on a later occasion, with reference to the Lord's Passion itself, they, nevertheless, hear the words: 'I have yet many things to say to you, but you cannot bear them now.'[27]

From such passages as these we learn that Holy Writ contains a store of knowledge as limitless as is the incapacity of human nature to grasp in this life the meaning of the holy mysteries. Even though more knowledge is always being acquired by everyone, it will ever fall short in all things of its rightful completeness until the time when that which is perfect being come, that which is in part will be done away.[28] Accordingly, one appellation is not adequate for expressing all the glories of God simultaneously, nor is any one entirely free from the handicap of incompleteness. If one would say 'God,' he fails to express the attribute of 'Father'; and in saying 'Father,' we leave out the idea of 'Creator.' Again, these names do not include the qualities of goodness, wisdom, power, and the rest of the attributes mentioned in Holy Scripture. Besides, if we understood the attribute 'Father' as applied to God entirely according to our ordinary acceptation of it, we are guilty of irreverence; for passion, effluxion, ignorance, infirmity, and other weaknesses of the kind are implied. A similar objection can be brought against the appellation 'Creator'; for with us this concept is associated with notions of

26 Matt. 13.11.
27 John 16.12.
28 1 Cor. 13.10.

time, material, tools, assistance—but a reverential idea of God must be purified of all these accretions insofar as this is possible for man. Even if all minds, in fact, should combine their researches and all tongues would concur in their utterance, never, as I have said, could anyone achieve a worthy result in this matter. Solomon, the wisest of men, presents this thought clearly to us when he says: 'I have said: I will be wise; and it departed farther from me';[29] not that it really fled but because wisdom appears unattainable particularly to those to whom knowledge has been given in an exceptionally high degree by the grace of God. Holy Writ, therefore, employs perforce a large number of names and words to convey a partial concept, and even this in an obscure manner, of the Divine Glory. I have neither the leisure nor the skill at present, however, to collect from the Holy Scripture, even at your urging, all the references made throughout to the Father and Son and Holy Spirit, but I think it will satisfy even your conscience if I place before you a few selected passages to show how our thoughts derive from the Scriptures and to provide grounds for certainty both for you yourselves and any others who desire to place their confidence in us; for, just as many proofs declare to us only one divine doctrine, so also, a fair-minded person will recognize in the few proofs I give the divine character which is in all.

We believe, therefore, and confess that there is one God, true and good, and that He is the Father Omnipotent from whom are all things, the God and Father of our Lord Jesus Christ. We believe in and confess His one, Only-begotten Son, our Lord and God, Jesus Christ, who only is true, by whom all things visible and invisible were made[30] and in whom they

---

29 Eccle. 7.24.
30 John 1.3; Col. 1.16.

all consist;[31] who in the beginning was with God and was God,[32] and afterward, according to the Scriptures, was seen upon the earth and conversed with men;[33] 'who being in the form of God thought it not robbery to be equal with God, but emptied himself. And in being born of a virgin, 'taking the form of a servant and in habit found as a man,'[34] He fulfilled according to the command of the Father all that was written concerning Him, becoming obedient unto death, even the death of the cross.[35] We believe and confess that, rising on the third day from the dead, according to the Scriptures, He was seen by His holy disciples and the others, as it is written;[36] that He ascended into heaven and sits on the right hand of the Father whence He will come at the end of time to raise up all men and to render to each according to his works;[37] that then the just will be received into life everlasting and into the kingdom of heaven and the sinners will be condemned to eternal punishment 'where their worm dieth not and the fire is not extinguished.'[38] We believe in and confess the Holy Spirit, the Paraclete, 'whereby we are sealed unto the day of redemption,'[39] the Spirit of truth,[40] 'the spirit of adoption of sons whereby we cry: Abba (Father),'[41] who worketh and divideth the gifts of God to every one according as He wills unto profit;[42] who teaches and brings to mind

31 Col. 1.17.
32 John 1.1.
33 Bar. 3.38.
34 Phil. 2.6,7.
35 Phil. 2.8.
36 1 Cor. 15.4,5.
37 Matt. 16.27.
38 Mark 9.43.
39 Eph. 4.30.
40 John 15.26.
41 Rom. 8.15.
42 1 Cor. 12.7,11.

whatever He hears from the Son;[43] who is good and shows the way to all truth and confirms all believers unto certain knowledge, true confession, pious worship, and adoration in spirit and truth[44] of God the Father and His Only-begotten Son, our Lord Jesus Christ, and of Himself. Each of these Names makes clearly evident to us the special character of the Person named and certain wholly specialized properties are reverently contemplated in each: in the Father, by virtue of His proper attribute, Father; in the Son, by the proper attribute, Son; and in the Holy Spirit, by His own special attribute. The Holy Spirit does not speak of Himself,[45] nor does the Son do aught of Himself,[46] but the Father sends the Son and the Son sends the Holy Spirit. So we believe and so we baptize, in the Name of the consubstantial Trinity, according to the command of our Lord Jesus Christ, who said: 'Going, teach ye all nations, baptizing them in the name of the Father and of the Son and of the Holy Ghost, teaching them to observe all things, whatsoever I have commanded you.'[47] If we observe these commandments, we show our love toward Him and we are rendered worthy to abide in it, as it is written;[48] but, if we do not observe them, we show conclusively that we are hostile to Him, for 'He that loveth me not,' says the Lord, 'keepeth not my words,'[49] and again: 'He that hath my commandments and keepeth them, he it is that loveth me.'[50]

I marvel exceedingly when I consider the words of our

43 John 14.26.
44 John 4.23.
45 John 16.13.
46 John 8.28.
47 Matt. 28.19.20.
48 John 15.10.
49 John 14.24.
50 John 14.21.

Lord Jesus Christ: 'Rejoice not that spirits are subject unto you, but rejoice that your names are written in heaven,'[51] and again: 'By this shall all men know that you are my disciples, if you have love one for another.'[52] Whereupon, the Apostle, showing the binding force of charity upon all men, declares: 'If I speak with the tongues of men and of angels and have not charity, I am become as sounding brass or a tinkling cymbal. And if I should have prophecy and should know all mysteries and all knowledge, and if I should have all faith, so that I could remove mountains, and have not charity, I am nothing';[53] and a little further on: 'whether prophecies shall be made void, or tongues shall cease or knowledge shall be destroyed,'[54] and so on; then he adds: 'And now there remain faith, hope, charity, these three; but the greatest of these is charity.'[55] In view of such declarations on the part of our Lord and the Apostle, I marvel, I say, how it is that men display such zeal and such intense absorption in the pursuit of goods that will come to an end and be destroyed, but have no regard for that which will remain, especially charity, the greatest of all goods, the distinguishing mark of the Christian. And not only this, but they show hostility to those who are zealous in its practice, and in fighting against them they fulfill the words of the Lord, namely, that they themselves do not enter in and those that are entering in they hinder.[56]

I beg and implore you, therefore, to be content with the words of the saints and of the Lord Himself and to desist from curious inquiry and unseemly controversies, to think on those things that are worthy of your heavenly calling, to live in a

51 Luke 10.20.
52 John 13.35.
53 1 Cor. 13.1,2.
54 1 Cor. 13.8.
55 1 Cor. 13.13.
56 Luke 11.52.

manner befitting the Gospel of Christ, relying on the hope of
eternal life and the heavenly kingdom prepared for all those
who keep the commandments of God the Father according
to the gospel of Jesus Christ our Lord in the Holy Spirit and
in truth. At the bidding of your piety, then, I have felt bound
in duty to declare and make clear before concluding my belief in these truths both for your benefit and through you for
those who are my brethren in Christ, so as to produce in
you and in them full conviction in the Name of our Lord
Jesus Christ and also to prevent anyone's mind from being
confused by the diverse methods of exposition we employ,
although always we are motivated by the necessity of opposing
the arguments trumped up by adversaries of the truth. My
aim, furthermore, is to see to it that no one becomes unsettled
by the opposition of those who attribute to me sentiments that
are alien to my mind, or who again and again falsely represent as my opinion the expression of their own wicked passions, in an effort to carry off to their side the more naive
[among their listeners]. These you must be wary of as enemies
to the evangelical and apostolic faith and charity. Recall the
words of the Apostle: 'But though we or an angel from heaven
preach a gospel to you besides that which we have preached
to you, let him be anathema.'[57] Thus, and by observing the
following warning also: 'Beware of false prophets'[58] and this
likewise: 'that you withdraw yourselves from every brother
walking disorderly, and not according to the tradition which
they have received of us,'[59]—we shall walk according to the
rule of the saints, 'built upon the foundation of the apostles
and prophets, Jesus Christ, our Lord himself being the chief
corner-stone; in whom all the building being framed together,

57 Gal. 1.8.
58 Matt. 7.15.
59 2 Thess. 3.6.

groweth up into an holy temple in the Lord.'[60] 'And may the
God of peace himself sanctify you in all things, that your whole
spirit and soul and body may be preserved blameless in the
coming of our Lord Jesus Christ. God is faithful who hath
called you, who also will do it,'[61] provided we keep His commandments by the grace of Christ in the Holy Spirit.

Considering that, for the present, enough has been said
above regarding a sound faith, I shall now try, in the Name
of our Lord Jesus Christ, to keep my promise with regard to
the Morals. Accordingly, whatever I have so far discovered
in the way of prohibitions or commended acts in scattered
passages throughout the New Testament, I have attempted
to the best of my ability to gather together into rules summar-
ized for the convenience of those who desire this service. With
each rule, also, I have coupled a listing by number of Scriptural passages comprised in the rule, as taken from the Gospels, from the Apostle, or the Acts. In this way, one who
reads the rule and sees, for example, the number 'one'
or 'two' cited with it, may consult the Scripture itself and,
looking up the passages quoted under the aforesaid number, find the testimony from which the rule was derived.
Furthermore, I intended at first to make a harmony with
quotations from the Old Testament for each passage of the
New Testament which accompanies the rules; but, since the
need was pressing and my brethren in Christ were urgently
demanding that I fulfill my promise of long standing, I recalled the words of Him who said: 'Give an occasion to a
wise man and wisdom shall be added to him.'[62] Consequently,
if anyone so desires, he will find a satisfactory starting point in
the testimonies that are cited for taking up the Old Testa-

---

60 Eph. 2.20,21.
61 1 Thess. 5.23,24.
62 Prov. 9.9.

ment and discovering for himself the harmony in all the Holy Scriptures, especially since, for the faithful and for those fully convinced of the truth of our Lord's words, one utterance alone is enough. I have, therefore, considered it sufficient also to cite a few only and not all the proofs to be found in the New Testament.

HEREWITH BEGINS THE *MORALS*

HAT THEY WHO BELIEVE in the Lord must first do penance according to the preaching of John and of our Lord Jesus Christ Himself; for they who do not penance now will receive a harsher sentence than those who were condemned before the time of the Gospel.

Cap. 1

Matthew [4.17]: 'From that time Jesus began to preach and to say: Do penance for the kingdom of heaven is at hand.' [11.20-22]: 'Then began he to upbraid the cities wherein were done the most of his miracles, for that they had not done penance. Woe to thee, Corozain, woe to thee, Bethsaida; for if in Tyre and Sidon had been wrought the miracles that have been wrought in you, they had long ago done penance in sackcloth and ashes. But it shall be more tolerable for Tyre and Sidon in the day of judgement than for you,' etc.

That this present life is the time for penance and for the remission of sins; in the life to come, the just judgment of retribution will take place.

Cap. 2

Mark [2.10]: 'But that you may know that the Son of man

71

hath power on earth to forgive sins, he sayeth,' *Matthew* [18.18,19]: 'Amen I say to you, whatsoever you shall bind upon earth, shall be bound in heaven: and whatsoever you shall loose upon earth shall be loosed in heaven. Again, Amen I say to you, that if two of you shall consent upon earth concerning anything whatsoever they shall ask, it shall be done to them by my Father who is in heaven,' *John* [5.28,29]: 'for the hour cometh wherein all that are in the graves shall hear his voice. And they that have done good things shall come forth unto the resurrection of life; but they that have done evil, unto the resurrection of judgment.' *Rom.* [2.4-6]: 'Or despisest thou the riches of his goodness and patience and long-suffering? Knowest thou not that the benignity of God leadeth thee to penance? But according to thy hardness and impenitent heart, thou treasurest up to thyself wrath against the day of wrath and of revelation and the just judgment of God who will render to every man according to his works.' *Acts* [17.30,31]: 'And God indeed having winked at the times of this ignorance, now declareth unto men that all should everywhere do penance, because he hath appointed a day wherein he will judge the world.'

That penitents should weep bitterly and show forth from their heart all the other appropriate works of penance.

Cap. 3

Matthew [26.75]: 'And Peter remembered the word of Jesus which he had said to him: Before the cock crow, thou wilt deny me thrice. And going forth he wept bitterly.' *2 Cor.* [7.6,7]: 'But he who comforteth the humble comforted us by the coming of Titus. And not by his coming only, but also by the consolation, wherewith he was comforted in you, relating to us your desire, your mourning, your zeal for me'; and a little further on [11]: 'For behold this selfsame thing, that you were made sorrowful according to God, how great carefulness it worketh in you; yea defence, yea indignation, yea fear, yea desire, yea zeal, yea revenge: in all things you have showed yourself to be undefiled in the matter.' *Acts* [19.18,19]: 'And many of them that believed came confessing and declaring their deeds. And many of them who had followed curious arts brought together their books and burnt them before all.'

That mere renouncement of sin is not sufficient for the salvation of penitents, but fruits worthy of penance are also required of them.

Cap. 4

Matthew [3.7-10]: 'And seeing many of the Pharisees and Sadducees coming to his baptism, he said to them: Ye brood of vipers, who hath shewed you to flee from the wrath to come? Bring forth therefore fruit worthy of penance. And think not to say within yourselves, We have Abraham for our father. For I tell you that God is able of these stones to raise up children to Abraham. For now the axe is laid to the root of the trees. Every tree therefore that doth not yield good fruit, shall be cut down and cast into the fire.'

That after departure from this life there is no opportunity for good deeds, since God in his forbearance has provided the present life for doing those things that please Him.

Cap. 5

Matthew [25.1-12]: 'Then shall the kingdom of heaven

be like to ten virgins, who taking their lamps went out to
meet the bridegroom and the bride. And five of them were
foolish and five wise. They who were foolish, having taken
their lamps, did not take oil with them. But the wise took oil
in their vessels with their lamps. And the bridegroom tarrying, they all slumbered and slept. And at midnight there was
a cry made: Behold the bridegroom cometh, go ye forth to
meet him. Then all those virgins arose and trimmed their
lamps. And the foolish said to the wise: Give us of your oil,
for our lamps are gone out. The wise answered, saying: Lest
perhaps there be not enough for us and for you, go ye rather
to them that sell, and buy for yourselves. Now whilst they
went to buy, the bridegroom came: and they that were ready,
went in with him to the marriage, and the door was shut.
But at last came also the other virgins, saying: Lord, Lord,
open to us. But he answering said: Amen I say to you, I know
you not.' *Luke* [13.24,25]: 'Strive to enter by the narrow
gate: for many, I say to you, shall seek to enter and shall not
be able. But when the master of the house shall be gone in
and shall shut the door, you shall begin to stand without and
knock at the door, saying: Lord, open to us. And he answering shall say to you: I know you not, whence you are.' *2 Cor.*
[6.2-4]: 'Behold, now is the acceptable time: behold, now
is the day of salvation. Giving no offence to any man that our
ministry be not blamed: but in all things let us exhibit ourselves as the ministers of God.' *Gal.* [6.10]: 'Therefore, whilst
we have time let us work good to all men.'

RULE TWO

That he who entangles himself in matters foreign to piety
cannot serve God.

Cap. 1

Matthew [6.24]: 'No man can serve two masters. For either he will hate the one and love the other: or he will sustain the one and despise the other. You cannot serve God and mammon.' *2 Cor.* [6.14-16]: 'Bear not the yoke with unbelievers. For what participation hath justice with injustice? Or what fellowship hath light with darkness? And what concord hath Christ with Belial? Or what part hath the faithful with the unbeliever? And what agreement hath the temple of God with idols?'

That he who would obey the Gospel must first be purged of all defilement of the flesh and the spirit that so he may be acceptable to God in the good works of holiness.

Cap. 2

Matthew [23.25,26]: 'Woe to you scribes and Pharisees, hypocrites: because you make clean the outside of the cup and of the dish, but within you are full of repine and uncleanness. Thou blind Pharisee, first make clean the inside of the cup and of the dish that the outside of them may become clean.' *2 Cor.* [7.1]: 'Having therefore these promises, dearly beloved, let us cleanse ourselves from all defilement of the flesh and of the spirit, perfecting sanctification in the fear of God.'

That he who has affection for anything in this life or allows anything to draw him away from God even slightly cannot become the Lord's disciple.

Cap. 3

Matthew [10.37,38]: 'He that loveth father or mother

more than me is not worthy of me; and he that loveth son
or daughter more than me is not worthy of me. And he that
taketh not up his cross and followeth me, is not worthy of me.'
[16.24,25]: 'If any man will come after me, let him deny
himself and take up his cross and follow me. For he that will
save his life, shall lose it.'

RULE THREE

That to love God with the whole heart has been declared
by the Lord to be the first and the greatest commandment of
the Law; and the second, to love one's neighbor as oneself.

Cap. 1

Matthew [22.37-39]: 'Jesus said to him: Thou shalt love
the Lord thy God with thy whole heart and with thy whole
soul and with thy whole strength and with thy whole mind.
This is the first and greatest commandment. And the second
is like to this: Thou shalt love thy neighbor as thyself.'

That, if anyone does not keep His commandments, it is
proof that he does not love God and His Christ; but the observance of the commandments of Christ in bearing the tribulations sent by Him even unto death is proof of love.

Cap. 2

John [14.21,24]: 'He that hath my commandments and
keepeth them, he it is that loveth me. He that loveth me not,
keepeth not my words.' [15.10]: 'If you keep my commandments you shall abide in my love; as I also have kept my
Father's commandments and do abide in his love.' *Rom.*
[8.35-37]: 'Who shall separate us from the love of Christ?

Shall tribulation? or distress? or persecution? or famine? or nakedness? or danger? or the sword? (As it is written: For thy sake we are put to death all the day long. We are accounted as sheep for the slaughter.) But in all these things we overcome, because of him that hath loved us,' etc.

RULE FOUR

That he who does His will gives honor and glory to God, but whoever trangresses His law dishonors Him.

Cap. 1

John [17.4]: 'I have glorified thee on the earth; I have finished the work which thou gavest me to do.' *Matthew* [5.16]: 'So let your light shine before men that they may see your good works and glorify your Father who is in heaven.' *Phil.* [1.10,11]: 'that you may be sincere and without offence unto the day of Christ, filled with the fruit of justice, through Jesus Christ, unto the glory and praise of God.' *Rom.* [2.23]: 'Thou that makest thy boast of the law, by transgression of the law dishonorest God.'

RULE FIVE

That we must be free from all enmity toward all men and love our enemies; and, when necessity requires, lay down our life for our friends with a love like that which God and His Christ had for us.

Cap. 1

Matthew [5.43,44]: 'You have heard that it hath been said to them of old, Thou shalt love thy neighbor and hate thy enemy. But I say to you, Love your enemies'; and a little later [48]: 'Be ye therefore perfect, as your heavenly Father is perfect.' *John* [3.16]: 'For God so loved the world as to give his only begotten Son.' [15.12,13] 'This is my commandment, that you love one another as I have loved you. Greater love than this no man hath, that a man lay down his life for his friends.' *Luke* [6.35,36]: 'and you shall be the sons of the Highest; for he is kind to the unthankful and to the evil. Be ye therefore merciful as your Father also is merciful.' *Rom.* [5.8,9]: 'But God commendeth his charity toward us; because when as yet we were sinners, Christ died for us.' *Eph.* [5.1,2]: 'Be ye therefore followers of God, as most dear children; and walk in love, as Christ also hath loved us and hath delivered himself for us, an oblation and a sacrifice to God.'

That the mark of the disciples of Christ is their love for one another in Him.

Cap. 2

John [13.35]: 'By this shall all men know that you are my disciples, if you have love one for another.'

That to wrong one's neighbor in any way or to cause him such disedification that his faith is destroyed is a sure sign that one does not possess the love of Christ for one's neighbor, even if what is done is allowed by the Scripture for a special reason.

Cap. 3

Rom. [14.15]: 'For if because of meat, thy brother be grieved, thou walkest not now according to charity. Destroy not him with thy meat for whom Christ died.'

That the Christian must serve even one who is vexed with him, in every way, at least in so far as he is able.

Cap. 4

Matthew [5.23,24]: 'If therefore thou offer thy gift at the altar and there thou remember that thy brother hath anything against thee, leave there thy offering before the altar and go first to be reconciled to thy brother: and then coming thou shalt offer thy gift.' *1 Cor.* [4.12,13]: 'we are reviled and we bless; we are persecuted and we suffer it. We are blasphemed and we entreat.'

That he who has the charity of Christ sometimes causes pain, even to one whom he loves, for his good.

Cap. 5

John [16.5-7]: 'And now I go to him that sent me, and none of you asketh me: Whither goest thou? But because I have spoken these things to you, sorrow hath filled your heart. But I tell you the truth: it is expedient to you that I go; for if I go not, the Paraclete will not come to you.' *2 Cor.* [7.7-9]: 'so that I rejoiced the more. For although I made you sorrowful by my epistle, I do not repent; and if I did repent, seeing that the same epistle (although but for a time) did make you sorrowful, now I am glad; not because you were made sorrowful, but because you were made sorrowful unto penance. For you were made sorrowful according to God, that you might suffer damage by us in nothing.'

RULE SIX

That we must speak fearlessly and without shame in the confession of our Lord Jesus and His doctrine.

Cap. 1

Matthew [10.27,28]: 'That which I tell you in the dark, speak ye in the light: and that which you heard in the ear, preach ye upon the housetops. And fear ye not them that kill the body, and are not able to kill the soul: but rather fear him that can destroy both soul and body in hell.' [32]: 'Every one therefore that shall confess me before men, I will also confess him before my Father who is in heaven.' *Luke* [9.26]: 'For he that shall be ashamed of me and of my words, of him the Son of man shall be ashamed, when he shall come in his majesty and that of the Father and of the holy angels.' *2 Tim.* [1.8]: 'Be not thou therefore ashamed of the testimony of our Lord, nor of me his prisoner: but labor with the gospel, like a good soldier of Jesus Christ.'

RULE SEVEN

That even if a man seem to confess the Lord and hear His words, but does not obey His commands, he is condemned, even though, by some divine concession, he be vouchsafed an endowment of spiritual gifts.

Cap. 1

Matthew [7.21-23]: 'Not every one that saith to me, Lord, Lord, shall enter into the kingdom of heaven: but he that doth the will of my Father who is in heaven. Many will say to me in that day, Lord, Lord, have not we prophesied in thy name and cast out devils in thy name and done many miracles in thy name? And then will I profess unto them, I never knew you: depart from me, you that work iniquity,' etc. *Luke* [6.46]: 'And why call you me, Lord, Lord, and do not the things which I say?' etc. *Titus* [1.16]: 'They profess that they know God: but in their works they deny him; being abominable, and incredulous, and to every good work reprobate.'

RULE EIGHT

That we must neither doubt nor hesitate respecting the words of the Lord, but be fully persuaded that every word of God is true and possible even if nature rebel; for therein is the test of faith.

Cap. 1

Matthew [14.25-31]: 'And in the fourth watch of the night, Jesus came to them walking upon the sea. And the disciples seeing him walking upon the sea, were troubled, saying: It is an apparition. And they cried out for fear. And immediately Jesus spoke to them, saying: Be of good heart: it is I, fear ye not. And Peter making answer, said: Lord, if it be thou, bid me come to thee upon the waters. And he said: Come. And Peter going down out of the boat, walked upon the water to come to Jesus. But seeing the wind strong, he was afraid; and when he began to sink, he cried out, saying: Lord, save me. And immediately Jesus stretching forth his hand took hold of him and said to him: O thou of little faith, why didst thou doubt?' *John* [6.53,54]: 'The Jews therefore strove among themselves, saying: How can this man give us his flesh to eat? Then he said to them: Amen, amen I say unto you: Except you eat the flesh of the Son of man and drink his blood, you shall not have life in you!' *Luke* [1.13]: 'But the angel said to him: Fear not, Zachary, for thy prayer is heard; and thy wife Elizabeth shall bear thee a son,' and shortly thereafter.' [18-20]: 'And Zachary said to the angel: Whereby shall I know this? For I am an old man and my wife is advanced in her days. And the angel answering

said to him: I am Gabriel, who stand before God, and am
sent to speak to thee and to bring thee these good tidings.
And behold thou shalt be dumb and shalt not be able to
speak until the day wherein these things come to pass, because
thou hast not believed my words, which shall be fulfilled in
their time.' *Rom.* [4.19-22]: 'And he was not weak in faith;
neither did he consider his own body now dead, whereas he
was almost an hundred years old, nor the dead womb of
Sarah. In the promise also of God he staggered not by distrust; but was strengthened in faith, giving glory to God;
most fully knowing that whatsoever he has promised, he is
able also to perform. And therefore it was reputed to him
unto justice.'

That he who in small matters does not trust in the Lord
is far more manifestly an unbeliever in things of greater
moment.

Cap. 2

John [3.12]:' If I have spoken to you earthly things and
you believe not; how will you believe if I shall speak to you of
heavenly things?' *Luke* [16.10]: 'He that is faithful in that
which is least, is faithful also in that which is greater: and
he that is unjust in that which is little, is unjust also in that
which is greater.'

That we should not rely on our own reasoning to the point
of rejecting the words of the Lord; but we must be convinced that the Lord's words are more worthy of credence
than our own fullest knowledge.

Cap. 3

Matthew [26.31, 33-34]: 'Then Jesus saith to them: All you shall be scandalized in me this night. And Peter answering said to him: Although all shall be scandalized in thee, I will never be scandalized. Jesus said to him: Amen I say to thee, that in this night before the cock crow, thou wilt deny me thrice.' [20-22]: 'But when it was evening, he sat down with his twelve disciples: and whilst they were eating, he said to them: I say to you that one of you is about to betray me. And they being very much troubled, began every one to say to him: Is it I, Lord?, *Acts* [10.13-15]: 'And there came a voice to him: Arise, Peter, kill and eat. But Peter said: Far be it from me, Lord, for I never did eat anything that is common and unclean. And the voice spoke to him again the second time: That which God hath cleansed, do not thou call common.' *2 Cor.* [10.4,5]: 'destroying counsels and every height that exalteth itself against the knowledge of God, and bringing into captivity every understanding unto the obedience of Christ.'

RULE NINE

That no one should be remiss in learning what pertains to his duty but should listen attentively and understand the words of the Lord and do His will.

Cap. 1

Matthew [15.15-18]: 'And Peter answering, said to him: Expound to us this parable. But Jesus said: Are you also yet without understanding? Do you not yet understand that whatsoever entereth into the mouth goeth into the belly and is cast out into the privy? But the things which proceed out of the mouth come forth from the heart and defile a man.'

[13.19]: 'When any one heareth the word of the kingdom
and understandeth it not, there cometh the wicked one and
catcheth away that which was sown in his heart: this is he
that received the seed by the wayside'; and a little farther on
[23]: 'But he that received the seed upon good ground is he
that heareth the word and understandeth and beareth fruit
and yieldeth, the one an hundredfold and another sixty, and
another thirty.' *Mark* [7.14]: 'And calling the whole multitude unto him, he said to them: Hear me and understand.'
Eph. [5.15-17]: 'See therefore how you walk circumspectly;
not as unwise, but as wise; redeeming the time, because the
days are evil. Wherefore become not unwise, but understanding what is the will of God.'

That we should not busy ourselves with matters which do
not concern us.

Cap. 2

John [13.27,28]: 'And after the morsel, Satan entered into
him. And Jesus said to him: That which thou dost, do quickly.
Now no man at the table knew to what purpose he said this
unto him.' *Acts* [1.6,7]: 'They therefore who were come together, asked him, saying: Lord, wilt thou at this time restore
again the kingdom to Israel? But he said to them: It is not
for you to know the times or moments, which the Father hath
put in his own power.'

That it is the duty of those who are zealous for God's good
pleasure to make inquiry as to what it is right for them to do.

Cap. 3

Matthew ⌊13.36]: 'And his disciples came to him, saying:
Expound to us the parable of the cockle of the field.' [19.16]:

'And behold one came and said to him: Good master, what good shall I do that I may have life everlasting?' *Luke* [3.7]: 'He said therefore to the multitudes that went forth to be baptized by him: Ye offspring of vipers, who hath shewed you to flee from the wrath to come?' And a little later [10]: 'And the people'—publicans and soldiers alike—'asked him, saying: What then shall we do?' *Acts* [2.37]: 'Now when they had heard these things, they had compunction in their heart and said to Peter and to the rest of the apostles: What shall we do, men and brethren?'

That he who is questioned must take care to give a worthy answer.

Cap. 4

Luke [10.25-29]: 'And behold a certain lawyer stood up, tempting him and saying: Master, what must I do to possess eternal life? But he said to him: What is written in the law? How readest thou? He answering, said: Thou shalt love the Lord thy God with thy whole heart, and with thy whole soul, and with all thy mind, and thy neighbor as thyself. And he said to him: Thou hast answered right; this do, and thou shalt live.' *Col.* [4.6]: 'Let your speech be always in grace seasoned with salt: that you may know how you ought to answer every man.'

That the condemnation of those who know and do not apply their knowledge is the more severe; but even sin committed in ignorance is not without risk.

Cap. 5

Luke [12.47,48]: 'And that servant who knew the will of his lord, and prepared not himself, and did not according to his will, shall be beaten with many stripes. But he that knew not and did things worthy of stripes, shall be beaten with few stripes.'

That the end of sin is death.

Cap. 1

John [3.36]: 'But he that believeth not the Son, shall not see life; but the wrath of God abideth on him.' *Rom.* [6.20,21]: 'For when you were servants of sin, you were free men to justice. What fruit therefore had you then in those things of which you are now ashamed? For the end of them is death.' And a little later [23]: 'For the wages of sin is death.' *1 Cor.* [15.56]: 'Now the sting of death is sin.'

That the fulfillment of the commandment of God is life everlasting.

Cap. 2

John [8.51]: 'Amen, amen I say to you: If any man keep my word, he shall not see death for ever.' *John* [12.49,50]: 'But he who sent me, the Father, he himself gave me commandment what I should say and what I should speak. And I know that his commandment is life everlasting.' *Rom.* [6.22]: 'But now being made free from sin, and becoming servants to God, you have your fruit unto sanctification, and the end, life everlasting.'

That the judgments of God ought not be lightly regarded, but feared even though retribution is not immediate.

Cap. 1

Matthew [10.28]: 'But rather fear him that can destroy both soul and body in hell.' *Luke* [12.45-47]: 'But if that servant shall say in his heart: My lord is long a-coming; and shall begin to strike the menservants and maidservants, and to eat and to drink and be drunk; the lord of that servant will come in the day that he hopeth not, and at the hour that he knoweth not, and shall separate him and shall appoint him his portion with unbelievers.' *John* [5.14]: 'Behold thou art made whole: sin no more, lest some worse thing happen to thee.' *Eph.* [5.6]: 'Let no man deceive you with vain words. For because of these things cometh the anger of God upon the children of unbelief.'

That he who has been chastised for his past sins and has obtained pardon prepares for himself a judgment of wrath more severe than the former judgment if he sin again.

Cap. 2

John [5.14]: 'Behold thou art made whole: sin no more, lest some worse thing happen to thee.'

That when any incur the judgment of the wrath of God, the rest should amend their ways in fear.

Cap. 3

Luke [13.1-6]: 'And there were present at that very time some that told him of the Galileans whose blood Pilate had mingled with their sacrifices. And Jesus answering said to them: Think you that these Galileans were sinners above all the men of Galilee, because they suffered such things? No, I say to you; but unless you shall do penance, you shall all likewise perish. Or those eighteen upon whom the tower fell in Siloe and slew them: think you that they also were debtors above all the men that dwelt in Jerusalem? No, I say to you; but except you do penance, you shall all likewise perish.' *Acts* [5.5]: 'And Ananias hearing these words, fell down and gave up the ghost. And there came a great fear upon all that heard it.' *1 Cor.* [10.10,11]: 'Neither do you murmur, as some of them murmured and were destroyed by the destroyer. Now all these things happened to them in figure; and they are written for our correction, upon whom the ends of the world are come.'

That frequently a man is even delivered up to evil works as punishment for past impiety.

Cap. 4

Rom. [1.28]: 'And as they liked not to have God in their knowledge, God delivered them up to a reprobate sense, to do those things which are not convenient.' *2 Thess.* [2.10,11]: 'Because they received not the love of the truth that they might be saved. Therefore God shall send them the operation of error, to believe lying.'

That the multitude of sinners does not arouse the solicitude of God, but he who is acceptable to Him, whether man or woman.

Cap. 5

Luke [4.25,26]: 'In truth I say to you, there were many widows in the days of Elias in Israel, when heaven was shut up three years and six months, when there was a great famine throughout all the earth. And to none of them was Elias sent but to Sarepta of Sidon, to a widow woman.' *1 Cor.* [10.1-5]: 'For I would not have you ignorant, brethren, that our fathers were all under the cloud and all passed through the sea. And all in Moses were baptized, in the cloud and in the sea; and all did eat the same spiritual food and all drank the same spiritual drink: (and they drank of the spiritual rock that followed them, and the rock was Christ). But with most of them God was not well pleased; for they were overthrown in the desert.'

RULE TWELVE

That every contradiction, even if it arise from a pious and amicable spirit, estranges the one dissenting from the Lord; but every word of the Lord ought to be received with complete assent.

Cap. 1

John [13.5-8]: 'And he began to wash the feet of the disciples and to wipe them with the towel wherewith he was girded. He cometh therefore to Simon Peter. And Peter saith to him: Lord, dost thou wash my feet? Jesus answered and said to him: What I do thou knowest not now, but thou shalt know hereafter. Peter saith to him: Thou shalt never wash my feet. Jesus answered him: If I wash thee not, thou shalt have no part with me.'

That we should not conform with human traditions to the extent of setting aside the command of God.

Cap. 2

Mark [7.5-8]: 'Then the Pharisees and scribes asked him:

Why do not thy disciples walk according to the tradition of the ancients, but they eat bread with unwashed hands? But he answering said to them: Well did Isaias prophesy of you hypocrites, as it is written: This people honoureth me with their lips but their heart is far from me. And in vain do they worship me, teaching doctrines and precepts of men. For leaving the commandment of God, you hold the tradition of men,' etc.

That we should observe everything without exception which has been handed down by the Lord through the Gospel and the Apostles.

Cap. 3

Matthew [28.19,20]: 'Going teach ye all nations; baptizing them in the name of the Father, and of the Son, and of the Holy Ghost; teaching them to observe all things whatsoever I have commanded you.' *Luke* [1.6]: 'And they were both just before God, walking in all the commandments and justifications of the Lord without blame.' [10.16]: 'He that heareth you, heareth me; and he that despiseth you, despiseth me.' *2 Thess.* [2.14]: 'Therefore, brethren, stand fast; and hold the traditions which you have learned as through us whether by word or by epistle.'

That no one may prefer his own will to the will of God, but in everything we must seek and do the will of God.

Cap. 4

John [5.30]: 'Because I seek not my own will, but the will of him that sent me, the Father.' *Luke* [22.41,42]: 'And kneeling down, he prayed saying: Father, if thou wilt, remove

this chalice from me: but yet not my will but thine be done.'
Eph. [2.3]: 'In which also we all conversed in time past, in
the desires of our flesh, fulfilling the will of the flesh and of
our thoughts, and were by nature children of wrath, even as
the rest.'

RULE THIRTEEN

That we must always be sober and ready in our zeal for the
works of God, being aware of the danger of a dilatory spirit.

Cap. 1

Luke [12.35-40]: 'Let your loins be girt, and lamps burning; and you yourselves like to men who wait for their lord,
when he shall return from the wedding: that when he cometh
and knocketh, they may open to him immediately. Blessed
are those servants whom the Lord when he cometh, shall
find watching. Amen, I say to you, that he will gird himself
and make them sit down to meat, and passing will minister
unto them. And if he shall come in the second watch, or come
in the third watch, and find them so, blessed are those servants. But this know ye, that if the householder did know
at what hour the thief would come, he would surely watch,
and would not suffer his house to be broken open. Be you then
also ready; for at what hour you think not, the Son of man
will come,' etc. *1 Thess.* [5.1-3]: 'But of the times and moments, brethren, you need not that we should write to you;
for yourselves know perfectly that the day of the Lord shall
so come as a thief in the night,' and shortly after [6]: 'Therefore, let us not sleep as others do; but let us watch and be
sober.'

That we should consider every season opportune for exercising zeal in that which is pleasing to God.

Cap. 2

John [9.4]: 'I must work the works of him that sent me, whilst it is day.' *Phil.* [2.12]: 'Wherefore, my dearly beloved, (as you have always obeyed, not as in my presence only, but much more now in my absence,) with fear and trembling work out your salvation.'

RULE FOURTEEN

That we should avoid unseasonable intrusions and discover the appropriate time for each word and deed.

Cap. 1

Matthew [9.14,15]: 'Then came to him the disciples of John, saying: Why do we and the Pharisees fast often, but thy disciples do not fast? And Jesus said to them: Can the children of the bridegroom mourn as long as the bridegroom is with them? But the days will come when the bridegroom shall be taken away from them, and then they shall fast in those days,' etc. *Gal.* [4.31-5.1]: 'So then, brethren, we are not the children of the bondwoman, but of the free; by the freedom, therefore, wherewith Christ has made us free. Stand fast and be not held again under the yoke of bondage.'

RULE FIFTEEN

That it is not right to neglect one's duty, relying on the good works of others.

Cap. 1

Matthew [3.8,9]: 'Bring forth therefore fruit worthy of penance. And think not to say within yourselves: We have Abraham for our father.'

That they who live with persons who are pleasing to God are in no way benefited if they are not perfecting their own will, even though in appearance they maintain a likeness to these.

Cap. 1

Matthew [25.1-4]: 'Then shall the kingdom of heaven be like to ten virgins, who taking their lamps went out to meet the bridegroom. And five of them were foolish and five wise. They who were foolish, having taken their lamps, did not take oil with them; but the wise took oil in their vessels with their lamps.' A little further on he adds concerning the foolish [11-13]: 'But at last came the other virgins saying: Lord, Lord, open to us. But he answering said: I say to you, I know you not.' *Luke* [17.34-37]: 'I say to you: in that night there shall be two men in one bed; the one shall be taken, and the other shall be left. Two women shall be grinding together; the one shall be taken, and the other shall be left. And they answering say to him: Where, Lord? Who said to them: Wheresoever the body shall be, thither will the eagles also be gathered together.'

That, having recognized the nature of this present time from the signs revealed to us by the Scriptures, we should dispose our affairs accordingly.

Cap. 1

Matthew [24.32]: 'And from the fig tree learn a parable: When the branch thereof is now tender and the leaves come forth, you know that summer is nigh. So you also, when you shall see all these things, know ye that it is nigh, even at the doors.' *Luke* [12.54-56]: 'When you see a cloud rising from the west, presently you say: A shower is coming: and so it happeneth. And when ye see the south wind blow, you say: There will be heat: and it cometh to pass. You hypocrites, you know how to discern the face of the heaven and of the earth; but how is it that you do not discern this time?' *1 Cor.* [7.29-31]: 'Already the time is short: so that they also who have wives should be as if they had none; and they that weep, as though they wept not; and they that rejoice, as if they rejoiced not; and they that buy, as though they possessed not; and they that use this world, as if they used it not: for the fashion of the world passeth away.'

RULE EIGHTEEN

That the commands of God should be carried out as the Lord enjoined; for he who is at fault in his manner of executing them is reprobate in the sight of God, even though he may seem to be complying with the command.

Cap. 1

Luke [14.12-14]: 'And he said to him also that had invited him: When thou makest a dinner or a supper, call not thy friends nor thy brethren nor thy kinsmen, nor thy neighbors who are rich; lest perhaps they also invite thee again, and a recompense be made to thee. But when thou makest a feast, call the poor, the maimed, the lame, and the blind; and thou shalt be blessed, because they have not wherewith to make thee recompense: for recompense shall be made to thee at the resurrection of the just.'

That we should not perform the command of God with a view to pleasing men or from any other earthly motive but in everything we should have as our aim, the good pleasure and the glory of God.

Cap. 2

Matthew [6.1,2]: 'Take heed that you do not your alms-deeds before men to be seen by them; otherwise you shall not have a reward of your Father who is in heaven. Therefore when thou dost an almsdeed, sound not a trumpet before men, as the hypocrites do in the synagogues and in the streets that they may be honored by men. Amen I say to you, they have received their reward,' etc. *1 Cor.* [10.31]: 'Therefore, whether you eat or drink, or whatsoever else you do, do all to the glory of God.' *1 Thess.* [2.4-6]: 'But as we were approved by God that the gospel should be committed to us: even so we speak, not as pleasing men, but God, who proveth our hearts. For neither have we used at any time the speech of flattery, as you know; nor taken an occasion of covetousness, God is witness; nor sought we glory of men, neither of you, nor of others.'

That the commands of the Lord should be carried out with an attentive mind and with good dispositions before God and men; for he who does not so is condemned.

Cap. 3

Matthew [23.25-27]: 'Woe to you, scribes and Pharisees, hypocrites; because you make clean the outside of the cup and of the dish, but within you are full of rapine and unclean-ness. Thou blind Pharisee, first make clean the inside of the cup and of the dish, that the outside of it may become clean.'

Rom. [12.8]: 'He that giveth, with simplicity.' *Phil.* [2.14]: 'Do ye all things without murmuring and hesitations.' *1 Tim.* [1.5,19]: 'Now the end of the commandment is charity from a pure heart and a good conscience . . . Having faith and a good conscience, which some rejecting have made shipwreck concerning the faith.'

That requital for the more important works is based on the prudent management of lesser ones.

Cap. 4

Matthew [25.23]: 'Well done, good and faithful servant; because thou hast been faithful over a few things, I will place thee over many things: enter thou into the joy of thy lord.' And shortly after [29]: 'For to everyone that hath shall be given, and he shall abound; but from him that hath not, that also which he seemeth to have, shall be taken away.' *Luke* [16.11,12]: 'If then you have not been faithful in the unjust mammon, who will trust you with that which is the true? And if you have not been faithful in that which is another's, who will give you that which is your own?'

That we should fulfill the commands of the Lord with insatiable desire, ever pressing onward toward greater achievement.

Cap. 5

Matthew [5.6]: 'Blessed are they that hunger and thirst after justice.' *Phil.* [3.13,14]: 'Brethren, I do not count myself to have apprehended. But one thing I do: forgetting the things that are behind, and stretching forth myself to those that are before, I press towards the mark, to the prize of the supernal vocation in Christ Jesus.'

That the commands of God should be executed, insofar as it is possible for the doer, in such a way as to give glory to God and to enlighten all men.

Cap. 6

Matthew [5.14-16]: 'You are the light of the world. A city seated on a mountain cannot be hid. Neither do men light a candle and put it under a bushel, but upon a candlestick that it may shine to all that are in the house. So let your light shine before men that they may see your good works and glorify your Father who is in heaven.' *Luke* [8.16]: 'Now no man lighting a candle covereth it with a vessel, or putteth it under a bed; but setteth it upon a candlestick, that they who come in may see the light.' *Phil.* [1.10,11]: 'That you may be sincere and without offence unto the day of Christ, filled with the fruit of justice, through Jesus Christ unto the glory and praise of God.'

RULE NINETEEN

That one who does the will of God should not be impeded whether he obeys in consideration of a divine command or of human reason, nor ought he permit any to hinder him even though they be his relatives, but he should abide by his decision.

Cap. 1

Matthew [3.13-15]: 'Then cometh Jesus from Galilee to the Jordan unto John to be baptized by him. But John stayed

him saying: I ought to be baptized by thee and comest thou
to me? And Jesus answering, said to him: Suffer it to be so
now. For so it becometh us to fulfill all justice,' etc.
[16.21-23]: 'From that time Jesus began to show to his disciples that he must go to Jerusalem and suffer many things
from the ancients and chief priests and scribes, and be put to
death and the third day rise again. And Peter taking him,
began to rebuke him saying: Lord, be it far from thee; this
shall not be to thee. But he turning, said to Peter: Go behind me, Satan, thou art a scandal unto me: because thou
savourest not the things that are of God, but the things that
are of men.' *Mark* [10.13,14]: 'And they brought to him
young children that he might touch them. And the disciples
rebuked them that brought them. Whom when Jesus saw,
he was displeased, and saith to them: Suffer the little children to come unto me, and forbid them not; for of such is
the kingdom of heaven.' *Acts* [21.10-14]: 'And as we tarried
there for some days, there came from Judea a certain prophet
named Agabus. Who, when he was come to us, took Paul's
girdle; and binding his own feet and hands, he said: Thus
saith the Holy Ghost: The man whose girdle this is, the Jews
shall bind in this manner in Jerusalem, and shall deliver him
into the hands of the Gentiles. Which when we had heard,
both we and they that were of that place, desired him that he
would not go up to Jerusalem. Then Paul answered and
said: What do you mean weeping and afflicting my heart?
For I am ready not only to be bound but to die also in
Jerusalem, for the name of the Lord Jesus. And when we
could not persuade him, we ceased, saying: The will of the
Lord be done.' *1 Thess.* [2.15,16]: 'Who both killed the Lord
Jesus and their own prophets and have persecuted us, and
please not God and are adversaries to all men; prohibiting

us to speak to the Gentiles that they may be saved, to fill up their sins always; for the wrath is come upon them to the end.'

That he should not be prevented who carries out a command of God without sincerity and yet maintains in appearance the full integrity of the Lord's teaching: because no one is wronged insofar as the act itself is concerned and sometimes certain persons may be benefited by it; yet such a one should be exhorted to have dispositions worthy of his good action.

Cap. 2

Matthew [6.2-4]: 'Therefore when thou dost an almsdeed, sound not a trumpet before thee as the hypocrites do in the synagogues and in the streets, that they may be honored by men. Amen I say to you, they have received their reward. But when thou dost alms, let not thy left hand know what thy right hand doth; that thy alms may be in secret and thy Father who seeth in secret will repay thee openly'; and, similarly, with regard to prayer, *Mark* [9.37-39]: 'John answered him, saying: Master, we saw one casting out devils in thy name, who followeth not us, and we forbade him because he followeth not us. But Jesus said: Do not forbid him. For there is no man that doth a miracle in my name and can soon speak ill of me. For he that is not against us is for us.' *Phil.* [1.15-18]: 'Some indeed even out of envy and contention; but some also for good will preach Christ. Some out of charity, knowing that I am set for the defence of the gospel; and some out of contention preach Christ not sincerely; supposing that they raise affliction to my bands. But what then? So that, by all means, whether by occasion, or by truth, Christ be preached; in this also I rejoice, yea and will rejoice.'

RULE TWENTY

That they who believe in the Lord should be baptized in the Name of the Father and of the Son and of the Holy Ghost.

Matthew [28.19]: 'Going teach ye all nations; baptizing them in the name of the Father and of the Son and of the Holy Ghost.' *John* [3.3]: 'Amen, amen I say to thee, unless a man be born again, he cannot see the kingdom of God'; and again [5]: 'Amen, amen I say to thee, unless a man be born of water and the Holy Ghost, he cannot enter into the kingdom of God.'

What is the nature or the function of baptism? The changing of the person baptized in thought and word and action and his transformation according to the power bestowed on him into that of which he has been born.

Cap. 2

John [3.6-8]: 'That which is born of the flesh is flesh, and that which is born of the Spirit is spirit. Wonder not that I said to thee, you must be born again. The Spirit breatheth where he will; and thou hearest his voice; but thou knowest not whence he cometh and whither he goeth; so is every one that is born of the Spirit.' *Rom.* [6.11]: 'Being dead to sin, but alive unto God in Christ Jesus.' [3-7]: 'All we who are baptized in Christ Jesus are baptized in his death; for we are buried together with him by baptism unto death; that as Christ is risen from the dead by the glory of the Father, so we also may walk in newness of life. For if we have been planted together in the likeness of his death, we shall also be in the likeness of his resurrection. Knowing this, that our old man is crucified with him, that the body of sin may be destroyed, to the end that we may serve sin no longer. For he that is dead is justified from sin.' *Col.* [2.11,12]: 'In whom also you are circumcised with circumcision not made by hand, in despoiling of the body of the sins of the flesh, but in the circumcision of Christ; buried with him in baptism in whom also you are risen again by the faith of the operation of God who hath raised him up from the dead.' *Gal.* [3.27-29]: 'For as many of you as have been baptized in Christ have put on Christ. There is neither Jew nor Greek: there is neither bond nor free: there is neither male nor female. For you are all one in Christ Jesus.' *Col.* [3.9-12]: 'Stripping yourselves of the old man with his deeds, and putting on the new, him who is renewed unto knowledge, according to the image of him that created him. Where there is neither Gentile nor Jew, circumcision nor uncircumcision, barbarian nor Scythian, bond nor free. But Christ is all, and in all.'

RULE TWENTY-ONE

That the receiving of the Body and Blood of Christ is also necessary for life everlasting.

Cap. 1

John [6.54,55]: 'Amen, amen I say unto you: Except you eat the flesh of the Son of man and drink his blood, you shall not have life in you. He that eateth my flesh and drinketh my blood hath everlasting life,' etc.

That he who undertakes to receive Communion, without observing the manner in which participation in the Body and Blood of Christ has been granted, derives no benefit therefrom; and he who communicates unworthily is condemned.

Cap. 2

John [6.54,55]: 'Amen, amen I say unto you: Except you eat the flesh of the Son of man and drink his blood, you shall not have life in you'; and a little further on [6.62-64]: 'But Jesus, knowing in himself that his disciples murmured at this, said to them: Doth this scandalize you? If then you shall see the Son of man ascend up where he was before? It is the spirit that quickeneth: the flesh profiteth nothing. The words that I have spoken to you are spirit and life.' *1 Cor.* [11.27-29]: 'Therefore, whosoever shall eat this bread, or drink this chalice of the Lord unworthily, shall be guilty of the body and of the blood of the Lord. But let a man prove himself: and so let him eat of the bread and drink of the chalice. For he that eateth and drinketh unworthily, eateth and drinketh judgment to himself, not discerning the body of the Lord.'

The manner in which we should eat the Body and drink the Blood of the Lord, for a commemoration of the obedience of the Lord even unto death, that they who live may no longer live for themselves but unto Him who died for them and rose again.

Cap. 3

Luke [22.19-20]: 'And taking bread he gave thanks and brake, and gave to them, saying: This is my body, which is given for you. Do this for a commemoration of me. In like manner the chalice also, after he had supped, saying: This is the chalice, the new testament in my blood, which shall be shed for you.' *1 Cor.* [11.23-26]: 'that the Lord Jesus, the same night in which he was betrayed, took bread, and giving thanks, broke, and said: Take ye, and eat: this is my body which is broken for you: this do for the commemoration of me. In like manner also the chalice, after he had supped, saying: This chalice is the new testament in my blood: this do ye, as often as you shall drink, for the commemoration of me. For as often as you shall eat this bread and drink the chalice, you shall show the death of the Lord, until he come.' *2 Cor.* [5.14,15]: 'For the charity of Christ presseth us: judging this, that if one died for all, then all were dead. And he died for all; that they also who live may not now live to themselves, but unto him who died for them and rose again' so that many may become one body in Christ . . . *1 Cor.* [10.16,17]: 'The bread which we break, is it not the partaking of the body of Christ? For we being many are one bread, one body, all that partake of one bread.'

That he who partakes of the Sacred Species should praise the Lord with hymns.

Cap. 4

Matthew [26.26]:. 'And whilst they were at supper, Jesus took bread, and blessed and broke: and gave to his disciples,' etc. To which he adds [30]: 'And a hymn being said, they went out unto Mount Olivet.'

RULE TWENTY-TWO

That committing sin estranges us from the Lord and leagues us with the Devil.

Cap. 1

John [8.34]: 'Amen, amen I say unto you: that whosoever committeth sin, is the servant of sin.' [44]: 'You are of your

father the devil, and the desires of your father you will do.'
Rom. [6.20]: 'For when you were the servants of sin, you
were free men to justice.'

That intimacy with the Lord is not to be explained in
terms of kinship according to the flesh but it is achieved by
alacrity in doing the will of God.

Cap. 2

John [8.47]: 'He that is of God, heareth the words of God.'
Luke [8.20-22]: 'And it was told him: Thy mother and thy
brethren stand without, desiring to see thee. Who answering,
said to them: My mother and my brethren are they who
hear the word of God and do it.' *John* [15.14]: 'You are my
friends, if you do the things that I command you.' *Rom.*
[8.14]: 'For whosoever are led by the Spirit of God, they are
the sons of God.'

RULE TWENTY-THREE

That he who is drawn into sin against his will should understand that, because he was voluntarily mastered by another
sin committed previously, he is now, as a consequence of this
first sin, led into another against his will.

Cap. 1

Rom. [7.14-20]: 'For we know that the law is spiritual;
but I am carnal, sold under sin. For that which I work, I
understand not. For I do not that good which I will; but the
evil which I hate, that I do. If then I do that which I will
not, I consent to the law, that it is good. Now then it is no
more I that do it, but sin that dwelleth in me. For I know that

there dwelleth not in me, that is to say, in my flesh, that which is good. For to will, is present with me; but to accomplish that which is good I find not. For the good which I will I do not; but the evil which I will not, that I do. Now if I do that which I will not, it is no more I that do it, but sin that dwelleth in me.'

RULE TWENTY-FOUR

That we must not lie, but in all things tell the truth.

Cap. 1

Matthew [5.37]: 'But let your speech be yea, yea: no, no; and that which is over and above these, is of evil.' *Eph.* [4.25]: 'Putting away lying, speak ye the truth every man with his neighbor . . .' *Col.* [3.9]: 'Lie not one to another.'

RULE TWENTY-FIVE

That we should not engage in fruitless or controversial discussions.

Cap. 1

2 Tim. [2.14]: 'Of these things put them in mind, charging them before the Lord: Contend not in words, for it is to no profit, but to the subverting of the hearers.' [23]: 'And avoid foolish and unlearned questions, knowing that they beget strifes.'

That idle words in which there is nothing beneficial ought not be spoken; for to speak or to perform even a good action without aiming to give edification is to grieve the Holy Spirit of God.

Cap. 2

Matthew [12.36]: 'But I say unto you, that every idle word that men shall speak, they shall render an account for it in the day of judgment.' *Eph.* [4.29,30]: 'Let no evil speech proceed from your mouth; but that which is good, to the edification of faith, that it may administer grace to the hearers. And grieve not the holy Spirit of God; whereby you are sealed unto the day of redemption.'

RULE TWENTY-SIX

That every word and deed should be ratified by the testimony of the Holy Scripture to confirm the good and cause shame to the wicked.

Cap. 1

Matthew [4.3,4]: 'And the tempter coming to him said: If thou be the Son of God, command that these stones be made bread. Who answered and said: It is written: Not in bread alone doth man live, but in every word that proceedeth from the mouth of God.' *Acts* [2.4]: 'And they were all filled with the Holy Ghost, and they began to speak with divers tongues, according as the Holy Ghost gave them to speak.' [12-17]: 'And they were all astonished and wondered, saying one to another: What meaneth this? But others mocking, said: These men are full of new wine. But Peter standing up with the eleven, lifted up his voice and spoke to them: Ye men of Judas, and all you that dwell in Jerusalem, be this known to you, and with your ears receive my words. For these are not drunk, as you suppose, seeing it is but the third hour of the day. But this is that which was spoken of by the prophet Joel: And it shall come to pass in the last days, (saith the Lord),

I will pour out my spirit upon all flesh, and they shall prophesy,' etc.

That appeals to what is natural or customary should also be employed for the ratification of what we do or say.

Cap. 2

Matthew [7.15-17]: 'Beware of false prophets, who come to you in the clothing of sheep, but inwardly they are ravening wolves. By their fruits you shall know them. Do men gather grapes of thorns or figs of thistles? Even so every good tree bringeth forth good fruit and the evil tree bringeth forth evil fruit.' etc. *Luke* [5.30,31]: 'But their scribes and Pharisees murmured, saying to his disciples: Why do you eat and drink with publicans and sinners? And Jesus answering, said to them: They that are whole need not the physician, but they that are sick.' *2 Tim.* [2.4,5]: 'No man, being a soldier to God, entangleth himself with secular businesses; that he may please him to whom he hath engaged himself. For he also that striveth for the mastery, is not crowned, except he strive lawfully.'

RULE TWENTY-SEVEN

That we should not be like those who are hostile to the Lord's teaching, but imitate God and His saints according to the power given us by Him.

Cap. 1

Matthew [20.25-28]: 'You know that the princes of the Gentiles lord it over them; and they that are the greater, exercise power upon them. It shall not be so among you: but whosoever will be the greater among you, let him be your minister; and he that will be first among you, shall be your servant, even as the Son of man is not come to be ministered unto, but to minister, and to give his life a redemption for many.' *Rom.* [12.2]: 'And be not conformed to this world; but be reformed in the newness of your mind, that you may prove what is the will of God.' *1 Cor.* [11.1]: 'Be ye followers of me, as I also am of Christ.'

RULE TWENTY-EIGHT

That we should not be readily and thoughtlessly carried away by those who make pretense of the truth, but we should recognize each from the sign given us by the Scriptures.

Cap. 1

Matthew [7.15,16]: 'Beware of false prophets, who come to you in the clothing of sheep, but inwardly they are ravening wolves. By their fruits you shall know them.' *John* [13.35]: 'By this shall all men know that you are my disciples, if you have love one for another.' *1 Cor.* [12.3]: 'Wherefore I give you to understand, that no man, speaking by the spirit of God, saith Anathema to Jesus.'

RULE TWENTY-NINE

That everyone should give evidence of his calling by his own works.

Cap. 1

John [5.36]: 'The works themselves which I do, give testimony of me, that the Father hath sent me.' [10.37,38]: 'If I do not the works of my Father, believe me not. But if I do, though you will not believe me, believe my works; that you may know and believe that the Father is in me, and I in the Father.' *2 Cor.* [6.3,4]: 'Giving no offense to any man, that our ministry be not blamed. But in all things let us exhibit ourselves as the ministers of God in much patience, in tribulations,' etc.

RULE THIRTY

That we should not profane holy things by mingling them with those meant for ordinary use.

Cap. 1

Matthew [21.12,13]: 'And Jesus went into the temple of God, and cast out all them that sold and bought in the temple and overthrew the tables of the money changers, and the chairs of them that sold doves; and he saith to them: It is written, My house shall be called the house of prayer; but you have made it a den of thieves.' *1 Cor.* [11.22]: 'What, have you not houses to eat and to drink in? Or despise ye the church of God; and put them to shame that have not?' [34]: 'If any man be hungry, let him eat at home; that you come not together unto judgment.'

That which is consecrated to God should be honored as holy as long as the will of God is fulfilled in it.

Cap. 2

Matthew [23.37,38]: 'Jerusalem, Jerusalem, thou that killest the prophets, and stonest them that are sent unto thee, how often would I have gathered together thy children, as the hen doth gather her chickens under her wings, and thou wouldst not? Behold, your house shall be left to you, desolate.'

RULE THIRTY-ONE

That objects set aside for those consecrated to God should not be usurped for others' use unless there be something superfluous.

Cap. 1

Mark [7.26-29]: 'For the woman was a Gentile, a Syrophoenician born. And she besought him that he would cast forth the devil out of her daughter. Who said: Suffer first the children to be filled; for it is not good to take the bread of the children, and cast it to the dogs. But she answered and said to him: Yea, Lord; for the whelps also eat under the table of the crumbs of the children. And he said to her: For this saying go thy way, the devil is gone out of thy daughter.'

RULE THIRTY-TWO

That to everyone should be rendered what is reasonably and fairly due him.

Cap. 1

Luke [20.21-25]: 'And they asked him, saying: Master, we know that thou speakest and teachest rightly; and thou dost not respect any person, but teachest the way of God in truth. Is it lawful for us to give tribute to Caesar, or no? But he considering their guile, said to them: Why tempt you me? Show me a penny. Whose image and inscription hath it? They answering, said to him, Caesar's. And he said to them: Render therefore to Caesar the things that are Caesar's: and to God the things that are God's.' *Rom.* [13.7,8]: 'Render therefore to all men their dues. Tribute, to whom tribute is due; custom, to whom custom: fear, to whom fear: honour, to whom honour. Owe no man anything, but to love one another.'

RULE THIRTY-THREE

That we should not give scandal.

Cap. 1

Matthew [18.6]: 'But he that shall scandalize one of these little ones that believe in me, it were better for him that a mill-stone should be hanged about his neck, and that he should be drowned in the depth of the sea.' And again [7]: 'Woe to that man by whom the scandal cometh.' *Rom.* [14.13]: 'But judge this rather, that you put not a stumbling block or a scandal in your brother's way.'

That whatever is opposed to the will of the Lord is scandal.

Cap. 2

Matthew [16.21-23]: 'From that time Jesus began to show to his disciples, that he must go to Jerusalem, and suffer many things from the ancients and chief priests and scribes and be put to death, and the third day rise again. And Peter taking him, began to rebuke him, saying: Lord, be it far from thee, this shall not be unto thee. Who turning, said to Peter: Go behind me, Satan, thou art a scandal unto me: because thou savorest not the things that are of God, but the things that are of men.'

That even a deed or word countenanced by the Scripture should be avoided whenever others would be emboldened thereby to commit sin by a similar act, or to relax their zeal for virtue.

Cap. 3

1 Cor. [8.4-13]: 'But as for the meats that are sacrificed to idols, we know that an idol is nothing in the world, and that there is no God but one. For although there be that are called gods, either in heaven or on earth (for there be gods many, and lords many); yet to us there is but one God, the Father, of whom are all things, and we unto him; and one Lord, Jesus Christ, by whom are all things and we by him. But there is not knowledge in every one. For some until this present, with conscience of the idol, eat as a thing sacrificed to an idol, and their conscience, being weak, is defiled. But meat doth not commend us to God. For neither, if we eat, shall we have the more; nor, if we eat not, shall we have the less. But take heed lest perhaps this your liberty become a stumbling block to the weak. For if a man see him that hath knowledge sit at meat in the idol's temple, shall not his conscience, being weak, be emboldened to eat those things which are sacrificed to idols? And through thy knowledge shall the weak brother perish, for whom Christ hath died? Now when you sin thus against the brethren, and wound their weak conscience, you sin against Christ. Wherefore if meat scandalize my brother, I will never eat flesh, lest I should scandalize my brother.' [9.4-7]: 'Have not we power to eat and drink? Have we not power to carry about a woman, a sister, as well as the rest of the apostles, and the brethren of the Lord, and Cephas? Or I only and Barnabas, have not we power to do this? Who serveth as a soldier at any time, at his own charges? Who planteth a vineyard, and eateth not of the fruit thereof? Who feedeth the flock, and eateth not of the milk of the flock?' etc.

That to avoid scandal even that which is not of necessity should be done.

Cap. 4

Matthew [17.23-36]: 'And when they were come to Capharnaum, they that received the didrachmas, came to Peter and said to him: Doth not your master pay the didrachmas? He said: Yes. And when he was come into the house, Jesus prevented him, saying: What is thy opinion, Simon? The kings of the earth, of whom do they receive tribute or custom? Of their own children, or of strangers? And he said: Of strangers. Jesus said to him: Then the children are free. But that we may not scandalize them, go to the sea, and cast in a hook: and that fish which shall first come up, take: and when thou hast opened its mouth, thou shalt find a stater: take that, and give it to them for me and thee.'

That as regards the will of the Lord, even if some take scandal, we must not let this hamper our freedom of action.

Cap. 5

Matthew [15.11-15]: 'Not that which goeth into the mouth defileth a man: but what cometh out of the mouth, this defileth a man. Then came his disciples, and said to him: Dost thou know that the Pharisees, when they heard this word were scandalized? But he answering, said: Every plant which my heavenly Father hath not planted, shall be rooted up. Let them alone; they are blind, and leaders of the blind. And if the blind lead the blind, both fall into the pit.' *John* [6.54]: 'Amen, amen I say unto you: Except you eat the flesh of the Son of man, and drink his blood, you shall not have life in you,' and a little further on [67,68]: 'After this, many of his disciples went back and walked no more with him. Then Jesus said to the twelve: Will you also go away?'

2 Cor. [2.15,16]: 'For we are the good odour of Christ unto God, in them that are saved, and in them that perish. To the one indeed the odour of death unto death; but to the others the odour of life unto life. And for these things who is sufficient?'

RULE THIRTY-FOUR

That each in his own degree should be as a pattern of good to others.

Cap. 1

Matthew [11.29]: 'Learn of me, because I am meek and humble of heart.' *2 Cor.* [9.2]: 'For I know your forward mind, for which I boast of you to the Macedonians. That Achaia also is ready from the year past, and your emulation hath provoked very many.' *1 Thess.* [1.6,7]: 'And you became followers of us, and of the Lord, receiving the word in much tribulation, with joy of the Holy Ghost; so that you were made a pattern to all that believe in Macedonia and in Achaia.'

RULE THIRTY-FIVE

That they who behold the fruit of the Holy Spirit in a man, who on every occasion maintains in his life a consistency with true piety, and do not ascribe this to the Holy Spirit but attribute it to the Adversary, commit blasphemy against the Holy Spirit Himself.

Cap. 1

Matthew [12.22-24, 28]: 'Then was offered to him one possessed with a devil, blind and dumb; and he healed him so that he spoke and saw. And all the multitudes were amazed, and said: Is not this the son of David? But the Pharisees hearing it, said: This man casteth not out devils but by Beezlebub, the prince of the devils. And Jesus, knowing their thoughts, said to them: If I by the Spirit of God cast out devils, then is the kingdom of God come among you.' To these words He adds subsequently [31,32]: 'Therefore I say to you: Every sin and blasphemy shall be forgiven men, but the blasphemy of the Spirit shall not be forgiven. And whosoever shall speak a word against the Son of man, it shall be forgiven him; but he that shall speak against the Holy Ghost, it shall not be forgiven him, neither in this world nor in the world to come.'

RULE THIRTY-SIX

That they who follow the Lord's teaching as their model should be received with all honor and carefulness for the glory of the Lord Himself; and he who neither hearkens to them nor receives them is condemned.

Cap. 1

Matthew [10.40]: 'He that receiveth you, receiveth me; and he that receiveth me, receiveth him that sent me.' [14,15]: 'And whosoever shall not receive you, nor hear your words, going forth out of that house or city shake off the dust from your feet. Amen, I say to you, it shall be more tolerable for the land of Sodom and Gomorrha in the day of judgement than for that city.' *John* [13.20]: 'He that receiveth whomsoever I send, receiveth me, and he that receiveth me receiveth him that sent me.' *Phil* [2.25]: 'But I have thought it necessary to send to you Epaphroditus, my brother and fellow labourer, and fellow soldier, but your apostle, and he that hath ministered to my wants'; and shortly after [29]: 'Receive him therefore with all joy in the Lord: and treat with honour such as he is.'

That ready service, according to our ability, even in very small things and even if it be rendered by women, is acceptable to God.

Cap. 1

Matthew [10.42]: 'And whosoever shall give to drink to one of these little ones a cup of cold water only in the name of a disciple, amen I say to you, he shall not lose his reward.' *Luke* [21.1-4]: 'And looking on, he saw the rich men cast their gifts into the treasury. And he saw also a certain poor widow casting in two brass mites. And he said: Verily I say to you, that this poor widow hath cast in more than they all. For all these have of their abundance cast into the offerings of God; but she of her want, hath cast in all the living that she had.' *Matthew* [26.6-10]: 'And when Jesus was in Bethania, in the house of Simon the leper, there came to him a woman having an alabaster box of precious ointment, and poured it on his head as he was at table. And the disciples seeing it, had indignation, saying: To what purpose is this waste? For this might have been sold for much, and given to the poor. and Jesus knowing it, said to them: Why do you trouble this woman? for she hath wrought a good work upon me.' *Acts* (Concerning Lydia) [16.15]: 'And when she was baptized and her household, she besought us, saying: If you have judged me to be faithful to the Lord, come into my house and abide there. And she constrained us.'

That the Christian should offer his brethren simple and unpretentious hospitality.

Cap. 1

John [6.8-11]: 'One of his disciples, Andrew, the brother of Simon, saith to him: There is a boy here, that hath five barley loaves and two fishes; but what are these among so many? Then Jesus said: Make the men sit down. Now there was much grass in the place. The men therefore sat down, in number about five thousand. And Jesus took the loaves; and when he had given thanks, he distributed to them that were set down. In like manner also of the fishes, as much as they would.' *Luke* [10.38-42]: 'And a certain woman named Martha received him into her house. And she had a sister called Mary, who sitting also at the Lord's feet, heard his word. But Martha was busy about much serving. Who stood and said: Lord, hast thou no care that my sister hath left me alone to serve? Speak to her, therefore, that she help me. And Jesus answering, said to her: Martha, Martha, thou art careful and art troubled about many things: few things— nay, one thing only is necessary. Mary hath chosen the best part which shall not be taken away from her.'

RULE THIRTY-NINE

That we should not be vacillating but steadfast in the faith and staunch in cleaving to the good things which are in the Lord.

Cap. 1

Matthew [13.20-21]: 'And he that received the seed upon stony ground is he that heareth the word, and immediately receiveth it with joy. Yet hath he not root in himself, but is only for a time: and when there ariseth tribulation and persecution because of the word, he is presently scandalized.' *1 Cor.* [15.58]: 'Therefore, my beloved brethren, be ye stead-

fast and unmoveable; always abounding in the work of the
Lord.' *Gal.* [1.6]: 'I wonder that you are so soon removed
from him that called you into the grace of Christ, unto
another gospel.'

That they who introduce erroneous doctrines, however
subtly, to delude or confound the unstable should not be
tolerated.

Cap. 1

Matthew [24.4,5]: 'Take heed that no man seduce you;
for many will come in my name saying, I am Christ: and
they will seduce many.' *Luke* [20.46,47]: 'Beware of the
scribes who desire to walk in long robes, and love salutations
in the marketplace, and the first chairs in the synagogues, and
the chief rooms at feasts; who devour the houses of widows,
feigning long prayer. These shall receive greater damnation.'
Gal. [1.8,9]: 'But though we, or an angel from heaven, preach
a gospel to you besides that which we have preached to you,
let him be anathema. As we said before, so now I say again:
If any one preach to you a gospel besides that which you have
received, let him be anathema.'

That whatsoever gives scandal must be eradicated, no
matter how essential and indispensable it may seem to be.

Cap. 1

Matthew [18.7-9]: 'Woe to that man by whom the scandal cometh. And if thy hand or thy foot scandalize thee, cut

it off and cast it from thee. It is better for thee to go into life maimed or lame, than having two hands or two feet to be cast into everlasting fire. And if thy eye scandalize thee, pluck it out and cast it from thee.'

That we should be indulgent to those who are somewhat weak in faith and carefully lead them on to perfection; but our indulgence, of course, should not cause us to fail in the observance of God's command.

Cap. 2

Matthew [12.20,21]: 'The bruised reed he shall not break: and the smoking flax he shall not extinguish: till he send forth judgment unto victory. And in his name the Gentiles shall hope.' *Rom* [14.1]: 'Now him that is weak in faith, take unto you.' *Gal.* [6.1,2]: 'And if a man be overtaken in any fault, you, who are spiritual, instruct such a one in the spirit of meekness, considering thyself, lest thou also be tempted. Bear ye one another's burdens and so you shall fulfill the law of Christ.'

RULE FORTY-TWO

That it is not to be thought that the Lord came to destroy the Law and the Prophets, but to fulfill them and to add that which is more perfect.

Cap. 1

Matthew [5.17]: 'Do not think that I am come to destroy the law or the prophets. I am not come to destroy but to fulfill.' *Rom.* [3.31]: 'Do we, then, destroy the law through faith? God forbid: but we establish the law.'

RULE FORTY-THREE

That as the Law prohibits wicked deeds, so the Gospel forbids harboring the vices themselves concealed in the soul.

Cap. 1

Matthew [5.21,22]: 'You have heard that it was said to them of old: Thou shalt not kill. And whosoever shall kill shall be in danger of the judgment. But I say to you, that whosoever is angry with his brother rashly shall be in danger of the judgement.' *Rom.* [2.28,29]: 'For it is not he is a Jew, who is so outwardly; nor is that circumcision which is outwardly in the flesh; but he is a Jew, that is one inwardly and the circumcision is that of the heart, in the spirit, not in the letter; whose praise is not of men, but of God.'

That as the law requires a partial, so the Gospel demands a full integrity for every good deed.

Cap. 2

Luke [18.22]: 'Sell all whatever thou hast, and give to the poor, and thou shalt have treasure in heaven; and come, follow me.' *Col.* [2.11]: 'In whom also you are circumcised with circumcision not made by hand, in despoiling of the body of the sins of the flesh, in the circumcision of Christ.'

That they who do not show forth a righteousness according to the Gospel greater than that prescribed by the Law cannot be accounted worthy of the kingdom of heaven.

Cap. 3

Matthew [5.20]: 'Unless your justice abound more than that of the scribes and Pharisees, you shall not enter into the kingdom of heaven.' *Phil.* [3.4-9]: 'If any other thinketh he may have confidence in the flesh, I more, being circumcised the eighth day, of the stock of Israel, of the tribe of Benjamin, an Hebrew of the Hebrews; according to the law, a Pharisee; according to zeal, persecuting the church; according to the justice that is in the law, conversing without blame. But the things that were gain to me, the same I have counted loss for Christ. Furthermore I count all things to be but loss for the excellent knowledge of Jesus Christ our Lord; for whom I have suffered the loss of all things, and count them but as dung that I may gain Christ and may be found in him, not having my justice, which is of the law, but that which is by the faith of Christ, which is the justice of God.'

RULE FORTY-FOUR

That the yoke of Christ is sweet and His burden light unto refreshment for those who submit to it; but all things alien to the teaching of the Gospel are heavy and burdensome.

Cap. 1

Matthew [11.28-30]: 'Come to me, all you that labor and are burdened, and I will refresh you. Take up my yoke upon you and learn of me, because I am meek and humble of heart, and you shall find rest to your souls. For my yoke is sweet and my burden light.'

RULE FORTY-FIVE

That they cannot be deemed worthy of the kingdom of heaven who do not imitate in their relations with one another the equality which is observed by children among themselves.

Cap. 1

Matthew [18.3]: 'Amen I say to you, unless you be converted and become as little children, you shall not enter into the kingdom of heaven.'

That he who desires to be deemed worthy of greater glory in the kingdom of heaven ought to love here on earth that which is lowly and meanest of all.

Cap. 2

Matthew [18.4]: 'Whosoever therefore shall humble himself, as this little child, he is the greater in the kingdom of heaven.' [20.26]: 'But whosoever will be the greater among you, let him be your minister.' *Mark* [10.44]: 'And whosoever will be first among you, shall be the servant of all.' *Phil* [2.3]: 'Let nothing be done through contention, neither by vainglory; but in humility, let each esteem others better than themselves.'

RULE FORTY-SIX

That we are obliged to show in more important matters a greater zeal, proportioned to that displayed in lesser ones.

Cap. 1

Luke [13.15-17]: 'Doth not every one of you, on the sabbath day, loose his ox or his ass from the manger, and lead them to water? And ought not this daughter of Abraham, whom Satan hath bound, lo, these eighteen years, be loosed from this bond on the sabbath day?' [18.1-7]: 'And he spoke a parable to them, that we ought always to pray and not to faint. There was a judge in a certain city, who feared not God nor regarded man. And there was a certain widow in that city, and she came to him, saying: Avenge me of my adversary. And he would not for a long time. But afterward he said within himself: Although I fear not God, nor regard man, yet because this widow is troublesome to me, I will avenge her, lest continually coming she weary me. And the Lord said: Hear what the unjust judge saith. And will not God revenge his elect who cry to him day and night?' *2 Tim.* [2.4,5]: 'No man, being a soldier to God, entangleth himself with secular businesses; that he may please him to whom he hath engaged himself. For he also that striveth for the mastery, is not crowned, except he strive lawfully.'

That relatively to those who manifest in lesser matters a fear born of faith and an alacrity proceeding from laudable desire, they who show themselves negligent or disdainful in concerns of greater moment shall be the more rigorously condemned.

Cap. 2

Luke [11.31]: 'The queen of the south shall rise in the judgment with the men of this generation, and shall condemn them; because she came from the ends of the earth to hear the wisdom of Solomon: and behold more than Solomon here.' *Matthew* [12.41]: 'The men of Ninive shall rise in judgment with this generation, and shall condemn it: because they did penance at the preaching of Jonas. And behold a greater than Jonas here.'

That he who exercises zeal in lesser matters should not regard lightly the more important ones; but he ought to observe the greater precepts in a preeminent manner and accomplish the lesser ones as well.

Cap. 3

Matthew [23.23,24]: 'Woe to you, scribes and Pharisees, hypocrites; because you tithe mint, and anise, and cummin, and have left the weightier things of the law: judgment and mercy and faith. These things you ought to have done, and not to leave those undone. Blind guides, who strain out a gnat and swallow a camel.'

RULE FORTY-SEVEN

That one ought not lay up treasure for himself on earth but in heaven; and the method to be followed in laying up treasure in heaven.

Cap. 1

Matthew [6.19,20]: 'Lay not up to yourselves treasures on earth: where the rust and moth consume, and where thieves break through and steal. But lay up to yourselves treasures in heaven: where neither the rust nor moth doth consume, and where thieves do not break through nor steal.' *Luke* [12.33]: 'Sell what you possess and give alms. Make to yourselves bags which grow not old, a treasure in heaven which faileth not.' *Luke* [18.22]: 'Sell all, whatever thou hast, and give to the poor and thou shalt have treasure in heaven.' *1 Tim.* [6.18,19]: 'To give easily, to communicate to others, to lay up in store for themselves a good foundation against the time to come, that they may lay hold on the true life.'

RULE FORTY-EIGHT

That we should be compassionate and generous; for they who are not such are denounced.

Cap. 1

Matthew [5.7]: 'Blessed are the merciful, for they shall obtain mercy.' *Luke* [6.30]: 'Give to everyone that asketh thee.' *Rom.* [1.31,32]: 'Without affection, without mercy, who having known the justice of God did not understand that they who do such things are worthy of death.' *1 Tim.*[6.18]: 'To give easily, to communicate to others.'

That whatever a man may possess over and above what is necessary for life, he is obliged to do good with, according to the command of the Lord who has bestowed on us the things we possess.

Cap. 2

Luke [3.11]: 'He that hath two coats, let him give to him that hath none: and he that hath meat, let him do in like manner.' *1 Cor.* [4.7]: 'For what hast thou that thou hast not received?' *2 Cor.* [8.14,15]: 'Let your abundance supply their want, that their abundance also may supply your want so that there may be an equality, as it is written: He that had much, had nothing over; and he that had little, had no want.'

That we should not be rich but poor according to the word of the Lord.

Cap. 3

Luke [6.20]: 'Blessed are ye poor, for yours is the kingdom

of God.' [24]: 'Woe to you that are rich, for you have your
consolation.' *2 Cor.* [8.2]: 'Their very deep poverty hath
abounded unto the riches of their simplicity.' *1 Tim.* [6.9,10]:
'For they that will become rich, fall into temptation and into
the snare [of the devil], and into many unprofitable and hurtful desires, which drown men into destruction and perdition.
For the desire of money is the root of all evils; which some
coveting have erred from the faith and have entangled themselves in many sorrows.'

That we should not be eager to have the necessities of life
in abundance, nor seek after luxury or satiety; but we should
be free from every form of avarice and ostentation.

Cap. 4

Luke [12.15]: 'Take heed and beware of all covetousness;
for a man's life doth not consist in the abundance of things
which he possesseth.' *1 Tim.* [2.9]: 'Adorning themselves not
with plaited hair, or gold, or pearls, or costly attire.' [6.8]:
'Having food and wherewith to be covered, with these we are
content.'

That no one should be anxious on account of his own need,
nor place his hope in the appurtenances of this life, but commend his affairs to God.

Cap. 5

Matthew [6.24-34]: 'You cannot serve God and mammon.
Therefore I say to you, be not solicitous for your life, what
you shall eat, nor for your body, what you shall put on. Is not
the life more than the meat: and the body more than the

raiment? Behold the birds of the air, for they neither sow, nor do they reap, nor gather into barns: and your heavenly Father feedeth them. Are not you of much more value than they? And which of you by taking thought, can add to his stature one cubit? And for raiment why are you solicitous? Consider the lilies of the field, how they grow: they labour not, neither do they spin. But I say to you, that not even Solomon in all his glory was arrayed as one of these. And if the grass of the field which is today and tomorrow is cast into the oven, God doth so clothe: how much more you, O ye of little faith? Be not solicitous therefore, saying, What shall we eat, or what shall we drink, or wherewith shall we be clothed? For after all these things do the heathens seek. For your Father knoweth that you have need of all these things. Seek ye therefore first the kingdom of God and his justice, and all these things shall be added unto you. Be not therefore solicitous for tomorrow; for the morrow will be solicitous for itself. Sufficient for the day is the evil thereof.' *Luke* [12.16-19]: 'The land of a certain rich man brought forth plenty of fruits. And he thought within himself, saying: What shall I do, because I have no room where to bestow my fruits? And he said: This will I do: I will pull down my barns, and will build greater; and unto them will I gather up all things that are grown to me, and my goods. And I will say to my soul: Soul, thou hast much goods laid up for many years, take thy rest; eat, drink, make good cheer,' etc. *1 Tim.* [6.17]: 'Charge the rich of this world not to be highminded nor to trust in the uncertainty of riches, but in God (who giveth us abundantly all things to enjoy).'

That we must be careful and solicitous regarding the needs of the brethren in accordance with the will of God.

Cap. 6

Matthew [25.34-36]: 'Come, ye blessed of my Father, possess you the kingdom prepared for you from the foundation of the world. For I was hungry and you gave me to eat; I was thirsty, and you gave me to drink; I was a stranger, and you took me in; naked, and you covered me; sick, and you visited me; I was in prison and you came to me'; and a little later [40]: 'Amen I say to you, as long as you did it to one of these my least brethren, you did it to me.' *John* [6.5]: 'When Jesus therefore had lifted up his eyes and seen that a very great multitude cometh to him, he said to Philip: Whence shall we buy bread that these may eat,' etc. *1 Cor.* [16.1,2]: 'Now concerning the collections that are made for the saints, as I have given order to the churches of Galatia, so do ye also. On the first day of the week let every one of you put apart with himself, laying up what it shall well please him; that when I come, the collections be not then to be made.'

That he who is able should work and give to those in need; for he who was unwilling to work was judged unworthy even to eat.

Cap. 7

Matthew [10.10]: 'The workman is worthy of his meat.' *Acts* [20.35]: 'I have showed you all things, how that so labouring you ought to support the weak, and to remember the word of the Lord, how he said: It is a more blessed thing to give rather than to receive.' *Eph.* [4.28]: 'He that stole, let him now steal no more; but rather let him labor, working with his hands the thing which is good, that he may have something to give to him that suffereth need.' *2 Thess.* [3.10]: 'When we were with you, this we declared to you: that if any man will not work, neither let him eat.'

RULE FORTY-NINE

That we should not resort to legal disputes with regard to the things of the body, even where its necessary covering is concerned.

Cap. 1

Luke [6.29,30]: 'To him that striketh thee on the right cheek, offer also the other. And him that taketh away from thee thy cloak, forbid not to take thy coat also. Give to every one that asketh thee, and of him that taketh away thy goods, ask them not again.' *1 Cor.* [6.1]: 'Dare any man, having a matter against another, go to be judged before the unjust, and not before the saints?' And a little further on [7,8]: 'Already indeed there is plainly a fault among you, that you have lawsuits one with another. Why do you not rather take wrong? Why do you not rather suffer yourselves to be defrauded? But you do wrong and defraud, and that to your brethren.'

That we should not contend with another nor take revenge, but, if possible, live in peace with all men, as the Lord commands.

Cap. 2

Matthew [5.38,39]: 'You have heard that it hath been said, An eye for an eye, and a tooth for a tooth. But I say to you not to resist evil; but if one strike thee on thy right cheek, turn to him also the other,' etc. *Mark* [9.49]: 'Have charity

among you; and also be at peace with one another.' *Rom.*
[12.17-19]: 'To no man rendering evil for evil. Providing
good things in the sight of all men. If possible, have peace
with all men. Revenge not yourselves, my dearly beloved, but
give place unto wrath.' *2 Tim.* [2.24]: 'But the servant of
the Lord must not wrangle, but be mild toward all men.'

That we ought not exact vengeance even for wrong done
to another from him who does the injury.

Cap. 3

Matthew [26.50-52]: 'Then they came up and laid hands
on Jesus and held him. And behold one of them that were
with Jesus, stretching forth his hand, drew out his sword;
and striking the servant of the high priest, cut off his ear.
Then Jesus saith to him: Put up again thy sword into its
place, for all that take the sword shall perish with the sword.'
Luke [9.52-56]: 'And he sent messengers before his face;
and going they entered into a city of the Samaritans, to
prepare for him. And they received him not, because his face
was of one going to Jerusalem. And when his disciples, James
and John had seen this, they said: Lord, wilt thou that we
command fire to come down from heaven and consume them
as it also did Elias? And turning he rebuked them, and they
went into another town.'

RULE FIFTY

That we should lead others along with ourselves to the
peace that is in Christ.

Cap. 1

Matthew [5.9]: 'Blessed are the peacemakers, for they shall be called the children of God.' *John* [14.27]: 'Peace I leave with you, my peace I give unto you.'

RULE FIFTY-ONE

That it is necessary to correct every fault in ourselves before we bring charges against another.

Cap. 1

Matthew [7.3-5]: 'And why seest thou the mote that is in thy brother's eye, and seest not the beam that is in thy own eye? Or how sayest thou to thy brother: Let me cast the mote out of thy eye; and behold a beam is in thy own eye? Thou hypocrite, cast out first the beam out of thy own eye, and then shalt thou see to cast out the mote out of thy brother's eye.' *Rom.* [2.1-3]: 'Wherefore thou art inexcusable, O man, whosoever thou art that judgest. For wherein thou judgest another, thou condemnest thyself. For thou dost the same things which thou judgest. For we know that the judgment of God is, according to truth, against them that do such things. And thinkest thou this, O man, that judgest them who do such things and dost the same, that thou shalt escape the judgment of God?'

RULE FIFTY-TWO

That we should not be indifferent to sinners, but mourn and grieve over them.

Cap. 1

Luke [19.41-43]: 'And when he drew near, seeing the city, he wept over it, saying: If thou also hadst known and that in this thy day, the things that are to thy peace; but now they are hidden from thy eyes.' *1 Cor.* [5.1-2]: 'It is absolutely heard that there is fornication among you, and such fornication as the like is not even mentioned among the heathens; that one should have his father's wife. And you are puffed up; and have not rather mourned, that he might be taken away from among you, that hath done this deed.' *2 Cor.* [12.21]: 'Lest again when I come to you, my God humble me; and I mourn many of them that sinned before, and have not done penance.'

That we should not bear with sinners in silence.

Cap. 2

Luke [17.3]: 'If thy brother sin against thee, reprove him,' etc. *Eph.* [5.11]: 'And have no fellowship with the unfruitful works of darkness, but rather reprove them.'

That we should tolerate association with sinners only for the purpose of recalling them to penitence, by every means short of sin.

Cap. 3

Matthew [9.10-13]: 'And behold many publicans and sinners came and sat down with Jesus and his disciples. And the Pharisees seeing it, said to his disciples: Why doth your master eat with publicans and sinners? But Jesus hearing it, said: They that are in health need not a physician, but they that are ill. Go then and learn what this meaneth, I will have mercy and not sacrifice. For I am not come to call the just but sinners to repentance.' *Luke* [15.1-4]: 'Now all the publicans and sinners drew near unto him to hear him. And the Pharisees and the scribes murmured, saying: 'This man receiveth sinners, and eateth with them. And he spoke to them this parable, saying: What man of you that hath an hundred sheep; and if he shall lose one of them, doth he not leave the ninety-nine in the desert, and go after that which was lost until he find it?' *2 Thess.* [3.14,15]: 'And if any man obey not our word by this epistle, note that man and do not keep company with him, that he may be ashamed; yet do not esteem him as an enemy, but admonish him as a brother.' *2 Cor.* [2.5-7]: 'And if anyone have caused grief, he hath not grieved me; but in part, that I may not burden you all. To him who is such a one, this rebuke is sufficient, which is given by many; so that on the contrary, you should rather forgive him and comfort him, lest perhaps such a one be swallowed up with overmuch sorrow.'

That, when every form of solicitude has been applied in their regard, we should avoid those who persist in their evil ways.

Cap. 4

Matthew [18.15-17]: 'If thy brother shall offend against thee, go, and rebuke him between thee and him alone. If he shall hear thee, thou shalt gain thy brother. And if he will not hear thee, take with thee one or two or more; that in the mouth of two or three witnesses every word may stand. And if he will not hear them, tell the church. And if he will not hear the church, let him be to thee as a heathen and a publican.'

RULE FIFTY-THREE

That a Christian should not bear a grudge, but from his heart should forgive those who have offended him.

Cap. 1

Matthew [6.14,15]: 'If you will not forgive men their of-fences, neither will your heavenly Father forgive you your offences; but if you forgive men their offences, your heavenly Father will also forgive you.'

RULE FIFTY-FOUR

That it is not right for us to judge one another in matters which are countenanced by the Scripture.

Cap. 1

Matthew [7.1,2]: 'Judge not, that you may not be judged. For with what judgment you judge, you shall be judged.' *Luke* [6.37]: 'Judge not and you shall not be judged. Con-demn not and you shall not be condemned.' *Rom.* [14.2-6]: 'For one indeed believeth that he may eat all things; but he that is weak, let him eat herbs. Let not him that eateth de-spise him that eateth not; and he that eateth not, let him not judge him that eateth; for God hath taken him to him. Who art thou that judgest another man's servant? To his own lord he standeth or falleth. And he shall stand; for God is able to make him stand. For one judgeth between day and day and another judgeth every day; let every man abound in his own sense. He that regardeth the day, regardeth it un-to the Lord. And he that doth not regard the day, to the Lord he regardeth it not. And he that eateth, eateth to the Lord; for he giveth thanks to God. And he that eateth not, to the Lord he eateth not, and giveth thanks to God;' and shortly after [12,13]: 'Therefore every one of us shall render account to God for himself. Let us not therefore judge one another any more.' *Col.* [2.16,17]: 'Let no man therefore judge you in meat or in drink, or in respect of a festival day, or of the new moon, or of the sabbaths, which are a shadow of things to come.'

That we should not quibble with regard to what is permitted by the Scripture.

Cap. 2

Rom. [14.22,23]: 'Blessed is he that condemneth not himself in that which he alloweth. But he that discerneth, if he eat, is condemned; because not of faith. For all that is not of faith is sin.' *Col.* [2.20-22]: 'If you be dead with Christ from the elements of the world, why do you yet decree as though living in the world? Touch not, taste not, handle not; which all are unto destruction by the very use, according to the precepts and doctrines of men.'

That we must not make judgments where doubtful matters are concerned.

Cap. 3

1 Cor. [4.5]: 'Therefore judge not before the time; until the Lord come, who both will bring to light the hidden things of darkness, and will make manifest the counsels of the hearts; and then shall every man have praise from God.'

That we should not judge out of consideration of persons.

Cap. 4

John [7.23,24]: 'If a man receive circumcision on the sabbath day, that the law of Moses may not be broken, are you angry at me because I have healed the whole man on the sabbath day? Judge not according to the appearance, but judge just judgment.'

That we ought not condemn anyone, even if his accusers be many, before making a careful study of his case in his presence.

Cap. 5

John [7.50,51]: 'Nicodemus said (he that came to him by night, who was one of them): Doth our law judge any man, unless it first hear him, and know what he doth?' *Acts* [25.14-16]: 'And as they tarried there many days, Festus told the king of Paul, saying: A certain man was left prisoner by Felix; about whom when I was at Jerusalem the chief priests and the ancients of the Jews, came unto me, desiring condemnation against him. To whom I answered: It is not the custom of the Romans to condemn any man, before that he who is accused have his accusers present and have liberty to make his answer, to clear himself of the things laid to his charge.'

RULE FIFTY-FIVE

That we must recognize and acknowledge every good as a gift and that even the patient endurance of suffering for Christ's sake is of God.

Cap. 1

John [3.27]: 'A man cannot receive anything, unless it be given him from heaven.' *1 Cor.* [4.7]: 'Or what hast thou that thou hast not received?' *Eph.* [2.8,9]: 'For by grace you are saved through faith, and that not of yourselves, for it is

a gift of God; not of works, that no man may glory.' *Phil.*
[1.28-30]: 'And this from God: for unto you it is given for
Christ, not only to believe in him, but also to suffer for him.
Having the same conflict,' etc.

That we should not accept in silence the benefactions of
God, but return thanks for them.

Cap. 2

Luke [8.38,39]: 'Now the man, out of whom the devils
were departed, besought him that he might be with him. But
Jesus sent him away, saying: Return to thy house, and tell
how great things God hath done to thee. And he went
through the whole city publishing how great things Jesus had
done to him.' *Luke* [17.12-19]: 'And as he entered into a certain town, there met him ten men that were lepers, who
stood afar off and lifted up their voice, saying: Jesus, master,
have mercy on us. Whom when he saw, he said: Go show
yourselves to the priests. And it came to pass, as they went,
they were made clean. And one of them, when he saw that
he was made clean, went back, with a loud voice glorifying
God. And he fell on his face before his feet, giving thanks;
and this was a Samaritan. And Jesus answering, said, Were
not ten made clean? And where are the nine? There is no
one found to return and give glory to God but this stranger.
And he said to him: Arise, go thy way; for thy faith hath
made thee whole.' *1 Cor.* [15.10]: 'But by the grace of God,
I am what I am.' *1 Tim.* [4.4]: 'Every creature of God is
good, and nothing to be rejected that is received with thanksgiving.'

That we should persevere in watching and prayer.

Cap. 1

Matthew [7.7,8]: 'Ask and it shall be given you: seek and you shall find; knock, and it shall be opened to you. For everyone that asketh, receiveth: and he that seeketh findeth: and to him that knocketh, it shall be opened, etc. *Luke* [18.1,2]: 'And he spoke also a parable to them, that we ought always to pray, and not to faint, saying: There was a judge in a certain city,' etc. *Luke* [21.34-36]: 'And take heed to yourselves, lest perhaps your hearts be overcharged with surfeiting and drunkenness, and the cares of this life, and that day come upon you suddenly. For as a snare shall it come upon all that sit upon the face of the whole earth. Watch ye therefore, praying at all times, that you may be accounted worthy to escape these things that are to come, and to stand before the Son of man.' *Col.* [4.2]: 'Be instant in prayer, watching in it with thanksgiving.' *1 Thess.* [5.16,17]: 'Always rejoice. Pray without ceasing.'

That we should give thanks to God even for the daily sustenance required by the body, before we partake of it.

Cap. 2

Matthew [14.19]: 'And taking the five loaves and the two fishes, giving thanks, he broke and gave to his disciples: and the disciples to the multitude.' *Acts* [27.35]: 'And when he had said these things, taking bread, he gave thanks to God in the sight of them all; and when he had broken it, he began to eat.' *1 Tim.* [4.4]: 'Every creature of God is good, and nothing to be rejected that is received with thanksgiving.'

That we should not recite long and repetitious prayers for things that are perishable and unworthy of the Lord.

Cap. 3

Matthew [6.7,8]: 'And when you are praying, speak not much, as the heathens. For they think that in their much speaking they may be heard. Be not you therefore like to them, for your heavenly Father knoweth what is needful for you, before you ask him.' *Luke* [12.29,30]: 'And seek not you what you shall eat, or what you shall drink; and be not lifted up on high. For all these things do the nations of the world seek. But your Father knoweth that you have need of these things.'

How we should pray, and with what dispositions of soul.

Cap. 4

Matthew [6.9,10]: 'Our Father who art in heaven, hallowed be thy name, Thy kingdom come, thy will be done,' etc. *Matthew* [6.33]: 'Seek ye therefore first the kingdom of God and his justice.' *Mark* [11.25]: 'When you shall stand to pray, forgive, if you have aught against any man.' *1 Tim.* [2.8]: 'I will therefore that men pray in every place, lifting up pure hands, without anger and contention.'

That we should pray for one another and for those who are preachers of the Word of Truth.

Cap. 5

Luke [22.31,32]: 'And the Lord said: Simon, Simon, behold Satan hath desired to have you, that he may sift you as wheat;

but I have prayed for thee, that thy faith fail not.' *Eph.* [6.18-20]: 'Praying at all times in the spirit; and in the same watching with all instance and supplication for all the saints and for me, that speech may be given me, that I may open my mouth with confidence to make known the mystery of the gospel. For which I am an ambassador in a chain, so that therein I may be bold to speak according as I ought.' *2 Thess.* [3.1]: 'For the rest, pray for us that the word of God may run and may be glorified in all, even as among you.'

That we should pray even for our enemies.

Cap. 6

Matthew [5.44,45]: 'Pray for them that persecute and calumniate you, that you may be the children of your Father who is in heaven.'

That no man ought to pray or prophesy with his head covered; and no woman, with uncovered head.

Cap. 7

1 Cor. [11.3-5]: 'But I would have you know that the head of every man is Christ; and the head of the woman is the man; and the head of Christ is God. Every man praying or prophesying with his head covered, disgraceth his head. But every woman praying or prophesying with her head not covered, disgraceth her head,' etc.

RULE FIFTY-SEVEN

That no one should entertain exalted notions of himself because of his own good deeds and hold others in disdain.

Cap. 1

Luke [18.9-14]: 'And to some who trusted in themselves as just and despised others, he spoke also this parable: Two men went up into the temple to pray, the one a Pharisee and the other a publican. The Pharisee standing prayed thus with himself: O God, I give thee thanks that I am not as the rest of men, extortioners, unjust, adulterers, as also is this publican. I fast twice in a week; I give tithes of all that I possess. And the publican, standing afar off, would not so much as lift up his eyes towards heaven, but struck his breast, saying: O God, be merciful to me a sinner. I say unto you, this man went down into his house justified rather than the other; because every one that exalteth himself shall be humbled; and he that humbleth himself shall be exalted.'

RULE FIFTY-EIGHT

That it must not be thought that the gift of God is purchased by money or by any other device.

Cap. 1

Acts [8.18-23]: 'And when Simon saw that by the imposition of the hands of the apostles, the Holy Ghost was given, he offered them money, saying: Give me also this power that on whomsoever I shall lay my hands, he may receive the Holy Ghost. But Peter said to him: Keep thy money to thyself, to perish with thee, because thou hast thought that the gift of God may be purchased with money. Thou hast no part nor lot in this matter. For thy heart is not right in the sight of God. Do penance therefore for this thy wickedness; and pray to the Lord that perhaps this thought of thy heart may be forgiven thee. For I see thou art in the gall of bitterness and in the bonds of iniquity.'

That according to the rule of faith God bestows gifts upon each man unto profit.

Cap. 2

Rom. [12.6]: 'And having different gifts, according to the grace that is given us, either prophecy, to be used according to the rule of faith.' *1 Cor.* [12.7-10]: 'And the manifestation of the Spirit is given to every man unto profit. To one indeed, by the Spirit, is given the word of wisdom; and to another, the word of knowledge, according to the same Spirit; to another, faith in the same Spirit; to another, the grace of healing; to another, prophecy; to another, the discerning of spirits; to another, divers kinds of tongues; to another, interpretation of speeches.'

That, since the gift of God is received as a free gift, it is our duty to share it freely and not make it a means of profit for self-gratification.

Cap. 3

Matthew [10.8,9]: 'Heal the sick, cleanse the lepers, cast out devils; freely have you received, freely give. Do not possess gold, nor silver, nor money in your purses.' *Acts* [3.6,7]: 'But Peter said: Silver and gold I have none; but what I have, I give thee: In the name of Jesus Christ of Nazareth, arise and walk. And taking him by the right hand, he lifted him up.' *1 Thess.* [2.5-8]: 'For neither have we used at any time the speech of flattery, as you know; nor taken an occasion of covetousness, God is witness; nor sought we glory of men, neither of you nor of others. Whereas we might have been burdensome to you, as the apostles of Christ; but we became little ones in the midst of you, as if a nurse should cherish her children: so desirous of you, we would gladly impart unto you not only the gospel of God but also our own souls, because you were become most dear unto us.'

That he who has received the first gift of God in a prudent manner and has diligently fostered it for the glory of God is deserving of other gifts also; but one who does not so is both deprived of the original gift and is not deemed worthy of that which has been prepared, and is delivered up to punishment.

Cap. 4

Matthew [13.10-14]: 'And his disciples came and said to him: Why speakest thou to them in parables? Who answered and said to them: Because to you it is given to know the mysteries of the kingdom of heaven; but to them it is not given. For he that hath, to him shall be given, and he shall abound: but he that hath not, from him shall be taken away that also which he hath. Therefore do I speak to them in parables, because seeing they see not, and hearing they hear not, neither do they understand. And the prophecy of Isaias is fulfilled in them.' [25.14-17]: 'For even as a man going into a far country, called his servants and delivered to them his goods; and to one he gave five talents, and to another two, and to another one, to every one according to his proper ability: and immediately he took his journey. And he that had received the five talents went his way, and traded with the same and gained other five. And.in like manner he that had received the two gained other two'; and shortly after [29,30]: 'For to every one that hath shall be given; but from him that hath not, that also which he hath shall be taken away. And the unprofitable servant cast ye out into the exterior darkness. There shall be weeping and gnashing of teeth.'

RULE FIFTY-NINE

That the Christian should not be attached to that glory which comes from men, nor claim for himself special honor, but should correct those who accord him such honor or who think too highly of him.

Cap. 1

Matthew [19.16,17]: 'And behold one came and said to him: Good master, what good shall I do that I may have life everlasting? Who said to him: Why callest thou me good? No one is good except one, God.' *John* [5.41]: 'I receive not glory from men'; and a little further on [44]: 'How can you believe, who receive glory one from another; and the glory which is from God alone, you do not seek? *Luke* [11.43]: 'Woe to you, Pharisees, because you love the uppermost seats in the synagogues, and salutations in the marketplace.' *1 Thess.* [2.5,6]: 'For neither have we used at any time the speech of flattery as you know; nor taken an occasion of covetousness, God is witness: nor sought we glory of men, neither of you nor of others.' *Acts* [10.25,26]: 'And it came to pass that when Peter was come in, Cornelius came to meet him, and falling at his feet adored. But Peter lifted him up, saying: Arise, I myself also am a man.' *Acts* [12.21-23]: 'And upon a day appointed, Herod being arrayed in kingly apparel, sat in the judgment seat and made an oration to them. And the people made acclamation, saying: It is the voice of a god and not of a man. And forthwith an angel of the Lord struck him, because he had not given the honour to God: and being eaten up by worms, he gave up the ghost.'

RULE SIXTY

That, inasmuch as the gifts of the Spirit are varied and

one individual cannot receive them all, nor all receive the same gift, everyone should soberly and thankfully remain content with the gift granted to him and all should be in accord with one another in the charity of Christ, as are the members of the body. Thus, he who is less richly endowed with gifts will not suffer discouragement by comparison with his superior in this regard; nor, indeed, should the more gifted be disdainful of his inferior. For they who are divided and at variance with one another are worthy of destruction.

Cap. 1

Matthew [12.25]: 'Every kingdom divided against itself shall be made desolate: and every city or house divided against itself shall not stand.' *Gal.* [5.15]: 'But if you bite and devour one another; take heed you be not consumed one of another.' *John* [17.20,21]: 'Not for them only do I pray, but for them also who through their word shall believe in me: that they all may be one, as thou, Father, in me and I in thee; that they also may be one in us.' *Acts* [4.32]: 'And the multitude of believers had but one heart and one soul; neither did any one say that aught of the things which he possessed was his own, but all things were common unto them.' *Rom.* [12.3-6]: 'For I say, by the grace that is given me, to all that are among you, not to be more wise than it behoveth to be wise, but to be wise unto sobriety, and according as God hath divided to every one the measure of faith. For as in one body, we have many members, but all the members have not the same office; so we being many, are one body in Christ, and every one members one of another; and having different gifts, according to the grace that is given us,' etc. *1 Cor.* [1.10]: 'Now I beseech you, by the name of our Lord Jesus Christ, that you all speak the same thing, and that there be no schisms among you; but that you be perfect in the same mind and in the same judgment.' *1 Cor.* [12.12,13]: 'For as the body is one and hath many members; and all the members of the body, whereas they are many, belonging to the one body, yet are one body, so also is Christ. For in one Spirit were we all baptized into one body, whether Jews or Gentiles, whether bond or free,' etc. *Phil.* [2.2-4]: 'That you all be of one mind, having the same charity, being of one accord, agreeing in sentiment. Let nothing be done through contention, neither by vain glory; but in humility, let each esteem others better than themselves; each one not considering the things that are his own, but those that are other men's.'

RULE SIXTY-ONE

That we should not be disdainful of those who administer the Lord's bounty, having regard to their lowliness, for with these especially God is well pleased.

Cap. 1

Matthew [11.25,26]: 'I confess to thee, O Father, Lord of heaven and earth, because thou hast hid these things from the wise and prudent, and hast revealed them to little ones. Yea, Father, for so hath it seemed good in thy sight.' [13.54-58]: 'Coming into his own country, he taught them in their synagogue, so that they wondered and said: How come this man by this wisdom and miracles? Is not this the carpenter's son? Is not his mother called Mary, and his brethren James and Joseph and Simon and Jude? And his sisters, are they not all with us? Whence therefore hath he all these things? And they were scandalized in his regard. But Jesus said to them: A prophet is not without honor, save in his own country, and in his own house. And he wrought not

many miracles, because of their unbelief.' *1 Cor.* [1.26-29]:
'For see your vocation, brethren, that there are not many
wise according to the flesh, not many mighty, not many noble;
but the foolish things of the world hath God chosen, that he
may confound the wise; and the weak things of the world
hath God chosen that he may confound the strong. And the
base things of the world and the things that are contemptible
hath God chosen, and things that are not, that he might
bring to nought things that are, that no flesh should glory
in the sight of God.'

RULE SIXTY-TWO

That they who believe in God and are baptized should
straightway prepare themselves for temptation even from their
own relatives and friends and even unto death, for one who is
not thus prepared is easily shaken in a sudden crisis.

Cap. 1

Matthew [3.16-4.1]: 'And Jesus being baptized, forthwith
came out of the water; and lo, the heavens were opened to
him, and he saw the Spirit of God descending as a dove and
coming upon him. And behold a voice from heaven, saying:
This is my beloved Son in whom I am well pleased. Then
Jesus was led by the Spirit into the desert, to be tempted by
the devil.' [10.16-18]: 'Behold I send you as sheep in the
midst of wolves. Be ye therefore wise as serpents and simple
as doves. But beware of men. For they will deliver you up
in councils and they will scourge you in their synagogues.
And you shall be brought before governors, and before kings
for my sake, for a testimony to them and to the Gentiles';
and, after a few intervening verses [21,22]: 'The brother
also shall deliver up the brother to death, and the father, the

son; and the children shall rise up against their parents, and shall put them to death. And you shall be hated by all men for my name's sake; but he that shall persevere unto the end, he shall be saved.' [38]: 'And he that taketh not up his cross and followeth me, is not worthy of me.' *John* [16.1-3]: 'These things have I spoken to you, that you may not be scandalized. They will put you out of the synagogue; yea, the hour cometh that whosoever killeth you will think that he doth a service to God. And these things will they do to you; because they have not known the Father, nor me,' etc. *Luke* [8.13]: 'Now they upon the rock, are they who when they hear, receive the word with joy; and these have no roots, for they believe for a while, and in time of temptation they fall away.' *2 Cor.* [1.8,9]: 'For I would not have you ignorant, brethren, of our tribulation which came to us in Asia that we were pressed out of measure above our strength, so that we were weary even of life. But we had in ourselves the answer of death, that we should not trust in ourselves but in God who raiseth the dead.' *2 Tim.* [3.12]: 'And all that will live godly in Christ Jesus, shall suffer persecution.'

That no one should place himself in the way of temptation before God permits, but we should pray not to fall into temptation.

Cap. 2

Matthew [6.9,10]: 'Thus therefore shall you pray: Our Father who art in heaven, hallowed be thy name. Thy kingdom come'; and shortly after [13]: 'And lead us not into temptation but deliver us from evil.' *John* [7.1-10]: 'After these things, Jesus walked in Galilee; for he would not walk in Judea, because the Jews sought to kill him. Now the Jews' feast of tabernacles was at hand. And his brethren said to him: Pass from hence and go into Judea, that thy disciples also may see thy works which thou dost. For there is no man that doth any thing in secret, and he himself seeketh to be known openly. If thou do these things, manifest thyself to the world. For neither did his brethren believe in him. Then Jesus said to them: My time is not yet come; but your time is always ready. The world cannot hate you; but me it hateth, because I give testimony to it, that the works thereof are evil. Go you up to this festival day, but I go not up to this festival day, because my time is not accomplished. When he had said these things, he himself stayed in Galilee. But after his brethren were gone up, then he also went up to the feast, not openly, but, as it were, in secret.' *Luke* [22.46]: 'Arise, pray, lest you enter into temptation.'

That we should retreat in good time before those who seek to ensnare us; yet, if any one be permitted to fall into temptation, he should pray for issue that he may be able to bear it and that the will of God may be done.

Cap. 3

Matthew [10.23]: 'And when they shall persecute you in this city, flee into another.' [12.14,15]: 'And the Pharisees, going out, made a consultation against him, how they might destroy him. But Jesus knowing it, retired from thence.' *John* [11.53,54]: 'From that day, therefore, they devised to put him to death. Wherefore Jesus walked no more openly among the Jews.' *Luke* [22.41,42]: 'And kneeling down, he prayed, saying: Father, if thou wilt, remove this chalice from me; but yet not my will but thine be done.' *1 Cor.* [10.13]: 'Let no temptation take hold on you but such as is human. And God is faithful who will not suffer you to be tempted above that which you are able; but will make also with temptation issue, that you may be able to bear it.'

That, in every temptation which assails him, the Christian should remember what is said in Holy Scripture regarding the evil which confronts him and so keep himself unharmed and set his adversaries at naught.

Cap. 4

Matthew [4.1-4]: 'Then Jesus was led by the spirit into the desert to be tempted by the devil. And when he had fasted forty days and forty nights, afterwards he was hungry. And the tempter coming said to him: If thou be the Son of God command that these stones be made bread. Who answered and said: It is written: Not in bread alone doth man live, but in every word that proceedeth from the mouth of God,' etc.

RULE SIXTY-THREE

That the Christian should not fear nor be distressed in difficult circumstances, and thus be distracted from his trust in God; but he should take courage as if the Lord were at hand directing his affairs and strengthening him against all his adversaries and as if the Holy Spirit were instructing him even as to the very replies he should make to his foes.

Cap. 1

Matthew [10.28-31]: 'Fear ye not them that kill the body,

and are not able to kill the soul, but rather fear him that can destroy both soul and body in hell. Are not two sparrows sold for a farthing? And not one of them shall fall on the ground without your Father. But the very hairs of your head are all numbered. Fear not therefore; better are you than many sparrows.' *Luke* [12.11,12]: 'And when they shall bring you into the synagogues, and to magistrates and powers, be not solicitous how or what you shall answer, or what you shall say. For the Holy Ghost shall teach you in the same hour what you must say.' *Mark* [4.37-40]: 'And there arose a great storm of wind, and the waves beat into the ship, so that the ship was filled. And he was in the hinder part of the ship, sleeping upon a pillow; and they awake him, and say to him: Master, doth it not concern thee that we perish? And rising up, he rebuked the wind, and said to the sea: Peace, be still. And the wind ceased, and there was made a great calm. And he said to them: Why are you fearful? Have you not faith yet?' *Acts* [5.17-21]: 'Then the high priest rising up and all they that were with him (which is the heresy of the Sadducees) were filled with envy. And they laid their hands on the apostles and put them in the common prison. But an angel of the Lord by night opening the doors of the prison and leading them out, said: Go, and standing speak in the temple to the people all the words of this life. Who, having heard this early in the morning, entered into the temple and taught.' *2 Cor.* [1.8]: 'For we would not have you ignorant, brethren, of our tribulation, which came to us in Asia'; and shortly after [10]: 'Who hath delivered and doth deliver us out of so great dangers: in whom we trust that he will yet also deliver us.'

RULE SIXTY-FOUR

That we should rejoice to suffer all things even unto death for the name of the Lord and for His commandments.

Cap. 1

Matthew [5.10-12]: 'Blessed are they that suffer persecution for justice' sake; for theirs is the kingdom of heaven. Blessed are ye when they shall revile you and persecute you and speak all that is evil against you, untruly, for my sake. Be glad and rejoice, for your reward is very great in heaven.' *Luke* [6.22,23]: 'Blessed shall you be when men shall hate you and when they shall separate you, and shall reproach you, and cast out your name as evil, for the Son of man's sake. Be glad in that day and rejoice; for behold your reward is great in heaven.' *Acts* [5.40-42]: 'And calling in the apostles, after they had scourged them, they charged them that they should not speak at all in the name of Jesus; and they dismissed them. And they indeed went from the presence of the council, rejoicing that they were accounted worthy to suffer reproach for the name of the Lord. And every day they ceased not in the temple and from house to house to teach and preach Christ Jesus.' *Col.* [1.23-25]: 'Whereof I, Paul, am made a minister. Who now rejoice in my sufferings for you, and fill up those things that are wanting of the sufferings of Christ in my flesh, for his body, which is the church.'

RULE SIXTY-FIVE

That it behooves us to make suitable requests in prayer, even if we are at the very point of death.

Cap 1

Matthew [27.46]: 'And about the ninth hour Jesus cried with a loud voice, saying: Eli, Eli, lamma sabacthani? That is, My God, my God, why hast thou forsaken me?' [*Luke* 23.46]: 'And Jesus, crying with a loud voice, said: Father, into thy hands I commend my spirit. And saying this, he gave up the ghost.' *Acts* [7.58,59]: 'And they stoned Stephen invoking and saying: Lord, lay not this sin to their charge. And when he had said this, he fell asleep.'

RULE SIXTY-SIX

That we must not fail those who fight in behalf of religion.

Cap. 1

John [16.31,32]: 'Jesus answered them: Do you now believe? Behold, the hour cometh and it is now come that you shall be scattered every man to his own, and shall leave me alone.' *2 Tim.* [1.15-18]: 'Thou knowest this, that all they who are in Asia, are turned away from me, of whom are Phigellus and Hermogenes. The Lord give mercy to the house of Onesiphorus, because he hath often refreshed me and hath not been ashamed of my chain; but when he was come to Rome, he carefully sought me and found me. The Lord grant unto him to find mercy of the Lord in that day; and in how many things he ministered unto me in Ephesus, thou very well knowest.' *2 Tim.* [4.16]: 'At my first answer no man stood with me, but all forsook me; may it not be laid to their charge.'

That we must pray for those who are tried by temptation.

Cap. 2

Luke [22.31,32]: 'Simon, Simon, behold Satan hath desired to have you, that he may sift you as wheat; but I have prayed for thee, that thy faith fail not.' *Acts* [12.5]: 'Peter therefore was kept in prison. But prayer was made without ceasing by the church unto God for him.'

RULE SIXTY-SEVEN

That to grieve for them that sleep ill befits those who have the assurance of the resurrection from the dead.

Cap. 1

Luke [23.27-28]: 'And there followed him a great multitude of people and of women, who bewailed and lamented him. But turning, he said to them: Daughters of Jerusalem, weep not over me.' *1 Thess.* [4.12,13]: 'And we will not have you ignorant, brethren, concerning them that are asleep, that you be not sorrowful even as others who have no hope. For if we believe that Jesus died, and rose again; even so them who have slept through Jesus, will God bring with him.'

RULE SIXTY-EIGHT

That we should not expect the needs peculiar to this life to continue after the resurrection; but we should realize that life in the next world is angelic and free from want.

Cap. 1

Luke [20.34-36]: 'Jesus answered and said to them: The children of this world marry and are given in marriage: but they that shall be accounted worthy of that world and of the resurrection from the dead shall neither be married nor take wives. Neither can they die any more; for they are equal to the angels and are the children of God, being children of the resurrection.' *1 Cor.* [15.35-38]: 'But some man will say: How do the dead rise again? or with what manner of body shall they come? Senseless man, that which thou sowest is not quickened except it die first. And that which thou sowest, thou sowest not the body that shall be; but bare grain, as of wheat, or of some of the rest. But God giveth it a body as he will'; and shortly after [42-44]: 'So also is the resurrection of the dead. It is sown in corruption, it shall rise in incorruption. It is sown in dishonour, it shall rise in glory. It is sown in weakness, it shall rise in power. It is sown a natural body, it shall rise a spiritual body.'

That we must not expect the coming of the Lord to be in a certain place or in a manner according to the flesh, but suddenly throughout the whole world in the glory of the Father.

Cap. 2

Matthew [24.23,24]: 'Then if any man shall say to you: Lo! here is Christ, or there, do not believe him; for there shall arise false Christs and false prophets and shall show great signs and wonders, insomuch as to deceive (if possible) even the elect.' *Mark* [13.23-26]: 'Take you heed, therefore; behold I have foretold you all things. But in those days after that tribulation, the sun shall be darkened and the moon shall not give her light. And the stars of heaven shall be falling down and the powers that are in heaven shall be moved. And then shall they see the Son of man coming in the clouds with great power and glory.' *1 Thess.* [4.14,15]: 'For this we say unto you in the word of the Lord, that we who are alive, who remain unto the coming of the Lord, shall not prevent them who have slept. For the Lord himself shall come down from heaven with commandment and with the voice of an archangel and with the trumpet of God; and the dead who are in Christ, shall rise first.'

RULE SIXTY-NINE

A list of acts which are forbidden and have a threat attached to them.

Cap. 1

Matthew [15.19,20]: 'For from the heart come forth evil thoughts, murders, adulteries, fornications, thefts, false testimonies, blasphemies. These are the things that defile a man.' [25.41-43]: 'Depart from me, you cursed, into everlasting fire which was prepared for the devil and his angels. For I was hungry and you gave me not to eat; I was thirsty and you gave me not to drink; I was a stranger, and you took me not in; naked, and you covered me not; sick and in prison, and you did not visit me.' *Luke* [6.24-26]: 'Woe to you that are rich; for you have your consolation. Woe to you that are filled; for you shall hunger. Woe to you that laugh; for you shall mourn and weep. Woe to you when all men shall bless you.' [21.34]: 'And take heed to yourselves, lest perhaps your hearts be overcharged with surfeiting and drunkenness, and the cares of this life and that day come upon you suddenly.' *Rom.* [1.28-30]: 'And as they liked not to have God in their knowledge, God delivered them up to a reprobate sense, to do those things which are not convenient; being filled with all iniquity, fornication, avarice, wickedness,' etc. [13.9]: 'For: Thou shalt not commit adultery: Thou shalt not kill: Thou shalt not steal: Thou shalt not covet: and if there be any other commandment,' etc. *1 Cor.* [6.9,10]: 'Do not err: neither fornicators, nor idolators, nor adulterers, nor effeminate, nor liers with mankind, nor covetous, nor drunkards, nor railers, nor extortioners, shall possess the kingdom of God.' *2 Cor.* [12.20]: 'Lest perhaps contention, envyings, animosities, dissensions, detractions, whisperings, swellings, seditions, be among you.' *Gal.* [5.19-21]: 'Now the works of the flesh are manifest, which are adultery, fornication, uncleanness, luxury, idolatry, witchcrafts, enmities, contention, emulations, wraths, quarrels, dissensions, sects, envies, murders, drunkenness, revellings, and such like. Of the which I foretell you, as I have foretold, that they who do such things shall not obtain the kingdom of God.' *Gal.* [5.26]: 'Let us not be made desirous of vain glory, provoking one another, envying one another.' *Eph.* [4.31]: 'Let all bitterness and anger, and indignation, and clamour, and blasphemy, be put away from you, with all malice.' [5.3,4]: 'But fornication and all uncleanness, or covetousness, let it not so much as be named among you, as becometh saints; or obscenity, or foolish talking, or scurrility, which is to no purpose.' *Col.* [3.5,6,8,9]: 'Mortify, therefore, your members which are upon the earth; fornication, uncleanness, lust, evil concupiscence, and covetousness, which is the service of idols. For which things the wrath of God cometh upon the children of unbelief. But now put you also all away: anger, indignation, malice, blasphemy, filthy speech out of your mouth. Lie not to one another.' *1 Tim.* [1.9-11]: 'But for the unjust and disobedient, for the ungodly, and for sinners, for the wicked and defiled, for murderers of fathers, and murderers of mothers, for manslayers, for fornicators, for them who defile themselves with mankind, for men-stealers, for liars, for perjured persons, and whatever other thing is contrary to sound doctrine, which is according

to the gospel of the glory of the blessed God, which hath
been committed to my trust.' *1 Tim.* [4.1-3]: 'In the last times
some shall depart from the faith, giving heed to spirits of error
and doctrines of devils, speaking lies in hypocrisy, and having
their conscience seared, forbidding to marry, to abstain from
meats which God hath created to be received with thanksgiving by the faithful, and by them that have known the
truth.' *1 Tim.* [6.3-5]: 'If any man teach otherwise, and consent not to the sound words of our Lord Jesus Christ and to
that doctrine which is according to godliness, he is proud,
knowing nothing, but sick about questions and strifes of
words; from which arise envy, contention, blasphemies, evil
suspicions, conflicts of men corrupted in mind, and who are
destitute of the truth, supposing gain to be godliness. Fly
such as these.' *2 Tim.* [3.1-5]: 'In the last days shall come
dangerous times. For men shall be lovers of themselves,
covetous, haughty, proud, blasphemers, disobedient to parents, ungrateful, wicked, without affection, without peace,
slanderers, incontinent, unmerciful, without kindness, traitors,
stubborn, puffed up, and lovers of pleasures more than of
God; having an appearance indeed of godliness, by denying
the power thereof. Now these avoid.' *Tit.* [3.3]: 'For we ourselves also were some time unwise, incredulous, erring, slaves
to divers desires and pleasures, living in malice and envy, hateful and hating one another.'

A list of acts that are approved and carry with them certain
promise of blessing.

Cap. 2

Matthew [5.3-12]: 'Blessed are the poor in spirit, for theirs
is the kingdom of heaven. Blessed are they that mourn, for

they shall be comforted. Blessed are the meek, for they shall possess the land. Blessed are they that hunger and thirst after justice, for they shall have their fill. Blessed are the merciful, for they shall obtain mercy. Blessed are the clean of heart, for they shall see God. Blessed are the peacemakers, for they shall be called the children of God. Blessed are they that suffer persecution for justice' sake, for theirs is the kingdom of heaven. Blessed are ye, when they shall revile you and persecute you and speak all that is evil against you untruly for my sake. Be glad and rejoice, for your reward is great in heaven.' *Matthew* [25.34-36]: 'Come, ye blessed of my Father, possess you the kingdom prepared for you from the foundation of the world. For I was hungry, and you gave me to eat; I was thirsty, and you gave me to drink; I was a stranger, and you took me in; naked and you covered me; sick and you visited me; I was in prison, and you came to me.' *Rom.* [12.7-21]: 'Or ministry in ministering; or he that teacheth, in doctrine; he that exhorteth, in exhorting; he that giveth, with simplicity; he that ruleth, with carefulness; he that showeth mercy, with cheerfulness. Let love be without dissimulation, hating that which is evil, cleaving to that which is good. Loving one another with the charity of brotherhood, with honour preventing one another. In carefulness, not slothful. In spirit fervent. Serving the Lord, Rejoicing in hope. Patient in tribulation. Instant in prayer. Communicating to the necessities of the saints. Pursuing hospitality. Bless them that persecute you; bless and curse not. Rejoice with them that rejoice; weep with them that weep. Being of one mind one towards another. Not minding high things but consenting to the humble. Be not wise in your own conceits. To no man rendering evil for evil. Providing good things in the sight of all men. If it be possible, as much as is in you, have peace with all men. Revenge not yourselves, my dearly beloved; but give place unto wrath, for it is written: Revenge is mine, I will repay, saith the Lord. But if thy enemy is hungry, give him to eat; if he thirst, give him to drink. Be not overcome by evil, but overcome evil by good.' *2 Cor.* [6.3-10]: 'Giving no offence to any man, that our ministry be not blamed; but in all things let us exhibit ourselves as the ministers of God, in much patience, in tribulations, in necessities, in distresses, in stripes, in prisons, in seditions, in labours, in watchings, in fastings, in chastity, in knowledge, in longsuffering, in sweetness, in the Holy Ghost, in charity unfeigned, in the word of truth, in the power of God; by the armour of justice on the right hand and on the left; by honour and dishonour, by evil report and good report; as deceivers, and yet true; as unknown, and yet known; as dying, and behold we live; as chastised and not killed; as sorrowful, yet always rejoicing; as needy, yet enriching many; as having nothing and possessing all things.' *2 Cor.* [13.11]: 'For the rest, brethren, rejoice, be perfect, take exhortation; be of one mind, have peace.' *Gal.* [5.22]: 'But the fruit of the Spirit is charity, joy, peace, patience, benignity, goodness, faith, mildness, continency, chastity.' *Eph.* [4.1-4]: 'I therefore, a prisoner in the Lord, beseech you that you walk worthy of the vocation in which you are called, with all humility and mildness, with patience supporting one another in charity; careful to keep the unity of the Spirit in the bond of peace. One body and one Spirit; as you are called in one hope of your calling.' *Eph.* [4.32]: 'And be ye kind to one another; merciful, forgiving one another, even as God hath forgiven you in Christ.' [5.1,2]: 'Be ye therefore followers of God, as most dear children; and walk in love as Christ also hath loved us, and hath delivered himself for us, an oblation and a sacrifice to God for an odour of sweetness.' *Phil.* [2.1-3]: 'If there be therefore any consolation in Christ, if any comfort of charity, if any society of the spirit, if any bowels of commiseration, fulfill ye my joy, that you be of one mind, having the same charity, being of one accord, agreeing in sentiment. Let nothing be done through contention, neither by vain glory.' *Phil.* [4.8,9]: 'For the rest, brethren, whatsoever things are true, whatsoever modest, whatsoever just, whatsoever holy, whatsoever lovely, whatsoever of good fame, if there be any virtue, and if there be any praise, think on these things. The things which you have both learned and received and heard and seen in me, these do ye.' *Col.* [3.1-3]: 'Therefore if you be risen with Christ, seek the things that are above; where Christ is sitting at the right hand of God. Mind the things that are above, not the things that are upon the earth. For you are dead, and your life is hid with Christ in God.' [12]: 'Put ye one therefore, as the elect of God, holy and beloved, the bowels of mercy, benignity, humility, mildness, patience.' *1 Thess.* [5.14-22]: 'Rebuke the unquiet, comfort the timorous, support the weak, be patient toward all men. See that none renders evil for evil to any man, but ever follow that which is good towards each other and towards all men. Always rejoice. Pray without ceasing. In all things give thanks; for this is the will of God in Christ Jesus concerning you all. Extinguish not the spirit. Despise not prophecies. But prove all things; hold fast that which is good. From all appearance of evil refrain yourselves.' *Tit.* [2.2-5]: 'That the aged men be sober, chaste, prudent, sound in faith, in love, in patience. The aged women, in like manner, in holy attire, not false accusers, not given to much wine, teaching well; that they may teach the young women to be wise, to love their husbands, to love their children, to be discreet, chaste, gentle, having a care of the house, obedient to their husbands, that the word of God be not blasphemed.' *Tit.* [3.1,2]: 'Admonish them to be subject to princes and powers, to obey at a word, to be ready to every good work, to speak evil of no man, not to be litigious, but gentle; showing all mildness toward all men.' *Heb.* [13.1-5]: 'Let the charity of the brotherhood abide in you, and hospitality do not forget; for by this some, being not aware of it, have entertained angels. Remember them that are in bands, as if you were bound with them; and them that labour, as being yourselves also in the body. Marriage honourable in all, and the bed undefiled. For fornicators and adulterers God will judge. Let your manners be without covetousness, contented with such things as you have.'

RULE SEVENTY

They who are entrusted with the preaching of the Gospel ought, after prayer and supplication, to appoint as deacons or priests blameless men whose past life has been investigated and found worthy.

Cap. 1

Matthew [9.37,38]: 'Then he saith to his disciples: The harvest indeed is great, but the labourers are few. Pray ye therefore the Lord of the harvest, that he send forth labourers into his harvest.' *Luke* [6.13-16]: 'And when day was come, he called unto him his disciples; and he chose twelve of them (whom also he named apostles): Simon, whom he surnamed Peter, and Andrew, his brother, James and John, Philip and Bartholomew, Matthew and Thomas, James the son of Alpheus, and Simon who is called Zelotes and Jude the brother of James, and Judas Iscariot, who was the traitor.' *Luke* [10.1,2]: 'And after these things the Lord appointed also other seventy-two; and he sent them two and two before his face into every city and place whither he himself was to come. And he said to them: The harvest indeed is great but the labourers are few. Pray ye therefore the Lord of the harvest, that he send labourers into his harvest.' *Acts* [1.1,2]: 'The former treatise I made, O Theophilus, of all things which Jesus began to do and to teach, until the day on which giving commandments by the Holy Ghost to the apostles whom he had chosen, he was taken up.' *Acts* [1.23-26:] 'And they appointed two, Joseph, called Barsabas, who was surnamed Justus, and Matthias. And praying they said: Thou, Lord, who knowest the hearts of all men, show whether of these two thou hast chosen to take the place of this ministry and apostleship from which Judas hath by transgression fallen, that he might go to his own place. And they gave them lots and the lot fell upon Matthias, and he was numbered with the eleven apostles.' *1 Tim.* [3.1-10]: 'If a man desire the office of a bishop, he desireth a good work. It behoveth therefore a bishop to be blameless, the husband of one wife, sober, prudent, of good behaviour, given to hospitality, a teacher, not given to wine, no striker, not greedy of filthy lucre but equitable, not quarrelsome, not covetous, but one that ruleth well his own house, having his children in subjection with all gravity. (But if a man know not how to rule his own house, how shall he take care of the church of God?) Not a neophyte, lest being puffed up with pride, he fall into the judgment and snare of the devil. Moreover, he must have a good testimony of them who are without, lest he fall into reproach and the snare of the devil. Deacons in like manner chaste, not double-tongued, not given to much wine, not greedy of filthy lucre; holding the mystery of faith in a pure conscience. And let these also first be proved; and so let them minister, having no crime.' *Tit.* [1.5-9]: 'For this cause I left thee in Crete, that thou shouldst set in order the things that are wanting and shouldst ordain priests in every city, as I also appointed thee; if any be without crime, the husband of one wife, having faithful children, not accused of riot, or unruly. For a bishop must be without crime, as the steward of God: not proud, not subject to anger, not given to wine, no striker, not greedy of filthy lucre, but given to hospitality, gentle, sober, just, holy, continent: embracing that faithful word which is according to doctrine that he may be able to exhort in sound doctrine and to convince the gainsayers.'

That we should not be careless with regard to ordinations and that they should not be held without careful deliberation; for that which has not been put to the test involves risk; also, that it is necessary to expose one who is detected in any misdemeanor so that he who has discovered this may not be an accomplice to the sin and that others may not be scandalized but may rather learn to fear.

Cap. 2

1 Tim. [5.22]: 'Impose not hands lightly upon any man, neither be partaker of other men's sins.' *1 Tim.* [5.19,20]: 'Against a priest receive not an accusation but under two or three witnesses. Then that sin reprove before all, that the rest also may have fear.'

That he who has been chosen should not of his own accord undertake the preaching of the Gospel, but wait for the time acceptable to God and begin his preaching when he has been assigned this duty; that, furthermore, he should preach to those to whom he has been sent.

Cap. 3

Matthew [10.5,6]: 'These twelve Jesus sent, commanding them, saying: Go yet not into the way of the Gentiles and into the city of the Samaritans enter ye not; but go ye rather to the lost sheep of the house of Israel.' *Matthew* [15.22-24]: 'And behold a woman of Canaan who came out of those coasts, crying out, said to him: Have mercy on me, O Lord, thou son of David; my daughter is grievously troubled by a devil. Who answered her not a word. And his disciples came and besought him, saying: Send her away for she crieth after us; and he answering, said: I was not sent but to the sheep that are lost of the house of Israel.' *John* [8.42]: 'For from God I proceeded and came; for I came not of myself but he sent me.' *Acts* [11.19]: 'Now they who had been dispersed by the persecution that arose on occasion of Stephen, went about as far as Phoenice and Cyprus and Antioch, speaking the word to none, but to the Jews only.' *Rom.* [1.1]: 'Paul, a servant of Jesus Christ, called to be an apostle, separated unto the gospel of God.' *Rom.* [10.14,15]: 'And how shall they hear without a preacher? And how shall they preach unless they be sent.' *1 Tim.* [1.1]: 'Paul, an apostle of Jesus Christ, according to the commandment of God our Saviour, and of Christ Jesus our hope.''

That he who has been called to the preaching of the Gospel should obey instantly and without delay.

Cap. 4

Luke [9.59-60]: 'But he said to another: Follow me. And he said: Lord, suffer me first to go out and to bury my father. And the Lord said to him: Let the dead bury their dead; but go thou and preach the kingdom of God.' *Gal.* [1.15-17]: 'But when it pleased God who separated me from my mother's womb and called me by his grace to reveal his Son in me that I might preach him among the Gentiles, immediately I condescended not to flesh and blood, neither went I to Jerusalem to the apostles who were before me; but I went to Arabia and again I returned to Damascus.'

That heterodoxy is forbidden.

Cap. 5

John [10.1,2]: 'Amen, amen I say to you: He that entereth not by the door into the sheepfold but climbeth up another way, the same is a thief and a robber. But he that entereth in by the door is the shepherd of the sheep'; and a little further on [7,8]: 'I am the door of the sheep. All others as many as have come are thieves and robbers; and the sheep heard them not.' *Gal.* [1.8,9]: 'But though we or an angel from heaven preach a gospel to you besides that which we have preached to you, let him be anathema. As we said before, so now I say again: If anyone preach to you a gospel, besides that which you have received, let him be anathema.' *1 Tim.* [6.3,4]: 'If any man teach otherwise and consent not to the sound words of our Lord Jesus Christ and to that doctrine which is according to godliness, he is proud, knowing nothing,' etc.

That the faithful should be instructed in all the precepts of the Lord in the Gospel and also those transmitted to us through the Apostles as well as all that are to be inferred therefrom.

Cap. 6

Matthew [28.19,20]: 'Going teach ye all nations, baptizing them in the name of the Father, and of the Son, and of the Holy Ghost; teaching them to observe all things whatsoever

I have commanded you.' *Acts* [16.4]: 'And as they passed through the cities, they delivered unto them the decrees for to keep, that were decreed by the apostles and ancients who were at Jerusalem.' *1 Tim.* [6.2]: 'These things teach and exhort.' *Tit.* [2.1]: 'But speak thou the things that become sound doctrine.'

That, if he who has been appointed to preach the doctrine of the Lord keep silence respecting anything which is necessary in order to please God, he is guilty of the blood of those who are thus endangered, whether by reason of their doing what is forbidden or of omitting the good they are obliged to do.

Cap. 7

Luke [11.52]: 'Woe to you, lawyers, for you have taken away the key of knowledge; you yourselves have not entered in, and those that were entering in, you hindered.' *Acts.* [18.5,6]: 'And when Silas and Timothy were come from Macedonia, Paul was earnest in preaching, testifying to the Jews, that Jesus is the Christ. But they gainsaying and blaspheming, he shook his garments and said to them: Your blood be upon your own heads. I am clean; from henceforth I will go unto the Gentiles.' *Acts* [20.26,27]: 'Wherefore I take you to witness this day, that I am clear from the blood of all men; for I have not spared to declare unto you all the counsel of God.'

That, when there is question of something not expressly commanded in the Scripture, each should be exhorted to follow the better course.

Cap. 8

Matthew [19.12]: 'There are eunuchs who were born so from their mother's womb; and there are eunuchs who were made so by men; and there are eunuchs who have made themselves eunuchs for the kingdom of heaven. He that can take, let him take it.' *1 Cor.* [7.25-27]: 'Now concerning virgins, I have no commandment of the Lord; but I give counsel, as having obtained mercy of the Lord to be faithful. I think, therefore, that this is good for the present necessity, that it is good for a man so to be. Art thou bound to a wife? Seek not to be loosed. Art thou loosed from a wife? Seek not a wife,' etc.

That no one is permitted to force others to do what he himself has not succeeded in accomplishing.

Cap. 9

Luke [11.46]: 'Woe to you lawyers also, because you load men with burdens which they cannot bear, and you yourselves touch not the packs with one of your fingers.'

That he who is a preacher of the Word should be proposed to the rest as a model of every virtue by first practicing what he teaches.

Cap. 10

Matthew [11.28,29]: 'Come to me, all you that labour and are burdened, and I will refresh you. Take up my yoke upon you and learn of me because I am meek and humble of heart.' *John* [13.12-15]: 'Then after he had washed the feet of his disciples, and taken his garments, being set down again, he said to them: Know you what I have done to you? You call me Master and Lord; and you say well, for so I am. If then I being your Lord and Master have washed your feet; you also ought to wash one another's feet. For I have given you an example, that as I have done to you, so you do also to one another.' *Acts* [20.35]: 'I have showed you all things, how that so labouring you ought to support the weak.' *1 Cor.* [11.1]: 'Be ye followers of me, as I also am of Christ.' *1 Tim.* [4.12]: 'Let no man despise thy youth; but be thou an example of the faithful in word, in conversation,' etc.

That he who is a preacher of the Word should not feel secure in his own righteousness, but should realize that the moral improvement of the faithful is the specific and preeminent function of the office committed to him.

Cap. 11

Matthew [5.13]: 'You are the salt of the earth. But if the salt lose its savor, wherewith shall it be salted? It is good for nothing any more but to be cast out and to be trodden on by men.' *John* [6.37-40]: 'All that the Father giveth to me shall come to me; and him that cometh to me, I will not cast out. Because I came down from heaven not to do my own will but the will of him that sent me, the Father. Now this is the will of him who sent me: that every one who seeth the Son and believeth in him, may have life everlasting.' *1 Thess.* [2.19,20]: 'For what is our hope, or joy, or crown of glory? Are not you in the presence of our Lord Jesus Christ at his coming? For you are our glory and joy.'

That the preacher of the Word should visit all the towns and cities in his charge.

Cap. 12

Matthew [4.23]: 'And Jesus went about all Galilee teaching in the synagogues and preaching the gospel of the kingdom, and healing all manner of sickness and every infirmity.' *Luke* [8.1]: 'And he travelled through the cities and towns preaching the kingdom of God and evangelizing; and the twelve with him.'

That all should be summoned to the hearing of the Gospel, that the Word must be preached with all candor, that the truth must be upheld even at the cost of opposition and persecution of whatever sort, unto death.

Cap. 13

Matthew [10.27,28]: 'That which I tell you in the dark, speak ye in the light: and that which you hear in the ear, preach ye upon the housetops. And fear ye not them that kill the body and are not able to kill the soul.' *Matthew* [22.8,9]: 'The marriage indeed is ready, but they that were invited were not worthy. Go ye therefore into the highways and as many as you shall find, call to the marriage.' *John* [18.20]: 'Jesus answered him: I have spoken openly to the world; I have always taught in the synagogue and in the temple, whither all the Jews resort; and in secret I have spoken nothing.' *Acts* [5.27-29]: 'And when they had brought them, they set them before the council. And the high priest asked them, saying: Commanding we commanded you, that you should not teach in this name; and behold, you have filled Jerusalem with your doctrine and you have a mind to bring the blood of this man upon us. But Peter and the apostles answering, said: We ought to obey God rather than men.' *Acts* [20.23,24]: 'Save that the Holy Ghost in every city witnesseth to me, saying that bands and afflictions wait for me. But I fear none of these things, neither do I count my life more precious than myself so that I may consummate my course and the ministry of the word which I received from the Lord Jesus to testify the gospel of the grace of God,' *1 Thess.* [2.1,2]: 'For yourselves know, brethren, our entrance in unto you, that it was not in vain; but having suffered many things before and been shamefully treated (as you know) at Philippi, we had confidence in our God to speak unto you the gospel of God in much carefulness.'

That we should pray for the spiritual advancement of the faithful and also return thanks for this favor.

Cap. 14

John [17.20,21]: 'And not for them only do I pray, but for them also who through their word shall believe in me; that they all may be one as thou, Father, in me and I in thee: that they also may be one in us'; and again [17.24]: 'Father, I will that where I am, they also whom thou hast given me may be with me.' *Luke* [10.21]: 'In that same hour, Jesus rejoiced in the Spirit and said: I confess to thee, O Father, Lord of heaven and earth, because thou hast hidden these things from the wise and prudent and hast revealed them to little ones. Yea, Father, for so it hath seemed good in thy sight.' *Rom.* [1.8,9]: 'First I give thanks to my God through Jesus Christ for you all, because your faith is spoken of in the whole world. For God is my witness whom I serve in my spirit in the gospel of his Son, that without ceasing I make a commemoration of you always in my prayers.' *Phil.* [1.8-11]: 'For God is my witness how I long after you in the bowels of Jesus Christ. And this I pray, that your charity may more and more abound in knowledge and in all understanding; that you may approve the better things, that you may be sincere and without offence unto the day of Christ, filled with the fruit of justice, through Jesus Christ, unto the glory and praise of God.'

That good actions performed with the grace of God ought to be made known also to others for His glory.

Cap. 15

Luke [9.10]: 'And the apostles, when they were returned, told him all they had done.' *Acts* [14.26]: 'And when they were come and had assembled the church, they related what great things God had done with them.' *Eph.* [6.21,22]: 'But that you also may know the things that concern me and what I am doing, Tychichus, my dearest brother and faithful minister in the Lord, will make known to you all things; whom I have sent to you for this same purpose that you may know the things concerning us.'

That we must be solicitous not only for those who are present but also for the absent and do all things as the work of edification may require.

Cap. 16

John [10.16]: 'And other sheep I have that are not of this fold; them also I must bring and they shall hear my voice, and there shall be one fold and one shepherd.' *1 Thess.* [3.1,2]: 'For which cause, forbearing no longer, we thought it good to remain at Athens alone; and we sent Timothy,

our brother, and the minister of God in the gospel of Christ
to confirm you and exhort you concerning your faith.'

That we should hearken to those who ask us to confer a
benefit.

Chap. 17

Matthew [9.18,19]: 'As he was speaking these things, behold a certain ruler came up and adored him, saying: Lord,
my daughter is even now dead; but come, lay thy hand upon
her and she shall live. And Jesus rising up, followed him.'
Acts [9.38,39]: 'And forasmuch as Lydda was nigh to Joppe,
the disciples hearing that Peter was there, sent unto him two
men, desiring him that he would not be slack to come unto
them. And Peter rising up, went with them.'

That they who accept the doctrine of truth should be confirmed in it by our visits.

Cap. 18

Acts [15.36]: 'And after some days, Paul said to Barnabas:
Let us return and visit our brethren in all the cities wherein
we have preached the word of the Lord to see how they do.'
1 Thess. [2.17,18]: 'But we, brethren, being taken away
from you for a short time, in sight, not in heart, have hastened
the more abundantly to see your face with great desire. For
we would have come unto you, I, Paul, indeed once and again,
but Satan hath hindered us'; and a little further on [3.1-3]:
'For which cause, forbearing no longer, we thought it good
to remain at Athens alone; and we sent Timothy, our brother
and the minister of God in the gospel of Christ, to confirm
you and exhort you concerning your faith; that no man should

be moved in these tribulations; for yourselves know that we are appointed thereunto.'

That it behooves him who loves the Lord to be solicitous in all charity and with every manifestation of zeal for those whom he teaches, even though it should be necessary for him to persevere unto death itself in his teaching both public and private.

Cap. 19

John [10.11]: 'The good shepherd giveth his life for his sheep.' *John* [21.15-17]: 'When therefore they had dined, Jesus saith to Simon Peter: Simon, son of John, lovest thou me more than these? He saith to him: Yes, Lord, thou knowest that I love thee. He saith to him: Feed my lambs. He saith to him again: Simon, son of John, lovest thou me? He saith to him: Yea, Lord, thou knowest that I love thee. He saith to him: Tend my sheep. He saith to him the third time: Simon, son of John, lovest thou me? Peter was grieved because he had said to him the third time: Lovest thou me? And he said to him: Lord, thou knowest all things; thou knowest that I love thee. Jesus saith to him: Feed my sheep.' *Acts* [20.7]: 'And on the first day of the week, when the disciples were assembled to break bread, Paul discoursed with them, being to depart on the morrow: and he continued his speech until midnight'; and shortly after [11]: 'Then going up and breaking bread and tasting, and having talked a long time to them, until daylight, so he departed.' [20-21]: 'How I have kept back nothing that was profitable to you, but have preached it to you, and taught you publicly, and from house to house, testifying both to Jews and Gentiles penance towards God, and faith in our Lord Jesus.' [31]: 'Therefore watch,

keeping in memory that for three years I ceased not with tears
to admonish every one of you night and day.' *1 Thess.* [2.9]:
'For you remember, brethren, our labour and toil; working
night and day, lest we should be chargeable to any of you,
we preached among you the gospel of God,' etc.

That the preacher of the Word should be compassionate
and merciful, especially toward those who are suffering distress
of soul.

Cap. 20

Matthew [9.11-13]: 'And the Pharisees seeing it, said to
his disciples: Why doth your master eat with publicans and
sinners? But Jesus hearing it, said: They that are in health
need not a physician, but they that are ill. Go then and learn
what this meaneth: I will have mercy and not sacrifice. For
I am not come to call the just, but sinners to repentance.'
Matthew [9.36]: 'And seeing the multitudes, he had compassion on them, because they were distressed, like sheep that
have no shepherd.'

That it is right to be kind and solicitous even with regard
to the bodily needs of those in our charge.

Cap. 21

Matthew [15.32]: 'I have compassion on the multitudes,
because they continue with me now three days, and have not
what to eat, and I will not send them away fasting lest they
faint on the way.' *Mark* [1.40,41]: 'And there came a leper
to him, beseeching him, and kneeling down said to him: If
thou wilt, thou canst make me clean. And Jesus, having
compassion on him, stretched forth his hand and touching

him, saith to him: I will. Be thou made clean.' *Acts* [6.1-3]:
'And in those days, the number of disciples increasing, there
arose a murmuring of the Greeks against the Hebrews for
that their widows were neglected in the daily ministrations.
Then the twelve, calling together the multitude of the disciples, said: It is not reason that we should leave the word
of God and serve tables. Look ye out from among you, brethren, seven men of good reputation, full of the Holy Ghost and
wisdom, whom we may appoint over this business.'

That the preacher of the Word should not be eager to busy
himself with minor matters, relaxing, meanwhile, the zeal
he is obliged to show in more important ones.

Cap. 22

Acts [6.2]: 'Then the twelve, calling together the multitudes of the disciples, said: It is not reason that we should
leave the word of God and serve tables'; and a little farther
on [4]: 'But we will give ourselves continually to prayer and
to the ministry of the word.'

That we should not be ostentatious nor traffic in the word
of doctrine by flattering our hearers in the interest of our
own pleasure or convenience; but it befits us to act as if we
were speaking for the glory of God in His very presence.

Cap. 23

Matthew [23.5-10]: 'And all their works they do for to be
seen of men. For they make their phylacteries broad and en-
large their fringes. And they love the first places at feasts and
the first chairs in the synagogues, and salutations in the
market place and to be called by men, Rabbi, Rabbi. Be not

you called Rabbi; for one is your master and all you are brethren. And call none your father upon earth; for one is your Father, who is in heaven; neither be ye called masters; for one is your master, Christ.' *John* [7.16-18]: 'My doctrine is not mine but his that sent me. If any man will do the will of him, he shall know of the doctrine, whether it be of God or whether I speak of myself. He that speaketh of himself seeketh his own glory: but he that seeketh the glory of him that sent him, he is true and there is no injustice in him.' *2 Cor.* [2.17]: 'For we are not, as many, adulterating the word of God: but with sincerity, but as from God, before God, in Christ we speak.' *1 Thess.* [2.3-7]: 'For our exhortation was not of error nor of uncleanness, nor in deceit; but as we were approved by God that the gospel should be committed to us, even so we speak, not as pleasing men, but God, who proveth our hearts. For neither have we used at any time the speech of flattery as you know, nor taken an occasion of covetousness, God is witness; nor sought we glory of men, neither of you nor of others, whence we might have been burdensome to you, as the apostles of Christ.'

That the preacher of the Word should not abuse his power by insolent or high-minded treatment of those in his care; but he should rather regard his position as a reason for showing humility toward them.

Cap. 24

Matthew [24.45-51]: 'Who, thinkest thou, is a faithful and wise servant whom his lord hath appointed over his family to give them meat in season? Blessed is that servant whom when his lord shall come he shall find so doing. Amen I say to you, he shall place him over all his goods. But if that evil servant shall say in his heart: My lord is long a-coming, and shall begin to strike his fellow-servants and shall eat and drink with drunkards; the lord of that servant shall come in a day that he hopeth not, and at an hour that he knoweth not: and shall separate him and appoint his portion with the hypocrites. There shall be weeping and gnashing of teeth.' *John* [13.13,14]: 'You call me Master and Lord; and you say well, for so I am. If then I being your Lord and Master have washed your feet; you also ought to wash one another's feet.' *Luke* [22.24-27: 'And there was also a strife amongst them, which of them should seem to be the greater. And Jesus said to them: The kings of the Gentiles lord it over them and they that have power over them are called benefactors. But you not so: but he that is the greater among you, let him become as the younger; and he that is the leader as he that serveth. For which is greater, he that sitteth at table, or he that serveth? Is not he that sitteth at table?' *Acts* [20.17-20]: 'And sending from Miletus to Ephesus, he called the ancients of the church. And when they were come to him, he said to them: You know from the first day that I came into Asia, in what manner I have been with you, for all the time, serving the Lord with all humility and with many tears and temptations which befell me by the conspiracies of the Jews.' *2 Cor.* [11.19-21]: 'For you gladly suffer the foolish; whereas you yourselves are wise. For you suffer if a man bring you into bondage, if a man devour you, if a man take from you, if a man be lifted up, if a man strike you on the face. I speak according to dishonour, as if we had been weak in this part.'

That we should not preach the Gospel in a spirit of strife or envy, or rivalry with anyone.

Cap. 25

Matthew [12.18,19]: 'Behold my servant whom I have chosen, my beloved, in whom my soul hath been well-pleased. I will put my spirit upon him and he shall show judgment to the Gentiles. He shall not contend nor cry out, neither shall any man hear his voice in the streets.' *Phil.* [1.15-17]: 'Some, indeed, even out of envy and contention; but some also for good will preach Christ. Some out of charity, knowing that I am set for the defence of the gospel. And some out of contention preach Christ not sincerely; supposing that they raise affliction to my bands.'

That human devices for enhancing style should not be employed in preaching the Gospel, lest they conceal the grace of God.

Cap. 26

Matthew [11.25]: 'I confess to thee, O Father, Lord of heaven and earth, because thou hast hid these things from the wise and prudent, and hast revealed them to little ones.' *1 Cor.* [1.17]: 'For Christ sent me not to baptize, but to preach the gospel: not in wisdom of speech, lest the cross of Christ should be made void.' [2.1-5]: 'And I, brethren, when I came to you, came not in loftiness of speech or of wisdom, declaring unto you the testimony of Christ. For I judged not myself to know anything among you but Jesus Christ, and him crucified. And I was with you in weakness, and in fear, and in much trembling. And my speech and my preaching was not in the persuasive words of human wisdom, but in showing of the Spirit and power; that your faith might not stand on the wisdom of men but on the power of God.'

That we should not think that we achieve success in preaching through our own devices, but we should rely entirely on God.

Cap. 27

2 Cor. [3.4-6]: 'And such confidence we have through Christ towards God. Not that we are sufficient to think anything of ourselves as of ourselves; but our sufficiency is from God, who also hath made us fit ministers of the new testament.' *2 Cor.* [4.7]: 'But we have this treasure in earthen vessels, that the excellency may be of the power of God and not of us.'

That one who is entrusted with the preaching of the Gospel should possess nothing more than is strictly necessary for him.

Cap. 28

Matthew [10.9,10]: 'Do not possess gold nor silver nor money in your purses; nor scrip for your journey, nor two coats, nor shoes, nor a staff; for the workman is worthy of his meat.' *Luke* [9.3]: 'Take nothing for your journey: neither staff, nor scrip, nor bread, nor money; neither have two coats.' *Acts* [20.33,34]: 'I have not coveted any man's silver, gold, or apparel as you yourselves know.' *2 Tim.* [2.4]: 'No man, being a soldier to God, entangleth himself with secular businesses; that he may please him to whom he hath engaged himself.'

That we should not lend our mind to worldly affairs in the interest of those who are free to occupy themselves with these matters.

Cap. 29

Luke [12.13,14]: 'And one of the multitude said to him: Master, speak to my brother that he divide the inheritance with me. But he said to him: Man, who hath appointed me judge or divider over you?' *2 Tim.* [2.4]: 'No man, being a soldier to God, entangleth himself with secular businesses,' etc.

That they who, to please their listeners, neglect to give a frank presentation of the will of God become the slaves of those they would please and abandon the service of God.

Cap. 30

John [5.44]: 'How can you believe, who receive glory one from another; and the glory which is from God alone, you do not seek?' *Gal.* [1.10]: 'If I yet pleased men, I should not be the servant of Christ.'

That the aim a teacher proposes to himself should be that of forming each one according to his level 'unto a perfect man, unto the measure of the age of the fulness of Christ.'

Cap. 31

Matthew [5.48]: 'Be you therefore perfect as your heavenly Father is perfect.' *John* [17.20,21]: 'Not for them only do I pray, but for them also who through their word shall believe in me; that they all may be one, as thou, Father, in me, and I in thee; that they also may be one in us.' *Eph.* [4.11-13]: 'And he gave some apostles and some prophets, and other some pastors and doctors, for the perfecting of the saints, for the work of the ministry, for the edifying of the body of

Christ: until we all meet into the unity of faith and of the knowledge of the Son of God, unto a perfect man, unto the measure of the age of the fullness of Christ.'

That we should instruct our adversaries in forbearance and mildness in the hope of their conversion until the full measure of solicitude has been exercised toward them.

Cap. 32

Matthew [12.19,20]: 'He shall not contend nor cry out neither shall any man hear his voice in the streets. The bruised reed he shall not break: and smoking flax he shall not extinguish: till he send forth judgment unto victory.' *2 Tim.* [2.24-26]: 'But the servant of the Lord must not wrangle; but be mild towards all men, apt to teach, patient, with modesty admonishing them that resist the truth; if peradventure God may give them repentance to know the truth, and they may recover themselves from the snare of the devil.'

That it is right to yield and not insist obstinately when, through fear or out of caution, some do not tolerate the presence of a preacher of the Word.

Cap. 33

Luke [8.37]: 'And all the multitude of the country of the Garasens besought him to depart from them, for they were taken with great fear. And he going into the ship, returned back again.'

That we should depart from those who through obstinacy do not receive the Gospel, not allowing ourselves to accept even corporeal necessities from them.

Cap. 34

Matthew [10.14]: 'And whosoever shall not receive you, nor hear your words, going forth out of that house or city, shake off the dust from your feet.' *Luke* [10.10,11]: 'But into whatsoever city you enter and they receive you not, going forth into the streets thereof, say: Even the very dust of your city that cleaveth to us, we wipe off against you. Yet know this, that the kingdom of God is at hand.' *Acts* [18.5,6]: 'And when Silas and Timothy were come from Macedonia, Paul was earnest in preaching, testifying to the Jews that Jesus is the Christ. But they gainsaying and blaspheming, he shook his garments and said to them: Your blood be upon your own heads; I am clean; from henceforth I will go unto the Gentiles.'

That we should abandon the incorrigible when we have exhausted all the resources of our solicitude in their regard.

Cap. 35

Matthew [23.37,38]: 'Jerusalem, Jerusalem, thou that killest the prophets and stonest them that are sent unto thee, how often would I have gathered together thy children, as the hen doth gather her chickens under her wings, and thou wouldst not? Behold your house shall be left to you, desolate.' *Acts* [13.46,47]: 'To you it behoved us to speak the word of God; but because you reject it and judge yourselves unworthy of eternal life, behold we turn to the Gentiles. For so the Lord hath commanded us: I have set thee to be the light of the Gentiles, that thou mayest be for salvation unto the utmost part of the earth.' *Tit.* [3.10,11]: 'A man that is a heretic after the first and second admonition, avoid; knowing that he that is such a one is subverted and sinneth, being condemned by his own judgment.'

That the integrity of the Lord's words must be maintained unswervingly toward all and in all circumstances, with no concession to our preferences.

Cap. 36

1 Tim. [5.21]: 'I charge thee before God and Christ Jesus and the elect angels, that thou observe these things without prejudice, doing nothing by declining to either side.'

That the preacher of the Word should say and do each thing after deliberation and close examination with a view to pleasing God, so as also to gain the approval and esteem due him from those in his care.

Cap. 37

Acts [20.18,19]: 'You know from the first day that I came into Asia, in what manner I have been with you for all the time, serving the Lord with all humility and with many tears and temptations'; and a little farther on [33,34]: 'I have not coveted any man's silver, gold, or apparel. You yourselves know that such things as were needful for me and them that are with me, these hands have furnished.' *1 Thess.* [2.10,11]: 'You are witnesses, and God also, how holily and justly and without blame we have been to you that believe, as you know.'

RULE SEVENTY-ONE

Prescriptions which refer jointly to bishops and priests.

Cap. 1

1 Tim. [3.1,2]: 'If a man desire the office of a bishop, he desireth a good work. It behoveth therefore a bishop to be blameless,' etc. *1 Tim.* [5.1,2]: 'An ancient man rebuke not, but entreat him as a father; young men, as brethren; old women, as mothers; young women, as sisters, in all chastity.' *2 Tim.* [2.22-24]: 'But flee thou youthful desires and pursue justice, faith, charity, and peace, with them that call on the Lord out of a pure heart. And avoid foolish and unlearned questions, knowing that they beget strifes. But the servant of the Lord must not wrangle, but be mild towards all men,' etc. *2 Tim.* [3.10,11]: 'But thou hast fully known my faith, doctrine, manner of life, purpose, longsuffering, patience, persecutions, afflictions.' *Tit.* [1.5,6]: 'For this cause I left thee in Crete that thou shouldst set in order the things that are wanting and shouldst ordain priests in every city as I also appointed thee, if any be without crime,' etc.

Concerning deacons.

Cap. 2

Acts [6.5,6]: 'And they chose Stephen, a man full of faith and of the Holy Ghost, and Philip and Prochorus and Nicanor' and the rest. 'These they set before the apostles; and they, praying, imposed hands upon them.' *1 Tim.* [3.8]: 'Deacons in like manner chaste, not double tongued, not given to much wine, not greedy of filthy lucre,' etc.

RULE SEVENTY-TWO

Concerning the hearers: that those hearers who are instructed in the Scriptures should examine what is said by the teachers, receiving what is in conformity with the Scriptures and rejecting what is opposed to them; and that those who persist in teaching such doctrines should be strictly avoided.

Cap. 1

Matthew [18.7-9]: 'Woe to that man by whom the scandal cometh. And if thy eye scandalize thee, pluck it out,' and similarly with regard to the hand and foot. *John* [10.1]: 'Amen, amen I say to you:. He that entereth not by the door into the sheepfold but climbeth up another way, the same is a thief and a robber'; and a little further on [10.5]: 'But a stranger they follow not, but fly from him because they know not the voice of strangers.' *Gal.* [1.8]: 'But though we or an angel from heaven preach a gospel to you besides that which you have received, let him be anathema.' *1 Thess.* [5.20-22]: 'Despise not prophecies. Prove all things; hold fast that which is good. From all appearance of evil refrain yourselves.'

That they who possess little knowledge of the Scriptures should recognize the distinctive mark of the saints by the fruits of the Spirit, receiving those who bear this mark and avoiding those who do not.

Cap. 2

Matthew [7.15,16]: 'Beware of false prophets who come to you in the clothing of sheep but inwardly they are ravening wolves. By their fruits you shall know them.' *Phil.* [3.17]: 'Be ye followers of me, brethren, and observe them who walk so as you have our model.'

That they who teach rightly the Word of Truth should be received even as the Lord, unto the glory of Him who has sent them, Jesus Christ our Lord.

Cap. 3

Matthew [10.40]: 'He that receiveth you, receiveth me.'
John [13.20]: 'He that receiveth whomsoever I send, receiveth me.' *Luke* [10.16]: 'He that heareth you, heareth me.'
Gal. [4.13,14]: 'And the temptation in my flesh, you despised not nor rejected, but received me as an angel of God, even as Christ Jesus.'

That they who heed not those who are sent by the Lord bring dishonor not only upon these latter, but upon Him also who sent them, and they draw down upon themselves a harsher judgment than that pronounced upon the people of Sodom and Gomorrha.

Cap. 4

Matthew [10.14,15]: 'And whosoever shall not receive you nor hear your words, going forth out of that house or city, shake off the dust from your feet. Amen I say to you, it shall be more tolerable for the land of Sodom and Gomorrha in the day of judgment than for that city.' *Luke* [10.16]: 'He that despiseth you, despiseth me.' *1 Thess.* [4.8]: 'Therefore, he that despiseth these things, despiseth not man, but God who also hath given his holy Spirit in us.'

That the teaching of the Lord's commandments should be received as having the power to procure eternal life and the kingdom of heaven; and also that we should put it into practice with a good will, even though it seem arduous.

Cap. 5

John [5.24]: 'Amen, amen I say unto you, that he who

heareth my word and believeth him that sent me, hath life everlasting and cometh not into judgment but is passed from death to life.' *Acts* [14.20-22]: 'And when they had preached the gospel to that city and had taught many, they returned again to Lystra, and to Iconium, and to Antioch, confirming the souls of the disciples and exhorting them to continue in the faith; and that through many tribulations we must enter into the kingdom of heaven.'

That reprimand and censure should be accepted as healing remedies for vice and as conducive to health; whence it is evident that they who feign indulgence in a spirit of flattery and do not upbraid the sinners cause them to suffer supreme loss and plot the destruction of that life which is their true life.

Cap. 6

Matthew [18.15]: 'But if thy brother shall offend against thee, go, and rebuke him between thee and him alone. If he shall hear thee, thou shalt gain thy brother.' *1 Cor.* [5.4,5]: 'You being gathered together and my spirit with the power of our Lord Jesus Christ, to deliver such a one to Satan for the destruction of the flesh, that the spirit may be saved in the day of the Lord Jesus.' *2 Cor.* [7.8-10]: 'Seeing that the same epistle (although but for a time) did make you sorrowful, now I am glad, not because you were made sorrowful, but because you were made sorrowful unto penance. For you were made sorrowful according to God, that you might suffer by us in nothing. For the sorrow that is according to God worketh penance, steadfast unto salvation.' *Tit.* [1.13]: 'Wherefore rebuke them sharply that they may be sound in the faith.'

RULE SEVENTY-THREE

That a husband must not separate from his wife nor a wife from her husband unless one of them be taken in adultery or is a hindrance to the other in the devout service of God.

Cap. 1

Matthew [5.31,32]: 'And it hath been said, Whosoever shall put away his wife, let him give her a bill of divorce. But I say to you, that whosoever shall put away his wife, excepting for the cause of fornication, maketh her to commit adultery; and he that shall marry her that is put away, committeth adultery.' *Luke* [14.26]: 'If any man come to me and hate not his father and mother and wife and children, and brethren, and sisters, yea and his own life also, he cannot be my disciple.' *Matthew* [19.9]: 'And I say to you, that whosoever shall put away his wife except it be for fornication and shall marry another, committeth adultery; and he that shall marry her that is put away, committeth adultery.' *1 Cor.* [7.10,11]: 'But to them that are married, not I, but the Lord commandeth that the wife depart not from her husband; and if she depart, that she remain unmarried, or be reconciled to her husband; and let not the husband put away his wife.'

That the husband may not put away his wife and marry another, nor may she who is put away by her husband marry another.

Cap. 2

Matthew [19.9]: 'And I say to you that whosoever shall put away his wife, except it be for fornication, and shall mary another, committeth adultery and he that shall marry her that is put away, committeth adultery.'

That husbands should love their wives with the love wherewith Christ has loved the Church, who delivered Himself
up for her, that He might sanctify her.

Cap. 3

Eph. [5.25,26]: 'Husbands, love your wives, as Christ
also loved the Church and delivered himself up for it, that
he might sanctify it, cleansing it by the laver of water in the
word of life'; and a little later [28]: 'So also ought men to
love their wives as their own bodies,' etc.

That wives should be subject to their husbands, as the
Church is to Christ, and thus do the will of God.

Cap. 4

Eph. [5.22-24]: 'Let women be subject to their husbands,
as to the Lord; because the husband is the head of the wife,
as Christ is the head of the church; and he is the saviour of
his body. Therefore as the church is subject to Christ, so also
let the wives be to their husbands in all things.' *Tit.* [2.4,5]:
'That they may teach the young women to be wise, to love
their husbands, chaste, having a care of the house, gentle,
obedient to their husbands, that the word of God be not blasphemed.'

That women should not adorn themselves for beauty's sake,
but they should be full of zeal and solicitude for good works,
regarding this as the true and appropriate adornment for
Christian women.

Cap. 5

1 Tim. [2.9,10]: 'In like manner women also in decent

apparel; adorning themselves with modesty and sobriety, not with plaited hair, or gold, or pearls, or costly attire, but as it becometh women professing godliness, with good works.'

That women should keep silence in church, but be zealous at home to inquire about the manner of pleasing God.

Cap. 6

1 Cor. [14.34,35]: 'Let women keep silence in the churches; for it is not permitted to them to speak, but to be subject. But if they would learn anything, let them ask their husbands at home. For it is a shame for women to speak in church.' *1 Tim.* [2.11-15]: 'Let the woman learn in silence, with all subjection. But I suffer not a woman to teach, nor to use authority over the man, but to be in silence. For Adam was first formed, then Eve. And Adam was not seduced; but the woman being seduced, was in the transgression. Yet she shall be saved through child-bearing, if she continue in faith, and love, and sanctification, with sobriety.'

RULE SEVENTY-FOUR

That a widow who enjoys sufficiently robust health should spend her life in works of zeal and solicitude, keeping in mind the words of the Apostle and the example of Dorcas.

Cap. 1

Acts [9.36]: 'And in Joppe there was a certain disciple named Tabitha, which by interpretation is called Dorcas. This woman was full of good works and almsdeeds which she did'; and a little farther on [39]: 'And all the widows stood about him weeping and showing him the coats and garments which

Dorcas made when she was with them.' *1 Tim.* [5.9,10]: 'Let a widow be chosen of no less than three-score years of age, who hath been the wife of one husband; having testimony for her good works, if she have brought up children, if she have received to harbour, if she have washed the saints' feet, if she have ministered to them that suffer tribulation, if she have diligently followed every good work.'

That the widow esteemed for the good works mentioned by the Apostle and accounted in the number of true widows should persevere day and night in prayer and supplication, with fasting.

Cap. 2

Luke [2.36,37]: 'And there was Anna, a prophetess, the daughter of Phanuel, of the tribe of Aser; she was far advanced in years, and had lived with her husband seven years from her virginity. And she was a widow until fourscore and four years; who departed not from the temple, by fastings and prayers serving night and day.' *1 Tim.* [5.5,6]: 'But she that is a widow indeed, and desolate, let her trust in God and continue in supplications and prayers night and day. For she that liveth in pleasures is dead while she is living.'

RULE SEVENTY-FIVE

That bond-servants should obey their masters according to the flesh with a right good will for the glory of God in whatever does not violate a commandment of God.

Cap. 1

Eph. [6.5-8]: 'Servants, be obedient to them that are your lords according to the flesh, with fear and trembling, in the simplicity of your heart, as to Christ: not serving to the eye, as it were pleasing men, but, as the servants of Christ doing the will of God from the heart, with a good will serving, as to the Lord and not to men. Knowing that whosoever good thing any man shall do, the same shall he receive from the Lord, whether he be bond or free.' *1 Tim.* [6.1,2]: 'Whosoever are servants under the yoke, let them count their masters worthy of all honour, lest the name of the Lord and his doctrine be blasphemed. But they that have believing masters, let them not despise them because they are brethren; but serve them the rather, because they are faithful and beloved, who are partakers of the benefit.' *Tit.* [2.9,10]: 'Exhort servants to be obedient to their masters in all things pleasing, not gainsaying, not defrauding, but in all things shewing good fidelity, that they may adorn the doctrine of God our Saviour in all things.'

That masters, mindful of the true Master, should, after the Lord's example, give in return to their bond-servants, insofar as they can, in the fear of God and out of clemency, whatever benefits they may receive from them.

Cap. 2

John [13.3-5]: 'Jesus, knowing that the Father had given him all things into his hands, and that he came from God and goeth to God, ariseth from supper and layeth aside his garments and having taken a towel girded himself. After that, he putteth water into a basin and began to wash the feet of the disciples and to wipe them with a towel wherewith he was girded'; and a little farther on [13-15]: 'You call me Master and Lord and you say well, for so I am. If then I, being your Lord and Master, have washed your feet, you also ought to wash one another's feet. For I have given you an example that as I have done to you, so you do also.' *Eph.* [6.9]: 'You, masters, do the same things to them, forebearing threatening, knowing that the Lord both of them and you is in heaven, and there is no respect of persons with him.'

RULE SEVENTY-SIX

That children should honor and obey their parents in all things wherein the command of God would not be violated.

Cap. 1

Luke [2.48]: 'And his mother said to him: Son, why hast thou done so to us? Behold thy father and I have sought thee sorrowing'; and a little farther on [51]: 'And he went down with them, and came to Nazareth and was subject to them.' *Eph.* [6.1-3]: 'Children, obey your parents in the Lord, for this is just. Honour thy father and thy mother, which is the first commandment with a promise: that it may be well with thee and thou mayest be long-lived upon the earth.'

That parents should rear their children with mildness and forbearance 'in the discipline and correction of the Lord,' and, insofar as may be, give them no occasion for anger or grief.

Cap. 2

Eph. [6.4]: 'And you, fathers, provoke not your children to anger; but bring them up in the discipline and correction of the Lord.' *Col.* [3.21]: 'Fathers, provoke not your children to indignation, lest they be discouraged.'

RULE SEVENTY-SEVEN

That virgins should be free from all solicitude for this world so that they may be able to give thanks to God without distraction of mind or body, in expectation of the kingdom of heaven.

Cap. 1

Matthew [19.12]: 'There are eunuchs who have made themselves eunuchs for the kingdom of heaven. He that can take, let him take it.' *1 Cor.* [7.32-35]: 'But I would have you to be without solicitude. He that is without a wife is solicitous for the things that belong to the Lord, how he may please God. But he that is with a wife is solicitous for the things of the world, how he may please his wife. The married woman and the virgin differ from each other. The unmarried woman thinketh on the things of the Lord, that she may be holy both in body and in spirit. But she that is married thinketh on the things of the world, how she may please her husband. And this I speak for your profit: not to cast a snare upon you, but for that which is decent and which may give you power to attend upon the Lord without impediment.'

RULE SEVENTY-EIGHT

That soldiers may not perform deeds of violence nor make false accusations.

Cap. 1

Luke [3.14]: 'And the soldiers also asked him, saying: And what shall we do? And he said to them: Do violence to no man, neither calumniate any man; and be content with your pay.'

That rulers are custodians of the decrees of God.

Cap. 1

Rom. [13.3,4]: 'For princes are not a terror to good works but to the evil. Wilt thou then not be afraid of the power? Do that which is good and thou shalt have praise from the same. For he is God's minister to thee for good. But if thou do that which is evil, fear; for he beareth not the sword in vain. For he is God's minister, an avenger to execute wrath upon him that doth evil.'

That it is right to submit to higher authority wherever a command of God would not be violated.

Cap. 2

Rom. [13.1-3]: 'Let every soul be subject to higher powers; for there is no power but from God; and those that are, are ordained of God. Therefore, he that resisteth the power, resisteth the ordinance of God; and they that resist, purchase to themselves damnation. For princes are not a terror to good works, but to the evil,' etc. *Acts* [5.29]: 'We ought to obey God rather than men.' *Tit.* [3.1]: 'Admonish them to be subject to princes and powers, to obey, and be ready to every good work.'

The qualities which the Scripture would have Christians possess as disciples of Christ, conformed only to the pattern of what they behold in Him or hear from Him.

Cap. 1

Matthew [11.29]: 'Take up my yoke upon you and learn of me.' *John* [13.13-15]: 'You call me Master and Lord; and you say well, for so I am. If then I being your Lord and Master have washed your feet: you also ought to wash one another's feet. For I have given you an example, that as I have done to you, so you do also.'

As sheep of Christ who hear the voice of their own Shepherd only and follow Him.

Cap. 2

John [10.27]: 'My sheep hear my voice and I know them and they follow me'; and above [10.5]: 'But a stranger they follow not, but fly from him because they know not the voice of strangers.'

As vine branches of Christ rooted in Him and in Him bringing forth fruit, doing and possessing only what is conformable to Him and worthy of Him.

Cap. 3

John [15.5]: 'I am the vine; you, the branches.'

As members of Christ, perfect in every observance of the Lord's commandments or in showing forth the gifts of the Holy Spirit in conformity with the dignity of their Head which is Christ.

Cap. 4

1 Cor. [6.15]: 'Know you not that your bodies are the members of Christ?' *Eph.* [4.15,16]: 'But doing the truth in charity we may in all things grow up in him who is the head, even Christ; from whom the whole body being compacted and fitly joined together by what every joint supplieth, according to the operation in the measure of every part, maketh increase of the body, unto the edifying of itself in charity.'

As a spouse of Christ, guarding their purity and walking according to the will of the Bridegroom alone.

Cap. 5

John [3.29]: 'He that hath the bride is the bridegroom.' *2 Cor.* [11.2]: 'For I have esspoused you to one husband that I may present you as a chaste virgin to Christ.'

As temples of God, holy, pure, and filled only with what pertains to the worship of God.

Cap. 6

John [14.23]: 'If any one love me he will keep my word and my Father will love him and we will come to him and will make our abode with him.' *2 Cor.* [6.16]: 'For you are the temple of the living God; for the Scripture saith: I will dwell in them and walk among them and I will be their God.'

As a sacrifice unto God, blameless and unspotted, in every member and part maintaining the integrity of divine worship.

Cap. 7

Rom. [12.1]: 'I beseech you, brethren, by the mercy of God that you present your bodies a living sacrifice, holy, pleasing unto God, your reasonable service.'

As sons of God formed to the image of God according to the measure vouchsafed to men.

Cap. 8

John [13.33]: 'Little children, yet a little while I am with you.' *Gal.* [4.19]: 'My little children, of whom I am in labour again, until Christ be formed in you.'

As light in the world, both so as to be non-receptive of evil and to illuminate those who come to them to receive knowledge of the truth, that they may become what they ought to be or give proof of what they are.

Cap. 9

Matthew [5.14]: 'You are the light of the world.' *Phil.* [2.15]: 'Among whom you shine as lights in the world.'

As salt in the earth, so that they may renew in spirit unto incorruption those who associate with them.

Cap. 10

Matthew [5.13]: 'You are the salt of the earth.'

As the word of life, confirming the hope of the true life by their mortification in the things of this life.

Cap. 11

Phil. [2.15,16]: 'Among whom you shine as lights in the world, holding forth the word of life to my glory in the day of Christ.'

What the Scripture would have those be who are entrusted with the preaching of the Gospel, as apostles and ministers of Christ and faithful dispensers of the mysteries of God, fulfilling to the letter in word and work the precepts of the Lord alone.

Cap. 12

Matthew [10.16]: 'Behold I send you as sheep in the midst of wolves.' [28.19]: 'Going teach ye all nations.' *1 Cor.* [4.1,2]: 'Let a man so account of us as of the ministers of Christ and the dispensers of the mysteries of God; but as for the rest, it is required among the dispensers that a man be found faithful.'

As heralds of the kingdom of heaven unto the ruin of him who wields empire over one who dies in sin.

Cap. 13

Matthew [10.7]: 'And going, preach, saying: The kingdom of heaven is at hand.' *2 Tim.* [4.1,2]: 'I charge thee before God and Jesus Christ, who shall judge the living and the dead by his coming and his kingdom: Preach the word of God.'

As the model or rule of piety unto the perfecting of all righteousness in the followers of the Lord and unto proof of iniquity in those who are guilty of the slightest disobedience.

Cap. 14

Phil. [3.13-16]: 'Forgetting the things that are behind, and stretching forth myself to those that are before, I press toward the mark, to the prize of the supernal vocation of God in

Christ Jesus. Let us therefore, as many as are perfect, be thus minded: and if in anything you be otherwise minded, this also God will reveal to you. Nevertheless, whereunto we are come, that we be of the same mind, let us also continue in the same rule.' *1 Tim.* [4.12]: 'Be thou an example of the faithful in word, in conversation, in charity, in faith, in chastity.' *2 Tim.* [2.15]: 'Carefully study to present thyself approved unto God, a workman that needeth not to be ashamed, rightly handling the word of truth.'

As the eye in the body, discerning good and evil, guiding the members of Christ as circumstances require with regard to each one.

Cap. 15

Matthew [6.22]: 'The light of thy body is thy eye. If therefore thy eye be single, thy whole body shall be lightsome.'

As shepherds of the sheep of Christ, not refusing to lay down their life for them if occasion require it, to the end that they may communicate to these the Gospel of God.

Cap. 16

John [10.11]: 'The good shepherd giveth his life for his sheep.' *Acts* [20.28]: 'Take heed to yourselves, therefore, and to the whole flock, wherein the Holy Ghost hath placed you bishops to tend the Church of God.'

As physicians who care for the maladies of the soul with great compassion, according to their knowledge of the doctrine of the Lord, to bring about health in Christ and perseverance.

Cap. 17

Matthew [9.12]: 'They that are in health need not a physician but they that are ill.' *Rom.* [15.1]: 'Now we that are stronger ought to bear the infirmities of the weak.

As fathers and nurses of children they themselves have begotten, who with fervent dispositions of love in Christ would not only impart the Gospel of God to them, but even give their lives for them.

Cap. 18

John [13.33]: 'Little children, yet a little while I am with you.' *1 Cor.* [4.15]: 'For in Christ Jesus, by the gospel, I have begotten you.' *1 Thess.* [2.7,8]: 'As if a nurse should cherish her children, so desirous of you, we would gladly impart unto you not only the gospel of God, but also our own souls, because you were become most dear unto us.'

As co-workers with God, devoting themselves completely and solely in behalf of the Church to those works only that are worthy of God.

Cap. 19

1 Cor. [3.9]: 'For we are God's coadjutors: you are God's husbandry; you are God's building.'

As husbandmen of the vines of God, who plant nothing alien to the vine which is Christ, nothing unfertile, but with all diligence foster that which is congenial and fruitful.

Cap. 20

John [15.1,2]: 'I am the true vine; and my Father is the husbandman. Every branch in me that beareth not fruit, he will take away; and every one that beareth fruit, he will purge it, that it may bring forth more fruit.' *1 Cor.* [3.6]: 'I have planted, Apollo watered, but God gave the increase.'

As builders of the temple of God, shaping each soul to be framed together upon the foundation of the Apostles and Prophets.

Cap. 21

1 Cor. [3.10,11]: 'According to the grace of God that is given to me, as a wise architect, I have laid the foundation and another buildeth thereon. But let every man take heed how he buildeth thereupon. For other foundation no man can lay but that which is laid, which is Christ Jesus.' *Eph.* [2.19-22]· 'Now, therefore, you are no more strangers and foreigners; but you are fellow citizens with the saints, and the domestics of God, built upon the foundation of the apostles and prophets, Jesus Christ himself being the chief corner stone, in whom all the building being framed together groweth up into an holy temple in the Lord, in whom you also are built together into an habitation of God in the Spirit.'

Cap. 22

What is the mark of a Christian? Faith working by charity. What is the mark of faith? A sure conviction of the truth of the inspired words, not to be shaken by any process of reasoning, nor by the alleging of natural requirements, nor by the pretences of false piety. What is the mark of a faithful soul?

To be in these dispositions of full acceptance on the authority of the words [of the Scripture], not venturing to reject anything nor making additions. For, if 'all that is not of faith is sin,' as the Apostle says,[1] and 'faith cometh by hearing and hearing by the word of God,'[2] everything outside Holy Scripture, not being of faith, is sin. What is the mark of charity toward God? To observe His commandments with a view to His glory. What is the mark of charity toward one's neighbor? Not to seek what is one's own but that which is to the advantage of the loved one both in body and soul. What is the mark of a Christian? To be born anew through baptism of water and the Spirit. What is the mark of one born of water? That he be dead and immovable with regard to all sin, as Christ died once and for all because of sin, as it is written: 'all we who are baptized in Christ Jesus are baptized in his death. For we are buried together with him by baptism unto death; knowing this, that our old man is crucified with him that the body of sin may be destroyed, to the end that we may serve sin no longer.'[3] What is the mark of one born of the Spirit? That he become in the measure granted him that of which he has been born, as it is written: 'That which is born of the flesh is flesh, and that which is born of the Spirit is spirit.'[4] What is the mark of him who has been born anew? That he strip off the old man with his deeds and cupidities and put on the new man, 'who is renewed unto knowledge, according to the image of him that created him.'[5] as it is written: 'As many of you as have been baptized in Christ have put on Christ.'[6] What is the mark of a Christian? That

1 Rom. 14.23.
2 Rom. 10.17.
3 Rom. 6.3,4,6.
4 John 3.6.
5 Col. 3.10.
6 Gal. 3.27.

he be purified of all defilement of the flesh and of the spirit
in the Blood of Christ, perfecting sanctification in the fear of
God and the love of Christ,[7] and that he have no blemish nor
spot nor any such thing; that he be holy and blameless[8] and so
eat the Body of Christ and drink His Blood; for 'he that
eateth and drinketh unworthily, eateth and drinketh judgment to himself.'[9] What is the mark of those who eat the
Bread and drink the Cup of Christ? That they keep in perpetual remembrance Him who died for us and rose again.
What is the mark of those who keep such remembrance? That
they live not for themselves but for Him who died for them
and rose again.[10] What is the mark of a Christian? That his
justice abound in all things more than that of the scribes and
Pharisees, according to the rule of the doctrine which has
been handed down in the Lord's Gospel.[11] What is the mark
of the Christian? That they love one another as Christ has
loved us.[12] What is the mark of a Christian? To set the Lord
always in his sight.[13] What is the mark of a Christian? To
watch daily and hourly and stand prepared in that state of
perfection which is pleasing to God, knowing that at what
hour he thinks not, the Lord will come.[14]

---

7 2 Cor. 7.1.
8 Eph. 5.27.
9 1 Cor. 11.29.
10 2 Cor. 5.15.
11 Matt. 5.20.
12 Eph. 5.2.
13 Ps. 15.8.
14 Luke 12.40.

AN ASCETICAL DISCOURSE

MAN WAS MADE after the image and likeness of God; but sin marred the beauty of the image by dragging the soul down to passionate desires. Now, God, who made man, is the true life. Therefore, when man lost his likeness to God, he lost his participation in the true life; separated and estranged from God as he is, it is impossible for him to enjoy the blessedness of the divine life. Let us return, then, to the grace [which was ours] in the beginning and from which we have alienated ourselves by sin, and let us again adorn ourselves with the beauty of God's image, being made like to our Creator through the quieting of our passions. He who, to the best of his ability, copies within himself the tranquility of the divine nature attains to a likeness with the very soul of God; and, being made like to God in the manner aforesaid, he also achieves in full a semblance to the divine life and abides continually in unending blessedness. If, then, by overcoming our passions we regain the image of God and if the likeness of God bestows upon us everlasting life, let us devote ourselves to this pursuit in preference to all others, so that our soul may never again be enslaved by any vice, but that our understanding may remain firm and unconquerable under the assaults of temptation, to the end that we may become sharers in the divine beatitude.

Now, an ally to the zeal of those who duly aspire to this gift is virginity. The grace of virginity, however, does not consist solely in abstaining from the procreation of children,

207

but our whole life, conduct and moral character 'should be virginal, illustrating in every action the integrity required of the virgin. It is possible, indeed, to commit fornication in speech, to be guilty of adultery through the eye, to be corrupted through the hearing, to receive defilement into the heart, and to transgress the bounds of temperance by want of control in partaking of food and drink. But he who keeps himself under restraint in all these matters, according to the rule of virginity, truly exhibits in himself the grace of virginity fully developed and in its perfection.

If, therefore, we desire, by the quelling of our passions to adorn the nature of our soul with the imprint of the beauty of God's likeness, that everlasting life may also be ours thereby, let us attend to ourselves that we may do nothing unworthy of our promise and thus incur the judgment pronounced upon Ananias.[1] It was within the power of Ananias not to dedicate his property to God in the beginning; but he consecrated his possessions to God by vow with a view to human glory, that he might be an object of admiration to men because of his munificence, and he also kept back a part of the price. This provoked the Lord's displeasure against him (of which Peter was the intermediary) to such a degree that he was not given time for repentance. Accordingly, before making a promise to live the religious life, anyone who wishes may lawfully and licitly follow the way of the world and freely submit to the yoke of wedlock. When, however, by his own consent, a man has been made subject to a prior claim, he should reserve himself for God as a kind of sacred votive offering, in fear of being condemned for sacrilege by defiling again, by an ordinary way of life, the body consecrated to God by vow. And I say this with not only one kind of passion in mind,

---

1 Acts. 5.1-5.

as some think, who would preserve the integrity of virginity by custody of the body alone, but with reference to every manifestation of a passionate inclination.

One who would reserve himself for God may not be defiled by any emotion savoring of this world. Anger, envy, bearing a grudge, deceit, insolence, arrogance, unseasonable talking, indolence in prayer, desire for goods one does not possess, negligence in observing the commandments, ostentation in dress, vain regard for one's appearance, meetings and conversations over and above what is necessary and fitting—all these must be most carefully avoided by one who has dedicated himself to God by virginity, because yielding to one of them is almost as perilous as falling into an expressly forbidden sin. All that springs from the passions mars in some way the purity of the soul and is an impediment in attaining to the divine life. He who has given up the world, therefore, must keep his attention fixed upon these considerations, so as in no way to defile himself, the vessel of God, by corrupting usage. This fact, moreover, should be especially borne in mind—he who has chosen the way of the angels by passing the confines of human nature has taken up a spiritual mode of life. Now, this is the special character of the angelic nature: to be free from the marriage yoke, not to be distracted by any created beauty, but to be constantly intent upon the divine countenance. Consequently, if he who has been raised to the rank of the angelic dignity suffers taint from human passions, he resembles a leopard's skin, the hair of which is neither entirely white nor wholly black, but because it is spotted with different colors is reckoned with neither black nor white. Let these words, therefore, in a very general way, serve as an exhortation to those who have chosen the life of chastity and discipline.

But since we ought to discuss particular features as well in this connection, it also is necessary to record briefly the follow-

ing points.They who are set apart from the ordinary life in
the world and follow a regimen more nearly approaching
the divine life should not undertake this discipline of their
own accord nor as solitaries. It is fitting that such a way of
life have a witness, that it may be free from base suspicion.
Just as the spiritual law would have no fewer than ten partake
of the mystic pasch, so they who practice the spiritual life in
common should properly exceed rather than fall short of this
number. There should be one leader appointed to command in
this admirable way of life, who has been chosen in preference
to the rest after a thorough examination of his life and character and consistently good conduct. Age should also be taken
into consideration where special honor is to be accorded. It
is somehow in keeping with man's nature that what is more
aged is more worthy of respect. Furthermore, this head should
exercise such authority, the brethren voluntarily obeying only,
in submissiveness and humility, as to prevent anyone in the
community from gainsaying his will when he gives any order
which would contribute to the honor and perfection of the
religious life.

As, according to the Apostle, authority established by God
is not to be resisted (for he declares that they who resist the
ordinance of God are condemned,[2]) so it is right in this case
also for the rest of the community to be persuaded that such
power is delegated the superior not accidentally but by the
divine will. Thus, with one member recommending all that
is useful and profitable to the soul and the others receiving
his good counsels with docility, advancement according to
God is without impediment. Since it is in every way fitting
that the community be obedient and under subjection to a
superior, it is therefore of the highest importance that the

---

2 Rom. 13.1,2.

one chosen as guide in this state of life be such that his life may serve as a model of every virtue to those who look to him, and, as the Apostle says, that he be 'sober, prudent, of good behaviour, a teacher.'[3] I am, consequently, of the opinion that his manner of life should be investigated, and not only as to whether he has reached old age in a chronological sense (for youthful traits of character can exist along with gray hair and wrinkles). Inquiry should be made, above all, as to whether his character and manners have grown gray through propriety, so that everything said and done by him may represent a law and a standard for the community. It is proper, moreover, for those who lead the monastic life to take thought for their livelihood, as the Apostle prescribes, so that they who work with their hands may eat their bread in honor.[4] And the work should be allotted at the direction of an older member well known for holiness of life, who will turn to account the works of their hands by procuring necessities with these so as to fulfill the command of providing bread with sweat and toil.[5] The reputation of the rest of the brethren should be kept unsullied and blameless by their not being required to go about in public to secure the necessities of life. The best rule and standard for a well-disciplined life is this: to be indifferent to the pleasure or pain of the flesh, but to avoid immoderation in either direction, so that the body may neither be disordered by obesity nor yet rendered sickly and so unable to execute commands. The same injury to the soul, indeed, results from both types of excess: when the flesh is not brought under subjection, natural vigor makes us rush headlong in the wake of our shameful impulses; on the other hand, when the body is relaxed, enfeebled and torpid,

---

3 1 Tim. 3.2.
4 2 Thess. 3.12.
5 Gen. 3.19.

it is under constraint from pain. With the body in such a condition, the soul is not free to raise its glance upward, weighed
down as it is in companionship with the body's malady, but
is, perforce, wholly occupied with the sensation of pain and
intent upon itself.

Our use [of material goods], therefore, should be regulated
by need. Wine, also, should not be held in abomination if it
is taken for curative purposes and is not craved beyond necessity. So, likewise, everything else should minister to the needs
and not to the cupidities of those who lead the ascetical life.
Prayer time should cover the whole of life, but since there
is absolute need at certain intervals to interrupt the bending
of the knee and the chanting of psalms, the hours appointed
for prayer by the saints should be observed. The mighty David
says: 'I rose at midnight to give praise to thee for the judgments of thy justification';[6] and we find Paul and Silas following his example, for they praised God in prison at midnight.[7]
Then too, the same Prophet says: 'Evening and morning and
at noon.'[8] Moreover, the coming of the Holy Spirit took
place at the third hour, as we learn in the Acts when, in
answer to the Pharisees who were jeering at the disciples
because of the diversity of tongues, Peter said that they were
not drunk who were speaking these words: 'seeing that it is
but the third hour.'[9] Again, the ninth hour recalls the Lord's
Passion, which took place that we might live.[10] But, since
David says: 'Seven times a day I have given praise to thee
for the judgments of thy justice,'[11] and the times for prayer
which have been mentioned do not make up this seven-fold

6 Ps. 118.62.
7 Acts 16.25.
8 Ps. 54.18.
9 Acts 2.15.
10 Matt. 27.45; Mark 15.33,34.
11 Ps. 118.164

apportionment, the mid-day prayer should be divided, one part being recited before the noon repast and the other afterward. In this way, the daily seven-fold praise of God distributed throughout the whole period of the day may become a pattern for us also. The entrances to the monasteries should be barred to women and not even all men should enter in, but only such as are permitted by the superior. Often, a want of discrimination regarding visitors introduces into the heart a succession of untimely conversations and fruitless tales, and from idle talk comes the further descent to idle and useless thought. This, therefore, should be the rule for all: The superior alone is to be asked and he alone is to give the response with regard to matters requiring speech; but the others are not to answer those prattlers who waste their time in vain discourses, so as to avoid being drawn along with them into a succession of idle words.

There should be a common supply room for all and nothing should be called private or personal to any individual— neither cloak, nor shoe, nor anything else required for the body. The use of these items should be under the authority of the superior, so that the articles from the common store may be allotted to each according to his need at the superior's direction.

The law of charity does not allow particular friendship or exclusive groups in community life, for particular affection inevitably works great harm to communal union. Consequently, all should regard one another with equal affection and one and the same degree of charity should prevail in the entire group. If any be found for any reason whatsoever to have an inordinate affection for a fellow religious, be he brother or kinsman or anyone else, he should be chastised as one who works detriment to the common good; for an excess of affection for one individual bears a strong implication of defect with regard to the others. The penalties imposed upon one found guilty of any fault ought to be proportioned to the offense, [e.g.], forbidding the offender to join in psalmody with his brethren, prohibiting him from taking part in common prayer, or ostracizing him from the common table. In this matter, the one in charge of general discipline will determine the penalty of the offender according to the gravity of his fault. The ministration to the community as a whole should be performed by two monks taking turns successively by the week in assuming full charge of necessary business, so that the reward of humility may belong to all in common and that it may be impossible for any one to outdo the rest of his brethren in giving service; also, that all may have a respite on equal terms, for the interchange of labor and intervals of rest prevents weariness from afflicting the laborers. The superior of the community is authorized to assign whom he will to make necessary journeys abroad and to appoint those who will remain at home and see to domestic concerns. Often, the fair flower of youth blooms forth somehow in the bodies of the young, even though they have been very markedly zealous in afflicting themselves in the practice of continency, and becomes the occasion of unruly desire for those whom they chance to meet. If, then, a brother is young as regards the vigor of his body, he should keep its charm and grace hidden until he reach a time of life when he may decorously show himself.

The brethren should betray no sign of anger, of unforgivingness, or envy, or contentiousness, whether in bearing, gesture, word, glance of the eye, expression of countenance, or by anything calculated to arouse a companion's ire. If anyone should commit one of these faults, even if he has first suffered an annoyance of this sort, he is not thereby sufficiently justified for involving himself in the offense; for evil at whatever point of time it is committed is evil just the same. Oaths of all kinds should be banished from the monastic company. Let a nod of the head or verbal assent take the place of an oath on the part of both speaker and hearer. If anyone should not trust a bare affirmation, he makes accusation against his own conscience as one who is insincere in speech, and for this reason he should be brought to account for his misdemeanor by the superior and be chastened by a salutary penalty. When the day is over and all labor of body and mind has come to an end, each one, before retiring, should examine his conscience in the intimacy of his own heart. And if anything untoward has occurred—a forbidden thought or an idle word, negligence in prayer or inattention in psalmody or desire of the ordinary life of the world—the fault should not be concealed, but confessed publicly, so that through the prayers of the community the malady of the one who has fallen prey to such an evil may be cured.

AN ASCETICAL DISCOURSE

THE ASCETICAL LIFE has one aim—the soul's salvation and all that can contribute to this end must be observed with as much fear as a divine command. The commandments of God themselves, indeed, have no other end in view than the salvation of him who obeys them. It therefore behooves those undertaking the ascetical life to enter upon the way of philosophy, stripped of all worldly and material things in the same manner as they who enter the bath take off all their clothing. The most important thing, consequently, and the chief concern for the Christian ought to be the stripping himself of the varied and diverse movements of the passions toward evil whereby the soul is defiled. Secondly, the renunciation of worldly possessions is of obligation for him who aspires to this sublime way of life, in as much as anxiety and solicitude for material interests engender much distraction for the soul. Whenever, therefore, a group of persons aiming at the same goal of salvation adopt the life in common, this principle above all others must prevail among them—that there be in all one heart, one will, one desire, and that the entire community be, as the Apostle enjoins, one body consisting of divers members.[1] Now this cannot be realized in any other way than by the enforcement of the rule that nothing is to be appropriated to anyone's exclusive use—neither cloak, nor vessel, nor anything else which is of use to the common life, so that each of these articles may be assigned to a need and not to an owner. Just

---

1 1 Cor. 12.12.

as a garment which is too small is unsuitable for a large person or one that is too ample for a slighter figure, but what is properly adapted to the individual is useful and appropriate, so everything else—bed, covering, warm clothing, footwear— should belong to the one who is strictly in need of these things, and not to an owner. As he who is wounded uses medicaments and not one who is sound, so also he who is in need of the things designed for bodily ease should enjoy them and not one who is living in luxury.

Furthermore, since the ways of men are varied and all are not in agreement as to what is useful, so, to avoid confusion resulting from each person's conducting himself according to his private whim, there should be someone placed in authority over the others who has been declared in the judgment of all eminent in intelligence, stability, and strictness of life, that his good qualities may be the common possession of all who follow his example. If several painters should depict the lineaments of one face, all the pictures would be alike, be- cause they would be likenesses of one and the same individual; similarly, if many types of character are intent upon the imitation of one model, all alike will bear the good impress of his life. Consequently, when a superior has been chosen, all private volition will give place and all, without exception, will follow the example of their head in obedience to the apostolic precept bidding every soul to be subject to higher powers and warning that 'they that resist purchase to them- selves damnation.'[2] True and perfect obedience of subjects to their superior is shown not only by their refraining from every untoward action in accordance with his advice, but also by their not doing even what is approved without his con- sent.

---

2 Rom. 13.1,2.

Now, continency and all corporal mortification are of some value, but, if a man following his private caprice do what is pleasing to himself and heed not the advice of his superior, his fault will be greater than the good he does; 'for he that resisteth the power, resisteth the ordinance of God.'[3] A greater reward, moreover, is accorded to obedience than to the virtue of continency. Thus, also, all should have the same mutual charity, equal in degree, for one another, as a man naturally feels for the members of his body in desiring an equal soundness in all the parts of it, since the pain of each member brings a like discomfort to the whole body. In the case of our bodies, however, although the pain of each afflicted member touches in equal measure the whole body, some members are regarded as more important than others (for we do not feel the same with respect to our eye and our toe, even if the pain is equally great in both). Even so, a like sympathy and love should be accorded all who live together in community on the part of each of the members; but there will be a higher esteem, and fittingly so, for those who contribute the greater service.

Since it is a matter of obligation that they love one another with absolutely equal affection, exclusive groups and factions are a detriment to the community; for he who loves one more than the others betrays his want of perfect love for those others. Unseemly quarreling, therefore, and particular affection alike, should be banished from the monastery, for enmity is engendered by wrangling and from the particular friendship and the faction arise suspicions and jealousies. In every instance, the loss of equality is the origin and foundation of envy and hatred on the part of those who are slighted thereby. On this account we have received a command from the Lord

---

3 *Ibid.*

to imitate the goodness of Him who maketh the sun to rise upon just and unjust.[4] As, therefore, God grants a share of light impartially to all, so His followers should send forth a ray of charity equally brilliant for all alike; for, wherever love falls short, hatred entirely supplants it. But if, as John says, 'God is charity,'[5] the Devil is necessarily hatred. As he who has love consequently has God, so he who has hate nurtures the Devil within himself.

The love of all toward all, therefore, should be equal and impartial, and each individual should be given his appropriate measure of honor. For those who are thus united, moreover, blood relationship will in no way claim a greater degree of love and not even the tie of blood in the case of a brother, son, or daughter according to the flesh will arouse a warmer affection for this blood relative than for the rest. He who follows nature in these matters makes it evident that he is not yet wholly withdrawn from nature, but is still subject to the rule of the flesh. Idle talking, also, and unseasonable distractions resulting from discoursing with one another should be forbidden. If, however, something conducive to spiritual advancement is involved, this only should be said and even that which is useful should be expressed in an orderly fashion at a suitable time by such persons as are entitled to speak. If it be an inferior, he should wait for the direction of his superior; but whisperings, a word in the ear, signs made by a nod of the head—all these should be outlawed, because whispering begets suspicion of slander and signs made by a nod are evidence to a brother of something secret and mischievous, and such things become the basis of hatred and suspicion. Whenever conversation is necessary, however, let

---

4 Matt. 5.45.
5 1 John 4.16.

the requirements of the situation determine the volume of the voice, so that we converse with one near at hand in a low tone and speak more loudly to one farther away. Whoever in giving advice or an order uses a very loud, piercing tone gives an impression of arrogance thereby and should not be in a religious community. Departure from the monastery, furthermore, is not permitted except for a duty or an emergency.

Since there are convents not only for men but for women who also profess virginity, all that has been said applies to both sexes alike. It is necessary to keep one thing in mind, however: This way of life demands on the part of women a greater and a more signal decorum in the observance of poverty, silence, obedience, and fraternal charity, a greater strictness with regard to going about in public, more caution in the matter of acquaintances, greater care in preserving mutual affection and avoiding factional groups; for in all these respects the lives of women who profess virginity should exhibit a more excellent zeal. She who is charged with the maintenance of discipline should not seek for what may be agreeable to her sisters, nor should she be eager for their gratitude for what is to their liking, but she should ever be grave, severe, dignified. She should bear in mind that she is to render an account to God for undue breaches of discipline in the common life. Nor should the individual sister seek to receive from her superior what is sweet and agreeable, but what is useful and beneficial. She should not dispute the orders given her (for such a practice becomes habitual and leads to rebellion), but as we receive the commands of the Lord without question, knowing that all of the Scripture is divinely inspired and of benefit to us, so also the members of the sisterhood should accept without distinction the commands of the superior. <u>They should perform all that is directed, not in a spirit of sadness and compulsion, but with alacrity, that their obedience may obtain a reward.</u> It is their duty to accept not only what is prescribed in the way of strict discipline, but, if their directress should forbid fasting or urge them to take nourishment to restore their strength or if she should prescribe any other relaxation demanded by necessity, they should fulfill all alike, convinced that her words are law. Whenever speech is required for reasons of necessity, whether with a man or with someone holding a position of authority or with another person who is able to be of service regarding a matter under question, the superior should be the one to speak, in the presence of one or two of the sisters whose manner of life and age now make it safe for them to appear and to speak in public. If any useful idea occur to someone privately, however, she should refer it to her superior and through the latter will be said all that needs to be said.

THE LONG RULES

Preface

SINCE BY GOD'S GRACE, we have gathered together in the Name of our Lord Jesus Christ—we who have set before ourselves one and the same goal, the devout life—and since you have plainly manifested your eagerness to hear something of the matters pertaining to salvation, I, for my part, am under obligation to proclaim the justifications of God, mindful as I am night and day of the Apostle's words, 'for three years I ceased not with tears to admonish every one of you night and day.'[1] Since, moreover, the present is the most opportune time and this place provides quiet and complete freedom from external disturbances, let us pray together that we may provide for our fellow servants their measure of wheat in due season,[2] and that you, on your part, may, like fertile soil, receive the word and produce in turn the fruit of justice, perfect and manifold, as it is written.[3] I implore you, then, by the charity of our Lord Jesus Christ who gave Himself for our sins,[4] let us at length apply our minds to the affairs of our souls and grieve for the vanity of our past life. Let us, on behalf of the rewards which are to come, take up the combat for the glory of God and of His Christ and of the adorable Holy Spirit. Let us not remain in our present state of negligence and passivity and, by ever postponing to the morrow and the future the beginning of the work, fritter away the time at hand by our

1 Acts 20.31.
2 Luke 12.42.
3 Matt. 13.23.
4 Tit. 2.14.

continued sloth. Then, being taken unprepared, with our hands empty of good works, by Him who demands our souls from us, we shall not be admitted to the joy of the nuptial chamber and we shall then bewail and lament the time of our life wasted in evil doing, when penance is no longer possible. 'Now is the acceptable time,' says the Apostle, 'now is the day of salvation.'[5] This is the time for repentance; the next life, for recompense. Now is the time to endure; then will be the day of consolation. Now, God is the Helper of such as turn aside from the evil way; then, He will be the dread and unerring Inquisitor of the thoughts and words and deeds of men. Now, we enjoy His longanimity; then, we shall know His just judgment, when we have risen, some unto never-ending punishment, others unto life everlasting, and everyone shall receive according to his works.[6] How long shall we defer our obedience to Christ, who has called us to His heavenly Kingdom? Shall we not rouse ourselves unto sobriety? Why will we not recall ourselves from our accustomed way of life to the strict observance of the Gospel? Why will we not place before our eyes that fearsome and manifest day of the Lord, when the kingdom of heaven will receive those who, because of their works, take their place on the right hand of the Lord, but the gehenna of fire and eternal darkness will envelop those who, because of their lack of good works, have been rejected and placed at the left hand. 'There,' He says, 'shall be weeping and gnashing of teeth.'[7]

We say, indeed, that we desire the kingdom of heaven, yet we are not solicitous for the means whereby it is attained. Although we suffer no hardship on behalf of the Lord's command, we, in the vanity of our minds, expect to achieve equal

---

5 2 Cor. 6.2.
6 Rom. 2.6.
7 Matt. 25.30.

honor with those who have resisted sin even unto death. What man who sits at home or slumbers during the sowing ever filled the fold of his garment with sheaves at the harvest? Who has gathered grapes from a vine which he has not planted and tended? They who labor possess the fruits. Rewards and crowns belong to the victors. Who would ever crown one who did not even strip himself for the combat with his adversary? According to the Apostle, indeed, it is necessary not only to conquer but to strive lawfully;[8] that is, not to neglect a small part even of what has been enjoined, but to carry out each detail as we have been commanded; for 'blessed is that servant whom when his lord shall come, he shall find'—not doing anything whatever, but 'so doing'[9] and again, 'If thou didst make thy offering well but didst not rightly divide it, thou didst sin.'[10] But, if we think that we have fulfilled some one of the commandments (I should not presume to say we actually had done so; for all the commandments form an interconnected whole, according to the valid sense of the Scripture, so that in breaking one commandment we necessarily violate the others also), we do not expect to be visited with wrath on the score of the commandments which we have transgressed, but we anticipate rewards for our alleged observance. The man who withholds one or two, perhaps, of the ten talents entrusted to him, but restores the rest, is not looked upon as generous for paying back the major part of the sum; by his withholding the lesser part he is shown to be unjust and avaricious. Withholding, do I say? When he who was entrusted with one talent subsequently gave back this same talent whole and entire as he had received it, he was condemned for not having added to what had been given

---

8 2 Tim. 2.5.
9 Luke 12.43.
10 Gen. 4.7 (Septuagint).

him.[11] He who has honored his father for ten years, and later on strikes him once only, is not esteemed as dutiful but is condemned as a parricide. 'Going,' says the Lord, 'teach ye all nations, teaching them' not to observe some things and neglect others, but 'to observe all things whatsoever I have commanded you.'[12] And the Apostle writes in a similar vein: 'Giving no offence to any man, that our ministry be not blamed; but in all things let us exhibit ourselves as ministers of God.'[13] Unless all were necessary to attain the goal of salvation, all the commandments would not have been written down, nor would it have been declared that all must be kept. What do all other righteous actions avail me if I am to be liable to hell-fire because I called my brother 'fool'?[14] What profit is there in being free from many masters if I am held in bondage by one? 'Whosoever committeth sin, is the servant of sin,' says the Scripture.[15] And what gain is there in not being afflicted with many maladies, if my body is being wasted by one?

Well, then, someone will say, will the large number of Christians who do not keep all the commandments practice the observance of some of them in vain? In this connection, it is well to recall blessed Peter, who, after he had performed so many good actions and had been the recipient of such great blessings, was told, upon his being guilty of one lapse only: 'If I wash thee not, thou shalt have no part with me.'[16] I shall not point out that his act bore no signs of indifference or contempt but was a demonstration of honor and reverence. But, someone might say, it is written: 'Everyone that shall

11 Matt. 25.24ff.
12 Matt. 28.19,20.
13 2 Cor. 6.3,4.
14 Matt. 5.22.
15 John 8.34.
16 John 13.8.

call upon the name of the Lord shall be saved,'[17] and, therefore, the very invocation of the Name of the Lord is sufficient to save him who invokes it. But let the objector hear also the words of the Apostle: 'How then shall they call on him in whom they have not believed?'[18] And, if you believe, hearken to the Lord saying: 'Not everyone that saith to me, Lord, Lord, shall enter into the kingdom of heaven; but he that doth the will of my Father who is in heaven.'[19] Certainly, whenever anyone does the will of the Lord, but not as God wills nor with dispositions of love for God, his zeal is to no purpose, according to the words of our Lord Jesus Christ Himself, who says: 'They act to be seen by men. Amen I say to you, they have received their reward.'[20] Wherefore, Paul the Apostle was taught to say: 'And if I should distribute all my goods to feed the poor and if I should deliver my body to be burned and have not charity, it profiteth me nothing.'[21] To sum up, I note the following three kinds of disposition which necessarily compel our obedience: we avoid evil through fear of punishment and take the attitude of a slave; or, seeking to obtain the reward, we observe the commandments for our own advantage and in this we are like hirelings; or else, for the sake of the virtuous act itself and out of love for Him who gave us the law, we rejoice to be deemed worthy to serve a God so good and so glorious and we are thus in the dispositions of sons. Nor will he who observes the commandments in fear and who is ever wary of incurring the penalty for sloth, keep some of the commandments laid upon him and neglect others, but he will regard the punishment of every act of disobedience as equally to be dreaded. For this reason he

---

17 Joel 2.32.
18 Rom. 10.14.
19 Matt. 7.21.
20 Matt. 6.5.
21 1 Cor. 13.3.

who is in all things fearful out of pious timidity is called
blessed,[22] and he stands firm in the truth who is able to say:
'I set the Lord always in my sight; for he is at my right hand
that I be not moved'[23]—meaning that he would overlook none
of the things that he is obliged to do. Again: 'Blessed is the
man that feareth the Lord.' Why? Because 'he shall delight
exceedingly in his commandments.'[24] It is not likely, then, that
they who fear will overlook any command or execute it carelessly. Yet, neither does the hireling will to disobey orders;
how would he receive the pay for his tending of the vine if he
did not do all that had been agreed? If by failing to provide
one necessary attention he renders the vine profitless to the
owner, who would pay a reward, so long as the damage remains, to him who wrought the mischief? The third form of
service is that prompted by love. Now, what son, having in
view his father's good pleasure and giving joy to his heart in
the more important matters, will wish to cause him pain as
regards even the most insignificant ones? And this filial devotion he will render even more earnestly when he recalls
the words of the Apostle: 'And grieve not the Holy Spirit of
God whereby you are sealed.'[25]

How, therefore, would they who break the greater number
of the commandments be classified—they who do not serve
God as their Father nor believe that He has promised great
rewards, nor submit to Him as Lord? 'If, then, I be a father,'
says the Prophet, 'where is my honor? And if I be a master,
where is my fear?'[26]—for he that feareth the Lord 'shall delight exceedingly in his commandments.'[27] 'By transgression of

---

22 Prov. 28.14.
23 Ps. 15.8.
24 Ps. 111.1.
25 Eph. 4.30.
26 Mal. 1.6.
27 Ps. 111.1.

the law,' says the Apostle, 'thou dishonourest God.'[28] How, then, if we prefer a life of pleasure to the life of obedience to the commandments, can we expect for ourselves a life of blessedness, fellowship with the saints, and the delights of the angelic company in the presence of Christ? Such expectations are truly the fantasies of a foolish mind. How shall I be worthy of the company of Job—I who do not accept even an ordinary mishap with thanksgiving? How shall I who am lacking in magnanimity toward my enemy stand in the presence of David? Or of Daniel, if I do not seek for God in continual continency and earnest supplication? Or of any of the saints, if I have not walked in their footsteps? What judge of a contest is so uninformed as to think that the victor and he who has not taken part in the contest should receive crowns of equal merit? What general ever summoned to an equal share in the spoils with the conquerors those who were not even present at the battle?

God is good, but He is also just, and it is the nature of the just to reward in proportion to merit, as it is written: 'Do good, O Lord, to those that are good and to the upright of heart. But such as turn aside into bonds, the Lord shall lead out with the workers of iniquity.'[29] He is merciful, but He is also a judge, for 'the Lord loveth mercy and judgment,' says the psalmist.[30] And he therefore also says: 'Mercy and judgment I will sing to thee, O Lord.'[31] We have been taught who they are upon whom He has mercy: 'Blessed are the merciful,' says the Lord, 'for they shall obtain mercy.'[32] You see with what discernment He bestows mercy, neither being merciful without judgment nor judging without mercy; for, the

---

28 Rom. 2.23.
29 Ps. 124.4,5.
30 Ps. 32.5.
31 Ps. 100.1.
32 Matt. 5.7.

Lord is merciful and just.'[33] Let us not, therefore, know God
by halves nor make His loving kindness an excuse for our
indolence; for this, His thunders, for this, His lightnings—
that His goodness may not be held in despite. He who causes
the sun to rise[34] also strikes men with blindness.[35] He who
sends the rain[36] also causes the rain of fire.[37] By the one He
manifests His goodness; by the other, His severity. For the
one let us love Him, for the other let us fear, that it may not
be said also to us: 'Or despisest thou the riches of his goodness
and patience and longsuffering? Knowest thou not that the
benignity of God leadeth thee to penance? But according to
thy hardness and impenitent heart, thou treasurest up to thyself wrath against the day of wrath.'[38]

Since, then, they cannot be saved who do not their works
according to the command of God and since no precept may
safely be overlooked (for it is great presumption to set ourselves up as critics of the Lawgiver by approving some of His
laws and rejecting others), let us who are striving to live the
devout life, who value the life of retirement and freedom from
worldly distractions as an aid to the observance of evangelical
doctrine, let us make it our common concern and resolve not
to allow any precept whatsoever to elude our vigilance. If the
man of God must be perfect (as it is written[39] and as our
words have already shown), it is all-important that he be
made perfect through the observance of every commandment
'unto the measure of the age of the fullness of Christ[40]; for,
according to divine law, an offering which is mutilated, even

---

33 Ps. 114.5.
34 Matt. 5.45.
35 2 Kings 6.18.
36 Zach. 10.1.
37 Gen. 19.24.
38 Rom. 2.4,5.
39 2 Tim. 3.17.
40 Eph. 4.13.

if it be pure, is unacceptable as a sacrifice to God. Whatever each one regards as wanting in himself, therefore, he should refer to the common consideration. That which is obscure can be more easily discerned by the earnest scrutiny of several persons, since, to be sure, God grants issue to the quest under the guidance and counsel of the Holy Spirit, according to the promise of our Lord Jesus Christ.[41] Consequently, as 'a necessity lieth upon me; for woe is unto me if I preach not the gospel,'[42] so upon you also rests a similar danger if you are remiss in discovering or languid and half-hearted in observing and fulfilling the precepts which have been handed down to us. The Lord says, therefore: 'The word that I have spoken, the same shall judge him in the last day.'[43] Again: 'And the servant who knew not the will of his lord and did things worthy of stripes, shall be beaten with few stripes; but he who knew and did not do nor prepared himself, according to his will, shall be beaten with many stripes.'[44]

Let us pray, therefore, that I may exercise the ministry of the Word blamelessly, and that my teaching may be fruitful in you. Knowing as we do that at the tribunal of Christ the words of the Holy Scripture will confront us (for He says: 'I will reprove thee and set thy sins before thy face'[45]), let us in all soberity attend to the words of the divine teaching and hasten to put them into practice, for we know not the day nor the hour when our Lord will come.[46]

---

41 John 14.26.
42 1 Cor. 9.16.
43 John 12.48.
44 Luke 12.47.
45 Ps. 49.21.
46 Matt. 24.42.

Q. 1. On order and sequence in the Lord's commandments.

Since the Scripture[1] has given us leave to propound questions, we require, first of all, to be informed as to whether the commandments of God have a certain order or sequence, as it were, so that one comes first, another, second, and so on; or whether all are interdependent and equal so far as precedence is concerned, so that one may begin at will wherever he likes, as with a circle.

R. Your question is an old one, proposed long ago in the Gospel when the lawyer came to the Lord and said: 'Master, which is the first commandment in the law?' And the Lord answered: 'Thou shalt love the Lord thy God with thy whole heart and with thy whole soul and with thy whole strength and with thy whole mind. This is the greatest and the first commandment. And the second is like to this: Thou shalt love thy neighbor as thyself.'[2] The Lord Himself, then, has established order in His commandments by designating the commandment of the love of God as the first and greatest commandment, and, as second in order and like to the first, but more as a fulfillment of it and as dependent upon it, the love of neighbor. With the aid of these and similar utterances which are handed down to us in the Holy Scripture, we can discover order and sequence in the whole series of the commandments.

Q. 2. Concerning the love of God, and showing that the inclination and the ability to keep the Lord's commandments belong to man by nature.

Speak to us first, therefore, of the love of God; for we have

---

1 Or, 'Since your words have given us leave'; cf. *PG* 31.906 n. 44.
2 Matt. 22.36-39.

heard that we must love Him, but we would learn how this may be rightly accomplished.

R. The love of God is not something that is taught, for we do not learn from another to rejoice in the light or to desire life, nor has anyone taught us to love our parents or nurses. In the same way and even to a far greater degree is it true that instruction in divine law is not from without, but, simultaneously with the formation of the creature—man, I mean— a kind of rational force was implanted in us like a seed, which, by an inherent tendency, impels us toward love. This germ is then received into account in the school of God's commandments, where it is wont to be carefully cultivated and skillfully nurtured and thus, by the grace of God, brought to its full perfection. Wherefore, we, also, approving your zeal as essential for reaching the goal, shall endeavor with the help of God and the support of your prayers, and as power is given us by the Spirit, to enkindle the spark of divine love latent within you. Now, it is necessary to know that, although this is only one virtue, yet, by its efficacy, it comprises and fulfills every commandment. 'If anyone love me,' says the Lord, 'he will keep my commandments.'[1] And again: 'On these two commandments dependeth the whole law and the prophets.'[2] Yet, we shall not undertake at this time to carry our discourse to its complete development (for in so doing, we should, inadvertently, make our discussion of one portion of the commandments embrace a full treatment of them), but, insofar as it is fitting and germane to the present purpose, we shall exhort you regarding the love we owe to God. First, however, we shall establish the fact that we have already received from God the power to fulfill all the com-

---

1 John 14.23.
2 Matt. 22.40.

mandments given us by Him, so that we may not take our
obligation in bad part, as though something quite strange
and unexpected were being asked of us, and that we may not
become filled with conceit, as if we were paying back something more than had been given us. By means of this power,
rightly and properly used, we pass our entire lives holily and
virtuously, but through a perverted use of it we gradually
fall prey to vice. Now, this is the definition of vice: the wrong
use, in violation of the Lord's command, of what has been
given us by God for a good purpose. Similarly, the definition
of the virtue which God requires of us is: the use with a good
conscience of these same gifts in accordance with the Lord's
command. This being the case, we shall apply the same principle also to charity. Having received, therefore, a command
to love God, we have possessed the innate power of loving
from the first moment of our creation. Of this, no external
proof is required, since anyone can discover it of himself and
within himself. We are by nature desirous of the beautiful,
even though individual conceptions of the beautiful differ
widely. Furthermore, we possess—without being taught—a
love for those who are near and dear to us, and we spontaneously render to our benefactors a full measure of good
will. Now, what is more admirable than Divine Beauty? What
reflection is sweeter than the thought of the magnificence of
God? What desire of the soul is so poignant and so intolerably
keen as that desire implanted by God in a soul purified from
all vice and affirming with sincerity, 'I languish with love.'[3]
Totally ineffable and indescribable are the lightning flashes
of Divine Beauty. Words do not adequately convey nor is the
ear capable of receiving [knowledge of them]. The rays of the
morning star, or the brightness of the moon, or the light of

---

3 Cant. 2.5.

the sun—all are more unworthy to be mentioned in comparison with that splendor and these heavenly bodies are more inferior to the true light than is the deep darkness of night, gloomy and moonless, to brightest noonday. This Beauty, invisible to the eyes of the flesh, is apprehended by the mind and soul alone. Whenever it cast its light upon any of the saints, it left them with an intolerable pain of longing, and they would say, weary of life on earth: 'Woe is me that my sojourning is prolonged,'[4] 'when shall I come and appear before the face of God?';[5] and again: 'to be dissolved and to be with Christ, a thing by far the better';[6] also: 'my soul hath thirsted after the strong living God'[7] and 'Now thou dost dismiss thy servant, O Lord.'[8] Since they felt the burden of this present life as an imprisonment, they were scarcely able to contain themselves under the impulses which the touch of Divine Love had made to stir within their souls. Indeed, by reason of their insatiable eagerness to enjoy the vision of Divine Beauty, they prayed that contemplation of the joy of the Lord would last as long as the whole of eternal life. Men are by nature, then, desirous of the beautiful. But, that which is truly beautiful and desirable is the good. Now, the good is God, and, since all creatures desire good, therefore, all creatures desire God.

So then, whatever is rightly done of free choice is also in us naturally, at least, in the case of those who have not perverted their rational faculty by iniquity. The love of God is, therefore, demanded of us as a strict obligation, and for a soul to fail in this is the most unendurable of all evils. Separation and estrangement from God are more unbearable than

---

4 Ps. 119.5.
5 Ps. 41.3.
6 Phil. 1.23.
7 Ps. 41.3.
8 Luke 2.29.

the punishment reserved for hell and more oppressive to the sufferer than the being deprived of light is to the eye, even if there be no pain in addition, or than the loss of its life is to an animal. If, moreover, the love of children for their parents is a natural endowment and if this love is noticeable in the behavior even of brute beasts, as well as in the affection of human beings in early infancy for their mothers, let us not appear to be less rational than infants or more savage than wild beasts by alienating ourselves from Him who made us and by being unloving toward Him. Even if we did not know what He is from His goodness, yet, from the very fact that we are made by Him, we ought to feel an extraordinary affection for Him and cling to a constant remembrance of Him, as infants do to their mothers. Furthermore, he who is our benefactor is foremost among those whom we naturally love. This gratitude is characteristic not of men only, but it is also felt by almost all animals, so that they attach themselves to those who have conferred some good upon them. 'The ox knoweth his owner,' says the Prophet, 'and the ass his master's crib.'[9] God forbid that what follows these words should be said of us: 'but Israel hath not known me and my people hath not understood.'[10] As for the dog and many other animals, I need not speak of the great affection they show toward those who rear them. Now, if we bear a natural love and good will toward our benefactors and undergo any kind of hardship to make a return for what was first rendered to us, what words can fitly treat of the gifts of God? So many are they in number as even to defy enumeration; so great and marvelous are they that a single one of them claims for the Giver all our gratitude. Some, therefore, I shall pass over, although

9 Isa. 1.3.
10 *Ibid.*

these in themselves show forth transcendent greatness and glory, yet, being surpassed by greater ones as are the stars by the rays of the sun, they appear to be of a less striking worth. I have not the leisure, in fact, to leave the surpassing benefits and measure from His lesser gifts the goodness of our Benefactor.

Let us, then, say nothing about the rising of the sun, the phases of the moon, climates, the alternation of the seasons, the water dropping from the clouds, other moisture rising from the earth, the sea itself, the whole earth and its produce, the creatures that live in the waters, those which inhabit the air, the countless varieties of animals—all beings destined to minister to our well-being. But what we may not pass over, even if we wished, that which it is quite impossible for one of sound mind and reason to be silent about—yet to speak of it adequately is more impossible—is the fact that God made man according to His image and likeness, that He deemed him worthy of the knowledge of Himself, that in preference to all the animals He adorned him with rationality, bestowed upon him the opportunity of taking his delight in the unbelievable beauties of paradise, and made him the chief of all the creatures on earth. Then, even after he was seduced by the serpent and fell into sin, and by sin into death and its attendant evils, God did not forsake him. First, He gave to him the Law as an aid, appointed angels to watch over and care for him, sent prophets to refute evil and teach virtue, checked his impulses toward vice by threats, aroused his eagerness for the good by promises, revealed again and again the fate of each of the two classes [the good and the wicked], by making a prejudgment in the case of divers persons so as to warn the rest. In addition to all these and other favors equally great, He did not turn away from man when he persisted in disobedience. We have not been deserted by the Lord's goodness, nor have we impeded His love for us by our stupidity in treating our Benefactor contumeliously through not comprehending the greatness of the favors bestowed—nay, we have even been recalled from death and restored to life again by our Lord Jesus Christ Himself. Even the manner in which this favor was granted calls for the greatest wonder: 'Who, being in the form of God, thought it not robbery to be equal with God; but emptied Himself, taking the form of a servant.'[11]

He has, moreover, taken upon Himself our infirmities and carried our sorrows.[12] He was crucified for us that we might be healed by His bruises.[13] He also redeemed us from the curse, 'being made a curse for us,[14] and endured the most ignominious death that He might restore us to the life of glory. Nor was He content with merely bringing back to life those who were dead, but He conferred upon them the dignity of divinity and prepared everlasting rest transcending every human concept in the magnitude of its joy.[15] What, therefore, shall we render to the Lord for all the blessings He has bestowed upon us?[16] He is so good, indeed, that He does not exact a recompense, but is content merely to be loved in return for His gifts. Whenever I call all these things to mind (if I may speak of my own feelings), I am struck by a kind of shuddering fear and a cold terror, lest, through distraction of mind or preoccupation with vanities, I fall away from God's love and become a reproach to Christ. For, he who now deceives us and endeavors by every artifice to induce us to forget our Benefactor through the attraction of worldly allure-

---

11 Phil. 2.6,7.
12 Isa. 53.4.
13 Isa. 53.5.
14 Gal. 3.13.
15 1 Cor. 2.9.
16 Ps. 115.12.

ments, leaping at us and trampling us down unto our soul's destruction, will then, in the presence of the Lord, reproach us with our insolence and will gloat over our disobedience and apostasy. He who neither created us nor died for us will count us, nevertheless, among his followers in disobedience and neglect of the commandments of God. This reproach to the Lord and this triumph of our Enemy appear to me more dreadful than the punishments of hell, because we provide the Enemy of Christ with matter for boasting and with cause for exulting over Him who died for us and rose again. Wherefore, we are in a very special sense His debtors, as it is written.[17] So much, then regarding the love of God. It is not my aim, as I said before, to exhaust the subject, for that is impossible, but to implant in your souls a brief and summary reminder which will keep the divine longing ever astir within them.

Q. 3. Of charity toward one's neighbor.

It would be logical to take up next the commandment which is second both in order and emphasis.

R. We have already said above that the law [of God] develops and maintains the powers existing in germ within us. And since we are directed to love our neighbor as ourselves, let us consider whether we have received from the Lord the power to fulfill this commandment also. Who does not know that man is a civilized and gregarious animal, neither savage nor a lover of solitude! Nothing, indeed, is so compatible with our nature as living in society and in dependence upon one another and as loving our own kind. Now, the Lord Himself gave to us the seeds of these qualities in anticipation of His requiring in due time their fruits, for He says: 'A new com-

---

17 Rom. 8.12.

mandment I give unto you: that you love one another.'[1] Moreover, wishing to animate our soul to the observance of this commandment, He did not require signs or wonders as the means of recognizing His disciples (although He gave the power of working these also in the Holy Spirit), but He says: 'By this shall all men know that you are my disciples, if you have love one for another.'[2] Further, He establishes so close a connection between the two great commandments that benefit conferred upon the neighbor is transferred to Himself: 'For I was hungry,' He says, 'and you gave me to eat,'[3] and so on, adding: 'as long as you did it to one of these my least brethren, you did it to me.'[4]

It is, accordingly, possible to keep the second commandment by observing the first, and by means of the second we are led back to the first. He who loves the Lord loves his neighbor in consequence. 'If anyone love me,' said the Lord, 'he will keep my commandments';[5] and again, He says: 'This is my commandment, that you love one another as I have loved you.'[6] On the other hand, he who loves his neighbor fulfills the love he owes to God, for He accepts this favor as shown to Himself. Wherefore, Moses, that faithful servant of God, manifested such great love for his brethren as to wish his name to be struck off the book of God in which it was inscribed, if the sin of his people were not pardoned.[7] Paul, also, desiring to be, like Christ, an exchange for the salvation of all, dared to pray that he might be an anathema from Christ for the sake of his brethren who were his kinsmen according to the flesh.[8] Yet, at the same time, he knew that

1 John 13.34.
2 John 13.35.
3 Matt. 25.35.
4 Matt. 25.40.
5 John 14.23.
6 John 15.12.
7 Exod. 32.32.
8 Rom. 9.3.

it was impossible for him to be estranged from God through his having rejected His favor for love of Him and for the sake of that great commandment; moreover, he knew that he would receive in return much more than he gave. For the rest, what has been said thus far offers sufficient proof that the saints did attain to this measure of love for their neighbor.

Q. 4. Of the fear of God.

R. For those newly entered upon the way of piety, the basic discipline acquired through fear is more profitable, according to the counsel of Solomon, wisest of men: 'The fear of the Lord is the beginning of wisdom.'[1] But, for you who have, as it were, passed through your infancy in Christ and no longer require milk but are able to be perfected according to the inner man by the solid nourishment of doctrine,[2] loftier precepts are needed whereby the whole truth of the love which is in Christ is brought to fulfillment. But, manifestly, you must be on your guard lest the superabundance of the gifts of God make you liable to a harsher judgment if you are ungrateful to the Giver; for He says: 'to whom they have committed much, of him they will demand the more.'[3]

Q. 5. On avoiding distraction.

R. This, at all events, must be recognized—that we can observe neither the commandment of the love of God itself nor that referring to our neighbor, nor any other commandment, if our minds keep wandering hither and yon. It is not possible to master an art or science if one is always starting on fresh subjects, nor even to excel in any single one without recognizing what pertains to the end in view; for one's action must be consistent with the aim, inasmuch as rational ends

---

1 Prov. 1.7.
2 Heb. 5.13,14.
3 Luke 12.48.

are not reached by irrelevant means. It is against the nature of things for one to become a master in metal working by practicing the potter's art, and athletic crowns are not won by enthusiasm for playing the flute. As each kind of mastery demands its own specific and appropriate training, so the discipline for pleasing God in accordance with the Gospel of Christ is practiced by detaching oneself from the cares of the world and by complete withdrawal from its distractions. Therefore does the Apostle, although allowing marriage and deeming it worthy of blessing, oppose to it his own preoccupation with the concerns of God, as if these two interests could not be compatible, saying, 'He that is without a wife is solicitous for the things that belong to the Lord, how he may please God. But he that is with a wife is solicitous for the things of the world, how he may please his wife.'[1] In the same manner, the Lord also bore witness to the guileless and single-hearted attitude of His disciples, when He said, 'You are not of this world.'[2] On the other hand, He declared that it is impossible for the world to have knowledge of God or even to receive the Holy Spirit, saying, 'Just Father, the world hath not known thee'[3] and 'the spirit of truth, whom the world cannot receive.'[4]

Whoever, therefore, would be truly a follower of God must sever the bonds of attachment to this life, and this is done through complete separation from and forgetfulness of old habits. Unless we wrest ourselves from both fleshly ties and worldly society, being transported, as it were, to another world in our manner of living, as the Apostle said: 'But our conversation is in heaven,'[5] it is impossible for us to achieve our

---

1 1 Cor. 7.32,33.
2 John 15.19.
3 John 17.25.
4 John 14.17.
5 Phil. 3.20.

goal of pleasing God, inasmuch as the Lord said specifically: 'So likewise every one of you that doth not renounce all that he possesseth cannot be my disciple.'[6] And having done this, we should watch over our heart with all vigilance[7] not only to avoid ever losing the thought of God or sullying the memory of His wonders by vain imaginations, but also in order to carry about the holy thought of God stamped upon our souls as an ineffaceable seal by continuous and pure recollection. In this way, we shall excel in the love of God which at the same time animates us to the observance of the Lord's commands, and by this, in turn, love itself will be lastingly and indestructibly preserved. The Lord proves this by saying on one occasion: 'If you love me, keep my commandments,'[8] and again: 'If you keep my commandments, you shall abide in my love,'[9] and with still greater importunity: 'as I have kept my Father's commandments and do abide in his love.'[10]

By these words He teaches us always to place before ourselves as our goal, in undertaking a task, the will of Him who has enjoined the work, and to direct our effort toward Him, as He says in another place: 'I came down from heaven, not to do my own will but the will of him that sent me, the Father.'[11] As the secular arts are directed toward certain specific aims and adapt their particular activities to these aims, so also, inasmuch as our actions have as their rule and guide the keeping of the commandments in a manner pleasing to God, it is impossible to do this with exactitude unless it be done as He wills who gave [the commandments]. And by our

---

6 Luke 14.33.
7 Prov. 4.23.
8 John 14.15.
9 John 15.10.
10 *Ibid.*
11 John 6.38.

painstaking zeal to do the will of God in our work, we shall be united to God through our memory. As the smith, when he is forging an axe, for example, thinks of the person who commissioned the task, and with him in mind calculates its shape and size, suiting his work to the wish of him who ordered it done (for if he is unmindful of this, he will fashion something quite different from what he was ordered to make), so the Christian directs every action, small and great, according to the will of God, performing the action at the same time with care and exactitude, and keeping his thoughts fixed upon the One who gave him the work to do. In this way, he fulfills the saying, 'I set the Lord always in my sight; for he is at my right hand, that I be not moved,'[12] and he also observes the precept, 'Whether you eat or drink or whatsoever else you do, do all to the glory of God.'[13] But he who departs from the strict observance of the commandment in performing his actions clearly shows that he has given small thought to God. Mindful, therefore, of the voice of Him who said: 'Do not I fill heaven and earth, saith the Lord?'[14] and again: 'Am I a God at hand and not a God afar off?';[15] also: 'Where there are two or three gathered together in my name, there am I in the midst of them,'[16] we should perform every action as if under the eyes of the Lord and think every thought as if observed by Him. Thus, fear will abide constantly within us who hate iniquity, as it is written,[17] contumely, pride, and the ways of the wicked, and charity will be made perfect,[18] fulfilling the words of the Lord: 'I seek not my own will but

---

12 Ps. 15.8.
13 1 Cor. 10.31.
14 Jer. 23.24.
15 Jer. 23.23.
16 Matt. 18.20.
17 Ps. 118.163
18 1 John 4.12.

the will of him that sent me, the Father.'[19] Our soul, also, will continue in the abiding conviction that good actions are acceptable to the Judge and Arbiter of our life and that the opposite conduct receives condemnation from Him. I think, moreover, it must be added that the Lord's commandments themselves cannot be performed with the intent of pleasing men. No one has recourse to an inferior, if he knows his superior is present. On the contrary, if it happen that an action is acceptable and pleasing to some illustrious personage while to one of lower degree it appears ill-advised and blameworthy, far more value is placed upon the approval of the superior and the inferior's disapproval is unheeded. But, if this is so among men, the soul that is truly prudent and sound and that possesses a firm conviction of the presence of God would surely not ever neglect to do what is pleasing to God and concern itself with the glory received from men, nor be careless of God's behests in subservience to human customs,[20] nor be ruled by common prejudice and influenced by honors and dignities. Such were the dispositions of him who said: 'The wicked have told me fables but not as thy law, O Lord,'[21] and again: 'And I spoke of thy testimonies before kings, and I was not ashamed.'[22]

Q. 6. Concerning the necessity of living in retirement.

R. A secluded and remote habitation also contributes to the removal of distraction from the soul. Living among those who are unscrupulous and disdainful in their attitude toward an exact observance of the commandments is dangerous, as is shown by the following words of Solomon: 'Be not a friend

---

19 John 5.30.
20 Mark 7.8.
21 Ps.118.85.
22 Ps. 118.46.

to an angry man and do not walk with a furious man; lest
perhaps thou learn his ways and take snares to thy soul.'[1]
The words of the Apostle, 'Go out from among them and be
ye separate, saith the Lord,'[2] bear also upon this point. Consequently, that we may not receive incitements to sin through
our eyes and ears and become imperceptibly habituated to it,
and that the impress and form, so to speak, of what is seen
and heard may not remain in the soul unto its ruin, and
that we may be able to be constant in prayer, we should before all things else seek to dwell in a retired place. In so
doing, we should be able to overcome our former habits
whereby we lived as strangers to the precepts of Christ (and
it is no mean struggle to gain the mastery over one's wonted
manner of acting, for custom maintained throughout a long
period takes on the force of nature), and we could wipe away
the stains of sin by assiduous prayer and persevering meditation on the will of God. It is impossible to gain proficiency
in this meditation and prayer, however, while a multitude of
distractions is dragging the soul about and introducing into it
anxieties about the affairs of this life. Could anyone, immersed
in these cares, ever fulfill that command: 'If any man will
come after me, let him deny himself'?[3] For, we must deny
ourselves and take up the Cross of Christ and thus follow Him.
Now, self-denial involves the entire forgetfulness of the past
and surrender of one's will—surrender which it is very difficult, not to say quite impossible, to achieve while living
in the promiscuity customary in the world. And in addition,
the social intercourse demanded by such a life is even an
obstacle to taking up one's cross and following Christ. Readi-

---

1 Prov. 22.24,25.
2 2 Cor. 6.17.
3 Luke 9.23.

ness to die for Christ, the mortification of one's members on this earth, preparedness for every danger which might befall us on behalf of Christ's Name, detachment from this life—this it is to take up one's cross; and we regard the obstacles springing from the habits of life in society as major impediments thereto.

And in addition to all the other obstacles, which are many, the soul in looking at the crowd of other offenders does not, in the first place, have time to become aware of its own sins and to afflict itself by penance for its errors; on the contrary, by comparison with those who are worse, it takes on, besides, a certain deceptive appearance of righteousness. Secondly, through the disturbances and occupations which life in society naturally engenders, the soul, being drawn away from the more worthy remembrance of God, pays the penalty of finding neither joy nor gladness in God and of not relishing the delights of the Lord or tasting the sweetness of His words, so as to be able to say: 'I remembered God and was delighted,'[4] and 'How sweet are thy words to my palate! more than honey to my mouth.'[5] Worse still, it becomes habituated to a disregard and a complete forgetfulness of His judgments, than which no more fatal misfortune could befall it.

Q. 7. On the necessity of living in the company of those who are striving for the same objective—that of pleasing God—and the difficulty and hazards of living as a solitary.

Since your words have convinced us that it is dangerous to live in company with those who hold the commandments of God in light regard, we consider it logical to inquire whether one who retires from society should live in solitude or with

---

4 Ps. 76.4.
5 Ps. 118.103.

brethren who are of the same mind and who have set before themselves the same goal, that is, the devout life.

R. I consider that life passed in company with a number of persons in the same habitation is more advantageous in many respects. My reasons are, first, that no one of us is self-sufficient as regards corporeal necessities, but we require one another's aid in supplying our needs. The foot, to cite an analogy, possesses one kind of power and lacks another, and without the co-operation of the other members of the body it finds itself incapable of carrying on its activity independently for any length of time, nor does it have wherewithal to supply what is lacking. Similarly, in the solitary life, what is at hand becomes useless to us and what is wanting cannot be provided, since God, the Creator, decreed that we should require the help of one another, as it is written,[1] so that we might associate with one another. Again, apart from this consideration, the doctrine of the charity of Christ does not permit the individual to be concerned solely with his own private interests. 'Charity,' says the Apostle, 'seeketh not her own.'[2] But a life passed in solitude is concerned only with the private service of individual needs. This is openly opposed to the law of love which the Apostle fulfilled, who sought not what was profitable to himself but to many that they might be saved.[3] Furthermore, a person living in solitary retirement will not readily discern his own defects, since he has no one to admonish and correct him with mildness and compassion. In fact, admonition even from an enemy often produces in a prudent man the desire for amendment. But the cure of sin is wrought with understanding by him who loves sincerely; for Holy Scripture says: 'for he that loveth correcteth

---

1 Eccli. 13.20.
2 1 Cor. 13.5.
3 1 Cor. 10.33.

betimes.'[4] Such a one it is very difficult to find in a solitude, if
in one's prior state of life one had not been associated with
such a person. The solitary, consequently, experiences the truth
of the saying, 'Woe to him that is alone, for when he falleth
he hath none to lift him up.'[5] Moreover, the majority of the
commandments are easily observed by several persons living
together, but not so in the case of one living alone; for, while
he is obeying one commandment, the practice of another is
being interfered with. For example, when he is visiting the
sick, he cannot show hospitality to the stranger and, in the
imparting and sharing of necessities (especially when the
ministrations are prolonged), he is prevented from giving
zealous attention to [other] tasks. As a result, the greatest
commandment and the one especially conducive to salvation
is not observed, since the hungry are not fed nor the naked
clothed. Who, then, would choose this ineffectual and unprofitable life in preference to that which is both fruitful and
in accordance with the Lord's command?

Besides, if all we who are united in the one hope of our
calling[6] are one body with Christ as our Head, we are
also members, one of another.[7] If we are not joined together
by union in the Holy Spirit in the harmony of one body, but
each of us should choose to live in solitude, we would not
serve the common good in the ministry according to God's
good pleasure, but would be satisfying our own passion for
self-gratification. How could we, divided and separated, preserve the status and the mutual service of members or our
subordinate relationship to our Head which is Christ? It is
impossible, indeed, to rejoice with him who receives an honor

---

4 Prov. 13.24.
5 Eccle. 4.10.
6 Eph. 4.4.
7 1 Cor. 12.12.

or to sympathize with him who suffers[8] when, by reason of their being separated from one another, each person cannot, in all likelihood, be kept informed about the affairs of his neighbor. In addition, since no one has the capacity to receive all spiritual gifts, but the grace of the Spirit is given proportionately to the faith of each,[9] when one is living in association with others, the grace privately bestowed on each individual becomes the common possession of his fellows. 'To one, indeed, is given the word of wisdom; and to another, the word of knowledge; to another, faith, to another, prophecy, to another, the grace of healing,'[10] and so on. He who receives any of these gifts does not possess it for his own sake but rather for the sake of others, so that, in the life passed in community, the operation of the Holy Spirit in the individual is at the same time necessarily transmitted to all. He who lives alone, consequently, and has, perhaps, one gift renders it ineffectual by leaving it in disuse, since it lies buried within him. How much danger there is in this all of you know who have read the Gospel.[11] On the other hand, in the case of several persons living together, each enjoys his own gift and enhances it by giving others a share, besides reaping benefit from the gifts of others as if they were his own.

Community life offers more blessings than can be fully and easily enumerated. It is more advantageous than the solitary life both for preserving the goods bestowed on us by God and for warding off the external attacks of the Enemy. If any should happen to grow heavy with that sleep which is unto death and which we have been instructed by David to avert with prayer: 'Enlighten my eyes that I never sleep in

8 1 Cor. 12.26.
9 Rom. 12.6.
10 1 Cor. 12.8,9.
11 Matt. 25.26ff.

death,[12] the awakening induced by those who are already on watch is the more assured. For the sinner, moreover, the withdrawal from his sin is far easier if he fears the shame of incurring censure from many acting together—to him, indeed, might be applied the words: 'To him who is such a one, this rebuke is sufficient which is given by many'[13]—and for the righteous man, there is a great and full satisfaction in the esteem of the group and in their approval of his conduct. If in the mouth of two or three witnesses, every word shall stand,[14] he who performs a good action will be far more surely corroborated by the testimony of many. Besides these disadvantages, the solitary life is fraught with other perils. The first and greatest is that of self-satisfaction. Since the solitary has no one to appraise his conduct, he will think he has achieved the perfection of the precept. Secondly, because he never tests his state of soul by exercise, he will not recognize his own deficiencies nor will he discover the advance he may have made in his manner of acting, since he will have removed all practical occasion for the observance of the commandments.

Wherein will he show his humility, if there is no one with whom he may compare and so confirm his own greater humility? Wherein will he give evidence of his compassion, if he has cut himself off from association with other persons? And how will he exercise himself in long-suffering, if no one contradicts his wishes? If anyone says that the teaching of the Holy Scripture is sufficient for the amendment of his ways, he resembles a man who learns carpentry without ever actually doing a carpenter's work or a man who is instructed in metal-working but will not reduce theory to practice. To such a one the Apostle would say: 'Not the hearers of the

12 Ps. 12.4.
13 2 Cor. 2.6.
14 Matt. 18.16.

law are just before God, but the doers of the law shall be justified.'[15] Consider, further, that the Lord by reason of His excessive love for man was not content with merely teaching the word, but, so as to transmit to us clearly and exactly the example of humility in the perfection of charity, girded Himself and washed the feet of the disciples.[16] Whom, therefore, will you wash? To whom will you minister? In comparison with whom will you be the lowest, if you live alone? How, moreover, in a solitude, will that good and pleasant thing be accomplished, the dwelling of brethren together in one habitation[17] which the Holy Spirit likens to ointment emitting its fragrance from the head of the high priest?[18] So it is an arena for the combat, a good path of progress, continual discipline, and a practicing of the Lord's commandments, when brethren dwell together in community. This kind of life has as its aim the glory of God according to the command of our Lord Jesus Christ, who said: 'So let your light shine before men that they may see your good works and glorify your Father who is in heaven.'[19] It maintains also the practice characteristic of the saints, of whom it is recorded in the Acts: 'And all they that believed were together and had all things common,'[20] and again: 'And the multitude of believers had but one heart and one soul; neither did anyone say that aught of the things which he possessed was his own, but all things were common unto them.'[21]

Q. 8. Of renunciation; whether we ought first of all give up everything and thus enter upon the devout life.

---

15 Rom. 2.13.
16 John 13.5.
17 Ps. 132.1.
18 Ps. 132.2.
19 Matt. 5.16.
20 Acts 2.44.
21 Acts 4.32.

R. Our Lord Jesus Christ, coupling elaborate exposition with much forceful demonstration, says to all: 'If any man come to me, let him deny himself and take up his cross and follow me.'[1] Again, He says: 'So, likewise, everyone of you that doth not renounce all that he possesseth, cannot be my disciple.'[2] This precept, we think, involves a number of necessary renunciations. Above all, we renounce the Devil and carnal affections, in having given up the things of our secret shame, ties of physical relationship, human friendships, and a mode of life that is inimical to the perfection of the Gospel of salvation. And what is still more necessary: he that has stripped off the old man with his deeds,[3] 'who is corrupted according to the desire of error,'[4] renounces himself. Also, he repudiates all worldly affections which could hinder him from reaching the goal of piety. Such a one, moreover, regards as his true parents those who have brought him forth by the Gospel[5] and looks upon as his brethren those who have received the same spirit of adoption, and he will deem all possessions foreign to him, as indeed they are. In short, he who is crucified to the world and to whom for the sake of Christ the whole world is crucified,[6] can no longer have any part in worldly concerns. Our Lord Jesus Christ depicted hatred of one's life and self-denial in their most vivid form when He said: 'If any man will come after me, let him deny himself and take up his cross'; and then He added: 'and follow me.'[7] Again: 'If any man come to me and hate not his father and mother and wife and children and brethren and sisters, yea, and his own life, also, he cannot be my disciple.'[8]

---

1 Matt. 16.24.
2 Luke 14.33.
3 Col. 3.9.
4 Eph. 4.22.
5 1 Cor. 4.15.
6 Gal. 6.14.
7 Matt. 16.24.
8 Luke 14.26.

Perfect renunciation, therefore, consists in not having an affection for this life and keeping before our minds the 'answer of death, that we should not trust in ourselves.'[9] But, a beginning is made by detaching oneself from all external goods: property, vainglory, life in society, useless desires, after the example of the Lord's holy disciples. James and John left their father Zebedee and the very boat upon which their whole livelihood depended.[10] Matthew left his counting house and followed the Lord, not merely leaving behind the profits of his occupation, but also paying no heed to the dangers which were sure to befall both himself and his family at the hands of the magistrates because he had left the tax accounts unfinished.[11] To Paul, finally, the whole world was crucified, and he to the world.[12]

Thus, a man who is strongly seized with the desire of following Christ can no longer be concerned with anything pertaining to this life, not even with the love of his parents or other relatives if this runs counter to the precepts of the Lord (for in this case these words apply: 'If any man come to me and hate not his father and mother,'[13] and so on); nor with human respect, so that he omits because of it any profitable act. This fault the saints repudiated when they said: 'We ought to obey God rather than men.'[14] He can no longer pay heed to the profane who jeer at his good works so as to be intimidated by their scorn. But, if a man would know more precisely and clearly the resoluteness united with desire which is characteristic of those who follow the Lord, let him recall the Apostle, who for our instruction related the circumstances of his own case, saying: 'If any thinketh he may have confi-

---

9 2 Cor. 1.9.
10 Mark 1.20.
11 Matt. 9.9.
12 Gal. 6.14.
13 Luke 14.26.
14 Acts 5.29.

dence in the flesh, I more, being circumcised the eighth day, of the stock of Israel, of the tribe of Benjamin, an Hebrew of the Hebrews, according to the law, a Pharisee, according to zeal, persecuting the Church of God; according to the justice that is in the law, conversing without blame. But the things that were gain to me, the same I have counted loss for Christ. Furthermore, I count all things to be but loss for the excellent knowledge of Jesus Christ, my Lord; for whom I have suffered the loss of all things and count them as dung that I may gain Christ.'[15] If—to say a daring thing, but the truth nevertheless—the Apostle likened to the excrement of the body, which we abominate and dispose of as quickly as possible, the very benefits of the law temporarily given by God, inasmuch as they are obstacles to the knowledge of Christ and that justice which is in Him and our conformation to His death, what could one say regarding the legislation of men? Why, furthermore, need we confirm our assertions by reasoning and by the examples of the saints, when we may quote as evidence the very words of the Lord and thereby put to shame the timorous soul? His testimony is clear and undeniable in the words: 'So likewise every one of you that doth not renounce all that he possesseth, cannot be my disciple.'[16] And elsewhere, after the words, 'If thou wilt be perfect,' He says first: 'go sell what thou hast and give to the poor,' and then adds: 'come, follow me.'[17] Again, to any thoughtful person, the parable of the merchant points clearly to the same idea. 'The kingdom of heaven,' says Jesus Christ, 'is like to a merchant seeking good pearls. Who, when he had found one pearl of great price, went his way and sold all that he had and bought it.'[18] It is evident that the precious

---

15 Phil. 3.4-8.
16 Luke 14.33.
17 Matt. 19.21.
18 Matt. 13.45,46.

pearl is meant to be an image of the heavenly kingdom, which the word of the Lord shows we cannot attain unless we give up in exchange for it all our possessions alike—wealth, fame, lineage, and anything else that is an object of desire for many.

Then, too, the Lord declared that it is impossible to achieve the wished-for end if the mind is distracted by a variety of cares, when He said: No man can serve two masters';[19] and again: 'You cannot serve God and mammon.'[20] Therefore, we should choose to have treasure in heaven alone, so that we may keep our heart there. 'For,' says Jesus Christ, 'where thy treasure is, there is thy heart also.'[21] If, then, we keep in reserve any earthly possessions or perishable wealth, the mind sinks down as into mire and the soul inevitably becomes blind to God and insensible to the desire for the beauties of heaven and the good things laid up for us by promise. These we cannot gain possession of unless a strong and single-minded desire leads us to ask for them and lightens the labor of their attainment. This, then, is renunciation, as our discourse defines it: the severance of the bonds of this material and transient life and freedom from human concerns, whereby we render ourselves more fit to set out upon the road leading to God. It is the unhindered impulse toward the possession and enjoyment of inestimable goods, 'more to be desired than gold and many precious stones.'[22] In short, it is the transference of the human heart to a heavenly mode of life, so that we can say: 'But our conversation is in heaven.'[23] Also—and this is the chief point—it is the first step toward the likeness to Christ, who, being rich, became poor for our sake.[24] Unless we attain

19 Matt. 6.24.
20 Ibid.
21 Matt. 6.21.
22 Ps.18.11.
23 Phil. 3.20.
24 2 Cor. 8.9.

to this likeness, it is impossible for us to achieve a way of life in accord with the Gospel of Christ. How, indeed, can we gain either contrition of heart or humility of mind or deliverance from anger, pain, anxieties—in a word, from all destructive movements of the soul—if we are entangled in the riches and cares of a worldly life and cling to others by affection and association? To put it briefly, by what process of logic is one who is not permitted to concern himself with necessary matters, such as food and clothing, allowed to be held in constraint by the evil cares of wealth, as if by thorns which prevent the seed planted by the Husbandman of our souls from bearing fruit; for our Lord says: 'that which was sown upon thorns are they who are choked with the cares and riches and pleasures of this life and yield no fruit.'[25]

Q. 9. Whether he who is admitted to the company of those consecrated to the Lord ought, with indifference, to entrust his property to incompetent or unjust relatives.

R. The Lord said: 'go, sell what thou hast, and give to the poor, and thou shalt have treasure in heaven; and come follow me';[1] and again: 'Sell what you possess and give alms.'[2] I think, however, that one who takes leave of his kinsmen for such a purpose need not adopt a careless attitude toward his property, but, aware that it is very dangerous to leave the management of it to relatives or to someone selected at random, he should try to keep a precise accounting of everything as being henceforward consecrated to the Lord and with all piety distribute it either personally, if this is possible and he has the necessary experience, or through the agency of per-

---

25 Luke 8.14.

---

1 Matt. 19.21.
2 Luke 12.33.

sons chosen after searching inquiry and who have proved their ability to handle the business with fidelity and intelligence. If he who is entrusted with a king's fortune negligently makes no effort at all to increase it when possible, he is not absolved from guilt even though he does not commit repeated thefts from the treasure already amassed. What condemnation, then, ought we to expect to fall upon those who are frivolous and improvident in the management of goods that are already consecrated to the Lord? Are they not liable to the sentence of doom pronounced upon the negligent, as it is written: 'Cursed be he that doth the work of the Lord negligently'[3]?

We must everywhere be on our guard lest, under pretext of observing one commandment, we break another. To quarrel or to contend with the unjust ill befits us, for 'a servant of the Lord must not wrangle.'[4] He who has been unfairly treated by his blood relatives ought to be mindful of the words of the Lord: 'There is no man who hath left house or brethren or sisters or father or mother or wife or children or lands,' and not this merely, but: 'for my sake and for the gospel, who shall not receive an hundred times as much, now in this time and in the world to come, life everlasting.'[5] Certainly, it is our duty to bear witness against the unjust of their sin of sacrilege, according to the Lord's precept: 'If thy brother shall offend against thee, go and rebuke him.'[6] The rules of piety, however, forbid entering into litigation with such persons before secular tribunals, as the following words show: 'If a man will contend with thee in judgment and take away thy coat, let go thy cloak also unto him,'[7] and: 'Dare any of you,

3 Jer. 48.10.
4 2 Tim. 2.24.
5 Mark 10.29,30.
6 Matt. 18.15.
7 Matt. 5.40.

having a matter against another, go to be judged before the unjust and not before the saints?'[8] Before the latter, then, we should hold the trial, taking greater account of our brother's salvation than of the advantage to our fortune; for the Lord also says: 'If he shall hear thee,' and He adds: 'thou shalt gain,' not wealth, but 'thy brother.'[9] Sometimes, also, for the sake of manifesting the truth, we agree to an inquiry when the author of the injustice himself issues the challenge to public arbitration, not initiating the matter ourselves but acceding to those who summon us to court, not seizing the opportunity to indulge our own wrathful feelings and our quarrelsomeness but manifesting the truth. In this manner we shall save our adversary also, even against his will, from evil consequences and we ourselves will not violate the commandment of God, being as His ministers, neither contentious nor avaricious, steadily intent upon the manifestation of truth and never overstepping the appointed limits of zeal.

Q. 10. Whether all applicants are to be received or only certain ones, and whether these are to be admitted at once or after probation, and what the nature of this period of trial should be.

R. Since our benevolent God and Saviour, Jesus Christ, proclaims and says: 'Come to me, all you that labor and are burdened and I will refresh you,'[1] it is hazardous to reject those who through us approach the Lord, wishing to take upon themselves His mild yoke and the burden of the counsels which lifts us up to heaven. Yet, to be sure, unwashed feet

---

8 1 Cor. 6.1.
9 Matt. 18.15.

---

1 Matt. 11.28.

should not be permitted access to holy doctrines. Our Lord Jesus Christ questioned the youth who came to Him as to his previous life and, learning that he had practiced virtue, bade him fulfill that which was still wanting to his perfection; only then did he offer him the opportunity of following Him. Thus, it is clearly our duty to inquire into the past life of candidates, and to those who have already in the past led a good life we should impart the more advanced training in perfection; those, on the other hand, who are turning from an evil life or have set out from a state of indifference toward the strict life of the knowledge of God should be carefully examined to make sure that they are not of unstable character and easily swayed in their decisions.

The fickleness of such persons renders them suspect, for, in addition to their receiving no benefit themselves, they are a cause of injury to the rest by spreading complaints, lies, and wicked slanders of our work. Inasmuch, however, as all things are set right by persevering diligence and since fear of the Lord prevails over all sorts of defects of the soul, these persons are not to be immediately rejected. They should be directed toward the practice of suitable disciplines, and if, their resolution having been tested by time and laborious probation, we find in them some indication of stability, they may be safely admitted. If this is not the case, they should be sent away while they are still externs, so that their period of trial may not be injurious to the community. But it is necessary to make a close examination to discover whether a man who has previously fallen into sin confesses with deep contrition his most secret sins and becomes an accuser of himself,[2] whereby he both puts to shame the companions of his wickedness and repudiates them in imitation of Him who said: 'Depart from

2 Prov. 18.17.

me, all ye workers of iniquity';[3] and in addition he makes his future life secure from a further fall into like sins. For the rest, there is a general method of trying all candidates to see whether they are prepared to undergo without false shame all humiliations, so that they accept even the most menial work if reason sanctions the performance of these tasks as good and useful. After each candidate has been proved a useful instrument for the Lord, so to speak, and ready for every good work by exhaustive scrutiny on the part of those competent to study such matters, let him be enrolled among those who have consecrated themselves to the Lord. To one, moreover, who has enjoyed any of the higher positions in society, and who aspires to imitate the humility of our Lord Jesus Christ, should be given tasks which may appear extremely humiliating to worldlings, to see whether he will prove himself to be a worker for God, wholehearted and unashamed.

Q. 11. Concerning slaves.

R. All bound slaves who flee to religious communities for refuge should be admonished and sent back to their masters in better dispositions, after the example of St. Paul who, althought he had begotten Onesimus through the Gospel, sent him back to Philemon.[1] The former he had convinced that the yoke of slavery, borne in a manner pleasing to the Lord, would render him worthy of the kingdom of heaven; the latter he not only urged to annul the threat against his servant, mindful of His words who is truly the Lord: 'If you forgive men their offenses, your heavenly Father will forgive you also your offenses,'[2] but also, in order that he might be

---

3 Ps. 6.9.

---

1 Philem. 1.12.
2 Matt. 6.14.

more kindly disposed toward him, he writes: 'For perhaps he therefore departed for a season from thee that thou mightest receive him again forever; not now as a servant but instead of a servant, a most dear brother.'[3] If, however, it should be the case of a wicked master who gives unlawful commands and forces the slave to transgress the command of the true Master, our Lord Jesus Christ, then it is our duty to oppose him, that the Name of God be not blasphemed by that slave's performing an act displeasing to God. This protest is rightly made when the slave concerned is reconciled to bearing the sufferings that afflict him by reason of his obeying God rather than men, as it is written,[4] or when they who have given him refuge accept in a manner pleasing to God the trials encountered by them on his behalf.

Q. 12. How married persons are to be received.

R. Those who are married and who apply for entrance to a life such as this should be asked whether they are doing this by mutual consent, according to the precept of the Apostle ('for,' he says, 'he hath not power of his own body'[1]), and if such be the case, the applicant should be received in the presence of several witnesses. Nothing should be preferred to obedience to God. If the partner should disagree and offer resistance, being less concerned for God's good pleasure, let the words of the Apostle be recalled to mind: 'But God hath called us in peace.'[2] And let the Lord's precept be fulfilled: 'If any man come to me, and hate not his father and mother and wife and children,' and so on, 'he cannot be my disciple';[3]

---

3 Philem. 1.15,16.
4 Acts. 5.29.

---

1 1 Cor. 7.4.
2 1 Cor. 7.15.
3 Luke 14.26.

for nothing should take precedence over obedience to God. We know of many cases, moreover, where the determination to lead a life of chastity prevailed with the aid of earnest prayer and unremitting penance; the Lord inducing those who had been quite obstinate, even, in many instances, by visiting them with bodily illness to give their consent to the right decision.

Q. 13. That silence is a useful discipline for novices.

R. Silence is indeed a good discipline for novices, because, in acquiring control of the tongue, they are at the same time giving sufficient proof of continency and, also, while they are keeping silence they will be earnest and attentive in learning, from those who know how to make use of speech, in what manner one ought to ask a question or make reply in particular cases. There is, indeed, a tone of voice, a moderateness in length, a propriety of time, and a specific appropriateness in the use of words which are especially characteristic of those leading the devout life, and these qualities cannot be taught to one who has not acquired them by constant practice. By reason of its restful quiet, silence induces forgetfulness of the past and provides leisure for learning what is good. Consequently, silence should be kept, except, of course, for the chanting of the psalms, unless some private need pertaining to the care of one's soul or an emergency in the task at hand should arise or some similar question require an answer.

Q. 14. Of those who consecrate themselves to God and then try to repudiate their promise.

R. Surely, everyone who has been admitted to the community and then has retracted his promise should be looked upon as a sinner against God, in whose presence and to whom he pledged his consent to the pact. But 'if a man shall sin against God,' says the Scripture, 'who shall pray for him?';[1] for, if he has consecrated himself to God and has afterward turned aside to another mode of life, he is guilty of sacrilege, by having committed the theft of himself and stolen an offering made to God. The brethren are justified in never again opening their door to these persons, even if they should apply for shelter on some occasion when they are merely in transit. The apostolic rule clearly directs us to avoid every disorderly and undisciplined person and not to associate with him, in order that he may be put to shame.[2]

Q. 15. At what age consecration of oneself to God should be permitted and at what time the profession of virginity should be regarded as safe.

R. Inasmuch as the Lord says: 'Suffer the little children to come unto me,'[1] and the Apostle praises him who has known the Holy Scripture from infancy[2] and also directs that childred be reared 'in the discipline and correction of the Lord,'[3] we deem every time of life, even the very earliest, suitable for receiving applicants. Indeed, those children who are bereft of their parents we should take in on our own initiative, so that we may become fathers of the orphans in emulation of Job.[4] Those who are under their parents' care and who are brought to us by them should be received before many witnesses so as not to give occasion [for blame] to those who are desirous of this, but that every unjust tongue uttering blasphemy against us may be stopped.[5] They should be received according to

1 1 Sam. 2.25.
2 2 Thess. 3.14.

1 Mark 10.14.
2 2 Tim. 3.15.
3 Eph. 6.4.
4 Job 29.12.
5 Ps. 62.12.

this method, but not immediately numbered and reckoned with the body of the community, in order that, in the event of their failing to persevere, they may not afterward heap reproaches on the devout life. They should be reared with all piety as children belonging to the entire community, but meals and quarters for both girls and boys should be separate, to avoid their being too familiar or too self-confident with their elders and, also, that through the rarity of their association with them, their reverence for their directors may be preserved. Furthermore, this separation would prevent their developing a readiness to commit faults when they see the more advanced in perfection incurring penalties for omissions in their duties (if at any time these should happen to be off their guard), and also keep them from being imperceptibly filled with conceit when they witness their elders repeatedly delinquent in that which they themselves do aright. There is no difference, indeed, between a child in years and one who is mentally a child; consequently, it is not surprising that the same faults are often discovered in both. Then, too, [by such an arrangement], the young would not, because of close association with older persons, come to act in a precocious and unbecoming manner by doing things which their elders carry off with decorum by reason of their age.

To maintain this economy, then, and to ensure decorous behavior in other respects, the children's quarters should be separate from those of the more advanced in perfection. Along with other advantages, the quarters inhabited by the monks will not be disturbed by the drilling which is necessary for the young in learning their lessons. The prayers assigned for recitation throughout the day should, however, be said in common by young and old. The young, on the one hand, are generally stimulated by the example of the more perfect, and, on the other, their elders are in no small measure assisted in their prayer by the children. But as regards sleep and rising, the hours, the quantity, and the quality of the meals, specific routines and diets appropriate for children should be arranged. Moreover, one who is advanced in years should be placed in charge of these little ones, a person of more than average experience and who has a reputation for patience. Thus, he will correct the faults of the young with fatherly kindness and give wise instruction, applying remedies proper to each fault, so that, while the penalty for the fault is being exacted, the soul may be exercised in interior tranquility. Has one of them, for example, become angry with a companion? According to the seriousness of his offense, he should be made to care for this comrade and wait on him; for the practice of humility fells, as it were, an angry spirit, while arrogance usually breeds anger within us. Has he partaken of food out òf time? Let him fast for most of the day. Has he been accused of eating immoderately or in an unseemly fashion? Let him be deprived of food at meal time and forced to watch the others who know how to eat properly, so that he may be at once punished by abstinence and taught proper decorum. Has he uttered an idle word, or insulted his neighbor, or told a lie, or said anything at all that is forbidden? Let him learn restraint in fasting and silence.

Their studies, also, should be in conformity with the aim in view. They should, therefore, employ a vocabulary derived from the Scriptures and, in place of myths, historical accounts of admirable deeds should be told to them. They should be taught maxims from Proverbs and rewards should be held out to them for memorizing names and facts. In this way, joyfully and with a relaxed mind, they will achieve their aim without pain to themselves and without giving offense. Under the proper guidance, moreover, attentiveness and habits of concentration would readily be developed in such students if they were continually questioned by their teachers as to where their thoughts were and what they were thinking about. A child of tender age, simple, candid, and unskilled in deceit, readily reveals the secrets of his soul; so as not to be continually caught in what is forbidden, he would avoid unsuitable thoughts, and, fearing the shame of a scolding, would instantly recall his mind from its follies.

While the mind is still easy to mold and as pliable as wax, taking the form of what is impressed upon it, it should be exercised from the very beginning in every good discipline. Then, when reason enters in and habits of choice develop, they will take their course from the first elements learned at the beginning and from traditional forms of piety; reason proposing that which is beneficial and habit imparting facility in right action. At this point, also, permission to make the vow of virginity should be granted, inasmuch as it is now to be relied upon, since it is the individual's own choice and the decision follows upon the maturing of reason. After this stage, too, rewards for good deeds and penalties for faults proportioned to the importance of the action are meted out by a fair arbiter. Furthermore, ecclesiastical officials should be called in as witnesses of the decision, so that through their presence, as well, the consecration of the person as a kind of votive offering to God may be sanctified and the act ratified by their testimony; 'for,' says the Scripture, 'in the mouth of two or three witnesses shall every word stand.'[6] In this way, also, the fervor of the brethren will suffer no disedification, for those who have so vowed themselves to God and afterward try to revoke such a vow will have no excuse for their shamelessness. On the other hand, one who does not wish to submit to the life of virginity, on the ground that he is incapable of devoting his

---

6 2 Cor. 13.1.

whole attention to the things of the Lord, should be dismissed in the presence of the same witnesses. He who makes such a vow, however, after a great amount of careful deliberation which he should be allowed to engage in privately for several days, so that we may not appear to be kidnapping him, should be received forthwith and made a member of the community, sharing the dwelling and daily life of the more advanced in perfection. Moreover—to add a point which we had forgotten and which is not out of place here—since certain trades must be practiced even from early childhood, whenever any children appear to have an aptitude for these, we should not oppose their remaining during the day with their instructors in the art. At nightfall, however, we should invariably send them back to their companions, with whom they must also take their meals.

Q. 16. Whether continency is necessary for one who would lead the religious life.

R. It is evident that the practice of continency is essential; first, from the fact that the Apostle includes continency among the fruits of the spirit[1] and, second, from his saying that a blameless ministry is achieved through this virtue, in these words: In labors, in watchings, in fastings, in chastity';[2] and elsewhere: 'in labor, and painfulness, in much watchings, in hunger and thirst, in fastings often';[3] and again: 'And everyone that striveth for the mastery, refraineth himself from all things.'[4] Chastisement of the body and bringing it under subjection are achieved by no other means as successfully as by the practice of continency; for the effervescent fires of youth, whose leapings can scarcely be controlled, are held in re-

---

1 Gal. 5.23.
2 2 Cor. 6.5,6.
3 2 Cor. 11.27.
4 1 Cor. 9.25.

straint by continency as with a bridle. According to Solomon, 'Delicacies are not seemly for a fool;'[5] and what is more foolish than for the flesh to indulge itself in delights and for youth to whirl about at will! Wherefore, the Apostle says: 'and make not provision for the flesh in its concupiscences;[6] likewise: 'she that liveth in pleasures is dead while she is living.'[7] Moreover, the example of the delights enjoyed by the rich man show that continency is necessary for us, that we may never hear what was said to the rich man: 'thou didst receive good things in thy lifetime.'[8]

The Apostle also showed how much incontinency is to be dreaded by including it among the signs of apostasy, when he said: 'in the last days shall come dangerous times. Men shall be lovers of themselves.'[9] Then, after enumerating several forms of iniquity, he adds: 'slanderers, incontinent.'[10] Also, for selling his birthright for one portion of food, Esau was charged with incontinency as the greatest of evils.[11] The first disobedience befell men as a consequence of incontinency. All the saints, on the contrary, were renowned for continency. The whole life of the saints and of the blessed, the example of the Lord Himself while He was with us in the flesh, are aids to us in this matter. Moses, through long perseverance in fasting and prayer,[12] received the law and heard the words of God, 'as a man is wont to speak to his friend,'[13] says the Scripture. Elias was deemed worthy of the vision of God when he also had practiced abstinence in like degree.[14] And what

5 Prov. 19.10.
6 Rom. 13.14.
7 1 Tim. 5.6.
8 Luke 16.25.
9 2 Tim. 3.1,2.
10 2 Tim. 3.3.
11 Gen. 25.33.
12 Deut. 9.9.
13 Exod. 33.11.
14 1 Kings 19.8.

of Daniel? How did he attain to the contemplation of marvels? Was it not after a twenty-day fast?[15] And how did the
three children overcome the power of the fire? Was it not
through continency?[16] As for John, his whole plan of life was
based on the practice of continency.[17] Even the Lord Himself
inaugurated His public manifestation with the practice of this
virtue.[18] By continency, however, we do not mean complete
abstinence from food (for this is to take one's life by violence),
but that abstinence from pleasures which aims at the thwart-
ing of the will of the flesh for the purpose of attaining to the
goal of piety.

In general, we who are instructed in the devout life are
bound to abstain from those pleasures which they enjoy who
lead a self-indulgent life. The practice of continency, therefore, does not have to do only with the delights of the table,
but extends also to the avoidance of all that represents an
impediment to us. One who is perfectly continent does not
control his appetite only to fall prey to the desire for human
fame. He does not gain mastery over shameful desires and
neglect to overcome his attachment to wealth as well as all
other base emotions, such as anger, dejection, and the rest of
the vices which are wont to enslave inexperienced souls. We
have noticed, indeed, that all the precepts—and this is especially observable with regard to continency—are interconnected and that it is almost impossible to observe one
separately from another. Thus, he is humble who is continent
regarding worldly glory, and he meets the evangelical standard
of poverty who is master of himself with respect to worldly
goods. He abstains from anger who exercises control over
wrath and indignation. Perfect continency also sets limits for

15 Dan. 10.3.
16 Dan. 1.8ff.
17 Matt. 3.4.
18 Matt. 4.2.

the tongue, boundaries for the eyes, and enjoins upon the ears an avoidance of curiosity in the use of the hearing. Anyone who does not observe these restraints is incontinent and undisciplined. Do you see how all the other precepts cluster about this one and are intertwined with it?

Q. 17. That laughter also must be held in check.

R. Those who live under discipline should avoid very carefully even such intemperate action as is commonly regarded lightly. Indulging in unrestrained and immoderate laughter is a sign of intemperance, of a want of control over one's emotions, and of failure to repress the soul's frivolity by a stern use of reason. It is not unbecoming, however, to give evidence of merriment of soul by a cheerful smile, if only to illustrate that which is written: 'A glad heart maketh a cheerful countenance';[1] but raucous laughter and uncontrollable shaking of the body are not indicative of a well-regulated soul, or of personal dignity, or self-mastery. This kind of laughter Ecclesiastes also reprehends as especially subversive of firmness of soul in the words: 'Laughter I counted error,'[2] and again: 'As the crackling of thorns burning under a pot, so is the laughter of fools.'[3] Moreover, the Lord appears to have experienced those emotions which are of necessity associated with the body, as well as those that betoken virtue, as, for example, weariness and compassion for the afflicted; but, so far as we know from the story of the Gospel, He never laughed. On the contrary, He even pronounced those unhappy who are given to laughter.[4] And let not the equivocal sense of the word 'laughter' deceive us, for it is a frequent practice in the Scriptures to call joy of spirit and the cheerful feel-

---

1 Prov. 15.13.
2 Eccle. 2.2.
3 Eccle. 7.7.
4 Luke 6.25.

ing which follows upon good actions, 'laughter.' Sara says, for instance: 'God hath made a laughter for me,'[5] and there is another saying: 'Blessed are ye that weep now, for you shall laugh';[6] likewise, the words of Job: 'And the true mouth he will fill with laughter.'[7] All these references to gaiety signify merriment of soul instead of hilarity. He, therefore, who is master of every passion and feels no excitement from pleasure, or at least, does not give it outward expression, but is steadfastly inclined to restraint as regards every harmful delight, such a one is perfectly continent—but, clearly, he is also at the same time free from all sin. Sometimes, moreover, even acts of a permissible and necessary kind are to be abstained from, when the abstinence is dictated by consideration of our brother's welfare. Thus, the Apostle says: 'If meat scandalize my brother, I will never eat flesh.'[8] And even though he could have gained his livelihood from preaching the gospel, he did not take advantage of this privilege lest he should offer any hindrance, as it were, to the Gospel of Christ.[9]

Continency, then, destroys sin, quells the passions, and mortifies the body even as to its natural affections and desires. It marks the beginning of the spiritual life, leads us to eternal blessings, and extinguishes within itself the desire for pleasure. Pleasure, indeed, is evil's special allurement, through which we men are most likely to commit sin and by which the whole soul is dragged down to ruin as by a hook. Whoever, then, is neither overcome nor weakened by it successfully avoids all sin through the practice of continency. If, however, a man escape almost all incitements to sin, but falls prey even to one, such a man is not continent, just as he is not in health who is

---

5 Gen. 21.6.
6 Luke 6.21.
7 Job 8.21.
8 1 Cor. 8.13.
9 1 Cor. 9.12.

suffering from only one bodily affliction and as he is not free who is under the authority of anyone, it matters not whom. Further, the other virtues are practiced in secret and are rarely displayed to men. But continency makes itself known as soon as we meet a person who practices it. As plumpness an a healthy color betoken the athlete, so leanness of body and the pallor produced by the exercise of continency mark the Christian, for he is the true athlete of the commandments of Christ. In weakness of body, he overcomes his opponent and displays his prowess in the contests of piety, according to the words, 'when I am weak, then am I powerful.'[10] So beneficial is it merely to behold the continent man making a sparing and frugal use of necessities, ministering to nature as if this were a burdensome duty and begrudging the time spent in it, and rising promptly from the table in his eagerness for work, that I think no sermon would so touch the soul of one whose appetites are undisciplined and bring about his conversion as merely his meeting with a continent man. Indeed, the reason we are enjoined to eat and drink to the glory of God[11] is, probably, so that our good works may shine forth even at table to the glory of our Father who is in heaven.[12]

Q. 18. That we should taste everything set before us.

R. It should also be laid down as essential that continency is inexorably demanded of combatants for godliness, so that they may bring the body into subjection; 'for every one that striveth for the mastery refraineth himself from all things.'[1] However, to avoid being classed with the enemies of God who

10 2 Cor. 12.10.
11 1 Cor. 10.31.
12 Matt. 5.16.

1 1 Cor. 9.25.

are seared in their conscience and, therefore, abstain from food which God has made for the faithful to partake of with thanksgiving,[2] we should taste each dish when occasion offers so as to indicate to those looking on that 'all things are clean to the clean'[3] and that 'every creature of God is good and nothing to be rejected that is received with thanksgiving; for it is sanctified by the word of God and prayer.'[4] The aim of continency must nevertheless be kept in mind also, to the extent that we satisfy our need with the plainer foods and those necessary to sustain life, avoiding the evil of taking our fill of them and abstaining absolutely from those foods whose sole purpose is to give delight. By acting thus we shall root out the affection for foods whose end is to give pleasure and we shall also cure those who are seared in their conscience as with a hot iron—at least, insofar as this is possible for us— protecting ourselves, meanwhile, from the suspicion of guilt in either direction; for 'why,' says the Apostle, 'is my liberty judged by another man's conscience?'[5] Continency betokens the man who has died with Christ and who mortifies his members that are upon the earth.[6] This virtue we know as the mother of chastity, the protector of health, the effective remover of obstacles to the fruitfulness of good works in Christ, since, according to the word of the Lord, the cares of this world, the pleasures of life, and other desires choke the word and it is thus rendered unfruitful.[7] From this virtue even the demons fly, as the Lord Himself teaches, saying: 'This kind is not cast out but by prayer and fasting.'[8]

---

2 1 Tim. 4.2,3.
3 Titus 1.15.
4 1 Tim. 4.4,5.
5 1 Cor. 10.29.
6 Col. 3.5.
7 Matt. 13.22.
8 Matt. 17.20.

Q. 19. In what measure continency must be practiced.

R. With regard to the affections of the soul, continency has only one rule: complete abstinence from all that tends to harmful pleasure. With reference to food, as individual needs vary according to age, employment, and physical condition, respectively, so, also, the manner of its use and the amount of it differ. It is not possible, therefore, to include under one rule all who are in the school of the devout life. In setting the norm for healthy ascetics, we allow for appropriate deviation on the part of superiors according to particular circumstances. Nor is it possible for one discourse to cover every individual case, but such only as are amenable to the common and general teaching. As regards nourishment to be given the sick for their relief or to one who is exceptionally weary from strenuous work or who is preparing to undertake a laborious task, such as a journey or some other work, superiors will prescribe according to the need, in conformity with the words: 'Distribution was made to each according as every one had need.'[1] It is also impossible to lay down a rule that the time for taking food as well as the manner of taking it and its quantity be the same for all. The objective, however—satisfying need—must be common to all alike. Filling the stomach to satiety, burdening it with food, is an act deserving of malediction as the Lord says: 'Woe to you that are filled now.'[2] Besides, such excess renders the body unfit for work, prone to sleep, and more susceptible to harm. Nor, to be sure, ought pleasure to be made an end in taking food, but the aim should be the sustaining of life for those who have renounced intemperate delights. To become a slave to the pleasures of the table is to make the stomach one's god. Since our body, ever being emptied and drained, needs to be filled (and for this reason our appetite

1 Acts 2.45.
2 Luke 6.25.

for nourishment is natural), right reason dictates as regards
the use of food that we replenish by dry or moist nourishment, as the need may be, what has been used up in order to
sustain animal life.

In consequence, then, whatever is calculated to relieve our
need with the least trouble, this is to be employed. This the
Lord Himself made evident on the occasion when He was
host to the weary multitude lest they faint on the way, as it
it written.[3] Although He could have enhanced the miracle in
the desert by using costly appurtenances, so frugal and simple
was the repast He prepared for them that the bread was of
barley and, besides the bread, there was [only] a little fish.[4]
He does not mention drink, since water which nature provides for all was sufficient for their need. But, according to the
advice of Paul to Timothy, even this beverage should be de-
clined if it be injurious to anyone because of physical weakness.[5] Nothing, in fact, that is known to be harmful should be
partaken of, for it is not reasonable to take food for nourishment which from within us would make war upon the body
and hinder it in the accomplishment of the precept. This same
principle ought to be our guide in accustoming the mind to
shun what is harmful, however alluring it may be. Furthermore, we should prefer by all means whatever is most easily
procurable and not concern ourselves with costly fare and seek
to obtain extravagant foods with expensive sauces on the pretext of continency. On the contrary, we should choose whatever
is easy to obtain in each region, cheap, and available for general consumption, and use only those imported foods that are
necessary to sustain life, like olive oil and similar products.
In addition, if something would be useful for the necessary

---

3 Matt. 15.32.
4 John 6.9.
5 1 Tim. 5.23.

relief of the sick, this, too, is permitted, if it can be procured without difficulty, disturbance, or distraction.

Q. 20. The rule to be followed in serving meals to guests.
R. Vainglory, the desire to please men, and acting for display are strictly forbidden to Christians under all circumstances, because even a man who observes the precept but does it for the purpose of being seen and glorified by men loses the reward for that observance. All manner of vainglory, consequently, is especially to be avoided by those who have embraced every kind of humiliation for the sake of the Lord's command. But, inasmuch as we see men of the world ashamed of the lowliness of poverty and at pains when they entertain guests to have every article of food both abundant and expensive, I fear that, unwittingly, we are being infected by the same vice and that we are ashamed to be found guilty of the poverty called blessed by Christ.[1] Just as it is not proper to provide ourselves with worldly trappings like a silver vessel, or a curtain edged with purple, or a downy couch, or transparent draperies, so we act unfittingly in contriving menus which deviate in any important way from our usual diet. That we should run about searching for anything not demanded by real necessity, but calculated to provide a wretched delight and ruinous vainglory, is not only shameful and out of keeping with our avowed purpose, but it also causes harm of no mean gravity when they who spend their lives in sensual gratification and measure happiness in terms of pleasure for the appetite see us also taken up with the same preoccupations which keep them enthralled. If, indeed, sensual pleasure is evil and to be avoided, we ought on no occasion indulge in it, for nothing that is condemned can at any time be beneficial. They who

---

1 Matt. 5.3.

live riotously and are anointed with the best ointments and drink filtered wine come under the denunciation of the Scripture.[2] Because she lives in pleasure, the widow is dead while she is living.[3] The rich man is debarred from paradise because he lived in luxury upon earth.[4] What, then, have we to do with costly appointments? Has a guest arrived? If he is a brother and follows a way of life aiming at the same objective as ours, he will recognize the fare we provide as properly his own. What he has left at home, he will find with us. Suppose he is weary after his journey. We then provide as much extra nourishment as is required to relieve his weariness.

Is it a secular person who has arrived? Let him learn through actual experience whatever things verbal instruction has not convinced him of, and let him be given a model and pattern of frugal sufficiency in matters of food. Let memories of Christian fare linger in his mind and of a poverty which, because of Christ, gives no cause for shame. If he will not learn this lesson, but adopts a mocking attitude, he will not discommode us a second time. Moreover, when we see the rich placing the enjoyment of sensual delights among the greatest blessings, we should grieve profoundly for them, because they are not aware that, in wasting their whole life in vanities and in making pleasure their god, they have already received their share of blessing in this life and that by living in luxury here they are preparing themselves to burn in the fire reserved for them hereafter. And if occasion ever offers, we should not hesitate to say this to their faces. But, if it should happen that we ourselves are also prone to the same vice of eagerly seeking, insofar as it lies in our power, for what pleases the palate and of making ostentation our aim, I am

---

2 Amos 6.6.
3 1 Tim. 5.6.
4 Luke 16.25.

afraid that we are destroying what we make profession of building up and that we condemn ourselves by the same acts for which we judge others. For we are making a pretense of living in this state of life and have transformed ourselves only in certain respects, unless, to be sure, we even change our outer garb when we associate with distinguished worldlings. If this is a base manner of action, far baser is it to alter our fare to suit the fastidious. The life of the Christian does not vary, inasmuch as its end—the glory of God—is ever the same; for Paul says, speaking in Christ: 'whether you eat or drink or whatsoever else you do, do all to the glory of God.'[5] The life of persons in the world, on the contrary, is complex and varied, adapting itself in diverse ways to gratifying the whims of every chance acquaintance.

If you also change your daily fare, then, for rare quality or abundance in food to please a brother's palate, you imply that he takes delight in sensual pleasure and you heap reproaches upon him for his gluttony by the very preparations you make, since you thus accuse him of finding pleasure in such things. In fact, have we not often guessed who or what sort of guest was expected, upon seeing the appearance and quality of the preparations? The Lord did not praise Martha for being anxious about much serving, but He said: 'Thou art careful and art troubled about many things; few things—nay, one thing only is necessary':[6] 'few things'—that is, for the preparation of the meal, and 'one thing'—that is, the purpose, namely, to satisfy need. You are well aware, also, of what sort of food the Lord Himself placed before the five thousand. Jacob, too, prayed to God as follows: 'If thou shalt give me bread to eat and raiment to put on.'[7] He did not say: 'If

---

5 1 Cor. 10.31.
6 Luke 10.41,42.
7 Gen. 28.20.

thou wilt give me delicacies and sumptuous appointments.'
And what says Solomon, wisest of men? 'Give me neither
beggary nor riches; give me only what is necessary and sufficient, lest being filled I should deny and say: 'Who sees me? Or
being poor, I should steal and forswear the name of my God';[8]
thus representing riches as satiety, poverty as a complete lack
of the necessities of life, and sufficiency as a state both free
from want and without superfluity. Sufficiency varies, however, according to physical condition and present need. One,
because of his work, requires more substantial food and a
larger amount. Another needs a lighter and more digestible
diet and suited in other ways to his weakness, but for all alike
it should be cheap and easily procured. In every case, care
must be taken for a good table, yet without overstepping the
limits of the actual need. This should be our aim in giving hospitality—that the individual requirements of our guests may be
cared for. The Apostle says: 'as if using this world and not
misusing it';[9] unnecessary expenditure, however, is misuse.
Have we no money? So be it. Are not our granaries filled?
What of it! We live from day to day. Our livelihood is the
work of our hands. Why, then, do we waste food given by God
for the poor to gratify the voluptuary, sinning thereby in two
ways: by intensifying for the former the sufferings of their
poverty and increasing the harmful results of satiety for the
latter.

*Q. 21. How one ought to conduct oneself with regard to
sitting and reclining at the midday meal or at supper.*

R. Since it is a precept of the Lord, who on all occasions
habituates us to humility, that we should take the lowest
place in reclining at meals, he who strives to do all according

8 Prov. 30.8,9.
9 1 Cor. 7.31.

to injunction must not neglect this precept.[1] If any world-lings, therefore, should recline with us, it behooves us to be an example in this matter by not exalting ourselves above others or seeking to have the first place. But when all who thus gather together are in pursuit of the same goal, each one, so that at every opportunity they may give proof of their humility, has an obligation of being beforehand in taking the last place, according to the Lord's command. To engage in rivalry and strife in this matter is unseemly, because it destroys good order and is a cause of tumult. Moreover, if we are not willing to yield to one another and conflict arises over it, we shall be classed with those who quarrel over the first places. In this sphere, also, prudently aware of and attentive to what befits us, we therefore should leave the order of seating to the one entrusted with this duty, as the Lord declared when he said that the arrangement of these matters pertains to the master of the house.[2] In this way, we shall support one another in charity,[3] doing all things decently and according to order.[4] Also, we will not give the impression, by stubborn and vigor-ous opposition, that we are trying to appear humble in order to impress the company or to win popular favor, but rather we will practice humility by being obedient. To engage in altercation, indeed, is a surer sign of pride than to accept the first place when we are directed to do so.

Q. 22. On the garb befitting a Christian.

R. Earlier in our discourse it was shown that humility, sim-plicity, thriftiness, and frugality in all things are necessary, so that we might have rare occasion for distraction on the score of our bodily needs. This end we must keep also before

1 Luke 14.10.
2 *Ibid.*
3 Eph. 4.2.
4 1 Cor. 14.40.

our minds in treating of clothing. If it behooves us to seek to
be last of all, clearly the last place is also to be preferred in
this connection. If men who are greedy for renown seek glory
for themselves even in the garments they wear, striving to
attract attention and arouse envy by reason of the splendor
of their dress, it is obvious that one who out of humility
has chosen to pass his life in the lowliest condition of all
ought to prefer for himself even in this particular the last and
the least. Just as the Corinthians were accused of despising,
because of their own expenditures for the public feasts, those
who had not the means for such expenditure,[1] so, in the case
of an ordinary and plain style of dress, he who is turned out
with an elaborateness above the ordinary, by contrast, as it
were, puts the poor man to shame. In the light of the Apostle's
words, 'not minding high things but consenting to the humble,'[2] let each consider for himself whom the Christian more
fittingly resembles—those who live in royal palaces and are
clothed in soft garments, or him, the messenger and herald of
the Lord's advent, than whom no greater born of woman has
arisen,[3] John, I mean, son of Zachary, whose garment was of
camel's hair.[4] The saints of old, moreover, also went about
clad in sheepskins and goatskins.[5]

Now, the Apostle sets the standard for the proper use of
clothing in one sentence when he says: 'Having food and
wherewith to be covered, with these we are content,'[6]—as if
mere covering alone were necessary for us. At any rate, let
us not fall any more into the forbidden boasting—not to speak
of something worse—which accompanies elaborate dress or

1 1 Cor. 11.22.
2 Rom. 12.16.
3 Matt. 11.8,11.
4 Matt. 3.4.
5 Heb. 11.37.
6 1 Tim. 6.8.

the vanity that is likewise prompted by it; for these vices creep subsequently into our lives through the pursuit of vain and worthless arts. The use made in the beginning of the clothing which God Himself gave to the needy has been revealed to us; for the Scripture says: 'God made for them garments of skins.'[7] Such garb was sufficient to cover their nakedness. Since, however, another purpose enters in—that of keeping warm by means of clothing—it is necessary to have both uses in mind: covering for decency's sake and for protection against mischief from the air. Yet, inasmuch as even from this point of view some garments are more useful than others, we should prefer whatever can be put to greater use, so that the principle of poverty may in no way be violated. We should, furthermore, not keep in reserve some garments to wear in public and others for use at home, nor, again, some to be worn in the day time, others at night, but we should contrive to have only one garment which can serve for all occasions: for suitable wear during the day and for necessary covering at night. This manner of acting unites us even in our appearance and the Christian is thus identified by the way he dresses as with a kind of special stamp, for all who aim at the same goal are alike in as many ways as possible. This distinctiveness in dress is also useful as giving advance notice of each of us, by proclaiming our profession of the devout life. Actions in conformity with this profession are, in consequence, expected from us by those whom we meet. The standard of indecorous and unseemly conduct is not the same for ordinary folk as for those who make profession of great aspirations. No one would take particular notice of the man in the street who would inflict blows on a passerby or publicly suffer them himself, or who would use obscene language, or loiter in the

7 Gen. 3.21.

shops, or commit other unseemly actions of this kind. These things are accepted as in keeping with the general course of life in the world. On the other hand, everyone takes notice of him who is bound by promise to strive for perfection, if he neglect the least part of his duty, and they heap reproaches upon him for it, fulfilling the words: 'and turning upon you, they tear you.'[8] A mode of dress, therefore, which denotes one's profession serves to fulfill the office of pedagogue, as it were, for the weak, to keep them from wrongdoing even against their will. As one style of dress bespeaks the soldier, another, a senator, a third, some other high position, so that the rank of these dignitaries can generally be inferred, so also it is right and proper that there be some mark of identity for the Christian which would bear out even as to his garments the good order spoken of by the Apostle. In one place, indeed, he directs that a bishop be a man of orderly behavior;[9] in another, he prescribes that women be clad in decent apparel,[10] the word 'decent' clearly being used in a sense that accords with the specific character of the Christian ideal. This same advice applies also to footwear. On every occasion, a style which is plain, easy to procure, and serviceable should be preferred.

Q. 23. Regarding the cincture.

R. The saints long before us have demonstrated the necessity of a cincture. John bound his loins with a leather girdle[1] as did Elias before him, for it is written (as though this article of dress were specifically proper to a man), 'a hairy man with

---

8 Matt. 7.6.
9 1 Tim. 3.2.
10 1 Tim. 2.9.

---

1 Matt. 3.4.

a girdle of leather about his loins.'[2] Peter also is clearly proved to have worn a girdle by the words of the angel who said to him: 'Gird thyself and put on thy sandals.'[3] It appears from the prophecy of Agabus that the blessed Paul also used a cincture: 'the man whose girdle this is, they shall so bind in Jerusalem.'[4] Job, too, was commanded by the Lord to gird himself. As if this were a kind of sign of virility and of readiness for action, He says to Job: 'Gird up thy loins like a man.'[5] That cinctures were in habitual use among the disciples of the Lord, moreover, is evident from the fact that they were forbidden to carry money in their girdles.[6] It is particularly necessary, also, that one who is about to engage in work be well girt up and unimpeded in his movements. He needs a cincture, therefore, by which his tunic may be gathered close to his body and he will work more comfortably and be more unhampered in his movements when his garment is well wrapped about him. The Lord, also, took a towel and girded Himself when He was preparing to minister to His disciples.[7] With regard to quantity of clothing we need say nothing, since this phase of the subject has been adequately treated above in the passage on poverty.[8] If he who has two tunics is commanded to share with him who has none,[9] the possession of several tunics for his own use clearly is not allowed. What relevance is there, then, in laying down precepts on the use of two tunics for those who are forbidden to possess them?

---

2 2 Kings 1.8.
3 Acts 12.8.
4 Acts 21.11.
5 Job 38.3.
6 Matt. 10.9.
7 John 13.4.
8 Cf. Q. 22.
9 Luke 3.11.

Q. 24. Now that sufficient instruction on these [other] matters has been imparted to us, it would befit us to learn how we ought to live with one another.

R. When the Apostle says: 'But let all things be done decently and according to order,'[1] I think that he refers to the decent and well-ordered way of life in the society of the faithful where the relationship which obtains among the members of the body is maintained. Thus, the one to whom general supervision is entrusted, who appraises what has already been accomplished and plans and provides for what is still to be done, exercises the function of the eye, so to speak. Another does the work of the ear or the hand in hearkening to orders and executing them, and so on for each member of the body. It is important to bear in mind, therefore, the analogy of the parts of the body, where heedlessness or failure to use the members for the end for which they were made by God, the Creator, brings each individual member into danger. If the hand and the foot, for instance, would not follow the guidance of the eye, the former would bring inevitable and fatal ruin upon the whole body and the latter would stumble or even be hurled over a cliff. If the eye would close so as not to see, it would necessarily perish along with the other members suffering the misfortune mentioned above. In the same way, it is hazardous for a superior to be delinquent, since he holds the position of arbiter in everything; for the subject it is injurious and detrimental to be disobedient—especially perilous is it if, in addition, he give scandal to the rest. Each one who shows in his own place a tireless zeal, fulfilling the Apostle's precept, 'In carefulness not slothful,'[2] merits praise for his alacrity; but, for negligence, he deserves the opposite, that is, unhappiness and woe; for the Prophet

---

1 1 Cor. 14.40.
2 Rom. 12.11.

says, 'Cursed be he that doth the work of the Lord negligently.'[3]

Q. 25. That a superior who does not upbraid the sinner is liable to a dreadful judgment.

R. He who is charged with general supervision should feel as if he is liable to an account for each individual under his care. He should bear in mind that if one of the brethren falls into sin, not having been forewarned by him of the ordinance of God, or if, having fallen, he remain in that state, uninstructed as to the manner of making amends, the blood of that one will be required at his hands, as it is written;[1]—especially if he neglect that which is pleasing to God, not through ignorance, but for flattery's sake, accommodating himself to each one's vices and relaxing strict discipline. The Scripture says: 'They that call thee blessed, the same deceive thee and destroy the way of thy steps,'[2] 'but he that troubleth you shall bear the judgment, whosoever he be.'[3] In order that this may not be our lot, let us observe the apostolic rule in our conversations with the brethren; 'For neither,' says St. Paul, 'have we used at any time the speech of flattery, as you know; nor taken an occasion of covetousness, God is witness; nor sought we glory of men, neither of you nor of others.'[4]

Whoever, then, is free from these faults may, perhaps, exercise a leadership free from error, at once profitable to himself and salutary for his subjects. He who acts with true charity and not for the sake of any human honors nor to avoid giving offense to sinners, and for that reason seeking to be agree-

---

3 Jer. 48.10.

---

1 Ezech. 3.20.
2 Isa. 3.12.
3 Gal. 5.10.
4 1 Thess. 2.5,6.

able and pleasant to them, will hold discourse with them sincerely and candidly, not choosing to adulterate the truth in any respect. The following words therefore, apply also to him: 'but we became little ones in the midst of you, as if a nurse should cherish her children, so desirous of you we would gladly impart to you not only the gospel of God but also our own souls.'[5] He who is not such a one is a blind guide, casting himself headlong over the precipice and drawing his followers after him.[6] From these words it can be seen how serious an evil it is to be the cause of a brother's error instead of bearing the responsibility for guiding him aright. It is also a sign that the commandment of love is not being observed, for no father abandons his child when he is about to fall into a pit or leaves him to his fate after he has fallen therein. Needless to say, it is far more dreadful to allow the soul to be destroyed after it has fallen into the pit of evils. The superior is obliged, therefore, to be vigilant on behalf of the souls of the brethren and as seriously concerned for the salvation of each one as if he himself were to render an account for him. He should, furthermore, be solicitous in manifesting his zeal for them even unto death, in accordance not only with the general precept of charity addressed to all by the Lord: 'that a man lay down his life for his friends';[7] but also, in conformity with the special application of it by him who said: 'being desirous of you, we would gladly impart unto you not only the gospel of God, but also our own souls.'[8]

Q. 26. That all matters, even the secrets of the heart, should be placed before the superior.

R. Every subject, if he intends to make any progress worth

---

5 1 Thess. 2.7,8.
6 Luke 6.39.
7 John 15.13.
8 1 Thess. 2.8.

mentioning and to be confirmed in a mode of life that accords with the precepts of our Lord Jesus Christ, ought not conceal within himself any movement of his soul, nor yet utter any thoughtless word, but he should reveal the secrets of his heart to those of his brethren whose office it is to exercise a compassionate and sympathetic solicitude for the weak. In this way, that which is laudable will be ratified and that which is worthy of rebuke will receive the correction it deserves, and by the practice of such co-operative discipline, we shall by a gradual advance attain to perfection.

Q. 27. That the superior himself, if he commit a fault, should be admonished by the more eminent among the brethren.

R. Just as it is the superior's duty to be the leader of the brethren in everything, so, in turn, if ever he is himself suspected of being guilty of a fault, it devolves upon the rest to call it to his attention. That good order may not be disturbed, however, those who are eminent by reason of age and sagacity should be assigned the task of giving the admonition. If, then, there be something deserving of correction, we have benefited our brother and ourselves through him, inasmuch as we are restoring to the straight path him who is an embodiment, as it were, of our rule of life and who should, by his own uprightness, be a reproach to our perversity. If, on the other hand, any are baselessly disturbed on his account, they will be disabused of the bad opinion they had entertained of him, when full information is supplied by a clarification of the matter which had caused groundless suspicions to arise.

Q. 28. What the attitude of all should be toward the disobedient.

R. All should certainly be compassionate at first toward

one who obeys the Lord's commands reluctantly, as toward an ailing member of their body. The superior, also, should endeavor by private exhortation to cure his weakness; but, if he persists in disobedience and is not amenable to correction, he should be severely reprimanded in the presence of the whole community and a remedy, together with every form of exhortation, should be administered. If he is neither converted after much admonition nor cures himself by his own actions with tears and lamentations, being, as the proverb has it, 'his own destroyer,'[1] we should, as physicians do, cut him off from the body of the brethren as a corrupt and wholly useless member. Physicians, indeed, are wont to remove by cutting or burning any member of the body they find infected with an incurable disease, so that the infection may not spread further and destroy adjacent areas one after the other. This we also must do in the case of those who show hostility or create obstacles to the observance of the Lord's commands, according to the Lord's own precept: 'If thy right eye scandalize thee, pluck it out and cast it from thee.'[2] Benevolence to such persons is like that mistaken kindness of Heli which he was accused of showing his sons, contrary to the good pleasure of God.[3] A feigned kindness to the wicked is a betrayal of the truth, an act of treachery to the community, and a means of habituating oneself to indifference to evil, since that saying is not fulfilled: 'Why have ye not rather mourned that he might be taken away from you that hath done this deed.'[4] On the other hand, the saying which follows necessarily comes to pass: 'A little leaven corrupteth the whole lump.'[5] 'Them that sin, reprove before all,' says the Apostle, and he imme-

1 Cf. *PG.* 31.988 n. 20.
2 Matt. 5.29.
3 1 Sam. 3.13.
4 1 Cor. 5.2.
5 1 Cor. 5.6.

diately adds the reason, saying: 'that the rest also may have fear.'[6]

In general, then, whoever refuses the remedy applied by the superior acts inconsistently even with himself; for, if he does not take kindly to being governed and his own will acts as his arbiter, why does he continue to live under a superior? Why does he take him as the director of his life? But, having allowed himself, once and for all, to be reckoned with the body of the community, if he has been judged a suitable vessel for the ministry, when a command appears to be beyond his strength, leaving the decision regarding this to the one who imposed the command, he should show himself obedient and submissive even unto death, remembering that the Lord became 'obedient unto death, even to the death of the cross.'[7] To rebel and to contradict, however, are indications of many evils: a weak faith, a doubtful hope, and a self-important and arrogant character. His disobedience, indeed, implies that he holds in contempt him who gave the order. On the other hand, one who trusts in the promises of God and keeps his hope fixed on these will never draw back from commands, however difficult to execute they may be, knowing that the sufferings of this time are not worthy to be compared with the future glory to be revealed.[8] Furthermore, one who is convinced that 'he that humbleth himself shall be exalted'[9] and bears in mind that 'that which is at present momentary and light of our tribulation worketh above measure exceedingly an eternal weight of glory,'[10] obeys with greater alacrity than he who gives the order expects.

---

6 1 Tim. 5.20.
7 Phil. 2.8.
8 Rom. 8.18.
9 Matt. 23.12.
10 2 Cor. 4.17.

Q. 29. Concerning one who performs his actions in an arrogant or critical spirit.

R. The work of a man who is given to murmuring or self-exaltation should certainly not be coupled with works done by the humble of heart and contrite of spirit. In general, the work of the former should have no value for the pious, 'for that which is high to men is an abomination before God.'[1] There is also another precept of the Apostle which reads: 'Neither do you murmur, as some of them murmured and were destroyed by the destroyer';[2] and again: 'not with sadness or of necessity.'[3] The work of such persons, therefore, even as a blemished sacrifice, should not be accepted, and to include it with the work of the rest is unholy. If those bringing strange fire to the altar were the objects of such mighty wrath,[4] how is it not perilous to accept with a view to observing the command work which proceeds from a spirit that is hateful to God? 'For what participation,' says the Apostle, 'hath justice with injustice? Or what part hath the faithful with the unbeliever?'[5] Wherefore it is said: 'Wicked is he that slayeth a calf in sacrifice to me, as if he should kill a dog; and he that offereth wheaten flour, as if it were swine's blood.'[6] Consequently, it is essential that the works of the sluggard and of the dissenter be rejected by the brethren. The superiors, also, should keep a close watch over this portion of the community that they may not violate the decree of Him who said, 'the man that walked in the perfect way, he served me. He that worketh pride shall not dwell in the

1 Luke 16.15.
2 1 Cor. 10.10.
3 2 Cor. 9.7.
4 Lev. 10.1,2.
5 2 Cor. 6.14,15.
6 Isa. 66.3.

midst of my house.'[7] Nor, furthermore, should superiors accept the work of one who allows sin to enter into his observance of the commandment or spoils his work by a lazy shrinking from toil or by the haughtiness which proceeds from exceptional achievement and which emboldens him to persist in his error by not permitting him to become aware of his own wickedness. It is of the greatest importance, then, that the superior be convinced that if he fails to offer his brother the proper guidance he will draw down upon himself heavy and inescapable wrath, for his blood will be required at his hands, as it is written.[8] The subject also should be prepared not to hesitate before any command, even the most difficult, persuaded that his reward will be great in heaven. Let the hope of glory, therefore, hearten him in his obedience, that the work of the Lord may be done with all joy and patient endurance.

Q. 30. The dispositions which ought to animate the superior in caring for the brethren.

R. His rank should not arouse feelings of pride in the superior, lest he himself lose the blessing promised to humility[1] or 'lest being puffed up with pride he fall into the judgment of the devil.'[2] On the other hand, let him be assured that added responsibility calls for greater service. He who ministers to many wounded persons, wiping away the matter from their wounds and applying medicaments appropriate to the particular injury involved, does not find a motive for pride in his ministrations, but rather for humility, anxiety, and energetic action. Far more thoughtful and solicitous ought he be who, as the servant of all and as being himself liable to an account

7 Ps. 100.6,7.
8 Ezech. 3.18.

1 Matt. 5.3.
2 1 Tim. 3.6.

on their behalf, performs the office of curing the spiritual weakness of his brethren. In this manner he will fulfill the aim which the Lord had in mind when He said: 'If any man desire to be first, he shall be the last of all and the minister of all.'[3]

Q. 31. That ministration from the superior should be accepted.

R. Corporal ministration should be accepted by inferiors from those who may hold the first place in the community. True humility imposes the duty of service upon the superior and shows the subject that to accept such ministration is not unfitting. The example of the Lord Himself, indeed, leads us to this conclusion, since He did not disdain to wash the feet of His disciples and they did not venture to resist Him in this. Peter, to be sure, refused at first because of his great reverence, but, as soon as he learned the penalty of disobedience, he immediately gave way. There is no reason, consequently, why the subject should fear that he is deviating from his ideal of humility if he accepts service from a superior. Many times, in fact, the service is given for his instruction and as a forceful example rather than as a response to some urgent need. He should, therefore, show himself truly humble by his obedience and imitation rather than commit an act of false pride and arrogance by raising objections in feigned humility. Contradiction betokens unruliness and self-will. Even more, it is an indication of pride and disdain, not of humility and obedience in all things. We must, therefore, obey him who said: 'supporting one another in charity.'[1]

---

3 Mark 9.34.

---

1 Eph. 4.2.

Q. 32. On the proper dispositions toward relatives according to the flesh.

R. Superiors should not allow those who have been permanently admitted to the community to be distracted in any way—by allowing them either to leave the company of their brethren and live in private on the pretext of visiting their relatives or to be burdened with the responsibility of caring for their relatives according to the flesh. The Scripture absolutely forbids the words 'mine' and 'thine' to be uttered among the brethren, saying: 'And the multitude of believers had but one heart and one soul; neither did anyone say that aught of the things which he possessed was his own.'[1] The parents or brothers of a member of the community, therefore, if they live piously, should be treated by all the brethren as fathers or other relative possessed in common: 'For whosoever shall do the will of my Father that is in Heaven, he is my brother and sister and mother,' says the Lord.[2] In our opinion, moreover, the care of these persons would devolve upon the superior of the community. If our relatives have become entangled in the usual concerns of the worldly life, we who are intent upon that which is decent and which may give us power to attend upon the Lord without impediment[3] have no common cause with them. In addition to being of no assistance to them, we would fill our own lives with confusion and anxiety and we would invite occasions of sin. Furthermore, it is not even proper to receive those among our former relatives who come for a visit if they hold the commandments in light esteem and are contemptuous of the works of piety, because they do not love the Lord, who said: 'He that loveth me not, keepeth not my words.'[4] 'But what

1 Acts. 4.32.
2 Matt. 12.50.
3 1 Cor. 7.35.
4 John 14.24.

participation hath justice with injustice? Or what fellowship hath light with darkness?"[5]

Besides, the utmost effort must be made entirely to remove occasions of sin from those still in the training school of virtues—the chief of those occasions being the remembrance of their former life in the world—so that it may never be said of them that in their hearts they have returned to Egypt.[6] This very often happens in prolonged conversations with their relatives according to the flesh. In general, therefore, neither these relatives nor any other extern should be allowed to talk with the brethren unless we are certain that their conversation will bring about the edification and perfection of the soul. If, however, it be necessary to hold discourse with those who have been once admitted, it should be done by those who have the gift of speaking, for the reason that they have the power to speak with understanding and to listen in such a way that their faith may be strengthened. The Apostle clearly teaches, indeed, that ability in speaking is not possessed by all but that this charism is accorded to few, saying: 'To one, indeed, by the Spirit is given the word of wisdom, and to another, the word of knowledge';[7] and in another place, he says: 'that he may be able to exhort in sound doctrine and to convince the gainsayers.'[8]

Q. 33 On the proper way to converse with consecrated women.

R. He who has renounced marriage once and for all will surely repudiate with even greater finality those cares which, the Apostle says, plague the married man, that is, how he

---

5 2 Cor. 6.14.
6 Num. 14.4.
7 1 Cor. 12.8.
8 Titus 1.9.

may please his wife,[1] and he will liberate himself entirely from all solicitude about giving pleasure to a woman, since he dreads the judgment of Him who said: 'God hath scattered the bones of them that please men.'[2] Nor will he, therefore, cultivate acquaintance even with a man for the purpose of giving him pleasure, but he will hold discourse with him when it is necessary so as to manifest that zeal for his neighbor which every person is obliged to show according to the command of God. Such discourse, however, should not be allowed indiscriminately to all who so desire, nor is every time and place suitable; but if, according to the Apostle's injunction, we would be without offence to Jews and Gentiles and the church of God[3] and would do all things decently and according to order[4] unto edification, it is necessary that the person, the time, the need, and the place be properly chosen and determined upon. By consideration of all these details, every shadow of evil suspicion will be avoided; evidence of dignity and chastity will be exhibited in every way by those permitted to visit with one another and to take counsel regarding the things that are pleasing to God, as these pertain either to the needs of the body or to the care of the soul. There should be, however, no less than two on each side participating in the discourse, for, to say the least, one person alone is easily exposed to suspicion and what is said under such conditions is not so readily corroborated; for the Scripture explicitly declares that every word stands in the presence of two or three.[5] But there should not be more than three, so as not hamper the zeal for energetic action which is inspired by the command of our Lord Jesus Christ.

---

1 1 Cor. 7.33.
2 Ps. 52.6.
3 1 Cor. 10.32.
4 1 Cor. 14.40.
5 Deut. 19.15.

If it be necessary that some others among the brethren
speak of or listen to something bearing on some private matter, the persons concerned should not themselves meet with
each other, but chosen representatives, persons of advanced
age, should discuss the business with selected older members of
the sisterhood and by their mediation the need for conversing
should be taken care of. The good order followed when women are to converse with men or vice versa should be also be
applied in the case of members of the same sex meeting with
one another. In addition to the qualities of gravity and piety
to be exhibited under all circumstances, they should be wise
in their questions and answers and trustworthy and prudent
in treating of the matters under discussion, thus fulfilling the
words: 'he shall order his words with judgment.'[6] By so
doing they will at once satisfy those who have submitted
their business to them and reach a settlement of the matters
under consideration. Certain other brethren should minister
to the sisters' bodily needs, and these also ought to be chosen
after careful deliberation. They should be of advanced age,
venerable and grave of aspect and deportment, so as not to
afflict the conscience of anyone with evil suspicions, 'for why
is my liberty judged by another man's conscience?'[7]

*Q. 34. Regarding the character of the persons who care for
the needs of the brethren.*

R. It is of the greatest importance that, of those who distribute necessary articles within the community, there will
be some in each department who are able to imitate the
conduct described in the Acts: 'Distribution was made to
every one, according as he had need.'[1] These should take

---

6 Ps. 111.5.
7 1 Cor. 10.29.

---

1 Acts 4.35.

great pains to be kind and tolerant to all and not give occasion for suspicions of favoritism or partiality, in obedience to the precept of the Apostle, who said: 'doing nothing by declining to either side.'[2] On the other hand, they should not act in a spirit of contentiousness, which the same Apostle condemns as unbefitting Christians, saying: 'If any man seem to be contentious, we have no such custom nor the church of God.'[3] The result of such contentiousness is that they deprive those with whom they are at variance of articles which they need and allot a superfluous amount to those to whom they happen to feel partial. Now, the former course is an indication of fraternal enmity, the latter, of particular affection, which is especially abhorrent because by it the union of charity among the brethren is torn asunder and is replaced by base suspicions, jealousies, strife, and a distaste for work.

They who have the office of distributing necessary articles to the community, therefore, are duty-bound to be absolutely free from particular affection and from aversion, both for the reasons just given and for many other pertinent ones of similar nature. They are obliged to take cognizance of such tendencies within themselves and to display such zeal—both they and those who engage in other forms of service to the community—as if they were ministering not to men but to the Lord Himself, who, because of His great goodness, regards as offered to Himself the honor and esteem shown to those who are consecrated to Him and who has promised in return the inheritance of the kingdom of heaven, saying: 'Come, ye blessed of my Father, possess you the kingdom prepared for you from the foundation of the world, for as long as you did it to one of these, my least brethren, you did it

---

2 1 Tim. 5.21.
3 1 Cor. 11.16.

to me.'[4] On the other hand, we must also keep in mind the danger of negligence, recalling him who said: 'Cursed be every man that doth the work of the Lord negligently.'[5] Not only are these cast out of the kingdom, but they also await that dread and terrible sentence of the Lord pronounced upon such persons: 'Depart from me, you cursed, into ever-lasting fire which was prepared for the devil and his angels.'[6] But, if they who bestow care and service find so much profit in their zeal and receive so harsh a judgment for negligence, how necessary it is that they who are the objects of their ministrations should strive to show themselves worthy to be called brethren of the Lord! This the Lord teaches us when He says: 'For whosoever shall do the will of my Father, that is in heaven, he is my brother and sister and mother.'[7]

That man, indeed, is in danger who does not throughout his whole life place before himself the will of God as his goal, so that in health he shows forth the labor of love by his zeal for the works of the Lord, and in sickness displays endurance and cheerful patience. The first and greatest peril is that, by not doing the will of God, he separates himself from the Lord and cuts himself off from fellowship with his own brethren; secondly, that he ventures, although undeserving, to claim a share in the blessings prepared for those who are worthy. Here, also, we must remember the words of the Apostle: 'And we helping do exhort you that you receive not the grace of God in vain.'[8] And they who are called to be brethren of the Lord should not receive in a wanton spirit so great a divine grace nor fall from so high a dignity through negli-

4 Matt. 25.34,40.
5 Jer. 48.10.
6 Matt. 25.41.
7 Matt. 12.50.
8 2 Cor. 6.1.

gence in doing the will of God, but, rather, obey the same Apostle, saying: 'I, a prisoner in the Lord, beseech you that you walk worthy of the vocation in which you are called.'[9]

Q. 35. Whether there should be several communities in the same parish.

R. The example of the members of the body which we have usefully applied so often is appropriate also to the question before us. Our discourse has shown that if the body is to be in good condition and rightly disposed for all its activities, the eyes, the tongue, and the other members which are essential and exercise the highest authority over the body are needed; yet it is difficult and no easy matter to find a soul having the capacity to act as an eye for a number of persons. If good discipline require that the brethren have a superior who is provident, experienced in speaking, sober and kindly, seeking after the justifications of God with a perfect heart,[1] how is it possible for a number of persons of such calibre to be found in the same parish? If it should ever happen, however, that two or three such are found (not an easy thing and we have never known it to happen), it would be far better if they shared responsibility with one another and lightened the burden so that, in the absence of one or the other or in the event of their being engaged or under any other circumstances whereby one superior happens to be absent from the community, the other might console the brethren for his absence; or, even apart from such emergencies, that one of them may go to another community which is in need of a director. Moreover, in order to reach the goal we have set for ourselves, experience in the ways of the world can help

9 Eph. 4.1.

1 1 Par. 28.9; Ps. 118.145.

us greatly. As in the world, those skilled in ordinary trades are jealous of their rivals, because the very nature of the situation imperceptibly engenders a spirit of competition, so also, even in a way of life such as ours, the same state of affairs frequently exists. Beginning with a rivalry in doing good and an eagerness to outdo one another either in hospitality to guests or in multiplying the number of their members or other activities of the kind, they, by degrees, fall to wrangling. Thereupon, instead of restful retirement, the brethren who stop at these monasteries enroute suffer great doubt and distress, since they are perplexed as to which group they should lodge with; for, showing preference causes hard feelings and it is impossible to satisfy both contenders, particularly if there happens to be need for haste. Then, too, these rivalries cause great distress to those who are entering upon their life in community, since they must select certain directors and the act of choosing certain ones at all implies rejection of the rest as unfit.

Directly at the start, then, they suffer harm through pride of intellect, because they are not conforming to what is being taught them, but are becoming accustomed to sit as habitual judges and critics of the community. Since, therefore, there is no admitted good and so much that is of an opposite nature in the separation of establishments, this segregation is from all points inexpedient. If there should be such a system already in operation, it should be quickly set to rights—particularly if ill effects have already been felt—for a continuance of such an arrangement will bring open strife. 'But if any man seem to be contentious,' says the Apostle, 'we have no such custom, nor the church of God.'[2] What objection will be raised to union? The procuring of the necessities? They are far more easily obtained in common, for one lamp and one heart and

---

2 1 Cor. 11.16.

all such things can suffice for the entire group, and in these matters, if anywhere, facility should in every way be sought, so as to reduce the number of necessary articles to be owned. Under the system of separate establishments, more persons are needed to supply the brethren with necessities from outside, but, when establishments are joined, only half as many are required. And how difficult it is to find a man who will not bring dishonor upon the Name of Christ and who, when he goes abroad, conducts himself with externs in a manner worthy of his profession is well known to you without any words of mine. Besides, how can they who remain separated and who by their not living in union arouse base suspicions against themselves, edify those who live the common life either by compelling them to live in peace, if this should be necessary, or by exhorting them to the observance of the other commandments? Moreover, we have heard the words of the Apostle to the Philippians: 'Fulfill ye my joy, that you be of one mind, having the same charity, being of one accord, agreeing in sentiment. Let nothing be done through contention, neither by vainglory; but in humility let each one esteem others better than themselves; each one not considering the things that are his own but those that are other men's.'

Now, what greater sign of humility is there than for the superiors of the community to submit to one another? If they are equal in spiritual gifts, their mutual exercise of virtue is the more beautiful. As the Lord Himself has given us the example by sending the disciples two and two,[4] so also, of these, one will be willing to yield joyfully and wholeheartedly to the other, calling to mind the words of the Lord: 'he that humbleth himself shall be exalted.'[5] But if one be

3 Phil. 2.2-4.
4 Mark 6.7.
5 Luke 18.14.

surpassed in spiritual gifts by the other, it is more virtuous for the weaker to be ruled by the stronger. Again, the maintenance of separate establishments would surely constitute manifest disobedience to the precept of the Apostle: 'each one not considering the things that are his own but those that are other men's.'[6] I think, indeed, that it is impossible for this injunction to be observed where there is separation, inasmuch as each section is privately occupied with the care of its own members and is without solicitude for the others, a state of affairs which is, as I said, clearly opposed to the apostolic precept. And since the saints mentioned in the Acts frequently testify to its observance, now by the words: 'And the multitude of believers had but one heart and one soul,'[7] and again: 'All they that believed were together and had all things common,'[8] there very evidently was no dwelling apart for any of them nor did each individual lead an independent life, but all were governed under one and the same supervision, even though their full number was five thousand; and, perhaps, many factors in their situation appeared in man's judgment to be obstructive of harmonious union. What rational grounds, then, permit those in a single parish who are so much less numerous to live separated from one another? Would it were possible that not only they who are in the same parish and are living together would remain thus united, but that many more communities of brethren now established in separated places would be governed in the unity of the Spirit and in the bond of peace[9] under the combined supervision of superiors who could firmly and wisely look after the interests of all.

6 Phil. 2.4.
7 Acts 4.32.
8 Acts 2.44.
9 Eph. 4.3.

Q. 36. Of those who leave the brotherhood.

R. Certainly, those who have made an irrevocable and reciprocal promise to live together cannot leave at will, inasmuch as their not persevering in what they have pledged comes from one of two causes: either from the wrongs suffered in living the common life or from an unsteadiness of resolution in him who is changing his course. But he who is withdrawing from his brethren because of injury sustained should not keep his motive to himself, but should make an open charge respecting the wrong done him, in the manner taught by the Lord, who said: 'If thy brother shall offend, go and rebuke him between thee and him alone,'[1] and so on. Then, if the amendment he desires is effected, he has gained his brethren and has not dishonored their union. But, if he sees that they persist in the evil and are not willing to make amends, he will report this to those empowered to judge in such cases, and then, after several have given testimony [if he cannot get redress], he may withdraw. In acting thus, he will not be separating himself from brethren but from strangers, for the Lord compares one who persists in evil to a heathen and publican: 'let him be to thee as the heathen and publican.'[2] If, however, by reason of the fickleness of his nature, he leaves the society of his brethren, let him cure his own weakness, or, if he will not do this, let the brotherhoods refuse to accept him. And if, by the Lord's command, one or another is attracted to some other establishment, such do not sever their relations, but they fulfill the ministry. Reason does not admit any other grounds for the brethren leaving their community; in the first place, because such withdrawal brings dishonor upon the Name of our Lord Jesus Christ, which is

1 Matt. 18.15.
2 Matt. 18.17.

the basis of their union; second, because it inevitably creates uneasiness in the conscience of each one as regards his neighbor, and mutual suspicions are aroused—both of which eventualities are clearly opposed to the Lord's precept: 'If thou offer thy gift at the altar, and there thou remember that thy brother hath anything against thee, leave there thy offering before the altar and go first to be reconciled to thy brother; and then, coming, thou shalt offer thy gift.'[3]

Q. 37. Whether prayer and psalmody ought to afford a pretext for neglecting our work, what hours are suitable for prayer, and, above all, whether labor is necessary.

R. Our Lord Jesus Christ says: 'He is worthy'—not everyone without exception or anyone at all, but 'the workman, of his meat,'[1] and the Apostle bids us labor and work with our own hands the things which are good, that we may have something to give to him that suffereth need.[2] It is, therefore, immediately obvious that we must toil with diligence and not think that our goal of piety offers an escape from work or a pretext for idleness, but occasion for struggle, for ever greater endeavor, and for patience in tribulation, so that we may be able to say: 'In labor and painfulness, in much watchings, in hunger and thirst.'[3] Not only is such exertion beneficial for bringing the body into subjection, but also for showing charity to our neighbor in order that through us God may grant sufficiency to the weak among our brethren, according to the example given by the Apostle in the Acts when he says: 'I have showed you all things, how that so laboring you

---

3 Matt. 5.23,24.

---

1 Matt. 10.10.
2 Eph. 4.28.
3 2 Cor. 11.27.

ought to support the weak,'[4] and again: 'that you may have something to give to him that suffereth need.'[5] Thus we may be accounted worthy to hear the words: 'Come, ye blessed of my Father, possess you the kingdom prepared for you from the foundation of the world. For I was hungry and you gave me to eat; I was thirsty and you gave me to drink.'[6]

But why should we dwell upon the amount of evil there is in idleness, when the Apostle clearly prescribes that he who does not work should not eat.[7] As daily sustenance is necessary for everyone, so labor in proportion to one's strength is also essential. Not vainly has Solomon written in praise: 'and she hath not eaten her bread idle.'[8] And again, the Apostle says of himself: 'neither did we eat any man's bread for nothing, but in labor and in toil we worked night and day';[9] yet, since he was preaching the Gospel, he was entitled to receive his livelihood from the Gospel. The Lord couples sloth with wickedness, saying: 'Wicked and slothful servant.'[10] Wise Solomon, also, praises the laborer not only in the words already quoted, but also, in rebuking the sluggard, associating him by contrast with the tiniest of insects: 'Go to the ant, O sluggard.'[11] We have reason to fear, therefore, lest, perchance, on the day of judgment this fault also may be alleged against us, since He who has endowed us with the ability to work demands that our labor be proportioned to our capacity; for He says: 'To whom they have committed much, of him they will demand the more.'[12] Moreover, because some use prayer

---

4 Acts 20.35.
5 Eph. 4.28.
6 Matt. 25.34,35.
7 2 Thess. 3.10.
8 Prov. 31.27.
9 2 Thess. 3.8.
10 Matt. 25.26.
11 Prov. 6.6.
12 Luke 12.48.

and psalmody as an excuse for neglecting their work, it is necessary to bear in mind that for certain other tasks a particular time is allotted, according to the words of Ecclesiastes: 'All things have their season.'[13] For prayer and psalmody, however, as also, indeed, for some other duties, every hour is suitable, that, while our hands are busy at their tasks, we may praise God sometimes with the tongue (when this is possible or, rather, when it is conducive to edification); or, if not, with the heart, at least, in psalms, hymns and spiritual canticles, as it is written.[14] Thus, in the midst of our work can we fulfill the duty of prayer, giving thanks to Him who has granted strength to our hands for performing our tasks and cleverness to our minds for acquiring knowledge, and for having provided the materials, both that which is in the instruments we use and that which forms the matter of the arts in which we may be engaged, praying that the work of our hands may be directed toward its goal, the good pleasure of God.

Thus we acquire a recollected spirit—when in every action we beg from God the success of our labors and satisfy our debt of gratitude to Him who gave us the power to do the work, and when, as has been said, we keep before our minds the aim of pleasing Him. If this is not the case, how can there be consistency in the words of the Apostle bidding us to 'pray without ceasing,'[15] with those others, 'we worked night and day.'[16] Nor, indeed, because thanksgiving at all times has been enjoined even by law and has been proved necessary to our life from both reason and nature, should we therefore be negligent in observing those times for prayer customarily established in communities—times which we have inevitably selected because each period contains a reminder peculiar to

---

13 Eccle. 3.1.
14 Col. 3.16.
15 1 Thess. 5.17.
16 2 Thess. 3.8.

itself of blessings received from God. Prayers are recited early in the morning so that the first movements of the soul and the mind may be consecrated to God and that we may take up no other consideration before we have been cheered and heartened by the thought of God, as it is written: 'I remembered God and was delighted,'[17] and that the body may not busy itself with tasks before we have fulfilled the words: 'To thee will I pray, O Lord; in the morning thou shalt hear my voice. In the morning I will stand before thee and will see.'[18] Again at the third hour the brethren must assemble and betake themselves to prayer, even if they may have dispersed to their various employments. Recalling to mind the gift of the Spirit bestowed upon the Apostles at this third hour, all should worship together, so that they also may become worthy to receive the gift of sanctity, and they should implore the guidance of the Holy Spirit and His instruction in what is good and useful, according to the words: 'Create a clean heart in me, O God, and renew a right spirit within my bowels. Cast me not away from thy face; and take not thy holy Spirit from me. Restore unto me the joy of thy salvation and strengthen me with a guiding spirit.'[19] Again, it is said elsewhere, 'Thy good spirit shall lead me into the right land';[20] and having prayed thus, we should again apply ourselves to our tasks.

But, if some, perhaps, are not in attendance because the nature or place of their work keeps them at too great a distance, they are strictly obliged to carry out wherever they are, with promptitude, all that is prescribed for common observance, for 'where there are two or three gathered together in my name,' says the Lord, 'there am I in the midst of

---

17 Ps. 76.4.
18 Ps. 5.4,5.
19 Ps. 50.12-14.
20 Ps. 142.10.

them.'[21] It is also our judgment that prayer is necessary at the
sixth hour, in imitation of the saints who say: 'Evening and
morning and at noon I will speak and declare; and he shall
hear my voice.'[22] And so that we may be saved from invasion
and the noonday Devil,[23] at this time, also, the ninetieth Psalm
will be recited. The ninth hour, however, was appointed as a
compulsory time for prayer by the Apostles themselves in
the Acts where it is related that 'Peter and John went up to
the temple at the ninth hour of prayer.'[24] When the day's
work is ended, thanksgiving should be offered for what has
been granted us or for what we have done rightly therein and
confession made of our omissions whether voluntary or involuntary, or of a secret fault, if we chance to have committed
any in words or deeds, or in the heart itself; for by prayer
we propitiate God for all our misdemeanors. The examination
of our past actions is a great help toward not falling into like
faults again; wherefore the Psalmist says: 'the things you say
in your hearts, be sorry for them upon your beds.'[25]

Again, at nightfall, we must ask that our rest be sinless and
untroubled by dreams. At this hour, also, the ninetieth Psalm
should be recited. Paul and Silas, furthermore, have handed
down to us the practice of compulsory prayer at midnight,
as the history of the Acts declares: 'And at midnight Paul and
Silas praised God.'[26] The Psalmist also says: 'I rose at midnight to give praise to thee for the judgments of thy justifications.'[27] Then, too, we must anticipate the dawn by prayer,
so that the day may not find us in slumber and in bed, accord-

21 Matt. 18.20.
22 Ps. 54.18.
23 Ps. 90.6.
24 Acts 3.1.
25 Ps. 4.5.
26 Acts 16.25.
27 Ps. 118.62.

ing to the words: "My eyes have prevented the morning; that I might meditate on thy words.'[28] None of these hours for prayer should be unobserved by those who have chosen a life devoted to the glory of God and His Christ. Moreover, I think that variety and diversity in the prayers and psalms recited at appointed hours are desirable for the reason that routine and boredom, somehow, often cause distraction in the soul, while by change and variety in the psalmody and prayers said at the stated hours it is refreshed in devotion and renewed in sobriety.

Q. 38. Now that our discourse has adequately demonstrated that prayer is not to be neglected and that labor is necessary, it remains that we should be taught what sort of trades are suitable to our profession.

R. It is not easy to make a selection of certain trades in particular, because different ones are pursued by various persons according to the nature of localities and the opportunities offered in each region. It can be laid down as a general rule, however, that those trades should be chosen which allow our life to be tranquil and undisturbed, involving no difficulty in the procuring of the materials proper to them, nor requiring much exertion in selling the articles produced, nor leading to unsuitable or harmful association with men or women. In all things we must keep in mind that our special aim is simplicity and frugality and we must avoid pampering the foolish and harmful desires of men by working for the ends sought after by them. In the art of weaving we should employ our skill to produce goods which are for common use in daily life, not in making articles which have been devised by persons of lax morals as a trap and a snare for the young.

---

28 Ps. 118.148.

Likewise, in practicing the art of the shoemaker, we should serve by our skill those who seek to satisfy their real needs. As for the arts of building, carpentry, the smith's trade, and farming—these are all in themselves necessary for carrying on life, and they provide much that is useful. They should not, therefore, be repudiated by us for any reason inherent in themselves, but, as soon as they cause us anxiety or sever our union with the brethren, we must turn away from them, choosing in preference the trades which allow us to lead recollected lives in constant attendance on the Lord and do not cause those who follow the practices of the devout life to be absent from psalmody and prayer or draw them away from other disciplinary practices. Those trades, then, which involve no detriment to the life we have undertaken are to be given a decided preference—agriculture especially, since its proper function is the procuring of necessities and farmers are not obliged to do much traveling or running about hither and thither; but its practice must comply with the condition we have laid down: that it does not cause us disturbance or trouble from neighbors or associates.

Q. 39. The method to be followed in selling our products and the manner in which we should make journeys.

R. We should take care not to dispose of our products in a distant market nor should we go about peddling them. Staying in one place is far more seemly and beneficial, both for mutual edification and for the strict observance of daily routine. Thus, we should prefer lowering the price of the articles to traveling about for the sake of a small profit. If experience shows, however, that the former expedient is impossible, we should choose localities and cities inhabited by devout men, so that our sojourn may not be without fruit for us. The brethren, moreover, should travel in groups to the designated fairs, each carrying the fruits of his own toil. They should start out together, so that the journey may be made with the recitation of prayers and psalms and so afford mutual edification. When they have arrived at their destination, they should choose the same lodging in the interest of mutual protection, and so as not to miss any of the hours for prayer, day or night, and also because transactions with persons who are difficult to deal with or avaricious pass off with less damage when handled by a group rather than by one individual. Even persons who are most given to violence do not wish to have many witnesses of their wrong-doing.

Q. 40. Concerning business transactions at public assemblies.

R. Reason tells us, however, that commercial transactions are unseemly in places where the shrines of the martyrs are located; for it does not befit Christians to appear at these shrines or in their environs for any other purpose than to pray and, by recalling to memory the saints' conflict unto death in behalf of piety, to be animated to a like zeal. They should be mindful, also, of the most dread wrath of the Lord, because, even though He is always and everywhere meek and humble of heart, as it is written,[1] yet He threatened with the scourge those—and those only—buying and selling in the temple,[2] because trafficking in merchandise changed this house of prayer into a den of thieves. Furthermore, when others are setting us an example of disregarding the practice which obtained among the saints, by making the shrines the occasion and place for a market and a fair and common trade instead of praying for one another, adoring God together, imploring His aid with tears, making satisfaction for their sins, thank-

---

1 Matt. 11.29.
2 John 2.15.

ing Him for His benefactions and strengthening their faith by
hearing words of exhortation (practices which we know to
have occurred within our own memory), we ought not to imitate them and confirm their unseemly conduct by also participating in such commercial pursuits. We should, on the contrary, imitate those assemblies described in the Gospel as taking place in the time of our Lord Jesus Christ and obey the
injunction of the Apostle as complying with the rule established by so illustrious a precedent. He writes as follows:
'When you come together, every one of you hath a psalm,
hath a doctrine, hath a revelation, hath a tongue, hath an
interpretation; let all things be done to edification.'[3]

Q. 41. Of authority and obedience.

R. Even in the case of authorized trades, the individual
ought not be permitted to follow the one he is skilled in or
the one he wishes to learn, but that for which he may be
judged suited. He who denies himself and completely sets
aside his own wishes does not do what he wills but what he
is directed to do. Nor, indeed, does reason permit that he
himself make choice of what is good and useful, since he has
irrevocably turned over the disposal of himself to others who
will appoint the task for which they in the Lord's Name may
find him suited. Whoever chooses a task conformed to his
personal wish brings accusation against himself; first, of self-
gratification; second, of preferring a certain trade for the sake
of worldly renown or hope of gain, or some such reason, or
of choosing the easier course out of sloth and indifference.
To be guilty of such faults, however, is an indication that a
man is not yet free from evil passions. Nor, to be sure, has he
practiced self-denial, since in his eagerness to give full play

---

3 1 Cor. 14.26.

to his own impulses he does not give up the things of this world, being still held captive by prospects of gain and renown. Neither has he mortified his members which are upon the earth,[1] since he does not endure fatigue in his labors, but betrays his own wilfullness by regarding his private judgment as more reliable than the appraisal of him on the part of several others. One who is master of a trade that is in no way objectionable to the community ought not abandon it, however, for to deem of no account that which is at one's immediate disposal is the sign of a fickle mind and an unstable will. And if a man is unskilled, he should not of himself take up a trade, but should accept the one approved by his superiors, so as to safeguard obedience in all things. Now, just as it has been shown to be unfitting that one should rely upon oneself, so it is forbidden also to refuse to submit to the decision of others. And if one is adept in a trade that is unacceptable to the community, he should be ready to renounce it in proof that he has no affection for anything in this world. To follow personal preference is, in the words of the Apostle, the act of one who has no hope;[2] but to be obedient in all things is worthy of approbation, since the same Apostle praises certain persons because 'they gave their own selves first to the Lord, then also to us, by the will of God.'[3]

For the rest, everyone should be devoted to his own trade, applying himself to it enthusiastically and accomplishing it blamelessly with ready zeal and careful attention, as if God were his overseer, so that he may ever be able to say in all honesty: 'Behold, as the eyes of servants are on the hands of their masters, so are our eyes unto the Lord our God';[4] but one should not work now at one kind of task, now at another.

---

1 Col. 3.5.
2 1 Thess. 4.12.
3 2 Cor. 8.5.
4 Ps. 122.2.

We are incapable by nature of following successfully a number of pursuits at the same time; to finish one task with diligent care is more beneficial than to undertake many and not complete them. If the mind is distracted by several occupations and passes from one to another, besides the fact that nothing is perfectly finished, such procedure betokens levity of character as already present or, if not that, as being inculcated. In case of necessity, however, one who has the ability may assist in other trades besides his own. Yet this also should not be done of one's own volition, but only upon being summoned, for we should have recourse to this expedient at the call of emergency and not on our own initiative; just as, in the case of our bodily members, we support ourselves with the hand when the foot is limping. Again, as it is not good to take up a trade on one's personal initiative, so, not to accept one that is appointed deserves censure, to prevent the vice of contumacy from being fostered or the limits of docility and obedience from being transgressed. Furthermore, the care of tools devolves, first of all, upon the artisan of each trade. If it should happen, however, that some oversight occur, those who first notice it should take the proper steps, on the ground that the tools are possessed by all in common; although their use is a private matter, the benefit from them is for all, and to regard the instruments of another's trade with disdainful indifference betrays a want of community spirit. It is not fitting, moreover, for those who follow trades to exercise such authority over their tools as not to permit the superior of the community to use them for whatever purpose he wishes, or that they should of themselves take the liberty of selling or exchanging them, or getting rid of them in any other way, or of acquiring others in addition to those they have. How could he who has irrevocably chosen not to be master even of his own hands and who has consigned to another the direction of their activity, how could he be consistent in maintaining full authority over the tools of his trade, arrogating to himself the dignity of mastership over them?

Q. 42. On the aim and the dispositions with which work-men should perform their tasks.

R. This we must also keep in mind—that he who labors ought to perform his task not for the purpose of ministering to his own needs thereby, but that he may accomplish the Lord's command: 'I was hungry and you gave me to eat,'[1] and so on. To be solicitous for oneself is strictly forbidden by the Lord in the words: 'Be not solicitous for your life, what you shall eat, nor for your body, what you shall put on,' and He adds thereto: 'for after all these things do the heathens seek.'[2] Everyone, therefore, in doing his work, should place before himself the aim of service to the needy and not his own satisfaction. Thus will he escape the charge of self-love and receive the blessing for fraternal charity from the Lord, who said: 'As long as you did it to one of these, my least brethren, you did it to me.'[3] Nor should anyone think that the Apostle is at variance with our words when he says: 'that working they would eat their own bread';[4] this is addressed to the unruly and indolent, and means that it is better for each person to minister to himself at least and not be a burden to others than to live in idleness. 'For we have heard,' he says, 'there are some among you who walk disorderly, working not at all, but curiously meddling. Now we charge them that are such, and beseech them by the Lord Jesus Christ, that, working with silence, they would eat their own bread.'[5] Again, that saying,

---

1 Matt. 25.35.
2 Matt. 6.25,32.
3 Matt. 25.40.
4 2 Thess. 3.12.
5 2 Thess. 3.11,12.

'we worked night and day lest we should be chargeable to any of you'[6] bears on the same point, inasmuch as the Apostle in the name of fraternal charity had burdened himself with labors in excess of those imposed upon him for the purpose of eliminating the disorderly. But, he who is striving eagerly for perfection should work night and day 'that he may have something to give to him that suffereth need.'[7]

A man who relies upon himself, however, or even upon the person whose duty it is to provide for his needs, and thinks that his own activity or that of his associate is a sufficient resource for his livelihood, runs the risk, as he places his hope in man, of falling under the curse which reads: 'Cursed be the man that trusteth in man and maketh flesh his arm and whose soul departeth from the Lord.'[8] Now, by the words, 'that trusteth in man,' the Scripture forbids a man to place his hope in another, and by the words, 'and maketh flesh his arm,' it forbids him to trust in himself. Either course is termed a defection from the Lord. Further, in adding the final issue of both: 'He shall be like tamaric in the desert and he shall not see when good shall come,'[9] the Scripture declares that for anyone to place his trust either in himself or in anyone else is to alienate himself from the Lord.

Q. 43. The manner in which tasks should be performed has been adequately set forth unless we should be led by the teaching of actual experience to make further inquiries. We request, however, a thorough analysis of the question as to what sort of persons superiors of the community should be and how they should govern their fellow religious.

---

6 2 Thess. 3.8.
7 Eph. 4.28.
8 Jer. 17.5.
9 Jer. 17.6.

R. This aspect of the matter has already been treated in a summary way, as it were; but, since you do well in wishing it clarified still further (for as the chief and leader is, so also, as a rule, is the subject wont to be), it is essential that we do not pass over this question in a cursory manner. So, then, the superior, mindful of the Apostle's precept: 'Be thou an example of the faithful,'[1] should make his life a shining model for the observance of every commandment of the Lord, so that there may be no excuse for those under his guidance to think the Lord's commands impossible or readily to be set aside. To consider first, then, that which is first in importance —he should be, by the love of Christ, so confirmed in humility that, even if he is silent, the example of his actions may afford more effective instruction than any words. If, indeed, the goal of Christianity is the imitation of Christ according to the measure of His Incarnation, insofar as is conformable with the vocation of each individual, they who are entrusted with the guidance of many others are obliged to animate those still weaker than themselves, by their assistance, to the imitation of Christ, as the blessed Paul says: 'Be ye followers of me, as I also am of Christ.'[2]

Superiors, therefore, should first make of themselves an exact copy of Him by practicing humility according to the standard set by our Lord Jesus Christ, for He says: 'Learn of me, because I am meek and humble of heart.'[3] Habitual mildness of manner, then, and humility of heart should characterize the superior. If the Lord was not ashamed to minister to His own servants and was willing to be a servant to earth and clay which He Himself had formed and shaped into a man ('For I am,' He says, 'in the midst of you as he that serveth'[4]),

---

1 1 Tim. 4.12.
2 1 Cor. 11.1.
3 Matt. 11.29.
4 Luke 22.27.

what must we do to our equals that we may deem ourselves to have arrived at the imitation of Him? So far, then, there is this one quality with which the superior should be endowed. Second, he should be kind and patient with those who from inexperience fall short in their duty, not failing to reprove them for their sins, but bearing gently with the intractable and applying remedies with all kindliness and moderation. He should likewise be competent in determining the kind of treatment required by the disorder, not scolding in a spirit of contempt, but admonishing and instructing with modesty, as it is written.[5] He should be sober in administering worldly goods, provident of the future, knowing how to contend with the strong and how to bear the infirmities of the weak and able to say and do all things unto the perfecting of his brethren. He should not take upon himself the office of superior of himself, but should be chosen by the heads of the other monasteries and he should be one who has in the past given sufficient proof of his character. 'And let these also first be proved,' says the Apostle, 'and so let them minister, having no crime.'[6] A person of this sort, therefore, ought to hold the office of superior; let him establish good order among the brethren, making an allotment of tasks according to the fitness of each member.

Q. 44. Who should be permitted to go on journeys and how they ought to be interrogated upon their return.

R. Permission for going abroad should be granted to him who is able to accomplish the journey without injury to his soul and with profit to his companions. If a suitable person is not available, it is better to endure every inconvenience and trouble, even to the point of death, in the lack of necessary supplies, rather than to allow certain injury to the soul for

---

5 2 Tim. 2.25.
6 1 Tim. 3.10.

the sake of physical comfort ('For it is good for me to die,' says the Apostle, 'rather than that any man should make my glory void'[1]). If this is true with regard to matters in which choice was permitted, how much more applicable is it to those involving a command! Yet, to be sure, the law of charity leaves us some recourse even here; for, if it should happen that in one community there be no one of the brethren who can be sent without risk, neighboring monasteries will supply what is lacking, making journeys in common and without separation from one another, in order that those who are weak in spirit or suffering from bodily illness may be kept safe through close union with their stronger companions. These arrangements should be made in advance by the superior, so that recourse may not be wanting at the very moment of emergency. After the return, moreover, examination should be made of the journey as to the incidents which occurred, the sort of persons met with by the traveler along the way, the discourse held with them, the musings of his soul, and as to whether he passed every day and night in the fear of God or went astray and violated any precept, either by yielding to external circumstances or by giving in to his own natural indolence.

Thereupon, what was rightly done should be accorded the seal of approval, but a fault should be corrected by appropriate and skillful instruction. Travelers will thus be more watchful because they are liable to account, and we shall not appear indifferent to their conduct even when they are separated from us. The history of the Acts, moreover, shows that this was also a customary practice with the saints, when it teaches us that Peter, upon his return to Jerusalem, gave an account to the faithful of his sojourn among the Gentiles[2] and that

---

1 1 Cor. 9.15.
2 Acts 11.4ff.

Paul and Barnabas, after their arrival, assembled the church and proclaimed all that God had done by them; and again, that the entire throng remained silent and listened to Barnabas and Paul relating the things God had wrought.[3] The chief point for us to keep in mind, however, is that running hither and thither, business transactions, and commercial profits should be entirely shunned by members of religious communities.

Q. 45. That there should be another person after the superior who, should the latter be on a journey or not at leisure, could take charge of the brethren.

R. Since it frequently happens by reason of physical weakness, or the necessity of travel, or some other circumstance, that the superior is absent from the community, some other person approved by him and by others who are competent to judge should be selected to take charge of the brethren in his absence, that there may be one person to address words of exhortation and solace to those who remain at home. This will also ensure that, when the superior is away, the brethren will not adopt a popular system of government, as it were, to the abrogation of the rule and traditional discipline, but will preserve established and approved customs unto the glory of God. By this arrangement, too, there will be some one person to give prudent answers to guests, so that they who require discourse may be edified by the admirable presentation of the subject and that the rank and file of the community may not be embarrassed. If all indiscriminately would hasten to seize the opportunity for talking, it would be both a source of distraction and a sign of disorder. The Apostle does not permit several persons to speak on the same ocasion, even though they are endowed with the gift of teaching, for he says; 'But

---

3 Acts 15.12.

if anything be revealed to another, let the first hold his peace.'[1] Again he demonstrates the absurdity of a lack of order in this regard when he says: 'If therefore the whole church come together into one place, and all speak with tongues and there come in unlearned persons or infidels, will they not say that you are mad?'[2]

Even if a stranger should address his inquiries through ignorance to some other person and although he who is questioned by mistake is able to make a satisfactory reply, yet, for the sake of good order, he should keep silence and direct the stranger to him whose function this is, as did the Apostles when the Lord was present. In this way, speech will be employed in a well-ordered and fitting manner. If in the treatment of bodily ills it is not permissible for everyone to use the knife for the cure of those who are ill, but the office of him who has learned the art after a long period of instruction, application, and experience in curing the sick, how is it at all reasonable for the ordinary person to be forward in offering his aid in affecting a cure that is wrought by the word? In this kind of ministration, the least defect works very great harm; for, if not even the distribution of bread is allowed to be made by all among the brethren indiscriminately and if this duty belongs to him who has been approved for the office, how much greater need there is that a person of superior competence, carefully and cautiously chosen, dispense spiritual nourishment to those who ask for it? It is, therefore, no venial act of arrogance for anyone to venture to answer casually and with assurance a question which has to do with the judgment of God and not refer it to the person whose function is the ministry of the word, who, being in all things faithful and a wise administrator, has been chosen

1 1 Cor. 14.30.
2 1 Cor. 14.23.

to give spiritual food in season[3] and order his words in judgment, as it is written.[4] If, however, something should escape him whose duty it is to give an answer, and another should observe this, he should not take issue with the former on the spot, but privately offer an apposite suggestion; for the former practice gives rise to insolence on the part of inferiors toward superiors. Therefore, even if one should make a helpful response, yet beyond the scope of his office, he is liable to penalties for unruly behavior.

Q. 46. That no one should conceal sins either in his own interest or for a brother's advantage.

R. According to the Lord's injunction, every sin must be made known to the superior, either by the sinner himself or by those who are cognizant of his fault, if they themselves are not able to effect a cure; for vice kept secret is a festering wound in the soul. We would not term a benefactor one who would confine deadly poisons inside our body, but him, rather, who draws them out by painful laceration, so that either the noxious matter is ejected by vomiting or, in any case, that the treatment may be readily indicated because the infection is made manifest. By the same token, it is surely clear that concealing sin contributes to the death of the sick man; 'for the sting of death is sin,' says the Scripture,[1] and also: 'Open rebukes are better than hidden love.'[2] Let no one, therefore, conceal a sin in behalf of another, lest fratricide take the place of fraternal charity; nor should anyone hide his own sins, ·'for

---

3 Luke 12.42.
4 Ps. 111.5.

---

1 1 Cor. 15.56.
2 Prov. 27.5.

he who doth not heal himself in his works,' says the Scripture, 'is brother to him that committeth outrage against himself.'[3]

Q. 47. Of those who do not accept these regulations.

R. Anyone who does not approve of the superior's prescriptions should take up the matter with him either publicly or in private, if his objection is a sound one and consonant with the Scriptures; if not, he should hold his peace and do the thing that was enjoined. And if he himself should suffer from embarrassment, he should employ others as his representatives in the matter, so that, if the injunction be in opposition to the Scriptures, he may save both himself and his brethren from harm. If, however, it be proved to be in accord with right reason, he would himself avoid a rash and hazardous dispute—'For he that discerneth,' says the Apostle, 'if he eat is condemned, because not of faith'[1]—and he would not lay a snare of disobedience for simpler souls; 'for it were better,' says the Lord, 'that a millstone should be hanged about his neck and that he should be drowned in the depth of the sea than that he should scandalize one of these little ones.'[2] And if some persist in their disobedience, finding fault in secret and not openly stating their grievance, thus becoming the cause of quarreling in the community and undermining the authority of the commands given, they should be dismissed from the community as teachers of disobedience and rebellion; for the Scripture says: 'Cast out the scoffer from the council and contention shall go out with him,'[3] and also: 'Put away the evil one from among yourselves,' for a little leaven corrupteth the whole lump.'[4]

---

3 Prov. 18.9.

---

1 Rom. 14.23.
2 Matt. 18.6.
3 Prov. 22.10.
4 1 Cor. 5.13,6.

Q. 48. That the superior's actions should not be curiously scrutinized, but everyone should concern himself with his own work.

R. In order that no one may fall readily into this vice of captious quarreling, to his own undoing and that of others, this rule should, in general, be followed in the community: that, in the first place, no one is to concern himself with the superior's method of administration or make curious inquiries about what is being done, with the exception of those who, by reason of their rank and sagacity, are closely associated with the superior. He, in turn, on his part, is bound to take counsel with these and to deliberate with them on community matters, in obedience to the advice of Him who said: 'Do all things with counsel.'[1] Certainly, if we have entrusted our souls to the guidance of a superior, as to one who is accountable to God, it is wholly absurd for us not to trust him in matters of trivial consequence, and thus become filled[2] with unbecoming suspicions of our brother and give occasion for suspicion to others also. In order that this may not come to pass, everyone should confine himself to the occupation which has been appointed him and devote himself entirely to his own concerns, not busying himself at all with the doings of others, after the example of the holy disciples of the Lord; for, although the affair of the Samaritan woman might have aroused suspicion, yet 'no man,' the Scripture tells us, 'said: What seekest thou? or, why talkest thou with her?'[3]

Q. 49. Of controversies in the community.

R. Now, with regard to disputes which arise among the brethren: Whenever certain individuals are in disagreement

---

1 Eccli. 32.24.
2 *auton . . . plerousthai;* it is probable that *autous,* i.e., *emas,* should be read. Cf. *PG* 31.1038 n. 92.
3 John 4.27.

on any matter, they should not contend with one another in a wrangling spirit, but refer the settlement to those who are more competent than they. Nevertheless, so that good order may not be disturbed by everyone constantly submitting his problems and so that there may arise no occasion for levity or foolishness, some one approved person should be empowered either to refer the disputed point to the community for general consideration or to bring it to the attention of the superior. In this way, the investigation of the question will be more fittingly and more intelligently carried on, for knowledge and experience are nowhere more essential than in matters of this kind. If no workman would entrust the use of his tools to unskilled persons, it is far more important to restrict the use of words to those who will be able to discern competently the proper time, place, and method of questioning, and who, by disputing reasonably and without rancor and by listening intelligently can make accurate contributions toward solving the problem unto general edification.

Q. 50. On the manner in which the superior should administer a rebuke.

R. The superior should not administer a rebuke to wrongdoers when his own passions are aroused; for, by admonishing a brother with anger and indignation, he does not free him from his faults but involves himself in the error. For this reason, the Apostle says: 'With modesty, admonishing them that resist.'[1] Nor should he become vehemently angry even when he himself is treated contumeliously, and, when he sees such treatment inflicted upon another, he should again show himself indulgent toward the sinner; but more than that, he ought, in the latter case, to manifest displeasure at the wrong done. By this difference in his conduct as regards himself and

---

1 2 Tim. 2.25.

another, he will avoid the suspicion of self-love and prove
that he does not hate the sinner but is repelled by the sin.
He who shows displeasure in a manner which is the reverse
of that which I have indicated clearly proves that he is displeased, not for God's sake, nor because of the offender's
peril, but because of his own love of honor and authority.
Zeal ought to be exercised for the glory of God, who is dishonored by the violation of His decree, but it is right to show
the mercy of fraternal charity on behalf of a brother who is
endangering his salvation by sin; for 'the soul that sinneth, the
same shall die.'[2] We should, however, be stirred to anger by
every sin as sin, reflecting the ardor of our feelings in the
severity of the penalty we impose.

*Q. 51. Of the manner in which the fault of the offender
should be corrected.*

R. The cure of those afflicted by evil passions should be
effected according to the method used by physicians. The
superior, therefore, must not become angry with the sick, but
he must wage war upon their malady by setting up a coun-
ter-irritant to the vice, curing the infirmity of the soul by
drastic measures, if need be. For example, vainglory should
be corrected by imposing practices of humility, idle talking,
by silence, excessive sleep, by watching in prayer, sloth, by
physical labor, intemperance at table, by fasting, murmuring,
by segregation, so that none of the brethren may desire to
work in partnership with the offender and that the work of
the others may not be coupled with his, as was said above,
unless, to be sure, he shows that he has been freed from his
vice by doing penance without shame. In that event, the work
which was done in a murmuring spirit should be accepted;
yet, not even then should it be put to the service of the breth-

---

2 Ezech 18.4.

ren but made use of in some other way. The reason for this has been adequately set forth above.[1]

Q. 52. On the dispositions in which punishment should be received.

R. If, as we have said, the superior should apply remedies to the weak in a dispassionate manner, so, in turn, those undergoing treatment should not look upon the penalties imposed on them as hostile acts, nor regard as despotic the solicitude shown them by the superior in a spirit of compassion for the salvation of their souls. It is shameful, indeed, that they who are sick in body place so much confidence in physicians that, even if these cut or burn or cause distress by their bitter medicines, they look upon them as benefactors, while we do not share this attitude toward the physicians of our souls when they secure our salvation for us by laborious discipline. The Apostle says, however: 'who is he then who can make me glad, but the same who is made sorrowful by me,'[1] and again: 'For behold this selfsame thing, that you were made sorrowful according to God, how great carefulness it worketh in you.'[2] It behooves one who looks to the end, therefore, to consider him a benefactor who causes us pain which is according to God.

Q. 53. How instructors in the arts will correct the blunders of the children.

R. It is the duty of those themselves who teach the arts to reprimand the faulty technique of their pupils and correct their mistakes. All offenses, however, which arise from perversity of character, such as disobedience and the spirit of

1 Cf. *supra,* Q. 29.

1 2 Cor. 2.2.
2 2 Cor. 7.11.

contradiction, laziness in performing tasks, idle talking, lying, or any other act forbidden to those who lead a religious life, should be referred to the person in charge of general discipline, so that he may determine the measure and the mode of treatment to be applied. The administering of a reprimand appertains to the cure of the soul; therefore, just as not everyone may practice the medical art, so no one should give a reprimand except he to whom the superior, after careful consideration, gives this permission.

Q. 54. That the superiors of the brotherhoods ought to consult with one another about the problems pertaining to their office.

R. It is a good plan that the heads of the communities should meet together occasionally at certain appointed times and places. At these assemblies they should lay before one another for consideration irregular situations, characters which are exceptionally difficult to deal with, details of their administration, so that, if any of them be delinquent in any respect, this may be revealed in an authoritative manner by the judgment of the group and that what has been rightly done may be ratified by their collective testimony.

Q. 55. Whether recourse to the medical art is in keeping with the practice of piety.

R. Each of the arts is God's gift to us, remedying the deficiencies of nature, as, for example, agriculture, since the produce which the earth bears of itself would not suffice to provide for our needs; the art of weaving, since the use of clothing is necessary for decency's sake and for protection from the wind; and, similarly, for the art of building. The same is true, also, of the medical art. In as much as our body is susceptible to various hurts, some attacking from without and some from within by reason of the food we eat, and since the body suffers affliction from both excess and deficiency, the medical art has been vouchsafed us by God, who directs our whole life, as a model for the cure of the soul, to guide us in the removal of what is superfluous and in the addition of what is lacking. Just as we would have no need of the farmer's labor and toil if we were living amid the delights of paradise, so also we would not require the medical art for relief if we were immune to disease, as was the case, by God's gift, at the time of Creation before the Fall. After our banishment to this place, however, and after we had heard the words: 'In the sweat of thy face shalt thou eat thy bread,'[1] through prolonged effort and hard labor in tilling the soil we devised the art of agriculture for the alleviation of the miseries which followed the curse, God vouchsafing us the knowledge and understanding of this art. And, when we were commanded to return to the earth whence we had been taken and were united with the pain-ridden flesh doomed to destruction because of sin and, for the same reason, also subject to disease, the medical art was given to us to relieve the sick, in some degree at least.

Now, the herbs which are the specifics for each malady do not grow out of the earth spontaneously; it is evidently the will of the Creator that they should be brought forth out of the soil to serve our need. Therefore, the obtaining of that natural virtue which is in the roots and flowers, leaves, fruits, and juices, or in such metals or products of the sea as are found especially suitable for bodily health, is to be viewed in the same way as the procuring of food and drink. Whatever requires an undue amount of thought or trouble or involves a large expenditure of effort and causes our whole life to revolve, as it were, around solicitude for the flesh must be avoided by Christians. Consequently, we must take great care to em-

---

1 Gen. 3.19.

ploy this medical art, if it should be necessary, not as making it wholly accountable for our state of health or illness, but as redounding to the glory of God and as a parallel to the care given the soul. In the event that medicine should fail to help, we should not place all hope for the relief of our distress in this art, but we should rest assured that He will not allow us to be tried above that which we are able to bear.[2] Just as in those days the Lord sometimes made clay, and anointed, and bade wash in Siloe, and on other occasions was content with the mere command: 'I will, be thou made clean,'[3] whereas He left some to struggle against their afflictions, rendering them more worthy of reward by trial, so it also is with us. He sometimes cures us secretly and without visible means when He judges this mode of treatment beneficial to our souls; and again He wills that we use material remedies for our ills, either to instil in us by the prolonged nature of the cure an abiding remembrance of the favor received, or, as I have said, to provide an example for the proper care of the soul. As in the case of the flesh it is essential to eliminate foreign elements and add whatever is wanting, so also, where the soul is concerned, it behooves us to rid ourselves of that which is alien to it and take unto ourselves that which is in accordance with its nature; for 'God made man right,'[4] and He created us for good works that we might walk in them.

Moreover, as in using the medical art we submit to cutting, burning, and the taking of bitter medicines for the cure of the body, so, also, in caring for our souls we must heal them by accepting the cut of the reproachful word and the bitter medicine of penalties. The prophetic writings, furthermore, utter this remonstrance to those who have not received ad-

---

2 1 Cor. 10.13.
3 John 9.6,7; Matt. 8.3.
4 Eccle. 7.30.

monition: 'Is there no balm in Gilead? or is there no physician there? Why then hath not the health of the daughter of
my people gone up?'[5] The fact, also, that chronic illnesses
persist over a long period and despite varied and painful remedies is a sign that we should amend the sins of the soul by
assiduous prayer, prolonged penance, and the severe disciplinary treatment which reason may advise as adequate for
the cure. Nor, because some sinners do not make good use of
the art of medicine, should we repudiate all the advantages
to be derived from it; for we need not straightway condemn
all the arts together merely because undisciplined pleasure-
seekers abuse the art of cookery, or baking, or weaving, for
the purpose of ministering to their own delight, by overstepping the limits of what is strictly necessary. On the contrary,
their abuse of these arts ought to be made evident by our demonstrating the proper use of them. Similarly with the medical
art—,we ought not commit outrage against a gift of God
by putting it to bad use. To place the hope of one's health
in the hands of the doctor is the act of an irrational animal.
This, nevertheless, is what we observe in the case of certain
unhappy persons who do not hesitate to call their doctors
their saviors. Yet, to reject entirely the benefits to be derived
from this art is the sign of a pettish nature. Just as Ezechias
did not regard the lump of figs as a primary cause of his re-
gaining his health[6] and did not consider this fruit responsible
for the cure of his body, but gave glory to God and added
thanksgiving for the creation of the figs, so, also, when we
suffer the blows of calamity at the hands of God, who directs
our life with goodness and wisdom, we first ask of Him
understanding of the reason He has inflicted the blows;
second, deliverance from our pains or patient endurance of

5 Jer. 8.22.
6 2 Kings 20.7.

them, to the end that, with the temptation, He may also grant issue so we may be able to bear it.[7]

When the favor of a cure is granted us, whether by means of wine mixed with oil, as in the case of the man who fell among the robbers,[8] or through figs, as with Ezechias, we are to receive it with thanksgiving. Besides, we shall view the watchful care of God impartially, whether it comes to us from some invisible source or by a physical agency, the latter, indeed, frequently engendering in us a livelier perception of the favor as coming from the hands of God. Very often, also, the diseases which we contracted were for our correction and the painful remedies we were obliged to submit to formed part of the instruction. Right reason dictates, therefore, that we demur neither at cutting nor at burning, nor at the pains caused by bitter and disagreeable medicines, nor at abstinence from food, nor at a strict regimen, nor at being forced to refrain from that which is hurtful. Nevertheless, we should keep as our objective (again I say it), our spiritual benefit, in as much as the care of the soul is being taught in the guise of an analogy. There is no small danger, however, that we will fall into the error of thinking that every kind of suffering requires medical relief. Not all sicknesses for whose treatment we observe medicine to be occasionally beneficial arise from natural causes, whether from faulty diet or from any other physical origin. Illness is often a punishment for sin imposed for our conversion; 'For whom the Lord loveth,' says the Scripture, 'he chastiseth';[9] again: 'Therefore are there many infirm and weak among you and many sleep. But if we would judge ourselves, we should not be judged. But whilst we are judged, we are chastised by the Lord that we be not

---

7 1 Cor. 10.13.
8 Luke 10.34.
9 Prov. 3.12.

condemned with the world.'[10] Consequently, when we who belong to this class have recognized our transgressions, we should bear in silence and without recourse to medicine all the afflictions which come to us, in accordance with the words: 'I will bear the wrath of the Lord because I have sinned against him.'[11] We should, moreover, give proof of our amendment by bringing forth fruits worthy of penance,[12] remembering the words of the Lord: 'Behold, thou art made whole; sin no more lest some worse thing happen to thee.'[13] Sometimes, also, sickness afflicts us at the request of the Evil One—our benevolent Master, condescending to enter into combat with him as if he were a mighty adversary and confounding his boasts by the heroic patience of His servants. This we learn in the case of Job.[14] Then, too, God places those who are able to endure tribulation even unto death before the weak as their model. Lazarus, for example, although afflicted with such painful wounds, never brought a charge against the rich man, nor made any request of him, nor became peevish at the condition of things; consequently, he came to rest in Abraham's bosom as one who had accepted misfortunes in his lifetime.[15] Again, we find another reason for sickness as applying to the saints. In the case of the Apostle, for instance, in order that he might not seem to exceed the limits of human nature and that no one might think him to possess anything exceptional in his nature (this notion the Lycaonians actually entertained and they brought garlands and oxen for sacrifice[16]), he calls attention to his pro-

---

10 1 Cor. 11.30-32.
11 Mich. 7.9.
12 Luke 3.8.
13 John 5.14.
14 Job 2.6.
15 Luke 16.20ff.
16 Acts 14.12.

longed struggles with an infirmity as a means of demonstrating the fact that he is human.[17]

What profit would there be for such men in having recourse to medicine? Would there not rather be danger that in their solicitude for the body they would be led astray from right reason? Certainly, as was said before, those who have contracted illness by living improperly should make use of the healing of their body as a type and exemplar, so to speak, for the cure of their soul; since abstention from that which is hurtful according to the rules of the medical art, the choosing of what is beneficial, the observance of prescriptions, are of advantage to us also [in the spiritual life].

Further, the very transformation of the body from sickness to health should be an incentive to us not to despair of the soul, as if it had not power to be restored again through penance from its sinful state to its proper integrity. So, then, we should neither repudiate this art altogether nor does it behoove us to repose all our confidence in it; but, just as in practicing the art of agriculture we pray God for the fruits, and as we entrust the helm to the pilot in the art of navigation, but implore God that we may end our voyage unharmed by the perils of the sea, so also, when reason allows, we call in the doctor, but we do not leave off hoping in God. It seems to me, moreover, that the medical art is no small aid to continency. I observe that this art prohibits sensual indulgence, it is opposed to satiety, it forbids as inexpedient an elaborate diet and an exaggerated liking for condiments. In general, it regards want as the mother of health, so that even in this particular its counsel is not without value for us. Therefore, whether we follow the precepts of the medical art or decline to have recourse to them for any of the reasons men-

---

17 2 Cor. 12.7.

tioned above, we should hold to our objective of pleasing God and see to it that the soul's benefit is assured, fulfilling thus the Apostle's precept: 'Whether you eat or drink or whatsoever else you do, do all to the glory of God.'[18]

---

18 1 Cor. 10.31.

CONCERNING BAPTISM

BOOK I

Chapter 1

That we should become disciples of the Lord before we are accounted worthy of holy Baptism

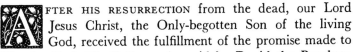 FTER HIS RESURRECTION from the dead, our Lord Jesus Christ, the Only-begotten Son of the living God, received the fulfillment of the promise made to Him by God, His Father, who said by David the Prophet: 'Thou art my son, this day have I begotten thee. Ask of me and I will give thee the Gentiles for thine inheritance, and the utmost parts of the earth for thy possession.'[1] And when He took unto Himself the disciples, He revealed to them first this power given to Him by the Father, saying: 'All power is given to me in heaven and in earth.'[2] Then he sent them forth with the words: 'Going therefore, teach ye all nations, baptizing them in the name of the Father and of the Son and of the Holy Ghost, teaching them to observe all things whatsoever I have commanded you.'[3] The Lord, in giving His command, however, said first: 'teach ye all nations,' and then added: 'baptizing them,' and so on. But you ask me for a discourse on the second part of the injunction and you say nothing regarding the first part. Now if I, in turn, did not give you a prompt answer, I would consider that I had violated

---

1 Ps. 2.7,8.
2 Matt. 28.18.
3 Matt. 28.19,20.

the precept of the Apostle, who had bidden us: 'Be ye ready to satisfy everyone that asketh you a reason.'[4] Consequently, I am going to impart to you the doctrine concerning Baptism according to the Lord's Gospel, which has an authority superior to the baptism of the blessed John. The passages which I shall cite, however, are only a few of the many references to this subject in the Holy Scriptures. But, in any event, I considered it necessary to have recourse to the order of things established by our Lord, so that you, also, first by understanding the force of the precept 'teach ye' and then by hearing in due course an exposition of the doctrine concerning this most glorious Baptism, might happily arrive at perfection, being instructed in the observance of all the precepts which the Lord gave to His own disciples, as it is written. In the passage just quoted, we heard Him say 'teach ye,' but now we must also mention what He says elsewhere regarding the same command. In this way, we first of all adopt a point of view that is pleasing to God; secondly, we observe a sequence that is both logical and fitting; thus avoiding, pursuant of our goal of God's good pleasure, a departure from the right interpretation [of His precept]. It is customary for the Lord to elucidate what is definitely laid down in one place by His utterances elsewhere. For instance: 'Lay up to yourselves treasures in heaven.'[5] Here is given the simple command. The manner of following it He reveals in another place: 'Sell what you possess and give alms. Make to yourselves bags which grow not old, a treasure in heaven which faileth not';[6] and there are many other instances of the same kind.

Now, a disciple, as we learn from the Lord Himself, is one who comes to the Lord for the purpose of following Him, that

4 1 Pet. 3.15.
5 Matt. 6.20.
6 Luke 12.33.

is, to hear His words, to believe in Him and obey Him as Master, King, Physician, and Teacher of truth, in the hope of gaining eternal life. Further, he must persevere in these dispositions, as it it written: 'then he said to those Jews who believed in him: If you continue in my word, you shall be my disciples indeed, and you shall know the truth, and the truth shall make you free.'[7] That is to say, we shall receive freedom of spirit from the cruel tyranny of the Devil by being delivered from the dominion of sin; for He says: 'whosoever committeth sin is the servant of sin.'[8] We shall also escape the sentence of death, as the Apostle Paul has told us: 'Him who knew no sin, he hath made sin for us, that we might be made the justice of God in him';[9] and again: 'For as by the disobedience of one man, many were made sinners; so also by the obedience of one, many shall be made just.'[10] In addition, one who believes in the Lord and who proves his fitness for instruction should learn both to repudiate all sin and to reject every pretext, however specious, which might distract him from the obedience which on many scores he owes to God. It is impossible, indeed, for one who commits sin or who has entangled himself in the affairs of this world, or who is solicitous even for the necessities of this life to serve—to say nothing of being the disciple of—that Lord who bade the young man sell his goods and give to the poor before He said to him: 'Come, follow me.'[11] More than this, He gave the young man that first injunction only after the latter had himself declared: 'All these have I kept.'[12] He had not yet received pardon for his sins, you see, nor had he been cleansed

---

7 John 8.31,32.
8 John 8.34.
9 2 Cor. 5.21.
10 Rom. 5.19.
11 Matt. 19.21.
12 Matt. 19.20.

by the Blood of our Lord Jesus Christ, but he was in the service
of the Devil and under the dominion of sin dwelling within
him. He was, therefore, unable to serve the Lord who proclaimed an unalterable decree when He said: 'Whoever committeth sin, is the servant of sin; now the servant of sin
abideth not in the house.'[13] Paul, too, speaking in Christ, bore
witness to this law when he wrote: 'But he who is the servant
of sin is a free man to justice.'[14] Again the Lord says: 'No
man can serve two masters,'[15] and so on. Furthermore, He
showed by His teaching, both specifically and by implication,
that they who are solicitous in supplying themselves with the
necessities of life cannot persevere in the service of God, not
to speak of being His disciples. And from this doctrine the
Apostle derived his fuller presentation: 'What participation
hath justice with injustice? Or what fellowship hath light with
darkness? And what concord hath Christ with Belial? Or what
part hath the faithful with the unbeliever? And what agreement hath the temple of God with idols?'[16] In another place,
he says directly, 'The flesh lusteth against the spirit and the
spirit against the flesh; for these are contrary one to another,
so that you do not the things that you would.'[17] Let us also
recall what he says in a passage which is meant to convey to
us a still deeper sense of shame: 'I know that the law is spiritual, but I am carnal, sold under sin. For that which I work,
I understand not. For I do not that good which I will; but
the evil which I hate, that I do. If then I do that which I will
not, I consent to the law, that it is good. Now then it is no
more I that do it, but sin that dwelleth in me.'[18] And after he

13 John 8.34,35.
14 Rom. 6.20.
15 Matt. 6.24.
16 2 Cor. 6.14-16.
17 Gal. 5.17.
18 Rom. 7.14-17.

has developed more fully the idea that it is impossible for one who is in the power of sin to serve the Lord, he plainly states who it is that redeems us from such a tyrannical dominion in the words: 'Unhappy man that I am, who shall deliver me from the body of this death? I give thanks to God through Jesus Christ, our Lord.'[19] Further on, he adds: 'There is now, therefore, no condemnation to them that are in Christ Jesus, who walk not according to the flesh.'[20]

More than this, his words in still another place clearly set forth the greatness of the benefit we have received through the loving-kindness of God in the Incarnation of our Lord Jesus Christ: 'For as by the obedience of one man, many were made sinners; so also, by the obedience of one, many shall be made just.'[21] In yet another passage, contemplating the still more wonderful benevolence of God in Christ, he says: 'Him who knew no sin, he hath made sin for us, that we might be made the justice of God in him.'[22] In view of these utterances and other similar ones, we are under the strictest obligation, unless we have received in vain the grace of God, [23] first, to free ourselves from the dominion of the Devil who leads a slave of sin into evils even against his will. Secondly, each of us, after denying himself present satisfactions and breaking off his attachment of this life, must become a disciple of the Lord, as He Himself said: 'If any man will come after me, let him deny himself and take up his cross and follow me.'[24] That is, 'let him become My disciple.' This same injunction He presents in a more extended, forceful and graphic form in the Gospel according to Luke, which

19 Rom. 7.24,25.
20 Rom. 8.1.
21 Rom. 5.19.
22 2 Cor. 5.21.
23 2 Cor. 6.1.
24 Matt. 16.24.

we shall speak of a little later. But we all escape the condemnation for our sins referred to above, if we believe in the
grace of God through His Only-begotten Son, our Lord Jesus
Christ, who said: 'This is my blood of the new testament,
which shall be shed for many unto remission of sins.'[25] The
Apostle also testified to this truth when he wrote: 'Love one
another as Christ also hath loved us and hath delivered himself for us, an oblation and a sacrifice to God;'[26] and again:
'Christ hath redeemed us from the curse of the law,'[27] and
so in many other passages. When pardon for his transgressions
is granted, then does man obtain of the Redeemer, Jesus
Christ, our Lord, deliverance from his sinful state and thereupon is he rendered fit to receive instruction. Not yet, however, is he worthy to follow that Lord (again I state) who
said to the young man: 'Sell what thou hast and give to the
poor' before He said: 'Come, follow me.'[28] And He gave Him
that first injunction only after the young man had affirmed
that he was free from the guilt of any sin by saying that he
had fulfilled all the commandments mentioned by the Lord.
It is clear, then, that in this connection, also, the right order
must be followed. We are taught not merely to care nothing
for our possessions and for the necessities of this life, but we
are even instructed to make no account of just claims as regards one another imposed upon us by law and nature: for
Jesus Christ says: 'He that loveth father or mother more
than me is not worthy of me.'[29] Moreover, these words must
be understood as referring similarly to any other close bonds
of intimacy, and surely they apply with far greater force to
more distant connections and to those outside the faith. Then

---

25 Matt. 26.28.
26 Eph. 5.2.
27 Gal. 3.13.
28 Luke 18.22.
29 Matt. 10.37.

He adds: 'He that taketh not up his cross and followeth me, is not worthy of me.'[30] And the Apostle who succeeded in doing this writes for our instruction: 'I am crucified to the world and the world to me.'[31] 'And I live, now not I; but Christ liveth in me.'[32]

Once more, let us call to mind the Lord's words which He spoke directly to each of us when to the man who said: 'Suffer me first to go and bury my father,' He replied: 'Let the dead bury their dead; but go thou and preach the kingdom of God.'[33] Another who said: 'Let me first arrange my affairs at home,' He rebuked with a stern threat, saying: 'No man, putting his hand to the plough and looking back, is fit for the kingdom of God.'[34] A human obligation, therefore, however honorable it may appear, if it retards us ever so slightly in rendering the whole-hearted obedience we owe to God, is to be repudiated by a person who wishes to become the Lord's disciple; compliance with it is the deserving object of a dire threat. The Lord again states this precept in more general terms when He says: 'If any man will come after me, let him deny himself and take up his cross and follow me.'[35] But if we recall the words of the Lord to him who said: 'Blessed is he that shall eat bread in the kingdom of God,'[36] we learn of a more terrible judgment of wrath and severity which deprives those who transgress the precept of every good hope. These are the Lord's words: 'A certain man made a great supper and invited many. And he sent his servant at the hour of supper to say to them that were invited that they should come, for now all things are ready. And they began

---

30 Matt. 10.38.
31 Gal. 6.14.
32 Gal. 2.20.
33 Luke 9.59,60.
34 Luke 9.61,62.
35 Matt. 16.24.
36 Luke 14.15.

all at once to make excuse. The first said to him: I have
bought a farm and I must go out and see it; I pray thee, hold
me excused. And another said: I have bought five yoke of
oxen and I go to try them; I pray thee, hold me excused.
And another said: I have married a wife, and therefore I
cannot come. And the servant, returning, told these things
to his lord. Then the master of the house, being angry, said
to his servant: Go out quickly into the streets and lanes of
the city, and bring in hither the poor, and the feeble, and the
blind and the lame. And the servant said: Lord, it is done
as thou has commanded, and yet there is room. And the
lord said to his servant: Go out unto the highways and hedges
and compel them to come in, that my house may be filled.
But I say unto you that none of those men that were invited
shall taste of my supper.'[37] Moreover, the Only-begotten Son
of the living God, sent by the Father not to judge the world
but to save the world,[38] true to Himself and faithful to the
will of the good God, His Father, associates with the decree of
His severity a doctrine whereby we might be made worthy
of becoming His disciples. He says: 'If any man come to me
and hate not his father and mother, and his wife and children and brethren and sisters, yea, and his own life also, he
cannot be my disciple.'[39] That sort of hatred is meant, of
course, which inculcates the virtue of piety by withdrawing us
from distractions, not the kind which leads us to contrive
hurtful schemes against another. 'And whosoever,' says the
Lord, 'doth not carry his cross and come after me, cannot
be my disciple.'[40] This, indeed, is the very agreement we make
when, in receiving the Baptism of water, we promise to be

37 Luke 14.16-24.
38 John 12.47.
39 Luke 14.26.
40 Luke 14.27.

crucified, to die, to be buried with Him, and so on, as it is written.[41]

In consideration of our weakness, however, God willed also to establish our hearts in full conviction of the truth by means of parables and, thereby, induce in us a readier obedience. He says, therefore: 'Which of you having a mind to build a tower, doth not first sit down and reckon the charges that are necessary, whether he have wherewithal to finish it; lest after he hath laid the foundation and is not able to finish it, all that see it begin to mock him, saying: This man began to build and was not able to finish. Or what king about to go to make war against another king, doth not first sit down and think whether he be able with ten thousand to meet him that with twenty thousand cometh against him? Or else, whilst the other is yet afar off, sending an embassy, he desireth conditions of peace. So, likewise, every one of you that doth not renounce all that he possesseth cannot be my disciple. Salt is good. But if the salt shall lose its savour, wherewith shall it be seasoned? It is neither profitable for the land nor for the dunghill, but shall be cast out. He that hath ears to hear, let him hear.'[42] If we have faith in these words, we will, first of all, with the grace of God, through our Lord Jesus Christ (unless we have received so great a grace in vain[43]), free ourselves from the tyranny of the Devil by refraining from every action that is pleasing to the Devil. Secondly, we will renounce not only the world and its concupiscences, but also the just claims we have on one another, and, even our life itself, whenever any of these things distracts us from the whole-hearted and immediate submission we owe to God. Then shall we be worthy to become disciples of the Lord. Furthermore, we

---

41 Rom. 6.4-11.
42 Luke 14.28-35.
43 2 Cor. 6.1.

learn from Moses and the Prophets, from the Evangelists and the Apostles, that all things visible and invisible were made in the beginning by God through His Only-begotten Son, our Lord Jesus Christ. By the events recounted in the Holy Scripture, also, we are taught the goodness of God and His severity in much patience, that His justice may be manifested and for our instruction. From the Scriptures we learn also of the prophecies concerning the Incarnation of Jesus our Lord and the paradoxical events which then occurred; of His glorious Resurrection from the dead, His Ascension, and most glorious Coming at the end of time; of the doctrines of piety, based on the hope of eternal life and the kingdom of heaven and wholly in accord with the Gospel and acceptable to God in the love of Christ Jesus, our Lord; of the judgment of just recompense rendered both to those who do what is forbidden or refuse to do that which is sanctioned, unto eternal punishment, and to those who live worthily, according to the Gospel of God, in sound faith, working by the charity of Christ,[44] in the expectation of life eternal and the kingdom of heaven which is in Christ Jesus, our Lord.

---

44 Gal. 5.6.

Chapter 2

How Baptism according to the Gospel of our Lord Jesus Christ is conferred

Since our Lord Jesus Christ has commanded us to love one another as He had loved us[1] and since He has taught us by the Apostle Paul to support one another in charity,[2] I readily accede to the request of Your Piety in Christ regarding the most glorious Baptism according to the Gospel of our Lord Jesus Christ, not as being competent to speak worthily on the subject but as making a small contribution, like the widow who cast in the two mites.[3] And I have need in this matter of the prayers of those who love Christ, that, by the grace of the good God and His Christ, the good Holy Spirit, reminding and instructing us regarding that which He hears from the Lord,[4] may direct our thoughts into the path of peace and sound doctrine, to the end that faith may be strengthened and that for you and for me may be fulfilled the saying: 'Give an occasion to a wise man and wisdom shall be added to him.'[5] Only we must bear in mind that instruction is necessary before we are worthy to receive this most admirable Baptism. Such was the command given to His disciples by our Lord and God, Jesus Christ, Only-begotten Son of the Living God. With a sense of obligation, therefore, we impart to you a few utterances singled out from the many sayings of our Lord Himself respecting those who wish to become disciples of Christ. And since He promises that we

1 John 13.34.
2 Eph. 4.2.
3 Luke 21.2.
4 John 14.26.
5 Prov. 9.9.

shall see the kingdom of God if we are born anew and that
by being born of water and the Holy Spirit we shall enter
into the kingdom of God,[6] I consider it necessary to add a
few of many references to the kingdom of heaven, that we
may in no way fail of its attainment. Indeed, one of our
sages has said that the little things in life are far from being
trivialities, and almost everyone knows this from practical
experience. Even so, we can become more firmly convinced of
the truth of this saying by noting the exactness of the prescriptions relating to priests and to animals brought for sacrifice.[7] If any small blemish was discovered or any mutilation,
not of all the bodily members, but, as it is written, of only
one part of a member—the lobe of the ear, for example—a
man would not be chosen for the priesthood and an animal
would not be acceptable for sacrifice. The Apostle says: 'Now
these things happened to them in figure; and they are written
for our correction, upon whom the ends of the world are
come.'[8] Moreover, the Lord clearly showed the superiority
[of the New Dispensation] in the words: 'There is here a
greater than the temple,'[9] and by saying: 'To whom they
have committed much, of him they will demand the more,'[10]
He indicated that we should take more meticulous care of
the soul than of the body.

And now let us speak of the kingdom of heaven. When our
Lord Jesus Christ ascended the mountain and began His
teaching by proclaiming the beatitudes, He first set forth that
beatitude which offers promise of the kingdom of heaven.
He said: 'Blessed are the poor in spirit, for theirs is the king-

---

6 John 3.5.
7 Lev. 22.21-31.
8 1 Cor. 10.11.
9 Matt. 12.6.
10 Luke 12.48.

dom of heaven.'[11] In the eighth beatitude, also, He says: 'Blessed are they that suffer persecution for justice' sake, for theirs is the kingdom of heaven.'[12] Again, in the parable of the shepherd, He prophesies the blessing that will be pronounced at the time of retribution, saying: 'Come, ye blessed of my Father, possess you the kingdom prepared for you from the foundation of the world. For I was hungry and you gave me to eat,'[13] and so on. At another time and place, as the context indicates, in the Gospel of Luke, He again sets forth the beatitudes, saying: 'Blessed are the poor in spirit, for theirs is the kingdom of heaven';[14] and yet again: 'Fear not, little flock, for it hath pleased your Father to give you a kingdom. Sell what you possess and give alms. Make to yourselves bags which grow not old, a treasure in heaven which faileth not.'[15] Such, then, are the means, whereby a man is rendered worthy of the kingdom of heaven. The indispensable requirements for entrance into the kingdom of heaven, however, are revealed by the Lord in the Gospel according to Matthew. He says: 'Unless your justice abound more than that of the scribes and Pharisees, you shall not enter into the kingdom of heaven,'[16] and again: 'Unless you be converted and become as little children, you shall not enter into the kingdom of heaven,'[17] and yet again, 'Whosoever shall not receive the kingdom of God as a little child shall not enter into it.'[18] Moreover, in the Gospel according to John, He says to Nicodemus: 'Unless a man be born again, he cannot see

---

11 Matt. 5.3.
12 Matt. 5.10.
13 Matt. 25.34,35.
14 Luke 6.20.
15 Luke 12.32,33.
16 Matt. 5.20.
17 Matt. 18.3.
18 Mark 10.15.

the kingdom of God';[19] also: 'Unless a man be born again of water and the Holy Ghost, he cannot enter into the kingdom of God.'[20]

With regard to all these requirements, one rule obtains: that if one is neglected, all are equally imperiled. If the Lord says: 'one jot or one tittle shall not pass of the law, till all are fulfilled,'[21] how much more will this be true of the Gospel, in as much as the Lord Himself says: 'Heaven and earth shall pass, but my words shall not pass.'[22] Wherefore, the Apostle James makes bold to say: 'Whosoever shall keep the whole law but offend in one point, is become guilty of all.'[23] This he inferred from the threat made by the Lord after He had proclaimed the beatitudes, after His testimonies to the state which transcends the human lot, after the prediction made to Peter: 'If I wash thee not, thou shalt have no part with me.'[24] The Apostle Paul, who filled up those things that were wanting of the sufferings of Christ for His body which is the Church,[25] tells us, speaking in Christ, what the offenses are for which, most of all, a man is deemed unworthy of heaven and for which he incurs the sentence of death, by his specific declaration: 'they who do such things are worthy of death.'[26] Why did he not say: 'they who do these things,' instead of saying: 'they who do such things shall not obtain the kingdom of God'?[27] Again, he says more generally: 'The unjust shall not obtain the kingdom of God,'[28] and similarly in other places. In the Gospel according to Luke, our Lord

---

19 John 3.3.
20 John 3.5.
21 Matt. 5.18.
22 Matt. 24.35.
23 James 2.10.
24 John 13.8.
25 Col. 1.24.
26 Rom. 1.32.
27 Gal. 5.21.
28 1 Cor. 6.9.

Jesus Christ Himself declared: 'No man putting his hand to the plow and looking back is fit for the kingdom of God.'[29] Here it must be observed that so dire and irrevocable a judgment is not pronounced upon many sins, but upon one—and this having to do with legitimate acts in which there was a delay ever so slight in giving to God the immediate and wholehearted obedience we owe Him on many grounds. By these and similar passages we are taught that all things must be perfectly and lawfully accomplished by those who have received the promise of the kingdom of heaven and that, if this perfect accomplishment be lacking, the gift of the kingdom is withheld. We learn, moreover, that everything which might prevent us from obtaining the kingdom of heaven is to be avoided and by this means we may hope to be accounted worthy of the promise. In our endeavors to become pleasing to God, we ought not only free ourselves from all iniquity, but we must also be perfect and blameless as regards every word of God. To this achievement the Apostle Paul, contemplating the great and ineffable love of God and His Christ toward us on behalf of our justification and salvation, exhorts us in the words: 'Giving no offence to any man, that our ministry be not blamed; but in all things let us exhibit ourselves as ministers of God.'[30]

As he who is poor in spirit cannot, by reason of the decree, enter the kingdom of heaven unless he has been born of water and the Holy Spirit,[31] so, on the other hand, unless the justice of that man 'abound more than that of the scribes and Pharisees,'[32] or if any other requirement be unfulfilled, he is not accounted worthy of the kingdom, because of another decree similar to that mentioned above. It is written: 'That

---

29 Luke 9.62.
30 2 Cor. 6.3,4.
31 John 3.5.
32 Matt. 5.20.

he might present it to himself, a glorious church, not having spot or wrinkle, or any such thing; but that it should be holy and without blemish.'[33] And there are many such utterance which, if they were diligently read, would convince us even more firmly that we must comply with every prescription in order to merit the kingdom of heaven. Further, that he who abounds in justice and who has been born anew has fulfilled the perfection of all righteousness comprised in the beatitudes and other prescriptions as well and that such a one is to be regarded as proficient in such righteous acts, the section on being born anew will, by the grace of God, prove a little further on. But since, as I said above, Your Piety's injunction requires of us a discourse on the most admirable Baptism according to the Gospel, I think it logical to follow what has been said regarding the kingdom of heaven with a brief instruction on the difference between the baptism according to Moses and that conferred by John. Then, at length, we may be accounted worthy, by the grace of God, to comprehend the pre-eminent dignity of the Baptism of our Lord Jesus Christ in its incomparable magnitude of glory. The Only-begotten Son of the living God declared that 'there is here a greater than the temple,' and 'a greater than Solomon here,' and 'a greater than Jonas here.'[34] The Apostle, also, after speaking first of the glory of Moses in the ministration of the law, a glory which the Jews were not able to approach, testifies [to this superiority] by adding the words: 'For even that which was glorious in this part was not glorified by reason of the glory that excelleth.'[35] John the Baptist, than whom there is no greater among them that are born of woman,[36] likewise bears witness [to the same truth] in the words: 'He must in-

33 Eph. 5.27.
34 Matt. 12.6,42,41.
35 2 Cor. 3.10.
36 Matt. 11.11.

crease, but I must decrease';[37] and again: 'I indeed baptize you in water unto penance, but he baptizes you in the Holy Ghost and fire,'[38] and so in many other places. The Holy Spirit is as far superior to water as He who baptizes in the Holy Spirit obviously is to him who baptizes in water. And this is true also of the Baptism itself. Wherefore, John himself, commended so highly and so frequently by the Lord, made the open and unabashed declaration: 'I am not worthy to loose the latchet of his shoe.'[39]

From all these proofs the superiority of the Baptism according to the Gospel of Christ becomes clearly evident. Even if it is not possible to comprehend it worthily, yet, according to our capacity and as God may grant us sufficiency, it is a pious and beneficial act to speak on this subject, using as our source the Scriptures themselves. The baptism which was handed down through Moses recognized, first, a difference in sins; for the grace of pardon was not accorded all transgressions; also, it required various sacrifices, it laid down precise rules for purification, it segregated for a time one who was in a state of impurity and defilement, it appointed the observance of days and seasons, and then baptism was received as the seal of purification. The baptism of John was far superior. It recognized no distinction of sins, nor did it require a variety of sacrifices, nor did it appoint strict rules for purification or any observance of days or seasons. Indeed, with no delay at all, anyone who had confessed his sins, however numerous or grave, had access at once to the grace of God and His Christ. He was baptized in the river Jordan and straightway received pardon for his sins. The Baptism of the Lord, however, surpasses all human powers of comprehension. It con-

---

37 John 3.30.
38 Matt. 3.11.
39 Mark 1.7.

tains a glory beyond all that man hopes or prays for, a pre-eminence of grace and power which exceeds the others more than the sun outshines the stars. More than this, if the words of the saints are recalled to mind, they prove even more conclusively its incomparable superiority. Yet, we must not therefore refrain from speaking of it, but, using the very utterances of our Lord Jesus Christ as our guides and groping our way, as it were, with a mirror and through the maze of an enigma, we must speak, not so as to diminish the greatness of the subject by an exposition made in weakness of body and with the aid of a reason that is set at naught, but so as to magnify by this means the greatness of the long-suffering and benevolence of the good God in tolerating our stammering attempts to speak about the prodigies of His love and grace in Christ Jesus.

Now, then, our Lord Jesus Christ says: 'Unless a man be born again, he cannot see the kingdom of God,'[40] and again: 'Unless a man be born again of water and the Holy Ghost, he cannot enter into the kingdom of God.'[41] After His resurrection from the dead (whereby He fulfilled in Himself the prophecy of David who said, speaking for God the Father: 'Thou art my son, this day have I begotten thee. Ask of me and I will give thee the Gentiles for thy inheritance and the utmost parts of the earth for thy possession';[42] and this actually took place and is evident to all)—[after His resurrection] as if in contradicition of His first command by which He forbade His disciples to go into the way of the Gentiles,[43] He further bade them: 'Going, teach ye all nations, baptizing them in the name of the Father and of the Son and of

---

40 John 3.3.
41 John 3.5.
42 Ps. 2.7,8.
43 Matt. 10.5.

the Holy Ghost.'[44] I think that we must by faith grasp and understand each of these words and speak, according as words are granted us in answer to the prayers of all, at the opening of our mouth.[45] It is written: 'If you do not believe, you shall not understand,'[46] and also: 'I have believed, therefore have I spoken.'[47] Now, I am of the opinion that the nouns and verbs and the content of the Holy Scriptures do not have as regards God and His Christ or the holy Prophets and Evangelists and Apostles the simple and conventional acceptation of ordinary use. On the contrary, we should examine them under the guidance of the Holy Spirit and with a pious intention, not all together but by parts, according as each may contribute to the exposition of sound doctrine. We should reflect upon them devoutly and direct our thoughts to a consideration of the rules and teachings of the devout life. It is most important that we be observant and attentive to every word and choose the sense that is in keeping with our heavenly calling. This we shall accomplish if, through the prayers of all, Jesus Christ, the Only-begotten Son of God, strengthen us, so that the words of the Apostle may be realized in us: 'I can do all things in Christ who strengtheneth me.'[48]

Now, then, the word 'anew,' I think, clearly means the repairing of the first birth in the defilement of sin. Job says: 'No one is free from stain, not even if his life last for one day.'[49] And David laments and says: 'I was conceived in iniquity and in sins did my mother conceive me.'[50] The Apostle also declares: 'For all have sinned and do need the glory of God, being justified freely by his grace, through the

---

44 Matt. 28.19.
45 Ps. 50.17.
46 Isa. 7.9.
47 Ps. 115.10.
48 Phil. 4.13.
49 Job 14.4 (Septuagint).
50 Ps. 50.7.

redemption that is in Christ Jesus, whom God hath proposed to be a propitiation through faith in his blood.'[51] Wherefore, the pardon of sins is also vouchsafed to them that believe, since the Lord Himself said: 'This is my blood of the new testament, which shall be shed for many unto remission of sins.'[52] The Apostle also adds another testimony: 'according to the purpose of his will, unto the praise of the glory of his grace, in which he hath graced us in his beloved Son; in whom we have redemption through his blood, the remission of sins according to the riches of his grace which hath superabounded in us.'[53] Imagine a statue which has been shattered into fragments and in which the glorious image of the king is no longer discernible. The wise artificer and skilled craftsman, seeking to regain the beauty of his work, shapes it anew and restores it to its former splendor. So it is with us. Afflicted as we are because of our disobedience to the command, as it is written: 'Man, when he was in honour did not understand; he is compared to senseless beasts and is become like to them,'[54] we have been recalled to our original glory as the image of God; for the Scripture says: 'God made man to the image and likeness of God.'[55] How this was done the Apostle teaches us, saying: 'Thanks be to God, that you were the servants of sin but have obeyed from the heart unto that form of doctrine into which you have been delivered.'[56] Just as wax applied to a carved mold is shaped exactly according to the form impressed upon the carved surface, so we, when we have submitted ourselves to the mold of doctrine according to the Gospel, are formed as re-

---

51 Rom. 3.23-25.
52 Matt. 26.28.
53 Eph. 1.5-8.
54 Ps. 48.13.
55 Gen. 1.27.
56 Rom. 6.17.

gards the inner man, fulfilling the words of the same Apostle
which he expresses in the form of a precept: 'stripping yourselves of the old man with his deeds, and putting on the new,
him who is renewed unto knowledge according to the image of
him that created him,'[57] and so in many other places.

The manner of our being born anew of water, Paul states
authoritatively when he says, speaking in Christ: 'Know you
not, brethren, that all we who are baptized in Christ Jesus
are baptized in his death? For we are buried together with
him by baptism unto death; that as Christ is risen from the
dead, so we also may walk in newness of life. For if we have
been planted together in the likeness of his death, we shall
be also in the likeness of his resurrection. Knowing this, that
our old man is crucified with him, that the body of sin may be
destroyed, to the end that we may serve sin no longer. For he
that is dead is justified from sin. Now if we be dead with
Christ, we believe that we shall live also together with Christ,
knowing that Christ rising again from the dead, dieth now no
more; death shall no longer have dominion over him. For in
that he died to sin, he died once; but in that he liveth, he
liveth unto God. So do you also reckon that you are dead to
sin but alive unto God in Christ Jesus.'[58] In all this, the nature
of our regeneration is viewed under the form of an analogy.
But it would be impossible to be born anew unless the grace
of God had first been vouchsafed us, as the Apostle himself
shows, not only in the words just quoted, but also in subsequent passages concerning Baptism, beginning with the
words: 'But God commendeth his charity towards us; because
when as yet we were sinners, Christ died for us; much more,
therefore, being now justified by his blood, shall we be saved
from wrath through him. For if, when we were enemies, we

---

57 Col. 3.9,10.
58 Rom. 6.3-11.

were reconciled to God by the death of his Son, much more, being reconciled, shall we be saved by his life.'[59]

And there are many passages of this sort which set forth with clarity and splendor the great, ineffable benevolence of God in freely pardoning our sins and granting us the means and the power of performing righteous acts for the glory of God and His Christ in the hope of gaining eternal life through Jesus Christ our Lord. Wherefore, the Apostle says: 'As by the offence of one, unto all men to condemnation; so also by the justice of one, unto all men to justification of life.'[60] Then, after an authoritative exposition in the verses which follow, he says: 'Know you not, brethren, that all we who are baptized in Christ Jesus are baptized in his death?'[61] For what purpose? That, grace being first granted us, we may fulfill our duties by faith through charity,[62] and, thus, the satisfaction of the divine love in Christ may be perfectly accomplished in us. And so there is need of a hard struggle, yet a lawful one,[63] lest we receive so great and precious a gift as the love of God in Christ to no avail; for the Apostle himself says: 'Him who knew no sin, he hath made sin for us that we might be made the justice of God in him. And we helping do exhort that you receive not the grace of God in vain.'[64] Furthermore, the Lord has said decisively: 'To whom they have committed much, of him they will demand the more.'[65] This obligation will be met and in a faultless manner if the prescriptions bearing upon what was said above and also those given in connection with the

---

59 Rom. 5.8-10.
60 Rom. 5.18.
61 Rom. 6.3.
62 Gal. 5.6.
63 2 Tim. 2.5.
64 2 Cor. 5.21; 6.1.
65 Luke 12.48.

subject of Baptism be scrupulously observed, and if we faithfully accept all that relates to these doctrines, by the power of the same grace of God through Jesus Christ our Lord, in grace of God; and, whatever we merit to understand, let us perform in the love of Christ who said: 'If you know these things, you will be blessed if you do them.'[66] 'A good understanding to all that do it,' declares the Prophet.[67] Indeed, the Only-begotten Son of the Living God Himself proclaimed a dire and inescapable condemnation when He said: 'He that knew the will of his lord and did it not, shall be beaten with many stripes';[68] and what is more, He does not even permit one who erred through ignorance to go unpunished.[69]

Now, to repeat what was said above, in order that familiar sayings and occurences may serve to bring us to a knowledge also of the salutary doctrine of Baptism, let us earnestly and in full certainty of truth study what they signify and apply their purport to our goal of the devout life. The effect of Baptism is, let us say, for the sake of the instruction to be derived from the parallel, like the change of color which occurs in wool when it is dipped into dye—or rather, that we may enkindle the light of knowledge unto the comprehension of the great Light, let us take John the Baptist for guide, who prophesied concerning the Lord: 'He shall baptize you in the Holy Ghost and fire,'[70] and use the comparison of iron dipped in fire whose flames are fanned by the wind. Under such conditions, the iron most readily betrays any dross it may contain and is very easily purified. After the iron is transformed not only in color but also in texture, its hardness and rigidity are rendered pliant, so that it becomes very malleable

---

66 John 13.17.
67 Ps. 110.10.
68 Luke 12.47.
69 Luke 12.48.
70 Matt. 3.11.

in the hands of the artisan and wonderfully adapts itself to the will of its master. Its dull black hue becomes extraordinarily bright, and it not only burns and shines itself, but illuminates and warms its surroundings. It necessarily follows, then, that he who has been baptized in fire, that is, in the word of doctrine which overcomes the malice of sin and makes manifest the grace of justifications, hates and abominates iniquity, as it is written,[71] and desires to receive purification through faith in the power of the Blood of our Lord Jesus Christ. He Himself said: 'This is my blood of the new testament, which shall be shed for many unto the remission of sins.'[72] The Apostle also declares: 'In whom we have redemption through his blood, the remission of sins.'[73] Such a one, moreover, will not only be cleansed from all iniquity and sin, but also from every stain of the flesh and the spirit.[74] Then, at length, baptized in the death of the Lord, he will desire to be conformed to His death, which is to die to sin, to himself and to the world. Thus, living according to the Incarnation and formed and molded in thought, word, and deed by the teaching of our Lord Jesus Christ, like wax by a carved surface, he may fulfill the words: 'Thanks be to God that you were the servants of sin, but have obeyed from the heart unto that form of doctrine into which you have been delivered.'[75] And so he will deserve to fulfill, likewise, those other words that have a bearing in this connection: 'buried together with him by baptism unto death.' For what purpose?—'that as Christ is risen from the dead by the glory of the Father, so we also may walk in newness of life.'[76] He who is dead must be buried, and he who is buried

71 Heb. 1.9.
72 Matt. 26.28.
73 Eph. 1.7.
74 2 Cor. 7.1.
75 Rom. 6.17.
76 Rom. 6.4.

in the likeness of death must rise again by the grace of God in Christ. No longer, because of sin, should he bear about in the inner man a countenance like a blackened kettle,[77] but, after his sins have been made manifest by fire and pardon has been granted through the Blood of Christ, he should shine forth in newness of life, by the justifications of Christ, more precious than any jewel.

And so, having put off the obduracy of disobedience, let us show docility and submission in observing the precepts. Let us send forth our light, fervent in spirit, and gain deliverance from the power of darkness which drags us down to death; 'for the wages of sin is death.'[78] Thus will the words of the Apostle be true in our regard also: 'Death is swallowed up in victory. O death, where is thy sting? O hell, where is thy victory?'[79] Let us, by obeying the Lord, the Sun of justice, become illuminated with His light and so be accounted worthy of understanding and power, that we may be justified in Him. And not only ought we ourselves to shine whiter than snow (for God does not deceive when He promises: 'If your sins be as scarlet, I shall make them white as snow'),[80] but we should give light also to those who come to us. We must pay heed to these words of the Lord: 'You are the light of the world,'[81] but it behooves us both to heed and act upon these others: 'So let your light shine before men, that they may see your good works and glorify your Father who is in heaven.'[82] Next, the Apostle, also, will give us direct testimony: 'among whom you shine as lights in the world, holding forth the word of life to my glory in the day of Christ.'[83]

---

77 Joel 2.6; Nah. 2.10.
78 Rom. 6.23.
79 1 Cor. 15.54,55.
80 Isa. 1.18.
81 Matt. 5.14.
82 Matt. 5.16.
83 Phil. 2.15,16.

But in what way will your newness of life be evident, not only
as compared with pagans and worldly men, but in the more
exacting comparison with those who are justified according to
the law? For, not only should we not endeavor to increase
our possessions and to acquire greater gains, as do men of
the world, but we should not even lay claim to the property
which has already been acquired and is our own. Let us be
zealous in giving to the needy over and above what the law
requires. Furthermore, we obey the command of our Lord
Jesus Christ: 'Be ye therefore merciful as your heavenly
Father also is merciful,'[84] not only by doing good to those who
are near and dear to us, but by including hostile and wicked
men also in our acts of kindness. Surely, we walk in newness
of life and achieve a justice more perfect than that of the
scribes and Pharisees when we obey these words of the Lord:
'It was said to them of old: An eye for an eye and a tooth for
a tooth. But I say to you not to resist evil; but if one strike
thee on thy right cheek, turn to him also the other. And if a
man will contend with thee in judgment and take away thy
coat, let go thy cloak also unto him. And whosoever will force
thee one mile, go with him other two.'[85] Not only are we to
refrain from taking revenge for offenses first committed
against us, as the scribes and Pharisees took revenge, for the
law of Moses permitted this, but we should display a forbearance greater than the offense and show in advance our
readiness to sustain other wrongs of equal or even greater
gravity. Thus do we achieve both aims together: death, in
that we are not moved to displeasure against him who inflicted the first blow upon us; newness of life in Christ, by
exposing ourselves to a second.

Moreover, is a man not dead to the Law if he does not

---

84 Luke 6.36.
85 Matt. 5.38-41.

seek to reclaim what has been taken from him? Does he not
live in Christ who lets go also his cloak? And we are taught
to observe likewise, in a measure over and above, all other
justice according to the Law. That we must not only be crucified to the world but also be dead to the law, we can learn
from the authoritative teaching of the Apostle Paul. In one
place, he says: 'I am crucified to the world and the world
to me.'[86] 'I live now not I, but Christ liveth in me.'[87] Elsewhere he declares, after showing that he had good reason
to boast of his observance of practices once in high repute
according to the law: 'Furthermore, I count all things to be
but dung that I may gain Christ and may be found in him,
not having my justice which is of the law, but that which
is of the faith of Christ Jesus which is of God, justice in
faith, that I may know him and the power of his resurrection and the fellowship of his sufferings, being made conformable to his death, if by any means, I may attain to the resurrection which is from the dead.'[88] Shortly after, he instructs
us very explicitly to share his sentiments: 'Let us, therefore,
as many as are perfect, be thus minded.'[89]

In still another place he speaks with greater vehemence, as
if expounding an indispensable doctrine: 'Therefore you
also are become dead to the law by the body of Christ, that
you may belong to another who is risen again from the dead,
that we may bring forth fruit to God. For when we were in
the flesh, the passions of sins which were by the Law did work
in our members, to bring forth fruit unto death. Now we are
loosed from the Law, dead to that wherein we were detained;
so that we should serve in newness of spirit and not in the

---

86 Gal. 6.14.
87 Gal. 2.20.
88 Phil. 3.8-11.
89 Phil. 3.15.

oldness of the letter.'[90] 'For the letter'—that is, the Law—
'killeth, but the spirit'—that is, the word of the Lord—
'quickeneth.'[91] As the Lord Himself says: 'the flesh profiteth
nothing; it is the spirit that quickeneth. My words are spirit
and life.'[92] The following admission of the Apostle offers
further testimony: 'To whom shall we go? Thou hast the
words of eternal life. And we have believed and have known
that thou art the Christ, the Son of the living God.'[93] If we
carefully heed these words, fully convinced of their truth, we
will be able to escape the terrible doom written by Moses in
threat and prophecy: 'The Lord thy God will raise up to thee
a prophet like unto me. Him thou shalt hear in all things
that he may command thee. And it will happen that every
soul that will not hear that prophet shall be destroyed utterly
from among the people.'[94] And John the Baptist, than whom
there was no greater among those born of women,[95] says
more directly and with greater severity: 'He that believeth
in the Son hath life everlasting; but he that believeth not the
Son shall not see life; but the wrath of God abideth on him.'[96]
Further, in order that this death and burial which takes place
in Baptism may not give rise to grief because of our anti-
cipating decay and destruction, and that the newness of life
may be shown to be a thing of greater promise than the sowing of seed, inasmuch as it confirms our hope of a glorious
resurrection, the Apostle adds his testimony: 'For if we have
been planted together in the likeness of his death, we shall
be also in the likeness of his resurrection.'[97] And if we, dying

90 Rom. 7.4-6.
91 2 Cor. 3.6.
92 John 6.64.
93 John 6.69,70.
94 Deut. 18.15,18,19.
95 Matt. 11.11.
96 John 3.36.
97 Rom. 6.5.

thus in a likeness of His death and being buried with Christ,
walk in the newness of life, we do not experience the corruption of death and our burial is only in semblance, as a planting of seed. By mortifying ourselves with regard to what is
forbidden and in manifesting the faith that 'worketh by
charity,'[98] we are made worthy to share the hope of the
Apostle and to say with him: 'But our conversation is in
heaven, from whence also we look for the Saviour, the Lord
Jesus Christ, who will reform the body of our lowness,
made like to the body of his glory according to the operation
whereby also he is able to subdue all things unto himself.'[99]
'And so shall we be always with the Lord,'[100] for our Lord
Jesus Christ Himself asks the Father, saying: 'Grant, Father,
that where I am, these also may be with me.'[101] And He
encourages us again with the same promise in the words:
'If any man (minister) to me, let him follow me; and where _Serves_
I am, there also shall my (minister) be.'[102] Paul the Apostle, _Servant_
prophesying in Christ, likewise testifies to this truth when he
writes: 'For this we say unto you in the word of the Lord,
that we who are alive, who remain unto the coming of the
Lord, shall not prevent them who have slept. For the Lord
himself shall come down from heaven with commandment,
and with the voice of an archangel, and with the trumpet of
God; and the dead who are in Christ shall rise first. Then we
who are alive, who are left, shall be taken up together with
them in the clouds to meet Christ, into the air, and so shall
we be always with the Lord.'[103]

In this manner, then, for those to whom the following

98 Gal. 5.6.
99 Phil. 3.20,21.
100 1 Thess. 4.16.
101 John 17.24.
102 John 12.26.
103 1 Thess. 4.14-16.

words now apply: 'For if we have been planted together in
the likeness of his death,' will be fulfilled at that time the
promise, 'we shall be also in the likeness of his resurrection';[104] 'for,' as the Apostle says elsewhere: 'if we be dead
with him, we shall live also with him. If we suffer, we shall
also reign with him.'[105] And, knowing that repetition will
foster conviction in his hearers, the Apostle inculcates a
firmer belief in the truth by a reiteration of the same ideas.
We hear him saying with reference to himself: 'To write the
same things to you, to me, indeed, is not wearisome but to
you is a safeguard.'[106] As we are told that Joseph twice interpreted the dream for King Pharaoh,[107] so the Apostle, like
Joseph in the story of the dream, presents his teaching on the
subject of Baptism by referring to considerations which he had
proposed before. He says: 'Knowing this, that our old man
is crucified with him, that the body of sin may be destroyed
to the end that we may serve sin no longer.'[108] By these words
we are taught that he who is baptized in Christ is baptized in
His death, and is not only buried with Christ and planted
together with Him, but is first of all crucified with Him. Thus
we are instructed that as he who is crucified is separated from
the living, so also he who has been crucified with Christ in the
likeness of His death is completely set apart from those who
live according to the old man; for the Lord charged us to
beware of false prophets,[109] and the Apostle says: 'And we
charge you, brethren, that you withdraw yourselves from every
brother walking disorderly and not according to the tradition
which they have received of us.'[110] The 'old man' mentioned

104 Rom. 6.5.
105 2 Tim. 2.11,12.
106 Phil. 3.1.
107 Gen. 41.1ff.
108 Rom. 6.6.
109 Matt. 7.15.
110 2 Thess. 3.6.

by the Apostle signifies, as if they represented his own members, all sin and defilement taken individually and together.

He who was crucified and condemned to death was separated from all the living who had in time past associated with Him and He was lifted above all that creeps upon the earth. He, likewise, who has been crucified with Christ through Baptism, is set apart therewith from all who live according to this world and His mind is elevated to heavenly converse so that he can truly say and with trust in Christ: 'But our conversation is in heaven.'[111] Again, the Apostle adds: 'For he that is dead is justified from sin';[112] that is to say, he is set free, he is delivered, he is cleansed of all sin; and not sin in word and deed only, but also of all passionate movements of the mind. In another place, he declares: 'And they that are Christ's have crucified their flesh with the vices and concupiscences.'[113] Surely, we who are baptized with water do crucify these things, since Baptism is an image of the Cross, of death, burial, and resurrection from the dead, as it is written. Again, the Apostle says: 'Mortify your members which are upon the earth'—by keeping, at least henceforward, your baptismal promises—'fornication, uncleanness, lust, evil concupiscence, and covetousness, which is the service of idols. For which things the wrath of God cometh'—and not content with this, he adds an all-embracing phrase, 'upon the children of unbelief.'[114] No longer, therefore, may a transient pleasure defile and harass the mind of one who has been planted together with Christ in the likeness of His death.[115] Furthermore, by hating and execrating all evil, even the vicious inclinations of the mind, the baptized soul shows forth purity of heart, as

---

111 Phil. 3.20.
112 Rom. 6.7.
113 Gal. 5.24.
114 Col. 3.5,6.
115 Rom. 6.5.

David says, 'the perverse heart did not cleave to me; and the malignant that turned aside from me, I would not know';[116] for, surely, he did not himself turn their way and go to them. Having been planted with Him in the likeness of His death, we will assuredly be raised up together with Christ (for the planting implies this eventuality). But in the present life, we are formed in the inner man according to the measure of the Incarnation in newness of life and obedience unto death, fully persuaded of the truth of His words, so that we may become worthy to say with truth: 'And I live, now not I, but Christ liveth in me.'[117] That this obtains also for the future life, the same Apostle has strongly affirmed in the words, 'For if we be dead with him, we shall live also with him. If we suffer, we shall also reign with him.'[118] Then he persuades us to the acceptance of these words, by adding in similar vein: 'For if we have been planted together in the likeness of his death, we shall be also in the likeness of his resurrection.'[119] Again, he presents the same doctrine regarding the Baptism according to the Gospel with greater urgency and force by adding the words: 'Christ, rising again from the dead, dieth now no more; death shall no more have dominion over him. For in that he died to sin, he died once; but in that he liveth, he liveth unto God. So do you also reckon, that you are dead to sin, but alive unto God in Christ Jesus.'[120]

In making this application of the dispensation of our Lord Jesus Christ Himself as regards the remission of sins through His Incarnation unto death, the Apostle teaches us explicitly and in a manner at once forceful and compelling that we are dead to sin but alive unto God in Christ Jesus. Therefore, as

116 Ps. 100.4.
117 Gal. 2.20.
118 2 Tim. 2.11,12.
119 Rom. 6.5.
120 Rom. 6.9-11.

Christ, having died for us and having risen again from the dead in our behalf, dies now no more, so also we, having been baptized unto the likeness of death, have died to sin and by the resurrection, as if from the dead, which is effected in Baptism, we live unto God in Christ Jesus and die no more, that is, we shall sin no more because 'the soul that sinneth, the same shall die.'[121] As death no longer had dominion over Him, so also sin will no longer have dominion over us, that is, we will no longer commit it. Since 'whosoever committeth sin is the servant of sin,'[122] we have been liberated completely from this servitude, as the Apostle declares, saying: 'And they that are Christ's have crucified their flesh with the vices and concupiscences.'[123] Let us, therefore, live to God in Christ Jesus who has set us free, as it is written: 'Christ hath redeemed us from the curse of the law, being made a curse for us.'[124] Our sins are remitted by a power superior to the law, namely, by the grace of our Lord Jesus Christ, as it is written: 'For as by the disobedience of one man, many were made sinners; so also, by the obedience of one, many shall be made just.'[125] 'Stand fast, therefore,' says the Apostle, 'and be not held again under the yoke of bondage.'[126] And as Christ Himself died once for sin, 'but in that he liveth, he liveth unto God,'[127] so also we, who have died once and for all to sin by the Baptism of water which is an image of the Cross and of death, should keep watch over ourselves and return no more to sin. Let us continue to live to God in Christ Jesus, who said: 'If any man minister to me, let him follow me.'[128] We must, therefore, first of all obey that precept which

---

121 Ezech. 18.4.
122 John 8.34.
123 Gal. 5.24.
124 Gal. 3.13.
125 Rom. 5.19.
126 Gal. 5.1.
127 Rom. 6.10.
128 John 12.26.

the Lord Himeslf gave us: 'So let your light shine before men, that they may see your good works and glorify your Father who is in heaven;'[129] and secondly, the Apostle's injunction: 'Whether you eat or drink or whatsoever else you do, do all to the glory of God.'[130] Each of these precepts will be fulfilled if, worthily disposed toward our celestial calling and living in a manner worthy of the Gospel of Christ, we can truly say: 'For the charity of Christ presseth us; judging this, that if one died for all, then all were dead; and Christ died for all, that they also who live may not now live to themselves, but unto him who died for them and rose again.'[131] Thus also is accomplished that word of the Lord: 'Abide in my love. If you keep my commandments, you shall abide in my love as I also have kept my Father's commandments and do abide in his love.'[132]

Furthermore, 'Giving no offense to any man that our ministry be not blamed,' in all things let us exhibit ourselves as the ministers of God.'[133] Let us show that the promise made at our Baptism was sincere and true, by heeding the following exhortations addressed by the Apostle to those who have been planted together with Christ and who have risen with Him: 'Let not sin, therefore, reign in your mortal body, so as to obey the lusts thereof. Neither yield ye your members as instruments of iniquity unto sin; but present yourselves to God as those that are alive from the dead, and your members as instruments of justice unto God.'[134] Again: 'Therefore if you be risen with Christ, seek the things that are above, where Christ is sitting at the right hand of God. Mind the things that

---

129 Matt. 5.16.
130 1 Cor. 10.31.
131 2 Cor. 5.14,15.
132 John 15.9,10.
133 2 Cor. 6.3,4.
134 Rom. 6.12,13.

are above, not the things that are upon the earth.'[135] In this careful analysis, represented by the few passages I have quoted, I think the Apostle designates this great prevenient grace of God's infinite benevolence as one for which we cannot make a return. It was first bestowed on us in the love of Christ Jesus, our Lord, whose obedience even unto death, as it is written,[136] wrought for us the remission of ours sins, deliverance from death in sin which endures forever, reconciliation with God, the power of becoming pleasing to God, a free gift of justice, companionship with the saints in eternal life, inheritance of the kingdom of heaven, and countless other blessings as a reward. With wisdom and forcefulness, the Apostle, making use of pertinent considerations, expounds for us the doctrine of the Baptism of water in the death of our Lord Jesus Christ. In the words which I have already quoted, he instructs us to keep watch over ourselves lest we receive so great and precious a grace in vain: 'Let not sin, therefore, reign in your mortal body, so as to obey the lusts thereof. Neither yield ye your members as instruments of iniquity unto sin, but present your-selves to God as those that are alive from the dead and your members as instruments of justice unto God,'[137] and so on.

Thus, he separates us completely from all sin and also from the justice according to the Law. On the other hand, he strongly urges toward the justice which is according to God, joining a dire threat with a blessed and desirable promise, as follows: 'For the wages of sin is death. But the grace of God, life everlasting in Christ Jesus, our Lord.'[138] Again, he tells us to imitate the Lord and rise superior to the justice of the Law when he adds the words: 'Know you not, brethren

---

135 Col. 3.1,2.
136 Phil. 2.8.
137 Rom. 6.12,13.
138 Rom. 6.23.

(for I speak to them that know the law), that the law with dominion over a man as long as he liveth? For the woman that hath a husband, whilst her husband liveth, is bound to the law. But if her husband be dead, she is loosed from the law of her husband. Therefore, while her husband liveth, she shall be called an adulteress, if she be with another man; but if her husband be dead, she is delivered from the law of her husband; so that she is not an adulteress if she be with another man. Therefore, my brethren, you also are become dead to the law by the body of Christ; that you may belong to another, who is risen again from the dead, that we may bring forth fruit to God. For when we were in the flesh, the passions of sins, which were by the law, did work in our members to bring forth fruit unto death. But now we are loosed from the law, dead to that wherein we were detained, so that we should serve in newness of spirit and not in the oldness of the letter,'[139] and so on. Here we are instructed to marvel at the unspeakable benevolence of God in Christ Jesus and with the greater fear to cleanse ourselves of every defilement of the flesh and the spirit.[140]

The difference between the spirit and the letter the Apostle explains succinctly in another place by comparing the Law and the Gospel, saying: 'For the letter killeth but the spirit quickeneth.'[141] By the 'letter' he means the Law, as is evident also from what precedes and follows. By the 'spirit' he means the Lord's doctrine, for the Lord Himself said: 'My words are spirit and life.'[142] If the justice according to the Law be zealously sought by those who have consecrated themselves to God by baptism and who have promised 'no longer to live to themselves, but unto him who died for them and rose

---

139 Rom. 7.1-6.
140 2 Cor. 7.1.
141 2 Cor. 3.6.
142 John 6.64.

again,'[143] the Apostle condemns such action as adultery. This is clearly shown by his words quoted above. What, then, should be said with regard to the observance of human traditions? Respecting the justice of the Law, the Apostle again speaks very forcefully as follows: 'Furthermore, I count all things to be but loss for the excellent knowledge of Jesus Christ, my Lord; for whom I have suffered the loss of all things and count them but as dung, that I may gain Christ and may be found in him, not having my justice which is of the law, but that which is of the faith of Christ Jesus, the justice which is of God.'[144] The denunciation of human observances is plainly expressed in the words of the Lord,[145] but, as regards particular counsels of human wisdom, the Apostle has instructed us to repudiate them with vigor. He says: 'For the weapons of our warfare are not carnal, but mighty to God unto the pulling down of fortifications, destroying counsels and every height that exalteth itself against the knowledge of God.'[146] Again, with reference to individual conceptions of justice in general, even if it is earnestly sought after for God's sake, he says: 'For I bear them witness that they have a zeal of God, but not according to knowledge. For they, not knowing the justice of God, and seeking to establish their own, have not submitted themselves to the justice of God.'[147] From this and similar utterances it is clear that they who would quibble about the judgments of God are condemned. It is written: 'Woe to you that are wise in your own eyes and prudent in your own conceits.'[148] Moreover, the Lord declares very explicitly that whoever does not

---

143 2 Cor. 5.15.
144 Phil. 3.8,9.
145 Matt. 15.3ff.
146 2 Cor. 10.4,5.
147 Rom. 10.2,3.
148 Isa. 5.21.

receive the kingdom of heaven as a little child shall not enter into it.[149] It is necessary, therefore, to be free from all alike— the concupiscences aroused by the Devil, worldly preoccupations, attention to human observances and to our own wishes, however specious and lawful they may seem, if they cause a delay ever so slight in the swift readiness with which we ought to accomplish the will of God. They who profess, through the Baptism which we are here considering, to be crucified with Christ, to be dead and buried, planted and raised up again with Him, may, then, be assured that they speak truly when they say: 'I am crucified to the world' (and in a far stronger sense to the Devil) 'and the world to me.'[150] 'And I live, now not I, but Christ liveth in me.'[151] In these words, the Apostle teaches us a greater justice than that of the Law, so that we may be judged worthy of the kingdom of heaven.

But perhaps we should now proceed to another consideration and, by our faith in Christ, to arrive at the knowledge and understanding of what it means to be baptized in the Name of the Father and of the Son and of the Holy Ghost. First of all, it is necessary to point out that the special glory of the Person named is signified by each Name. Secondly, it must be borne in mind that the Lord Himself revealed the significance of Baptism in the Name of the Holy Spirit when He said: 'That which is born of the flesh is flesh and that which is born of the Spirit is spirit.'[152] Thus, with the familiar instance of the continuity of reproduction which obtains in carnal birth as an illustration, we may acquire a clear and accurate understanding of religious doctrine. We know, indeed, and are fully convinced that just as that which is born

---

149 Matt. 18.3.
150 Gal. 6.14.
151 Gal. 2.20.
152 John 3.6.

of flesh shares the nature of that of which it has been born, so also, we who are born of the Spirit are, necessarily, spirit. But this spirit is not according to that great glory of the Holy Spirit which cannot be comprehended by the human mind, but it is according to the glory which is in the distribution to every man for his profit of the gifts of God, through His Christ.[153] It is mysteriously discerned also in the operation of all these gifts and in other instances, by words, likewise; as when we recall to memory the commandments of God which were proclaimed through our Lord Jesus Christ and teach these commandments, for Christ Himself says: 'He himself will teach you all things and bring all things to your mind, whatsoever I shall have said to you.'[154] Then, too, the Apostle tells us at greater length what the attitudes of mind are whereby a man becomes spirit. In one place, he writes: 'but the fruit of the spirit is charity, joy, peace, patience,'[155] and so on. Previously, he had said: 'But if you are led by the spirit you are not under the law,'[156] and in another place: 'If we live in the Spirit, let us also walk in the Spirit.'[157] And yet again, he says: 'And having different gifts according to the grace of God that is given us, either prophecy, to be used according to the rule of faith, or ministry in ministering,'[158] and so on.

In these and other passages of the kind, then, the Lord says that they who are born of the Spirit become spirit. The Apostle again testifies to the same truth when he says: 'For this cause I bow my knees to the Father of our Lord Jesus Christ, of whom all paternity in heaven and earth is named,

---

153 1 Cor. 12.7.
154 John 14.26.
155 Gal. 5.22.
156 Gal. 5.18.
157 Gal. 5.25.
158 Rom. 12.6.

that he would grant you, according to the riches of his glory, to be strengthened by His Spirit with might unto the inward man.'[159] And if, living in the Spirit, we also walk in the Spirit,[160] thus becoming receptive of the Holy Spirit, we shall be enabled to confess Christ; because, 'no man can say the Lord Jesus but by the Holy Ghost.'[161] In this way, therefore the Lord, both by His own words and also through the Apostle, taught that they who are born of the Spirit become spirit. And in this spiritual regeneration we shall again imitate birth according to the flesh, in that, first, we change our abode and alter our ways by strengthening the inner man in spirit, so that we can say: 'But our conversation is in heaven.'[162] While we draw our body along upon the earth like a shadow, we keep our souls in the company of heavenly spirits. Secondly, we change our companions, for David says: 'The man that in private detracted his neighbor, him did I persecute. With him that had a proud eye and an insatiable heart, I would not eat. My eyes were upon the faithful of the earth, to sit with me; the man that walked in the perfect way, he served me. He that worketh pride shall not dwell in the midst of my house; he that speaketh unjust things did not prosper before my eyes,'[163] and similarly in other places. The Apostle, likewise, gravely admonishes us: 'if any man that is named a brother be a fornicator, or covetous, or a server of idols, or a railer, or a drunkard, or an extortioner, with such a one, not so much as to eat.'[164]

And in making such prescriptions regarding matters of this kind, the same Apostle tells us again and again, clearly and definitely, the sort of persons with whom we should associate,

159 Eph. 3.14-16.
160 Gal. 5.25.
161 1 Cor. 12.3.
162 Phil. 3.20.
163 Ps. 100.5-7.
164 1 Cor. 5.11.

prefacing his words by speaking of the great and glorious grace of Christ's mercy. He says: 'For he is our peace, who hath made both one, and breaking down the middle wall of partition, the enmities in his flesh; making void the law of commandments contained in decrees; that he might make the two in himself into one new man, making peace; and might reconcile both to God in one body by the cross, killing the enmities in himself. And coming, he preached peace to you that were afar off, and peace to them that were nigh. For by him we have access both in one Spirit to the Father. Now, therefore, you are no more strangers and foreigners but you are fellow citizens with the saints and the domestics of God, built upon the foundation of the Apostles and Prophets, Jesus Christ himself being the chief corner stone; in whom all the building being framed together, groweth up into an holy temple in the Lord.'[165] And so, planted together with Christ in the likeness of His death, baptized in the Name of the Holy Spirit, born anew as to the inner man in newness of mind, and built upon the foundation of the Apostles and Prophets, we may be made worthy to be baptized in the Name of the Only-begotten Son of God and merit to receive the great grace of which the Apostle speaks when he says: 'As many of you as have been baptized in Christ have put on Christ.'[166] 'There is neither Gentile nor Jew, circumcision nor uncircumcision, barbarian nor Scythian, bond nor free. But Christ is all and in all.'[167]

Now, it follows necessarily that he who has been born is also clothed. Consider, for example, a drawing tablet. It may be fashioned of any sort of material; it may be irregularly cut or the surface may be left unplaned. If it bears a drawing of

165 Eph. 2.14-21.
166 Gal. 3.27.
167 Col. 3.11.

the king's likeness, the difference in material—whether it be wood or gold or silver—does not affect the drawing. The accurate resemblance of the image to its model and its artistic and meticulous presentation make the difference in material pass unnoticed, however obvious this difference may be. The spectators are moved to admire the excellence of the likeness itself, and this becomes more prized than all the king's power and sovereignty. The case is the same with one who is baptized, whether he be Jew or Gentile, male or female, slave or free, Scythian or barbarian, or anyone else bearing the name of any other race. As soon as he has put off the old man with his deeds in the blood of Christ and, by Christ's teaching in the Holy Spirit, has put on the new, created according to God in justice and holiness of truth,[168] and is renewed unto knowledge according to the very image of the Creator, he becomes worthy to win the divine approval, of which the Apostle speaks when he says: 'And we know that to them that love God, all things work together unto good, to such as, according to his purpose, are called. For, whom he foreknew, he also predestinated to be made conformable to the image of his Son; that he might be the firstborn amongst many brethren.'[169]

Then, when the soul has been clothed with the Son of God, it becomes worthy of the final and perfect stage and is baptized in the Name of the Father Himself of our Lord Jesus Christ, who, according to the testimony of John, gave the power to be made the sons of God.[170] It is written: 'Go out from the midst of them and be ye separate and touch not an unclean thing; and I will receive you and you will be sons and daughters to me, sayeth the Lord Almighty.'[171] This

168 Eph. 4.22-24.
169 Rom. 8.28,29.
170 John 1.12.
171 2 Cor. 6.17-18.

power is granted by the grace of our Lord Jesus Christ Himself, Only-begotten Son of the living God, in whom 'neither circumcision availeth anything nor uncircumcision, but faith that worketh by charity,' as it is written.[172] Through this grace we successfully accomplish that command which is added to the precept of baptism by the same Jesus Christ, our Lord. He says: 'teaching them to observe all things, whatsoever I have commanded you.'[173] Moreover, the Lord Himself declared that the observance of His commands is the proof of our love for Him, saying: 'If you love me, keep my commandments';[174] and again: 'He that hath my commandments and keepeth them, he it is that loveth me';[175] and yet again: 'If any one love me, he will keep my word and my Father will love him.'[176] And with still greater force and importunity He says: 'Abide in my love. If you keep my commandments, you shall abide in my love; as I also have kept my Father's commandments and do abide in his love.'[177] Now, if the observance of the commandments is the essential sign of love, it is very greatly to be feared that, without love, even the most effective action of the glorious gifts of grace and that of the most sublime powers and of faith itself and the commandment which make a man perfect will be of no avail; for Paul the Apostle himself declares in Christ: 'If I speak with the tongues of men and of angels, and have not charity, I am become as sounding brass, or a tinkling cymbal. And if I should have prophecy and should know all mysteries and all knowledge, and if I should have all faith, so that I could remove mountains, and have not charity, I am nothing.

---

172 Gal. 5.6.
173 Matt. 28.20.
174 John 14.15.
175 John 14.21.
176 John 14.23.
177 John 15.9,10.

And if I should distribute all my goods to feed the poor and
if I should deliver my body to be burned and have not
charity, it profiteth me nothing.'[178] In expressing himself in
such a definitive manner, I believe the Apostle had in mind
the words of the Lord: 'Many will come in that day, saying:
Lord, Lord, have not we prophesied in thy name and cast out
devils in thy name and done many miracles in thy name, and
did we not eat and drink in thy presence and didst thou not
teach in our streets? And he will answer them: I never knew
you; depart from me, you that work iniquity.'[179]

It is evident, therefore, and undeniable that, without
charity, even though ordinances are obeyed and righteous acts
are performed, even though the commandments of the Lord
have been observed and great wonders of grace effected, they
will be reckoned as works of iniquity, not for any cause inherent in the acts of righteousness or the charisms themselves,
but because they who perform these acts have as their aim
the gratification of their own will, 'supposing,' as the Apostle
says in one place, 'gain to be godliness.'[180] In another place,
he says: 'Some, indeed, out of envy and contention, but some
also for good will preach Christ. And some out of contention
preach Christ not sincerely, supposing that they raise affliction
to my bands';[181] and also: 'For we are not as many, adulterating the word of God.'[182] Again, he puts the matter nega-
tively: 'For neither have we used at any time the speech of
flattery toward you, nor taken an occasion of covetousness,
God is witness; nor sought we glory of men, neither of you
nor of others. Whereas we might have been burdensome to
you as the apostles of Christ.'[183] In the light of these and

---

178 1 Cor. 13.1-3.
179 Matt. 7.22,23; Luke 13.26,27.
180 1 Tim. 6.5.
181 Phil. 1.15,17.
182 2 Cor. 2.17.
183 1 Thess. 2.5-7.

similar passages, the justice of the Lord's decree becomes evident: 'depart from me, all ye workers of iniquity';[184] whereby, using the free gifts of God, you do your own will; as if a man should turn to a murderous purpose the instruments and remedies proper to the medical art and meant to heal and to promote health and well-being. In so doing, you do not obey the precept of the Apostle: 'Whether you eat or drink or whatsoever else you do, do all to the glory of God.'[185] On all counts, then, solicitude for the inner man is of the first importance, that the mind may be free from distraction and, as it were, be identified with the aim of giving glory to God. Thus, we will obey the Lord's command: 'Make the tree good and its fruit good';[186] again: 'Thou blind Pharisee, first make clean the inside of the cup and of the dish, that the outside may become clean.'[187] Let us bring forth fruit from the abundance of a good heart, one a hundred, one, sixty, and another, thirtyfold,[188] by words or deeds directed to the glory of God and His Christ, being careful not to grieve the Holy Spirit.[189] So let us avoid the condemnation of this same Lord, who said: 'Woe to you because you are like to whited sepulchres, which outwardly appear beautiful, but within are full of dead men's bones and of all filthiness. So you also outwardly indeed appear to men just; but inwardly you are full of hypocrisy and iniquity.'[190]

It is necessary, therefore, to receive instruction before Baptism, having first removed any impediment to learning and so making ourselves fit to receive the instruction. Our Lord Jesus Christ Himself confirms this assertion by His example

184 Luke 13.27.
185 1 Cor. 10.31.
186 Matt. 12.33.
187 Matt. 23.26.
188 Matt. 13.8.
189 Eph. 4.30.
190 Matt. 23.27,28.

and also by the formal injunction: 'So every one of you that
doth not renounce all that he possesseth cannot be my disciple';[191] and again by the precept: 'If any man will come
after me, let him deny himself and take up his cross and
follow me';[192] and yet again, by the definitive declaration:
'He that taketh not up his cross daily and followeth me, is
not worthy of me.'[193] By such flaming words as these from the
lips of our Lord Jesus Christ—who said also: 'I am come to
cast fire upon the earth and what will I but that it be
kindled?'[194]—the malice of sin is revealed and the excellence
of good actions performed for the glory of God and His
Christ is also made manifest. We, therefore, share with all
our hearts in the desire and the confession of the Apostle:
'Unhappy man that I am, who shall deliver me from the
body of this death. I give thanks to God through Jesus Christ,
our Lord,'[195] who said: 'This is my blood of the new testament, which shall be shed for many unto remission of sins.'[196]
The Apostle testifies to the same truth in the words: 'In whom
we have redemption through his blood, the remission of
sins.'[197] And then we are ready for the Baptism of water,
which is a type of the cross and of death, burial, and resurrection from the dead. Then we make and keep the covenants
which the same Apostle ratifies in his treatment of Baptism
with the words: 'Knowing that Christ rising again from the
dead, dieth now no more; death shall no more have dominion
over him. For in that he died to sin, he died once; but in that
he liveth, he liveth unto God. So do you also reckon that you
are dead to sin but alive unto God in Christ Jesus, our Lord.

191 Luke 14.33.
192 Matt. 16.24.
193 Matt. 10.38; Luke 9.23.
194 Luke 12.49.
195 Rom. 7.24,25.
196 Matt. 26.28.
197 Col. 1.14.

Let not sin, therefore, reign in your mortal body, so as to obey the lusts thereof. Neither yield ye your members as instruments of iniquity unto sin; but present yourselves to God, as those that are alive from the dead, and your members as instruments of justice unto God,'[198] and so on.

Whoever, therefore, is worthy to be baptized in the Name of the Holy Spirit and who has been born anew undergoes a change of abode, habits, and associates, so that, walking by the Spirit we may merit to be baptized in the Name of the Son and to put on Christ. For one who has been born should be deemed worthy of clothing, as the Apostle said: 'For as many of you as have been baptized in Christ have put on Christ';[199] and again: 'stripping yourselves of the old man with his deeds, and putting on the new, him who is renewed unto knowledge, according to the image of him that created him, where there is neither Gentile nor Jew.'[200] Then, having put on the Son of God who gives us power to become children of God, we are baptized in the Name of the Father and are called sons of God who commanded and declared, as the Prophet has said: 'Therefore, go out from among them and be ye separate, saith the Lord, and touch not an unclean thing: and I will receive you; and I will be a Father to you and you shall be my sons and daughters, saith the Lord almighty.[201] And the Apostle says: 'Having therefore these promises, dearly beloved, let us cleanse ourselves from all defilement of the flesh and of the spirit, perfecting sanctification in the fear of God.'[202] Again, he exhorts us in the words: 'Do ye all things without murmurings and hesitations, that you may be blameless and sincere children of God, without re-

---

198 Rom. 6.9-13.
199 Gal. 3.27.
200 Col. 3.9-11.
201 Isa. 52.11; 2 Cor. 6.17,18.
202 2 Cor. 7.1.

proof in the midst of a crooked and perverse generation;
among whom you shine as lights in the world, holding forth
the word of life to my glory in the day of Christ';[203] and yet
again: 'Therefore, if you be risen with Christ, seek the things
that are above, where Christ is sitting at the right hand of
God; mind the things that are above, not the things that
are upon the earth. For you are dead and your life is hid with
Christ in God. When Christ shall appear, who is our life, then
you also shall appear with him in glory.'[204] And this was
promised by the Lord Himself when He said: 'Then shall the
just shine as the sun.'[205]

Chapter 3

*That he who has been regenerated through Baptism should
thenceforth be nourished by participation in the
Holy Mysteries*

By the grace of the good God and by recalling the words
of the Only-begotten Son of the living God and of His saints,
Evangelists, Prophets, and the Apostles, who have ably ex-
pounded to us the doctrine of Baptism according to the Gospel
of our Lord Jesus Christ, we have learned that the Baptism of fire is opposed to all evil but complacent to the justice which is according to Christ. It engenders hatred of
iniquity and desire of virtue. And by the Blood of Christ,
through faith, we have been cleansed from all sin, and by
water we were baptized in the death of the Lord. We have
made an avowal, as it were, in writing, that we are dead to
sin and to the world, but alive unto justice.[1] Thus, baptized

---

203 Phil. 2.14-16.
204 Col. 3.1-4.
205 Matt. 13.43.

---

1 1 Pet. 2.24.

in the Name of the Holy Spirit, we were born anew. Having been born, we were also baptized in the Name of the Son, and we put on Christ. Then, having put on the new man according to God, we were baptized in the Name of the Father and called sons of God. Hereafter, therefore, we require to be nourished with the food of eternal life which, again, the Only-begotten Son of God gave to us when He said: 'Not in bread alone doth man live, but in every word that proceedeth from the mouth of God.'[2] Moreover, He taught us the manner in which this comes to pass, in the words: 'My meat is to do the will of him that sent me, the Father.'[3]

Once again, repeating the word 'Amen,' to confirm what He had said and to induce conviction in His hearers, He says: 'Amen, amen I say unto you: Except you eat the flesh of the Son of man and drink his blood, you shall not have life in you. He that eateth my flesh and drinketh my blood hath everlasting life; and I shall raise him up in the last day. For my flesh is meat indeed and my blood is drink indeed. He that eateth my flesh and drinketh my blood, abideth in me, and I in him.'[4] And a little further on we find the words: 'Many, therefore, of his disciples, hearing His words, said: This saying is hard and who can hear it? But Jesus knowing in himself that his disciples murmured at this, said to them: Doth this scandalize you? If then you shall see the Son of man ascend up where he was before? It is the spirit that quickeneth; the flesh profiteth nothing. The words that I have spoken to you are spirit and life. But there are some of you that believe not. For Jesus knew from the beginning who they were that did not believe, and who he was that would betray him. And he said: Therefore did I say to

---

2 Matt. 4.4.
3 John 4.34.
4 John 6.54-57.

you that no man can come to me, unless it be given him by
my Father. After this many of his disciples went back and
walked no more with him. Then Jesus said to the twelve:
Will you also go away? And Simon Peter answered him: Lord,
to whom shall we go? Thou hast the words of eternal life, and
we have believed and have known that thou art the Christ,
the Son of the living God.'[5]

Furthermore, near the end of the Gospels, it is written:
'Jesus, therefore, took bread and blessed and broke, and gave
to his disciples and said: Take ye and eat. This is my body
which is broken for you. Do this for a commemoration of me.
And taking the chalice, he gave thanks and gave to them,
saying: Drink ye all of this. For this is my blood of the new
testament which shall be shed for many unto the remission
of sins. Do this for a commemoration of me.'[6] The Apostle
testifies to these words when he says: 'For I have received of
the Lord that which also I delivered unto you, that the Lord
Jesus, the same night in which he was betrayed, took bread,
and giving thanks, broke and said: Take ye and eat. This is
my body, which shall be delivered for you; this do, for the
commemoration of me. In like manner, also, the chalice, after
he had supped, saying: This chalice is the new testament
in my blood. This do ye, as often as you shall drink, for the
commemoration of me. For as often as you shall eat this
bread and drink the chalice, you shall show the death of the
Lord until he come.'[7] In what way are these words useful
to us? They help us, when eating and drinking, always to
remember Him who died for us and rose again; thus, we are
certain to learn how to follow before God and His Christ
the teaching handed down by the Apostle, in the words: 'For

---

5 John 6.61-70.
6 Matt. 26.26-28; Luke 22.19,20.
7 1 Cor. 11.23-26.

the charity of Christ presseth us; judging this, that if one died for all, then all were dead; and Christ died for all, that they also who live may not now live to themselves, but unto him who died for them and rose again.'[8] Now, a man may eat and drink, that is to say, in the imperishable commemoration of Jesus Christ, our Lord, who died for us and rose again, but not accomplish that which constitutes the main significance of the commemoration—the Lord's obedience even unto death, according to the teaching of the Apostle which has just been quoted: 'For the charity of Christ presseth us; judging this, that if one died for all, then all were dead' (a fact we acknowledged by receiving Baptism), 'and Christ died for all, that they who live may not now live to themselves, but unto him who died for them and rose again.' Such a one, however, gains no benefit, for, according to the Lord's declaration, 'the flesh profiteth nothing.'[9]

Furthermore, a person of this sort brings down upon himself the condemnation of the Apostle, who says: 'He that eateth and drinketh unworthily, eateth and drinketh judgment to himself, not discerning the body of the Lord.'[10] This dire sentence is aimed not only against one who approaches the Holy Mysteries unworthily, defiled in the flesh and the spirit[11]—for, indeed, in so approaching he becomes guilty of the Body and Blood of the Lord[12]—but against him who eats and drinks negligently and to no profit by not fulfilling in his commemoration of Jesus Christ, our Lord, who died for us and rose again, these words of the Apostle: 'the charity of Christ presseth us; judging this, that if one died for all,

---

8 2 Cor. 5.14,15.
9 John 6.64.
10 1 Cor. 11.29.
11 2 Cor. 7.1.
12 1 Cor. 11.27.

then all were dead,' and so on. Such a person, if he thoughtlessly and idly makes void so precious and so great a blessing and approaches as if without thankfulness a mystery so sublime, is liable to the charge of negligence, for the Lord did not even permit those who utter an idle word to escape with impunity.[13] Moreover, His condemnation of negligence was most severe upon the man who kept his talent whole and entire in idleness.[14] Besides, the Apostle teaches us that even one who utters a good word, but not unto edification, grieves the Holy Spirit.[15] In this way, then, we ought to understand the condemnation of the man who eats and drinks unworthily. And if one grieving his brother because of meat falls away from charity,[16] without which even the greatest gifts of God's grace and the greatest acts of righteousness are of no avail,[17] what should be said of one who ventures to eat the Body and drink the Blood of our Lord Jesus Christ carelessly and without profit, grieving the Holy Spirit profoundly thereby, and who dares to eat and drink without being constrained by charity, so as to determine not to live to himself but unto Him who died for us and rose again, Jesus Christ, our Lord?[18] He, therefore, who approaches the Body and Blood of Christ in commemoration of Him who died for us and rose again must be free not only from all defilement of flesh and spirit, in order that he may not eat and drink unto judgment, but he must actively manifest the remembrance of Him who died for us and rose again, by being dead to sin, to the world, and to himself, and alive unto God in Christ Jesus, our Lord.

---

13 Matt. 12.36.
14 Matt. 25.25-29.
15 Eph. 4.29,30.
16 Rom. 14.15.
17 1 Cor. 13.1ff.
18 2 Cor. 5.15.

BOOK II

Q. 1. Whether everyone who has received Baptism according to the Gospel of our Lord Jesus Christ is obliged to be dead to sin and to live unto God in Christ Jesus.

R. All of us who desire the kingdom of God are, by the Lord's decree, under an equal and rigorous necessity of seeking after the grace of Baptism. He said: 'Unless a man be born again of water and the Holy Ghost, he cannot enter into the kingdom of God.'[1] By the same token, we are all equally bound to hold the same doctrine regarding Baptism; for the Apostle says to all alike, who are baptized: 'Know you not, brethren, that all we who are baptized in Christ Jesus, are baptized in his death? For we are buried together with him by baptism into death; that as Christ is risen from the dead by the glory of the Father, so we also may walk in newness of life,'[2] and so on. In another place, he teaches this doctrine more explicitly and in a manner more calculated to arouse feelings of reverence: 'As many of you as have been baptized in Christ, have put on Christ. There is neither Jew or Greek; there is neither bond nor free; there is neither male or female, for you are all one in Christ Jesus.'[3] And again, he says to all: 'In whom also you are circumcised with circumcision not made by hand, in despoiling of the body of the sins of the flesh, but in the circumcision of Christ; buried with him in baptism, in whom also you are risen again by the faith.'[4] Everyone, therefore, who has received the Baptism of the Gospel ought to live in accordance with the Gospel, by reason also of what the Apostle said in

---

1 John 3.5.
2 Rom. 6.3,4.
3 Gal. 3.27,28.
4 Col. 2.11,12.

yet another place: 'I testify again to every man circumcising himself, that he is a debtor to do the whole law.'[5]

It has been clearly demonstrated, then, that all who have received the one Baptism, as it is written,[6] are equally bound to fulfill in the manner of Him who died for us and rose again the words of the Apostle: 'For the charity of Christ presseth us; judging this, that if one died for all, then all were dead. And Christ died for all, that they also who live may not now live to themselves, but unto him who died for them and rose again.'[7] If one who has been circumcised in any part of his body, according to the circumcision of Moses, is a debtor to the whole Law, how much greater is the obligation when one is circumcised according to the circumcision of Christ, whereby the entire body is despoiled of the sins of the flesh, as it is written,[8] to accomplish the words of the Apostle: 'I am crucified to the world and the world to me.'[9] 'And I live, now not I, but Christ liveth in me.'[10] He, therefore, who is truly baptized in conformity with the teaching of the Apostle, unto the death of Christ, has rendered himself dead to the world and far more so to sin, according to the words of the Apostle with reference to Baptism: 'our old man is crucified with him, that the body of sin may be destroyed to the end that we may serve sin no longer.'[11] Such a one has indeed concluded an inviolable agreement to follow the Lord in all things, that is, to live wholly to God, in the complete fulfillment of the Apostle's words: 'I beseech you, therefore, brethren, by the mercy of God, that you present your bodies a living sacrifice, holy, pleasing unto God, your reasonable ser-

---

5 Gal. 5.3.
6 Eph. 4.5.
7 2 Cor. 5.14,15.
8 Col. 2.11.
9 Gal. 6.14.
10 Gal. 2.20.
11 Rom. 6.6.

vice,'[12] and so on. Again: 'Let not sin, therefore, reign in your mortal body, so as to obey the lusts thereof. Neither yield ye your members as instruments of iniquity unto sin, but present yourselves to God, as those that are alive from the dead, and your members as instruments of justice unto God.'[13] And yet again, with reference to the same doctrine, he says: 'There is neither Jew nor Greek; there is neither bond nor free; there is neither male nor female. For you are all one in Christ Jesus.'[14] Thus, we all, as one, may become worthy to hear the words: 'Come, then, good servant, thou wert faithful over a few things; I will place thee over many things. Enter thou into the joy of thy lord.'[15] These words we shall be accounted worthy to hear, if every one of us, wherever called and to whatever state assigned, increases manyfold by exceptional diligence and untiring zeal the grace allotted to him, as it is written.[16]

Q. 2. Whether it is safe for one who has not freed his heart from a consciousness of iniquity, uncleanness, or defilement to perform sacerdotal functions.

R. Moses was both giving an ordinance to his contemporaries and admonishing us when he wrote in the law which was given him by God: 'And the Lord spoke to Moses, saying: Say to Aaron: Whosoever of thy seed throughout your families hath a blemish, he shall not approach to offer gifts to his God, because no one who hath a blemish shall approach.'[17] Then, in the verses following, he explains what constitutes a blemish: No one shall approach who has had

---

12 Rom. 12.1.
13 Rom. 6.12,13.
14 Gal. 3.28.
15 Matt. 25.21.
16 Eph. 4.7.
17 Lev. 21.16,17,21.

carnal intercourse with strangers nor if any part of his body
be mutilated, even though the deformity does not so much
hamper effective action as mar his comeliness or physical
integrity. But the Lord, when He says: 'There is here a greater
than the temple,'[18] teaches us that he who dares to handle as
a priest the Body of the Lord who gave Himself for us as an
oblation and 'a sacrifice to God for an odor of sweetness'[19]
is guilty of an impiety as much greater than the former as
the Body of the Only-begotten Son of God is superior to rams
and bulls. Now, this is said not by way of comparison, for in
this case there can be no comparison of excellence. Then,
too, the blemish or mutilation is not here considered with reference to bodily members, but is determined by the justifications of the devout life according to the Gospel. That is,
a blemish is present whenever a commandment is partially or
incompletely observed or fulfilled in a manner not pleasing
to God; some human consideration, like a wound or leprosy,
manifesting itself upon the observance. It is, therefore, always
essential, but especially at the time of celebrating so holy
a mystery to observe this precept of the Apostle: 'Having
therefore these promises, dearly beloved, let us cleanse ourselves from all defilement of the flesh and of the spirit, perfecting sanctification in the fear of God,'[20] 'giving no offense
to any man, that our ministry be not blamed; but in all
things let us exhibit ourselves as the ministers of God.'[21] Thus
may a man become worthy to perform the sacred rites of
the ministry of the Lord according to the Gospel of God.

---

18 Matt. 12.6.
19 Eph. 5.2.
20 2 Cor. 7.1.
21 2 Cor. 6.3,4.

*Q. 3 Whether one who is not free from every defilement
of the flesh and of the spirit may safely eat the Body of the
Lord and drink His Blood.*

R. God in the Law appointed the supreme penalty for those
who dare to touch holy things when in a state of impurity, for
the following words written figuratively for the men of old
are meant for our correction.'[22] 'And the Lord spoke to Moses,
saying: Speak to Aaron and to his sons, that they beware of
those things that are consecrated of the children of Israel and
defile not the name of the things sanctified to me which they
offer. I am the Lord. Say to them and to their posterity: Every
man of your race that approacheth to those holy things that
the children of Israel have consecrated to the Lord, and
in whom there is uncleanness, shall perish from my face. I am
the Lord.'[23] If a threat so grave was pronounced against those
who merely approached things consecrated by men, what
would be said against one who ventured to draw near to such
a great and holy mystery. For, in the measure that He was
superior who was greater than the temple, according to the
Lord's words,[24] so much more awesome and dread is the act of
daring to touch the Body of Christ when the soul is defiled
as compared with handling rams and bulls. The Apostle says:
'Therefore, whosoever shall eat the bread or drink the chalice of the Lord unworthily, shall be guilty of the body and
of the blood of the Lord.'[25] Then, presenting the penalty in a
manner at once more striking and more awe-inspiring through
repetition, he says: 'But let a man prove himself and so let
him eat of the bread and drink of the chalice. For he that
eateth and drinketh unworthily, eateth and drinketh judgment

---

22 1 Cor. 10.11.
23 Lev. 22.1-3.
24 Matt. 12.6.
25 1 Cor. 11.27.

to himself, not discerning the body of the Lord.'[26] And if one who is in a state of uncleanness only (and from the law we learn in figure the proper nature of uncleanness) incurs so dire a condemnation, how much more severe a penalty will one bring upon himself who, being in a state of sin, is guilty of presumption toward the Body of the Lord! Let us be free, therefore, from all defilement (the difference between defilement [*molusmós*] and uncleanness [*akatharsía*] being clear to persons of intelligence) and so approach the Holy Mysteries that we may avoid the condemnation of those who killed the Lord; for 'whosoever shall eat the bread or drink the chalice of the Lord unworthily, shall be guilty of the body and of the blood of the Lord.' And let us come to the possession of eternal life as He promised, Jesus Christ, our Lord and God, who is without deceit, if only, in eating and drinking, we will be mindful of Him who died for us and if we will accomplish the Apostle's words: 'For the charity of Christ presseth us; judging this, that if one died for all, then all were dead. And Christ died for all, that they who live may not now live to themselves but unto him who died for them and rose again.'[27] And this is our pledge in Baptism.

Q. 4. Whether we must believe every word of God and comply with it, fully persuaded of the validity of what is said, even though some word or act on the part of the Lord Himself or of the saints seem to be in contradiction.

R. This question is quite unworthy of anyone who claims to believe in our Lord Jesus Christ, Only-begotten Son of the living God, through whom all things, visible and invisible were made,[28] inasmuch as He speaks the words which He

---

26 1 Cor. 11.28,29.
27 2 Cor. 5.14,15.
28 Col. 1.16.

hears from the Father. We must give an answer, however, in obedience to the words of the Apostle: 'Be ye ready to satisfy every one that asketh you a reason of the faith which is in you.'[29] Yet, lest by drawing upon our own knowledge we may only perplex our hearers, let us call to mind the Lord's own words: 'Amen, amen I say unto you, one jot or one tittle shall not pass of the law till all be fulfilled.'[30] Again: 'It is easier for heaven and earth to pass, than one tittle of the law to fall.'[31] And if a greater than Solomon is here and a greater than Jonas is here[32] it follows that we should say a greater than Moses is here. The Apostle, after telling us how the Jews could not approach the glory of Moses, compares this with the glory of our Lord Jesus Christ, adding: 'that which was glorified in this part was not glorified by reason of the glory that excelleth. For if that which is done away was glorious, much more that which remaineth is in glory.'[33] But, even if we are taught by this passage to discern and acknowledge the words of the Gospel, with unhesitating faith, as valid and certain, let us yet recall those other words of the Lord: 'Heaven and earth shall pass, but my words shall not pass.'[34] Above all others, then, the Lord's words suffice to establish our hearts in the Holy Spirit, our Guide, so that they remain firm and unwavering in accepting every word which proceedeth from the mouth of God.[35] But, in order that we might further assist the weak, it would seem fitting to bring before you one or two out of many additional proofs. David says: 'All his commandments are faithful, confirmed for ever and

29 1 Pet. 3.15.
30 Matt. 5.18.
31 Luke 16.17.
32 Matt. 12.41,42.
33 2 Cor. 3.10,11.
34 Matt. 24.35.
35 Deut. 8.3.

ever, made in truth and equity.'[36] Again: 'the Lord is faithful in all his words and holy in all his works,'[37] and there are many more in the same vein. Jehu says in the Book of Kings: 'See that there hath not fallen to the ground any word of the Lord.'[38]

Now, with reference to those passages in the Gospel which seem to involve some contradiction, it is better for each one to reproach himself as not yet having arrived at an understanding of the riches of the wisdom,[39] and to remind himself of the fact that it is difficult to penetrate the inscrutable judgments of God, than to become liable to a charge of presumption and audacity and to hear addressed to him the words: 'Impious is he who sayeth to the king: Thou art transgressing the law'[40] and 'Who shall accuse against the elect of God?'[41] Although the solution of the greater number of difficulties seems clear to the majority, yet, as regards those passages which appear to involve a contradiction, we are obliged to follow this rule: Whenever a word or act seems opposed to the precept everyone must obey the precept and not search the depths of the riches and the wisdom[42] nor make excuses in sins.[43] This course of action is pleasing to God, and from the Holy Scriptures we have learned that it is a secure way. Moreover, if one precept appear to be in opposition to another, by studying their content and by reading the passage as a whole, we shall discover, at length, that they are not incompatible and we shall demean ourselves as each precept requires for the attainment of our heavenly vocation. Toward

---

36 Ps. 110.8.
37 Ps. 144.13.
38 2 Kings 10.10.
39 Rom. 11.33.
40 Job 34.18.
41 Rom. 8.33.
42 Rom. 11.33.
43 Ps. 140.4.

this goal both precepts are directed, now in healing our ills, and now in promoting our advancement toward the perfection in which is the accomplishment of God's good pleasure. For instance, the Lord said on one occasion: 'No one lights a lamp and hides it under a bushel, but upon a lampstand and it shines to all that are in the house. So let your light shine before men, that they may see your good works and glorify your Father who is in heaven.'[44] At another time He said: 'But when thou dost an alms, let not thy left hand know what thy right hand doth.'[45]

You could find many passages of this sort in the writings of the evangelists and the Apostle. Now, then, if a command be given and the manner of carrying it out is not added, let us obey the Lord, who says: 'Search the Scriptures.'[46] Let us follow the example of the Apostles who questioned the Lord Himself as to the interpretation of His words, and learn the true and salutary course from His words in another place. For example, we learn the meaning of the words: 'Lay up to yourselves treasures in heaven'[47] from the advice given to the young man when the Lord said: 'Sell what thou hast and give to the poor and thou shalt have treasure in heaven';[48] and, also, from the words He addressed to those who desired to inherit the kingdom of heaven: 'Fear not, little flock, for it hath pleased your Father to give you a kingdom. Sell what you possess and give alms. Make to yourselves bags which grow not old, a treasure in heaven which faileth not.'[49] And if danger attend our observance of the command which is our glory, let us call to mind the words of the Apostle: 'It is good for me to die, rather than that any man should make my

---

44 Matt. 5.15,16.
45 Matt. 6.3.
46 John 5.39.
47 Matt. 6.20.
48 Matt. 19.21.
49 Luke 12.32,33.

glory void.'[50] Elsewhere, he says at greater length: 'Who shall separate us from the love of Christ? Shall tribulation or distress or persecution or famine or nakedness or danger or the sword,'[51] and so on. Here we are instructed in stronger terms to obey the commandments and to show more abundantly our love for the Lord who said: 'If any one love me, he will keep my word,'[52] and so in many other places. For the rest, we are taught to imitate the Apostle and cry out: 'O the depth of the riches of the wisdom and of the knowledge of God! How incomprehensible are his judgments and how unsearchable his ways! For who hath known the mind of the Lord?'[53] who came down from heaven and announced the words of His Father to us. In Him it is necessary and salutary to place our trust, as children in their parents, as boys in their teachers, according to the words of our Lord Jesus Christ Himself: 'Whosoever shall not receive the kingdom of God as a little child, shall not enter into it.'[54]

Q. 5. Whether our failure to obey every word of God merits His anger and our destruction, even though a threat is not specifically attached to each word.

R. The question whether disobedience to any word [of God] is deserving of His wrath and our destruction has been treated at greater length in the letter on concord.[55] Yet, to cite on this occasion one or two passages from the many bearing on this subject, let us hear the words of John the Baptist: 'He that believeth in the Son hath life everlasting; but he that believeth not the Son' (and that which is not restricted is all-

---

50 1 Cor. 9.15.
51 Rom. 8.35.
52 John 14.23.
53 Rom. 11.33,34.
54 Mark 10.15.
55 *De judicio Dei* (?).

inclusive) 'shall not see life, but the wrath of God abideth on him.'[56] The Lord Himself affirmed in a definitive manner that 'one jot or one tittle of the law shall not pass until all be fulfilled.'[57] If this is true of the law, it is far more true of the Gospel, as the Lord Himself declared many times. Now, as to [whether disobedience remains seriously culpable], even though a threat is not specifically attached to each word, I think that for the faithful it suffices to recall the Lord's words in that part of His teaching following the pronouncement of the beatitudes, where He enumerates a long series of prohibitions, to some of which He attaches a threat, saying: 'whosoever is angry with his brother shall be in danger of the judgment. And whosoever shall say: Raca, shall be in danger of the council. And whosoever shall say: 'Thou fool, shall be in danger of hell-fire,'[58] and there are many more such instances. To other precepts, however, He does not attach a threat, as when He said: 'Whosoever shall look on a woman to lust after her, hath already committed adultery with her in his heart';[59] and also: 'But I say to you not to swear at all';[60] and a little farther on: 'But let your speech be yea, yea; no, no, and that which is over and above these is of evil.'[61] Many such precepts He gave without adding a specific penalty, inasmuch as He had earlier made a more general pronouncement regarding all: 'Unless your justice abound more than that of the scribes and Pharisees, you shall not enter into the kingdom of heaven.'[62] Near the end of His discourse He adds: 'Every one that heareth these my words and doth them not shall be like to a foolish man that built

---

56 John 3.36.
57 Matt. 5.18.
58 Matt. 5.22.
59 Matt. 5.28.
60 Matt. 5.34.
61 Matt. 5.37.
62 Matt. 5.20.

his house upon the sand, and the rain fell and the floods came and the winds blew, and they beat upon that house and it fell and great was the fall thereof.'[63]

In other passages, also, where He enumerated a long list of sins, He did not affix to each the punishment reserved for it, considering as sufficient His frequent statements referring in general to all sins. Since, however, weaker souls need help, let us call to mind the words of the Apostle as well; for he, too, in imitation of the Lord said in one place: 'if any man that is named a brother be a fornicator or covetous or a server of idols or a railer or a drunkard or an extortioner, with such a one, not so much as to eat.'[64] Again: 'Lie not to one another,'[65] and in still another place: 'Let all anger and indignation and clamour and blasphemy be put away from you with all malice.'[66] And he frequently gave such precepts as these without adding a threat. In one place, however, he adds the penalty in a general way: 'Do not err; neither fornicators nor idolators nor adulterers nor the effeminate nor liers with mankind nor thieves, nor covetous nor drunkards nor railers nor extortioners shall possess the kingdom of God.'[67] Elsewhere, again, he writes in more detail: 'And as they liked not to have God in their knowledge, God delivered them up to a reprobate sense, to do those things which are not convenient. Being filled with all iniquity, fornication, malice, avarice, wickedness, full of envy, murder, contention, deceit, malignity, whisperers, detractors, hateful to God, contumelious, proud, haughty, inventors of evil things, disobedient to parents, foolish, dissolute, without affection, without fidelity,

63 Matt. 7.26,27.
64 1 Cor. 5.11.
65 Col. 3.9.
66 Eph. 4.31.
67 1 Cor. 6.9,10.

without mercy. Who, having known the justice of God, did not understand that they who do such things are worthy of death; and not only they that do them, but they also that consent to them that do them. Wherefore, thou are inexcusable, O man, whosoever thou art, that judgest. For wherein thou judgest another, thou condemnest thyself. For thou dost the same things which thou judgest,'[68] and so in many threats of punishment are not attached to each individual other places. It is evident from these passages that, even if form of disobedience, we are obliged to admit that whoever violates even one command inevitably invokes against himself the general verdict; for our Lord Jesus Christ declared: 'He that despiseth me and receiveth not my words hath one that judgeth him; the word that I have spoken, the same shall judge him in the last day.'[69] And the words which follow are even more frightening. John the Baptist, too, than whom there was no greater, offers clear and precise testimony: 'he that believeth not the Son shall not see life; but the wrath of God abideth on him.'[70] This thought is a familiar one in the Scriptures, even in the Old Testament. For, although Moses, who was the writer of a great part of the Law, did not add to it a threat against the transgressor or the negligent, a general malediction upon all violators is introductory to the announcement of a most frightful penalty: 'Cursed be every man that abideth not in all that is written in the book of this law';[71] and elsewhere: 'Cursed be he that doth the work of the Lord negligently.'[72] If he is accursed who does the work of the Lord negligently, what does he deserve who does it not?

---

68 Rom. 1.28-2.1.
68 John 12.48.
70 John 3.36.
71 Deut. 27.26.
72 Jer. 48.10.

Q. 6. Whether disobedience consists in doing what is forbidden or in neglecting to do that which is commended.

R. Our Lord Jesus Christ, in strongly confirming His judgment regarding this point, was pleased to teach us the fear of His ordinances by example as well as by words. In so doing, He both corrected past error and established our hearts in sound faith, since conviction is better produced by actual practice. He says, first of all: 'Unless your justice abound more than that of the scribes and Pharisees, you shall not enter into the kingdom of heaven.'[73] Then, after completing the presentation of His doctrine in regard to this matter, He adds His verdict together with an example: 'Every one that heareth these my words and doth them not, shall be like a foolish man that built his house upon the sand, and the rain fell and the floods came and the winds blew, and they beat upon that house and it fell, and great was the fall thereof.'[74] Again: 'A certain man had a fig tree planted in his vineyard, and he came seeking fruit on it and found none. And he said to the dresser of the vineyard: Behold, for these three years, I come seeking fruit on this fig tree and I find none. Cut it down, therefore. Why cumbereth it the ground?'[75] Elsewhere, He expresses His condemnation more vividly: 'Depart from me, you cursed, into everlasting fire which was prepared for the devil and his angels.'[76] Then He alleges, not the commission of any forbidden act, but the omission of commended ones, saying: 'For I was hungry and you gave me not to eat; I was thirsty and you gave me not to drink,'[77] and so on. Many such passages might one find to prove that not only are they who do wicked things worthy of death, for whom

73 Matt. 5.20.
74 Matt. 7.26,27.
75 Luke 13.6,7.
76 Matt. 25.41.
77 Matt. 25.42.

also the inextinguishable fire has been prepared,[78] but that, along with these, they are condemned who leave good works undone or who perform them negligently; for it is written: 'Cursed be every man who does the work of the Lord negligently.'[79]

It also would be appropriate to remind those who have received the pardon of their sins through Baptism of the words of John: 'Ye brood of vipers, who hath showed you to flee from the wrath to come? Bring forth, therefore, fruit worthy of penance. And think not to say within yourselves: We have Abraham for our father. For I tell you that God is able of these stones to raise up children to Abraham. For now the axe is laid to the root of the trees. Every tree, therefore, that doth not yield good fruit shall be cut down and any evil committed, but only of omission in performing the cast into the fire.'[80] There is no mention in these words of duties of piety. If everyone who does the work of the Lord negligently is accursed because he does not act with becoming zeal, how much greater is the curse upon him who refrains from doing any good at all! Justly, indeed, are the following words addressed to such persons: 'Depart from me, you cursed, into everlasting fire, which was prepared for the devil and his angels.'[81] And so, from all this, it is evident that great promptness and untiring zeal united with a good and simple intention are indispensable in carrying out the precepts of our Lord Jesus Christ, that we also may be worthy of the blessing promised by our Lord Jesus Christ, the Only-begotten Son of the Living God: 'Blessed are they that hunger and thirst after justice, for they shall have their fill.'[82]

---

78 Mark 9.43.
79 Jer. 48.10.
80 Matt. 3.7-10.
81 Matt. 25.41.
82 Matt. 5.6.

Q. 7. Whether it is possible, or pleasing, or acceptable to God for one who is a servant of sin to perform a meritorious act according to the rule of piety followed by the saints.

R. In the Old Testament, God says: 'The sinner that sacrificeth an ox to me is as if he should brain a dog; he that offereth the finest wheaten flour, as if he should offer swine's blood.'[83] He also prescribed great carefulness with regard to that which is offered in sacrifice, and imposed a dreadful penalty upon the trangressor. In the New Testament, however, the Lord Jesus Christ Himself said in the Gospel: 'Whosoever committeth sin is the servant of sin';[84] and: 'No man can serve two masters';[85] and also: 'You cannot serve God and mammon.'[86] Again, He said most explicitly: 'So likewise every one of you that doth not renounce all that he possesseth cannot be my disciple.'[87] Now, if His verdict is such respecting matters which are not of obligation, what is to be said of those that are forbidden? Speaking through the Apostle, the Lord says: 'Bear not the yoke with unbelievers. For what participation hath justice with injustice? Or what fellowship hath light with darkness? And what concord hath Christ with Belial? Or what part hath the faithful with the unbeliever? And what agreement hath the temple of God with idols?'[88] These words clearly indicate an act which is absolutely forbidden and is displeasing to God and perilous for one who would venture to commit it. I exhort you, therefore, let us make the tree good and its fruit good, as the Lord teaches,[89] and let us cleanse first the inside of the cup and of

---

83 Isa. 66.3 (Septuagint).
84 John 8.34.
85 Matt. 6.24.
86 *Ibid.*
87 Luke 14.33.
88 2 Cor. 6.14-16.
89 Matt. 12.33.

the dish and then the outside will be entirely clean.[90] Taught by the Apostle, let us purify ourselves of every defilement of the flesh and of the spirit[91] and then let us achieve perfect holiness in the love of Christ, that we may become pleasing to God and acceptable to the Lord, so as to gain the kingdom of heaven.

Q. 8 Whether the work enjoined by the command is acceptable to God if the manner of performing it is not in conformity with the divine ordinance.

R. We learn the answer to this question, and at the same time a rule, so to speak, for dealing with every question of this sort, from the Old Testament where God says in His own Person, as it were: 'If rightly thou didst make thy offering, but didst not rightly divide it, thou hast sinned. Peace; his turning is unto thee.'[92] These words show that not only is an offering which is improperly made unacceptable, but such an action is imputed as sin to him who has made the offering. From the simile used by the Apostle we can learn, by a human illustration, as it were, the inviolable rule of piety which is to be applied in general to all cases. The Apostle says: 'He also that striveth for the mastery is not crowned except he strive lawfully.'[93] Moreover, we can adduce—and we do it with deeper reverence—the rule given by our Lord Jesus Christ Himself when He said: 'Blessed is that servant whom when his lord shall come, he shall find so doing.'[94] In using the word 'so' the Lord shows that He excludes from His blessing one who does not perform his actions as we can accurately be taught and fully persuaded to do by

90 Matt. 23.26.
91 2 Cor. 7.1.
92 Gen. 4.7 (cf. Septuagint).
93 2 Tim. 2.5.
94 Matt. 24.46.

many stories and sayings in both the Old and New Testament. Not 'so doing' means acting inappropriately as regards the place, the time, the person, the matter involved, or in a manner intemperate or disorderly, or with improper dispositions.

First, let us consider how an act is performed inappropriately as to place. The Apostle, using a familiar example in order to present his point in a more lucid manner and to assist his hearers toward an understanding of the proprieties of the devout life, says: 'Doth not even nature itself teach you that a man, indeed, if he nourish his hair, it is a shame unto him? But if a woman nourish her hair, it is a glory to her,'[95] and so on. Properly, then, we should follow the customary ways of nature as regards the necessities of this life. For, even though life is sustained by eating and drinking, what prudent man would wish to eat and drink in the public square? Or who would see fit to sow seed on rocks and so lose both the seed and the fruit it is expected to produce? And so, one could think of many actions which would be performed in the wrong place to our peril and even to our condemnation. Recalling once more the words of the Apostle: 'All these things happened to them in figure; and they are written for our correction upon whom the ends of the world are come,'[96] let us see whether acts sanctioned by God with reference to the devout life do not maintain a distinctiveness which cannot be ignored, even though they also have something in common. Certain acts were appointed to be done at Jerusalem, and persons who nonetheless performed them elsewhere did so at their peril. Other actions were even more strictly localized because, both in the temple and at the altar, certain rites were prescribed for the divine service which were

---

95 1 Cor. 11.14,15.
96 1 Cor. 10.11.

different from those assigned to Jerusalem or other places. No one dared to perform actions appointed for the temple and the altar in other parts of Jerusalem, nor were the acts prescribed for other places permitted also in the temple. And for us, also, there is risk involved in observing the command in an unsuitable place, especially if we should celebrate the mysteries of the priesthood in unhallowed places; for such an act would constitute a sin of contempt on the part of the celebrant and would scandalize others in various ways, because of the varying deficiencies in the knowledge which people in general possess.

But, someone may say: Why, then, did the Apostle declare, 'I will, therefore, that men pray in every place'?[97] Certainly, the Lord gives the authority for praying in every place, in the words: 'neither in Jerusalem nor on this mountain shall you adore the Father.'[98] And the words of the Apostle are legitimate, because the word 'every' does not include places designated for human usage or for unclean and shameful deeds, but they do take in the region from the confines of Jerusalem to every place in the world duly appointed, in conformity with the prophecy of sacrifice,[99] that is, consecrated to God, for the celebration of the glorious mystery. Although we have heard the words of the Prophet: 'You shall be called priests of God,'[100] not all should usurp the power of this priesthood and ministry, nor is one to arrogate to himself the gift bestowed upon another. Each of the faithful should remain within the proper limits of the gift granted him by God. The Apostle teaches us this by saying to all: 'I beseech you, therefore, brethren, by the mercy of God, that you present your bodies a living sacrifice, holy, pleasing unto God,

---

97 1 Tim. 2.8.
98 John 4.21.
99 Mal. 1.11.
100 Isa. 61.6.

your reasonable service. And be not conformed to this world; but be reformed in the newness of your mind, that you may prove what is the good, the acceptable, and the perfect will of God.'[101] Moreover, he clearly allots to each the form of ministry which is suitable for him and forbids him to encroach upon another's province, when he says: 'For I say by the grace of God that is given me to all that are among you, not to be more wise than it behoveth to be wise, but to be wise unto sobriety and according as God hath divided to every one the measure of faith.'[102] Furthermore, with the good order which obtains among the members of the body for the purpose of comeliness and security as his model, he prescribes the good order which should exist among us with regard for the diversity of gifts and which is pleasing to God in the love of Christ Jesus. For he says: 'As in one body we have many members, but all the members have not the same office, so we being many are one body in Christ and every one members one of another. And having different gifts, according to the grace that is given us, either prophecy to be used according to the rule of faith, or ministry in ministering,'[103] and so on.

Now, if they who strive together toward the same goal, that of pleasing God, and who are so intimately united with one another in the love of Christ are yet not permitted to overstep the proper limits of their gifts, ought we not exert the greatest care in isolating from holy places those that are used for practices which are alien and hostile to holiness? From all the quotations from the Holy Scripture and other proofs of this sort, as well as from the examples given above, we must conclude that an action which is done in an unfitting place has an effect contrary to the one intended. As to actions

---

101 Rom. 12.1,2.
102 Rom. 12.3.
103 Rom. 12.4-7.

done at an inopportune time, we can hear our Lord Jesus Christ Himself speaking to us: 'Therefore shall the kingdom of heaven be like to ten virgins, who, taking their lamps, went to meet the bridegroom and the bride. And five of them were foolish and five, wise. But the five foolish, having taken their lamps, did not take oil with them; but the wise took oil in their vessels with the lamps. And the bridegroom tarrying, they all slumbered and slept. And at midnight there was a cry made: Behold the bridegroom cometh, go ye forth to meet him. Then all those virgins arose and trimmed their lamps. And the foolish said to the wise: Give us of your oil, for our lamps are gone out. The wise answered, saying: Lest perhaps there be not enough for us and for you, go ye rather to them that sell and buy for yourselves. Now whilst they went to buy, the bridegroom came; and they that were ready went in with him to the marriage, and the door was shut. But at last came also the other virgins, saying: Lord, Lord, open to us. But he, answering, said to them: Amen, I say to you, I know you not. Watch ye, therefore, because you know not the day nor the hour.'[104]

Now, then, since I realize that instruction concerning this decree carries greater strength and conviction when it is stated repeatedly and forcefully, I shall add a quotation on the same subject from another place. The Lord Himself says: 'many shall seek to enter and shall not be able. But when the master of the house shall be gone in and shall shut the door, you shall begin to say: Lord, open to us. And he, answering, shall say to you: I know you not, whence you are.'[105] 'Therefore, I say to you, be you also ready, because at what hour you think not, the Son of man will come,'[106] and similarly in

104 Matt. 25.1-13.
105 Luke 13.24,25.
106 Matt. 24.44.

many other places. If we must call to witness the Apostle, also, we shall hear him quoting the words of the Prophet: 'In an acceptable time I have heard thee.'[107] Then, of himself, the Apostle adds the following words: 'Behold, now is the acceptable time; behold, now is the day of salvation.'[108] Again: 'Therefore, whilst we have time, let us work good to all men, but especially to those that are of the household of the faith.'[109] If still another witness is needed, let us recall the words of David: 'For this shall every one that is holy pray to thee in a seasonable time.'[110] Solomon, likewise, declared in a general way: 'all things good in their time.'[111]

In the Old Testament, as, for instance, in the case of Core and the men who dared to enter the priesthood without being called to it and by the severity of the wrath which came upon them to their utter destruction,[112] we see how grave a thing it is to do that which is unsuitable as regards the person. Moreover, we were instructed by the Lord Himself to be on our guard in this respect, when He said to the disciples: 'I was not sent but to the sheep that are lost of the house of Israel,'[113] and to the woman: 'It is not good to take the bread of children and cast it to the dogs.'[114] Again, in the Old Testament, we find an example of an act performed unsuitably with respect to the material involved, when, although a command to offer sacrifice of undefiled and sound and unblemished victims had been given, the offering was not made of such. Regarding a sacrifice of this kind, God said: 'Offer it to thy prince if he will be pleased wtih it, or if he will

---

107 Isa. 49.8.
108 2 Cor. 6.2.
109 Gal. 6.10.
110 Ps. 31.6.
111 Eccle. 3.11.
112 Num. 16.31ff.
113 Matt. 15.24.
114 Mark 7.27.

regard thy face.'[115] We are taught the same truth, furthermore, in the New Testament by our Lord Jesus Christ Himself, who quotes the prophecy of Isaias against the Jews: 'Well did Isaias prophesy of you, saying: This people honoreth me with their lips, but their heart is far from me. And in vain do they worship me, teaching doctrines and precepts of men.'[116] The Apostle also testifies to the awareness of the Jews, but condemns them for the inconsistency of their justice: 'For I bear them witness, that they have a zeal of God but not according to knowledge. For they, not knowing the justice of God and seeking to establish their own, have not submitted themselves to the justice of God.'[117] Therefore, the Apostle, truly desirous of pleasing God, after recounting the justifications of the law which he had fully accomplished, adds: 'Furthermore, I count all things to be but loss for the excellent knowledge of Jesus Christ, my Lord; for whom I have suffered the loss of all things and count them but as dung, that I may gain Christ and may be found in him, not having my justice which is of the law, but that which is of the faith of Christ Jesus, which is of God, justice by faith; that I may know him,'[118] and so on. By utterances such as these, therefore, we are taught to be exceedingly careful never to associate considerations of human justice with the rule for pleasing God laid down by our Lord Jesus Christ.

As to measure in our actions, I think it is sufficient to remind ourselves of the words of our Lord Jesus Christ in order to comprehend the difference in the standard of the old law of charity ('for it is written: Thou shalt love thy neighbor as thyself').[119] The Lord said: 'A new commandment I give

---

115 Mal. 1.8.
116 Mark 7.6,7.
117 Rom. 10.2,3.
118 Phil. 3.8-10.
119 Matt. 19.19.

unto you: that you love one another as I have loved you.'[120]
'Greater love than this no man hath that a man lay down his
life for his friends.'[121] In general, one can understand the
doctrine concerning all justifications from the rule laid down
by the Lord Himself: 'Unless your justice abound more than
that of the scribes and Pharisees, you shall not enter into the
kingdom of heaven.'[122]

An act is performed in a disorderly, inconsistent manner
when a man puts that which is of the first importance in the
second or third place and thinks that what is third in order
should rank first. For example, to him who said: 'All these
have I kept from my youth,' the Lord gave the command:
'Sell what thou hast and give to the poor and take up thy
cross and come, follow me.'[123] Suppose that the second
injunction, 'Come, follow me,' were to be given to one who
had not kept the commandments, which must be observed as
a prerequisite condition [for receiving the invitation]. Again,
the Lord says: 'If any man will come after me, let him deny
himself and take up his cross and follow me.'[124] What if someone were to place the command to follow first? Or, despite
the fact that the Lord adds after a long instruction: 'So likewise every one of you that doth not renounce all that he possesseth cannot be my disciple,'[125] suppose that someone should
imagine that he was a disciple before he had fulfilled the
preliminary requirements. We must, therefore, obey the injunction of the Apostle: 'Let all things be done decently and
according to order.'[126]

Now let us consider how an act is performed in improper

120 John 13.34.
121 John 15.13.
122 Matt. 5.20.
123 Matt. 19.20,21.
124 Matt. 16.24.
125 Luke 14.33.
126 1 Cor. 14.40.

dispositions. The Lord said of those who give alms with the intention of pleasing men or who perform any other good deed so as to be seen by men: 'Amen I say to you they have received their reward.'[127] With still greater severity does He represent the iniquity of those who fulfill the command of God from human motives, by showing that not only does such action fail of its reward, but that its perpetrator merits punishment, since he acts not from a motive of piety but with a view to pleasing men or for some other gratification: to satisfy avarice or to further an enterprise. These motives the Apostle also denounces, and the Lord condemns such persons with a still greater harshness when He says: 'Many will come in that day, saying: Lord, Lord, have not we prophesied in thy name, and cast out devils in thy name, and done many miracles, and eaten and drunk in thy presence, and hast thou not taught in our streets? And then will I answer them, saying: Depart from me, I know you not where you are, ye workers of iniquity.'[128] From statements of this sort, it is evident that even if a man makes effective use of the gifts of grace, even if he obeys the commandments, but does not perform these acts in the dispositions and for the end prescribed by the Lord in the words: 'So let your light shine before men that they may see your good works and glorify your Father who is in heaven,'[129] he deserves to hear that answer given by the Lord.

The Apostle Paul also says, speaking in Christ: 'Whether you eat or drink or whatsoever else you do, do all to the glory of God.'[130] And the Lord's answer prompted him to say, also: 'If I speak with the tongues of men and of angels and have not charity, I am become as sounding brass or a tinkling cymbal. And if I should have prophecy and should know all

127 Matt. 6.5.
128 Matt. 7.22,23; Luke 13.26,27.
129 Matt. 5.16.
130 1 Cor. 10.31.

mysteries, and if I should have all faith, so that I could remove mountains and have not charity, I am nothing. And if I should distribute all my goods to feed the poor and if I should deliver my body to be burned and have not charity, it profiteth me nothing.'[131] And in another place he says more generally but with greater force: 'If I yet pleased men, I should not be the servant of Christ.'[132]

If you require evidence from the Old Testament also, to convince you that the judgment of God in this manner [is as I have represented it], Moses says: 'Thou shalt love the Lord thy God with thy whole heart and with thy whole mind and with thy whole strength,'[133] and 'Thou shalt love thy neighbor as thyself.'[134] To this the Lord adds: 'On these two commandments dependeth the whole law and the prophets.'[135] The Apostle also bears witness in the words: 'Love, therefore, is the fulfilling of the law.'[136] Moreover, they who do not observe these commands and perform the acts of justification which derive from them are liable to punishment, as Moses declares in the words: 'Cursed be every man that abideth not in all that is written in this book.'[137] And David says: 'If I have looked at iniquity in my heart, the Lord will not hear me.'[138] In another place, also, he says: 'There have they trembled for fear where there was no fear; for God hath scattered the bones of them that please men.'[139] There is need, then, of much diligence and of ceaseless care, lest, perhaps, in carrying out the commandment improperly as

131 1 Cor. 13.1-3.
132 Gal. 1.10.
133 Deut. 6.5.
134 Lev. 19.18; Matt. 19.19.
135 Matt. 22.40.
136 Rom. 13.10.
137 Deut. 27.26.
138 Ps. 65.18.
139 Ps. 52.6.

regards any of the details we have discussed, we may not only lose a reward so great and so blessed but also become the objects of threats so dire.

Q. 9. Whether we ought to associate with transgressors or have any part in the unfruitful works of darkness, when such persons or works are not under our charge.

R. Wicked, indeed, is every man who does not keep the whole law or who violates even one commandment. For, by the omission of only a small part, the whole is imperilled. That which is almost accomplished is yet not accomplished. For example, one who has almost died is not dead, but still lives. He who is almost alive does not live, but is still dead, and one who is on the point of entering has not entered, as for instance, the five virgins. In the same way, he who almost observed the law did not observe it, but is a transgressor. With regard to transgressors, therefore, even if they be relatives, we must obey the Apostle, who says in one place: 'if any man that is named a brother be a fornicator or covetous or a drunkard or a railer or an extortioner, not so much as to eat with such a one.'[140] Here it is to be noted that the Apostle does not segregate from the common life only the man who transgresses in all these ways, but also the one who commits any one of these offenses. He does not say 'with this one,' but 'with such a one.' In another place, he says: 'Mortify your members which are upon the earth: fornication, uncleanness, lust, evil concupiscence, and covetousness, which is the service of idols. For which things the wrath of God cometh' (and he adds in a general way) 'upon the children of unbelief.'[141] 'Be ye not therefore partakers with them.'[142] Again: 'that you

---

140 1 Cor. 5.11.
141 Col. 3.5,6.
142 Eph. 5.7.

with draw yourselves from every brother walking disorderly and not according to the tradition which they have received of us,'[143] and similarly elsewhere.

So that we may know clearly what is meant by not having a share in the works which do not bear fruit, let us first inquire as to what sort of actions merit the attribute 'unfruitful'—whether those only that are forbidden or such also as are commendable but are not performed in good dispositions. In the Old Testament, the Prophet, comparing the saints to a tree, says: 'which shall bring forth its fruit in due season.'[144] Solomon declares: 'The work of the just is unto life but the fruit of the wicked is sin';[145] and Osee: 'Sow for yourselves in justice, reap the fruit of life.'[146] Micheas says: 'And the land shall be made desolate because of the inhabitants thereof, and for the fruit of their devices.'[147] Other Prophets also have much to say on this subject. But, even though their words shine with the brightness of a lamp, the true Light, the Sun of justice, our Lord Jesus Christ Himself, expresses the matter more clearly in the words: 'A good tree cannot bring forth evil fruit, neither can an evil tree bring forth good fruit.'[148] and similarly elsewhere. So, then, since we have the name 'fruit' applied to contrary ideas, let us further inquire as to what sort of trees bear no fruit and as to which works the Apostle terms unfruitful. The significance of barren trees is clarified for us by John the Baptist, who said to those who had merited to receive Baptism for the remission of their sins and who had been cleansed from every stain of guilt: 'Bring forth therefore fruit worthy of penance,'[149] and, a little further on, he adds: 'Every tree

143 2 Thess. 3.6.
144 Ps. 1.3.
145 Prov. 10.16.
146 Osee 10.12 (Septuagint).
147 Mich. 7.13.
148 Matt. 7.18.
149 Matt. 3.8.

therefore that doth not yield good fruit shall be cut down and cast into the fire.'[150] The Lord, however, gives us clearer instruction in the words He will address to those who stand at His right hand: 'Come, ye blessed of my Father, possess you the kingdom prepared for you from the foundation of the world,'[151] and, in the words which follow, He makes mention of their good fruit. Those on His left hand, however, He consigns to 'the everlasting fire, prepared for the devil and his angels.'[152] He does not blame these for committing sin, but for omitting to do good works: 'For I was hungry,' He says, 'and you gave me not to eat,'[153] and so on. Their omission, moreover, causes these souls to share the fate of sinners who are called by the Lord the Devil's angels.

Since, therefore, the difference has been made evident between the trees bearing fruits which are of opposite kinds and those that bear none at all, let us examine further what the Apostle means by unfruitful works. Upon consideration of the matter, I find the link, which is needed between the man who observes the commandment of God lawfully and in a manner pleasing to Him and the one who commits evil and him who does neither, in those who do good, but in a manner displeasing to God for any of the reasons previously mentioned —in discussing the question whether the observance of a command is acceptable if such compliance is improperly carried out and in a manner not conformable to the requirements of the command.[154] Respecting these persons, the Lord said: 'they have their reward.'[155] Consider the case of the five foolish virgins. On the testimony of the Lord Himself, they were virgins and had trimmed their lamps and lighted them; that

150 Matt. 3.10.
151 Matt. 25.34.
152 Matt. 25.41.
153 Matt. 25.42.
154 See above, Q. 8.
155 Matt. 6.5.

is, they had done the same things as the wise virgins and they also went out to meet the Lord, showing themselves in every way as zealous as the wise. Yet, merely because they had not enough oil in their vessels, they failed of their purpose and were kept from entering the place where the bridegroom was.[156] So, also, with the one who was left of the two in the mill-house and of the two in the same bed.[157] The Lord is silent as to the reason for this, perhaps in order to show that, in every case, the least failure in propriety—and particularly, as the Apostle taught, in true charity[158] — renders an act displeasing. Since, then, we see how works become unfruitful, let us take care not to violate in any way the laws of the contest which aims to win the divine pleasure. In everything, let us exhibit ourselves as ministers of God,[159] and not this only, but let us be careful not to enter into such associations as Paul, speaking in Christ, has explicitly forbidden, saying: 'Have no fellowship with the unfruitful works of this darkness'; and, by adding: 'but rather reprove them,'[160] he taught us how we are to conduct ourselves in this abstention.

Now let us consider what it is to have fellowship and study the forms it takes.

I recall from Proverbs: 'Come with us, let us be sharers in blood';[161] and from the Apostle: 'You are all partakers of my joy'[162] and 'communicating to my tribulation.'[163] Also: 'Let him that is instructed in the word communicate to him that instructeth him in all good things.'[164] Again: 'If thou didst

---

156 Matt. 25.1ff.
157 Luke 17.34,35.
158 1 Cor. 13.1-3.
159 2 Cor. 6.4.
160 Eph. 5.11.
161 Prov. 1.11.
162 Phil. 1.7.
163 Phil. 4.14.
164 Gal. 6.6.

see a thief, thou didst run with him; and with adulterers thou
hast been a partaker';[165] 'thou shalt reprove thy brother
openly, and not incur sin through him';[166] and also: 'these
things hast thou done and I was silent. Thou thoughtest unjustly that I should be like to thee; but I will reprove thee and
set before thy face.'[167] As I recall these passages and other
similar ones, I am led to the opinion that fellowship in work
consists in mutual assistance toward the same objective. According to this, fellowship of thought would entail sharing
the sentiments of the one doing the work and taking pleasure
in it with him. Another variety of fellowship, overlooked by
most persons, is revealed by an accurate reading of the Holy
Scriptures. According to this kind of fellowship, one neither
actually performs a work in association with another nor
shares his dispositions, but, although aware of the malice
in the mind directing the work, one yet remains silent and
does not make open accusation as is required both by the
passages quoted above and also by the words of the Apostle
to the Corinthians: 'You have not mourned that he might
be taken away from you, that hath done this deed';[168] and he
adds: 'a little leaven corrupteth the whole lump.'[169] Let us
fear, therefore, and obey the Apostle when he says: 'Purge out
the old leaven, that you may be a new paste.'[170] Now, one
who with a good intention cooperates with another in a good
work and is unconscious of the wickedness of his partner's
dispositions and aim, such a one does not incur guilt in lend-
ing his assistance. Since he did not share the other's dispositions, but was keeping himself within the rule of the love of

165 Ps. 49.18.
166 Lev. 19.17.
167 Ps. 49.21.
168 1 Cor. 5.2.
169 1 Cor. 5.6.
170 1 Cor. 5.7.

God, he shall receive his own proper reward according to his own work, as our Lord Jesus Christ showed in the example of the man left in the bed and the woman left in the mill-house.[171] The difference between those who are entrusted to us and those who are not has to do with the obligation we have of watching over them and not with fellowship in sin. My solicitude is specifically due only those under my charge and participation in evil and in unfruitful works is forbidden to the same degree in all instances.

Q. 10 Whether it is always dangerous to give scandal.

R. I consider it necessary, first of all, to know what scandal is; then, the difference in the persons and the means whereby scandal is given; and, finally, to discover in this way wherein danger lies and where not. Now, scandal, as I am led to infer from the Scriptures, is everything that draws us away from true piety toward any form of defection, or introduces error, or fosters impiety; or, in general, everything which hinders us from observing God's command even unto death. If, however, what is said or done is good in itself, but infirmity in the agent makes his word or deed a source of harm, he is not liable to accusation from those who have taken scandal, since he said or did that which was good as regards edification. This the Lord indicated in the words: 'Not that which goeth into the mouth defileth a man; but what cometh out of the mouth, this defileth a man.'[172] On the other hand, to those who had taken scandal He said: 'Every plant which my heavenly Father hath not planted shall be rooted up';[173] also: 'He that eateth my flesh and drinketh my blood, hath everlasting life';[174] and, a little further on: 'No man can come

171 Luke 17.34,35.
172 Matt. 15.11.
173 Matt. 15.13.
174 John 6.55.

to me, unless it be given him by my Father.'[175] Thereupon, some turned these words to their own ruin, as the Scripture says: 'And many of the disciples, hearing this word, went back and walked no more with him. Then Jesus said to the twelve: Will you also go away? And Simon Peter answered him: Lord, to whom shall we go? Thou hast the words of eternal life, and we have believed and have known that thou art the Christ, the Son of the living God.'[176] Those of sound faith made use of these words to strengthen their faith and obtain eternal salvation, but the weak in understanding or faith, owing to their own wickedness, made them a cause of ruin, as it is written concerning the Lord: 'This child is set for the fall and for the resurrection of many.'[177] This was not said because of a contradiction existing within Himself, but with reference to the hostile views of those who would interpret His doctrine; as the Apostle says: 'To the one, indeed, the odor of life unto life; but to the others, the odor of death unto death.'[178]

Now, if that which is said or done is evil in itself, then he who says or does it is liable to the charge both of committing sin himself and of giving scandal, even if he to whom the scandal is given does not take it as such. This is illustrated in the case of Peter, to whom the Lord said, when Peter was protesting against His fulfilling His ministry of obedience even unto death: 'Go behind me, Satan, thou art a scandal unto me.' The reason added by the Lord, although brief, teaches us the general characteristics of scandal: 'because thou savorest not the things that are of God, but the things that are of men.'[179] From this we know that every attitude

---

175 John 6.66.
176 John 6.67-70.
177 Luke 2.34.
178 2 Cor. 2.16.
179 Matt. 16.23.

of mind which is contrary to the judgment of God constitutes a scandal, and, when such an attitude is, further, put
into action, it incurs the same penalty as homicide, according
to the words of the Prophet Osee: 'the priests have hidden
the way, they have slain Sichem, for they have wrought
wickedness among the people.'[180] On the other hand, if it is
a case of some act that is licit in itself, and harm comes of it
and it causes scandal to those who are weak in faith or understanding, he who has performed such an action is guilty
of scandal. The Apostle says of those who act thus and do not
spare the weak: 'Now when you sin thus against the brethren
and wound their weak conscience, you sin against Christ.'[181]
Consequently, either when something is done which is intrin-
sically evil and scandal results, or if the performance of a licit
act and one within our sphere of competence causes scandal
to one who is weak in faith or knowledge, then the penalty is
clear and unescapable. It is that dreadful condemnation pronounced by the Lord: 'It were better for him that a mill-
stone were hanged about his neck and he be cast into the
sea than that he should scandalize one of these little ones.'[182]
We have discussed this point more fully in former investi-
gations where the nature of those who take scandal was also
more closely studied. In this connection, the Apostle says
even with reference to legitimate actions: 'It is good not to
eat flesh and not to drink wine nor anything whereby thy
brother is offended or scandalized or made weak.'[183] Again,
in another place, he says: 'Every creature of God is good and
nothing to be rejected that is received with thanksgiving.'[184]
Yet, he also declares: 'I will never eat flesh lest I should

180 Osee 6.9 (Septuagint)
181 1 Cor. 8.12.
182 Luke 17.2.
183 Rom. 14.21.
184 1 Tim. 4.4.

scandalize my brother.'[185] Now, if such be the judgment of
permissible acts, what should be said of these that are forbidden? The Apostle gives us a general rule to follow: 'Be
without offense to the Jews and to the Gentiles, and to the
church of God; as I also in all things please all men, not
seeking that which is profitable to myself but to many that
they may be saved.'[186]

*Q. 11. Whether it is right or safe to refuse to obey any of
the prescriptions made by God or to put obstacles in the way
of one who has been commanded to execute these, or to be
tolerant of those who are offering such hindrance, especially
if the person who is interfering be a relative, or if some specious pretext impede the accomplishment of the precept.*

R. In view of the Lord's words, 'learn of me, because I am
meek and humble of heart,'[187] it is clear that we are more
solidly instructed in all things when we recall the words of our
Lord Jesus Christ Himself, Only-begotten Son of the living
God. When, therefore, John the Baptist said to Him: 'I ought
to be baptized by thee and comest thou to me?'[188] He replied:
'Suffer it to be so now, for so it becometh us to fulfill all
justice.'[189] Again, in the presence of the disciples, when Peter
decried the sufferings which the Lord prophesied He must
undergo in Jerusalem, He said with great displeasure: 'Go
behind me, Satan, thou art a scandal unto me; because thou
savourest not the things that are of God, but the things that
are of men.'[190] On another occasion, when Peter, moved by
reverence toward his Master, refused His ministration, the

---

185 1 Cor. 8.13.
186 1 Cor. 10.32,33.
187 Matt. 11.29.
188 Matt. 3.14.
189 Matt. 3.15.
190 Matt. 16.23.

Lord again said: 'If I wash thee not, thou shalt have no part with me.'[191] And, if the soul requires further assistance from examples taken from persons like ourselves, let us recall the words of the Apostle: 'What do you mean, weeping and afflicting my heart? For I am ready not only to be bound but to die also in Jerusalem, for the name of the Lord Jesus.'[192] Who could be more estimable than John or more sincere than Peter, or what motives could have been more reverential than those which they alleged? I know, furthermore, that neither Moses, that holy man, nor the Prophet Jonas, continued to be blameless before God when they entertained thoughts that were contrary to obedience. By these examples we are taught not to gainsay nor to offer hindrance nor suffer others to do so. And, if the Scriptures teach beyond a doubt that we dare not perform these particular actions or others like them, how much greater is our obligation to follow the example of the saints with regard to the rest, when they say: 'We ought to obey God rather than men,'[193] and also: 'If it be just to hear you rather than God, judge ye, for we cannot but speak the things which we have seen and heard.'[194]

Q. 12. Whether each individual must be solicitous for all in all circumstances, or only for those under his charge, and, with regard to these latter, whether he must act according to the gift allotted to him by God through the Holy Spirit.

R. Our Lord Jesus Christ, Only-begotten Son of God, by whom all things visible and invisible were made,[195] declared: 'I am not sent but to the sheep that are lost of the house of

---

191 John 13.8.
192 Acts 21.13.
193 Acts 5.29.
194 Acts 4.19,20.
195 Col. 1.16.

Israel';[196] and to His disciples He said: 'As the Father hath sent me, I also send you.'[197] He also admonishes them: 'Go ye not into the way of the Gentiles and into the city of the Samaritans, enter ye not.'[198] Then, after He had fulfilled the prophecy regarding Himself which David spoke as if in the person of God the Father: 'Thou art my son, this day have I begotten thee. Ask of me and I will give thee the Gentiles for thy inheritance and the utmost parts of the earth for thy possession,'[199] He bids His Apostles: 'Going, therefore, teach ye all nations.'[200] How much more strictly ought each one of us obey the Apostle when he writes admonishing us 'not to be more wise than it behoveth to be wise, but to be wise unto sobriety and according as God hath divided to every one the measure of faith![201] Furthermore, we should patiently await the time and the issue he proposes to us when he says again: 'Brethren, let every man wherein he was called, therein abide.'[202] The Apostle himself practiced very meticulously what he preached to others, for he says: 'they gave to me and Barnabas the right hands of fellowship, that we should go unto the Gentiles, and they unto the circumcision.'[203]

But, if ever the call of the love of God or of neighbor should require us to supply some deficiency, he who answers the summons will have the reward of voluntary obedience. This call is addressed to us when the love of God and His Christ demands that we fulfill this precept of the Lord: 'A new commandment I give unto you: that you love one

---

196 Matt. 15.24.
197 John 20.21.
198 Matt. 10.5.
199 Ps. 2.7,8.
200 Matt. 28.19.
201 Rom. 12.3.
202 1 Cor. 7.24.
203 Gal. 2.9.

another as I have loved you.'[204] 'Greater love than this no man
hath, that a man lay down his life for his friends.'[205] We are
called to love of neighbor either when a person in authority
needs our support or when those in his charge require that
some necessity be supplied. The Apostle says: 'Let no man
seek his own, but that which is another's.'[206] The love which
is according to Christ seeks not its own.[207] Elsewhere, the
Apostle says: 'edify one another as you also do.'[208] If a man
does not accomplish in word and work the mission upon
which he was sent, he is therefore guilty of the blood of those
who have not heard the Gospel, and he is unable to say with
the Apostle, addressing the Ephesian elders: 'I am clean from
this time of the blood of all of you. For I have not spared
to declare unto you all the counsel of God.'[209] And whoever
is able to do more than what is enjoined, unto the edification of faith in the love of Christ, will have a recompense
for this, as the Apostle intimated when he said: 'For if I
do this thing willingly, I have a reward; but if against my
will, a dispensation is committed to me.'[210]

*Q. 13 Whether it is necessary to suffer every kind of trial,
even to the point of risking death, in fulfilling our duty of
obedience to God, especially in caring for those committed
to us.*

R. Our Lord Jesus Christ, the Only-begotten Son of the
living God, through whom all things visible and invisible
were made,[211] who has life even as the Father who gave it

204 John 13.34.
205 John 15.13.
206 1 Cor. 10.24.
207 1 Cor. 13.5.
208 1 Thess. 5.11.
209 Acts 20.26,27.
210 1 Cor. 9.17.
211 Col. 1.16.

to Him and who received all power from the Father, when
they approached to seize Him and lead Him to death that
we might have justice and eternal life, went to meet death
with great alacrity, saying: 'behold the Son of man shall be
betrayed into the hands of sinners. Rise up, let us go. Behold,
he that will betray me is at hand.'[212] Moreover, as it is written in the Gospel according to John: 'Jesus, therefore, knowing all things that should come upon him, went forth and said
to them: Whom seek ye? They answered him: Jesus of
Nazareth. Jesus saith to them: 'I am he';[213] and, a little further on, He says: 'I have told you that I am he. If therefore
you seek me, let these go their way.'[214] How much more willingly, therefore, should we bear with the trials which beset
us in the natural course of things! By triumphing thus over
the assaults of our enemies for the sake of obedience to God,
we will glorify God, for we will cheerfully accept the annoy-
ances which appear to be brought upon us by our enemies,
inasmuch as we will have attained to the high purpose of him
who said: 'Unto you it is given for Christ, not only to believe
in him, but also to suffer for him.'[215] The Acts, in relating
the hardships of the Apostles, tell of how they accepted contumely and death with joy that they might fulfill their mission
of preaching according to the Lord's command.[216]

Furthermore, the Apostle means to instruct us when he
says: 'Who shall separate us from the love of God? Shall
tribulations? or distress? or persecution? or hunger? or nakedness? or danger? or the sword? (as it is written, For thy sake
we are put to death all the day long. We are accounted as
sheep for the slaughter). But in all these things we overcome

---

212 Mark 14.41,42.
213 John 18.4,5.
214 John 18.8.
215 Phil. 1.29.
216 Acts 4,5.

because of him that hath loved us. For I am sure that neither death nor life nor angels nor principalities nor powers nor dominations nor things present nor things to come nor height nor depth nor any other creature shall be able to separate us from the love of God which is in Christ Jesus.'[217] The observance of the commandments is, therefore, inextricably and completely bound up with the charity which is in Christ, as the words of the Lord Himself show: 'If any one love me, he will keep my word, but he that keepth not my words, loveth me not';[218] and also: 'You are my friends if you do the things that I command you.'[219] Moreover, the command that we love one another is a new one and His own, and this command the Apostle fulfills when he says: 'So desirous of you, we would gladly impart unto you not only the gospel of Christ, but also our own souls; because you were become most dear unto us.'[220] Keeping our gaze fixed upon Christ, therefore, let us, by glorious imitation of Him, increase our zeal. And thinking upon the saints, let us receive instruction from them to the full extent of our capacity, so that, rendered ever more zealous by them and observing every commandment of the Lord without spot or blame even unto death, we may attain to life everlasting and possess the kingdom of heaven, as He who cannot deceive has promised, Jesus Christ, our Lord and God, Only-begotten Son of the living God.

---

217 Rom. 8.35-39.
218 John 14.23,24.
219 John 15.14.
220 1 Thess. 2.8.

HOMILY ON THE WORDS,
'GIVE HEED TO THYSELF'

OD WHO CREATED US has granted us the faculty of speech that we might disclose the counsels of our hearts to one another and that, since we possess our human nature in common, each of us might share his thoughts with his neighbor, bringing them forth from the secret recesses of the heart as from a treasury. If we were passing through this life with our minds bared for all to see, we should, in thinking, make direct and immediate contact with one another. But, inasmuch as the mind carries on its processes of thought beneath a covering of flesh, nouns and verbs are needed to make known the secrets of the mind. As soon, therefore, as our mental faculty frames a meaningful utterance, it is conveyed by words, as by a ferry, and, flying through the air, it passes from the speaker to the auditor. If the passage of our words is attended by a deep tranquility and calm, they weigh anchor in the ears of our disciples, as in a peaceful haven, untroubled by storms. But, if a noisy protest on the part of our hearers, like an angry surge of the sea, oppose our words, they will be dispersed in the midst of their course through the air and, like a ship, they will be wrecked. By your silence, therefore, assure tranquility for my discourse. It may, perchance, prove to have something useful in it and worth carrying away. The word of truth is hard to catch and it can easily elude the inattentive listener. For this reason, the Holy Spirit wills that our words be concise and brief so as to express much in little and by condensation to make what is said easy

431

to retain in the memory. It is the natural function of speech neither to veil its meaning with obscurity nor to flow aimlessly about the subject in a wordy and inept manner. These faults, indeed, are avoided in the words which we have just quoted from one of the Books of Moses and which attentive listeners among you will recall perfectly, unless the very brevity of the quotation caused you, perhaps, to miss my citing of it. It ran as follows: 'Give heed to thyself, lest perhaps a wicked thought steal in upon thee.'[1]

We men are easily prone to sins of thought. Therefore, He who has formed each heart individually,[2] knowing that the impulse received from the intention constitutes the major element in sin, has ordained that purity in the ruling part of our soul be our primary concern. That faculty by which we are especially prone to commit sin surely merits great care and vigilance. As the more provident physicians offset physical weakness by precautionary measures taken in advance, so the Protector of us all and the true Physician of our souls takes possession first and with stronger garrisons of that part of the soul which He knows is most liable to sin. The actions performed by the body require time, favorable opportunity, physical exertion, assistance, and other accessories. The movements of the mind, however, take place independently of time; they are performed without weariness; they are accomplished effortlessly; every occasion is appropriate for them. For instance, some haughty person having nothing but contempt for decorum, although wearing outwardly the appearance of sobriety, may be sitting in the midst of persons who are admiring him for his virtue. Suppose that this man has run off in his thoughts, by a secret movement of the heart, to a place of sin. In imagination he beholds the objects of his

1 Deut. 15.9.
2 Ps. 32.15.

desire; he fashions the image of some shameful rendezvous entirely within the secret workshop of his heart and within himself he draws vivid pictures of sensual pleasure. He has, unwitnessed, committed a secret sin, which will remain unknown to all until the coming of Him who will reveal the hidden things of darkness and make manifest the counsels of the hearts.[3] Beware, therefore, 'lest perhaps a wicked thought steal in upon thee.' For, 'he who looks upon a woman to lust after her hath already committed adultery with her in his heart.'[4] The actions of the body, therefore, are retarded by many impediments, but he who sins in his intention has committed a transgression that is accomplished with the swiftness of thought. Where the lapse into sin is sudden, therefore, the power of swift protection has been granted us, 'lest perhaps,' as the Scripture declares, 'a wicked thought steal in upon thee.' And now, let us return to the theme of our discourse.

'Give heed to thyself,' says the Scripture. Every animal has been endowed by God, the Creator of all things, with an interior power of self-protection. You would find upon careful observation that, as a rule, brute beasts have an instinctive aversion for what would be harmful to them. On the other hand, they are drawn by a certain natural attraction to the enjoyment of whatever is beneficial. Consequently, God, who is also our Teacher, has given to us this great precept, so that we may acquire by the aid of reason what animals have by their very nature and that we may do knowingly, by the attentive and diligent application of our reason, that which animals do instinctively. Moreover, in obeying this precept, we become vigilant custodians of the resources God has bestowed on us, avoiding sin as the beasts shun noxious foods and following after justice as they seek for pasturage. 'Give

3 1 Cor. 4.5.
4 Matt. 5.28.

heed to thyself' that you may be able to distinguish between the injurious and the salutary. Now, inasmuch as the faculty of attention has a double aspect—referring, in one sense, to an absorption in visible objects and, in another sense, to an intellectual gaze at incorporeal realities—if we should assert that this precept has to do with the action of our bodily eyes, we should be indicating at the start that it cannot be obeyed. How could one encompass his whole person with a glance? The eye does not apply its power of sight to itself. It cannot view the head nor is it acquainted with the back, or the face, or the arrangement of the internal organs. Yet, to say that the precepts in the Scripture are impossible to fulfill is impious. It remains, therefore, to interpret the precept as referring to a mental action. 'Give heed to thyself'— that is, examine yourself from all angles. Keep the eye of your soul sleeplessly on guard, for 'Thou art going in the midst of snares.'[5] Traps set by the enemy lie concealed everywhere. Look about you in all directions, therefore, 'that you may be saved as a swallow from the traps and as a bird from the snare.'[6] The deer cannot be caught with traps because of the keenness of his vision; whence its name, deriving from its own sharpsightedness (oxudorkías). A bird, if alert, easily flies out of the range of the huntsman's snare. See to it, then, that you are not more remiss than the animals in protecting yourself. Never let yourself be caught in the snares of the Devil and so become his prey, the captured plaything of his will.[7]

'Give heed to thyself'—that is, attend neither to the goods you possess nor to the objects that are round about you, but to yourself alone. We ourselves are one thing; our possessions

---

5 Eccli. 9.20.
6 Prov. 6.5.
7 2 Tim. 2.26.

another; the objects that surround us, yet another. We are soul and intellect in that we have been made according to the image of the Creator. Our body is our own possession and the sensations which are expressed through it, but money, crafts, and other appurtenances of life in this world are extraneous to us. What, then, does the Scripture mean by this precept? Attend not to the flesh nor seek after its good in any form— health, beauty, enjoyment of pleasures, or longevity—and do not admire wealth and fame and power. Do not consider the accessories to your temporal existence to be of great consequence and thus, in your zealous concern for these things, neglect the life which is of primary importance to you. 'Give heed to thyself,' that is, to your soul. Adorn it, care for it, to the end that, by careful attention, every defilement incurred as a result of sin may be removed and every shameful vice expelled, and that it may be embellished and made bright with every ornament of virtue. Examine closely what sort of being you are. Know your nature—that your body is mortal, but your soul, immortal; that our life has two denotations, so to speak: one relating to the flesh, and this life is quickly over, the other referring to the soul, life without limit. 'Give heed to thyself'—cling not to the mortal as if it were eternal; disdain not that which is eternal as if it were temporal. Despise the flesh, for it passes away; be solicitous for your soul which will never die.

Acquire an exact understanding of yourself, that you may know how to make a suitable allotment to each of the two sides of your nature: food and clothing to the body and to the soul, the doctrines of piety, training in refined behavior, the practice of virtue, and the correction of vice. Do not fatten the body unduly and do not try to acquire physical bulk 'for the flesh lusteth against the spirit and the spirit against the

flesh; for these are contrary one to another.'[8] Take care never
to provide the lower part of your nature with great power of
dominion by adding weight to the flesh. As with scales, where,
if you depress one side, the other is necessarily raised, so, in
the case of the body and soul, excess in one inevitably causes
defect in the other. If the body is sleek and corpulent, the
mind, by a necessary consequence, is weak and languid in
carrying on the activity proper to it. If, on the other hand,
the soul is in good case and has been developed to its proper
stature by the practice of virtue, the body suffers a correspond-
ing deterioration.

This precept, moreover, is at once useful to the sick and
highly appropriate also to those who are in good health. In
the case of physical illness, physicians exhort their patients
to give heed to themselves and neglect nothing which pertains
to their cure. The Scripture, likewise, the physician of our
souls, restores to health a soul afflicted by sin with this brief
remedy: 'Give heed, therefore, to thyself,' that you may be
given assistance toward your recovery proportioned to the
gravity of your transgression. Sin is a serious and difficult
matter. You require frequent confession, bitter tears, prolonged vigils, constant fasting. A fault is light and support-
able; the penance done for it should be equally so. Only
'give heed to thyself' that you may recognize the state of health
or sickness in your soul. Many persons, from lack of attentiveness, contract serious and even incurable diseases and they
are not even aware that they are ill. But, even to those in good
health, this admonition is of no small assistance as regards
their actions. Thus, the same remedy heals the sick and establishes the sound in more perfect health. Every one of us, indeed, who is instructed in the Holy Scripture is the administrator of some one of those gifts which, according to the

---

8 Gal. 5.17.

Gospel, have been apportioned to us. In this great household of the Church not only are there vessels of every kind—gold, silver, wooden, and earthen[9]—but also a great variety of pursuits. The house of God, which is the Church of the living God,[10] has hunters, travelers, architects, builders, farmers, shepherds, athletes, soldiers. To all of these this short admonition will be appropriate, for it will produce in each proficiency in action and energy of will. You are a hunter sent forth by the Lord, who says: 'Behold, I send many hunters and they shall hunt them upon every mountain.'[11] Take good care, therefore, that your prey does not elude you, so that, having captured them with the word of truth, you may bring back to the Saviour those who have been made wild and savage by iniquity. You are a wayfarer, like to him who prayed: 'Direct my steps.'[12] 'Give heed to thyself' that you swerve not from the path, that you decline neither to the right nor the left.[13] Keep to the King's highway. The architect should lay the firm foundation of faith which is Jesus Christ, and let the builder look to his materials: not wood, nor hay, nor stubble, but gold, silver, precious stones.[14] If you are a shepherd, take care that none of your pastoral duties is neglected. And what are these duties? To bring back that which is lost, to bind up that which was broken, to heal that which is diseased.[15] If a farmer, dig around the unfriutful fig tree and administer remedies that will promite fecundity.[16] If a soldier, 'labor with the gospel, war a good warfare'[17] against the

9 2 Tim. 2.20.
10 1 Tim. 3.15.
11 Jer. 16.16.
12 Ps. 118.133.
13 Deut. 17.20.
14 1 Cor. 3.11,12.
15 Ezech. 34.16.
16 Luke 13.8.
17 2 Tim.1.8; 1 Tim. 1.18.

spirits of wickedness.[18] 'Take unto you all the armor of God'[19] against the desires of the flesh. Do not 'entangle yourself in secular businesses that you may please him to whom you have engaged yourself.'[20] If an athlete, 'give heed to thyself' lest you violate any of the laws for athletes, for no one is crowned except he strive lawfully.[21] Like Paul, run, fight, and strike with the fist.[22] Keep the eye of your soul unwaveringly alert, like a skillful boxer. Shield your vital parts with your hand. Keep your gaze fixed upon your opponent. In the race, stretch forth yourself to the things that are before;[23] 'So run that you may obtain';[24] do battle with your invisible adversaries.[25] Such a one this precept would have you be as long as you live, neither losing heart nor resting, but soberly and vigilantly maintaining a watch over yourself.

Time does not permit me to continue enumerating the various pursuits followed by those who are united in labor for Christ's Gospel and how the meaning of the precept applies to them all. 'Give heed to thyself': be sober, thoughtful, careful to preserve what you have and provident of the future. Do not lose by negligence that which you already possess and do not promise yourself the enjoyment of what is is not yours and perhaps never will be, as if you already possessed it. Is not this weakness of imagining that something hoped for is already possessed a natural trait in the young by reason of the frivolity of their minds? Whenever they are at leisure or in the stillness of night, they conjure up airy fantasies and are borne along the course of every extravagant fancy by the

18 Eph. 6.12.
19 Eph. 6.13.
20 2 Tim.2.4.
21 2 Tim. 2.5.
22 1 Cor. 9.26.
23 Phil. 3.13.
24 1 Cor. 9.24.
25 Eph. 6.12.

agility of their minds. They promise themselves fame, a brilliant marriage, model offspring, a good old age, universal esteem. Then, despite the fact that there is no foundation for such hopes, their minds swell nigh to bursting with dreams of achievements which men regard as supreme. They build fine large houses and fill them with all sorts of precious treasures. They encompass as great an area of land as their idle imagination could conceive of as set apart from the whole of creation. They store the produce therefrom in granaries fashioned by their vanity. To all this they add herds of cattle, a countless throng of slaves, civil magistracies, positions of national leadership, military commands, battles, triumphs, royal power itself. And, although they attain to all these glories only in vain fantasy, they imagine, by reason of their excessive folly, that they are in actual and present possession of their hopes. Now, day-dreaming is a malady which commonly afflicts an idle and indolent mind; in order to restrain, as with a bridle, this mental flightiness, this swelling conceit of thought, the Scripture bids us obey that great and wise precept: 'Give heed to thyself.' Do not promise yourself non-existent possessions, but administer to advantage the things that are yours.

Furthermore, I think that the Lawgiver has intended that this exhortation also should eliminate a very common human vice. It is easier for every one of us to busy ourselves with affairs that do not concern us than to look after our own. In order that we might not be guilty of this, the Scripture says [in effect]: Cease meddling with the affairs of another. Beware of spending your time in scrutinizing another's weakness. 'Give heed to thyself,' that is, turn the gaze of your soul toward self-scrutiny. Many there are, indeed, who, according to the Lord's words, see the mote in their brother's eye and see not the beam in their own.[26] You should, therefore, be constantly

---

26 Matt. 7.3.

440 SAINT BASIL

examining whether your life conforms to this teaching. But, do not look around outside yourself to see whether you can discover some blemish, as did that stern and boastful Pharisee who stood justifying himself and despising the publican. Continually examine yourself as to whether you have committed any sin of thought, or whether your tongue has been guilty of any lapse by running ahead of your thought, or whether there has been any heedless or involuntary action on the part of your hands. If you find many defects in your way of living (as, being human, you surely will), say with the publican: 'O God, be merciful to me a sinner.'[27]

'Give heed, therefore, to thyself.' This admonition, like a prudent counselor who keeps reminding you of the nature of things human, will be a useful ally when you are enjoying brilliant success and your whole life moves along like a stream. Even when you are cast down by adversities, it might profitably be recited again and again by your heart, that you may not be reduced to ignoble repining by despair; just as, in the former instance, it would keep you from being exalted through vanity to an overweening pride. Is your wealth your boast? Or are you proud of your lineage? Do you find cause for glory in your native land or in physical comeliness, or in the honors universally accorded you? 'Give heed to thyself,' for you are mortal; 'for dust thou art and unto dust thou shalt return.'[28] Pass in review those persons who have enjoyed positions of eminence before you. Where are they who held the civil magistracies? Where, the peerless orators? Where are they who had charge of the national assemblies—the famous breeders of horses, the generals, the officials, the sovereigns? Have not all of these fallen to dust? Have they not all become legend? Is it not true that a few bones are the memorial to

27 Luke 18.11-13.
28 Gen. 3.19.

the life of these men? Look down into their graves and see if
you are able to discern which is the slave and which the master; which the pauper, and which the rich man. Distinguish,
if you can, the captive from the king, the strong man from
the weak, the comely from the ill-favored. If you remember
your nature, you will never yield to vanity and you will be
mindful of yourself if you give heed to yourself.

On the other hand, suppose you are an ignoble and undis-
tinguished person, poor and of lowly origin, without home or
city, sick, in need of daily sustenance, in dread of the powerful, cowering before everyone because of your abject condition; 'but he that is poor,' says the Scripture, 'beareth not
reprehension.'[29] Yet, do not despair nor cast aside every good
hope because your present state is quite unenviable. Rather,
turn your thoughts to the blessings already granted you by
God and to those reserved by promise for the future. First of
all, you are a man, the only one of all living beings to have
been formed by God.[30] Is not this enough to call forth the
most ecstatic joy in a man who reasons intelligently—that you
have been formed by the very Hands of God who created all
things? Secondly, having been made according to the image
of the Creator, you are able to arrive at a dignity equal to that
of the angels by leading a good life. You have been given a
mind capable of understanding, through which you gain
knowledge of God. You investigate, with the aid of your
reason, the nature of existing things. You pluck the fruit,
exceedingly sweet, of wisdom. All the animals on land, wild
and tame, all those that live in the waters, all that fly through
the air of this earth serve you and are subject to you. Have
you not invented arts and founded cities, and devised all the
tools which minister to necessity and luxury? Has not your

---

29 Prov. 13.8.
30 Gen. 2.7.

rational faculty made it possible for you to sail the seas? Do not earth and waters yield nourishment for you? Do not air and sky and wheeling stars show forth to you their array? Why, then, are you dejected because you do not possess a horse with a silver bridle? You have the sun as a torchbearer, lighting your way in swiftest course all day long. The lustre of gold and silver is not yours, but you have the moon to shed her great beams of light around you. You do not mount a carriage inlaid with gold, but you have your feet, a vehicle belonging to you alone and adapted to you by nature. Why, then, do you admire those who have a full purse, but who need the feet of others to convey them from place to place? You do not take your slumber upon an ivory couch, but you have the ground which is more valuable than quantities of ivory. Sweet is the rest taken upon it and swiftly come by and free from care. You do not lie beneath a gilded roof, but you have the sky glittering overhead in all its expanse with the indescribable beauty of the stars. And these wonders are of a mortal kind; those which I shall now mention are still greater. For your sake, a God dwelt among men,[31] there was a distribution of the Holy Spirit,[32] death was destroyed,[33] hope of resurrection was confirmed,[34] a divine precept was given for leading a life of perfection, the way to God was shown by the commandments,[35] the kingdom of heaven was prepared,[36] and crowns of justice[37] were made ready for him who has not fled from the labors to be undergone on behalf of virtue.

Now, if you give heed to yourself, you will discover all this

31 John 1.14.
32 Heb. 2.4.
33 1 Cor. 15.26,55.
34 1 Cor. 15.12,22.
35 Matt. 19.17,21.
36 Matt. 25.34.
37 2 Tim. 4.8.

about yourself and still more. You will not be made disconsolate by your deficiencies, but you will take pleasure in what you do possess. This precept will be of great assistance if you keep it before your mind on all occasions. For example, suppose that anger overrules your reason and you are quite carried away by your wrath, so that you utter unseemly words and act in a rude and savage manner. If you give heed to yourself, you will control your wrath as you would an unruly and refractory young horse, laying on the blows of reason, like a lash. You will also govern your tongue and you will not use violence against the one who is provoking you to anger. Again, suppose evil desires are pricking your soul like goads and are subjecting you to wanton and licentious impulses. If you give heed to yourself, you will remember that this present delight will end in bitterness, and also that the pleasurable excitement now experienced by the body under the influence of sensual delight will beget the venomous worm that punishes us forever in hell.[38] If, moreover, you bear in mind that flesh by ardor will become the mother of everlasting fire,[39] lustful pleasure will be straightway put to flight and marvelous inner peace and quietness of soul will take its place, as the noisy clamor of giddy maid-servants is hushed at the entrance of a discreet mistress.

'Give heed to thyself,' then—and bear in mind that one part of your soul is rational and intelligent, the other emotional and non-rational. Authority belongs to the former by nature and to the latter, submission and obedience to the reason. Never, therefore, allow your mind to become the bound slave of the passions, nor permit the passions to rise up against reason and usurp power over the soul. In short, scrupulous attention to yourself will be of itself sufficient to

---

38 Isa. 66.24; Mark 9.43,45,47.
39 Matt. 25.41.

guide you to the knowledge of God. If you give heed to yourself, you will not need to look for signs of the Creator in the
structure of the universe; but in yourself, as in a miniature
replica of cosmic order, you will contemplate the great wisdom
of the Creator. From the incorporeal soul within you, learn
that God is incorporeal and without local determination.
Your soul, likewise, does not have local habitation as a dominant principle of its existence, but, because of its association
with the body, it abides in a place. Believe that God is invisible
from a consideration of your own soul. Your soul cannot be
apprehended with bodily eyes. It has neither color, nor shape,
nor any physical determination, but it is discernible by its
operations alone. Do not, therefore, seek as regards God that
cognition which is gained through the faculty of sight, but,
supporting faith by the reason, keep your apprehension of
Him a spiritual activity. Marvel at the manner in which the
Artificer has joined the powers of the soul with the body so
that they permeate it from end to end, bringing the most
widely separated parts of it into alliance and uniting them all
under one impulse of the breath. Consider, also, what this
power is which the soul imparts to the body and what sympathy the body renders the soul in return; how, on the one
hand, the body is given life by the soul and how the soul, on
the other hand, is the recipient of pains from the body. Reflect upon the stores of learning contained in the mind and
ask yourself why it is that, when additional information enters in, it does not obscure the knowledge previously acquired,
but our recollections remain clear and distinct, inscribed upon
the ruling part of the soul as upon a bronze tablet. Think of
how the soul destroys the beauty properly belonging to it by
yielding to carnal passion and how, on the contrary, it re-
covers the likeness to its Creator through the practice of virtue, after it has been purified from the shame of iniquity.

Having thus contemplated your soul, direct your attention, if you will, to the structure of your body. Admire the appropriateness with which the most skillful Artificer has fashioned it as a dwelling place for the rational soul. Of all living creatures, man alone He has made to stand erect, so that you may perceive from your very aspect that your life has a celestial origin. All quadrupeds keep their gaze fixed upon the ground and bow their heads toward their stomach. Man, however, was made to look upward so that he might not dally with the pleasures of the table nor with lustful desires, but devote his whole energy to his journey heavenward. Moreover, the Creator placed man's head at the highest point of his body and made it the seat of the principal senses. Here are located in close proximity sight, hearing, taste, and smell. And, although they are thus confined to so small an area, no one of them impedes the action of its neighbor. The eyes, of course, hold the topmost point of vantage, so that they may survey the entire body. Posted as they are under their little headlands, so to speak, they enjoy a full and unobstructed view. The sense of hearing, on the contrary, is not directly exposed to its stimulus, but the sounds in the air reach it by a circuitous route. This arrangement is dictated by the highest wisdom, so that while the voice, twisting its way along the tortuous windings of the ears, may pass through—or rather, sound within—nothing from outside which could act as an obstruction to this sense may be able to steal its way in. Study, also the nature of your tongue. Observe how soft and supple it is and how, because of its power of varied and intricate movement, it can meet every requirement of language. Think of your teeth, which serve both as instruments for the voice in providing the tongue with a sturdy fulcrum and also act as aids in the taking of food, some of the teeth cutting the food and others grinding it. And so, when you have gone over all these points with suitable reflections upon each, when you have, in addition, studied the process of breathing, the manner in which the heart conserves its warmth, the organs of digestion and the veins, you will discern in all of these wonders the inscrutable wisdom of the Creator; so that you will be able to say with the Prophet: 'Thy knowledge is become wonderful'[40] from the study of myself. Give heed, therefore, to thyself,' that you may give heed to God, to whom be glory and empire for ever and ever. Amen.

40 Ps. 138.6.

HOMILY 10

Against Those Who Are Prone to Anger

N THE CASE of medical precepts, the benefit to be derived from them, provided that these maxims are apposite and in accordance with the laws of the medical art, is most effectually demonstrated by the test of experience. The same is true of spiritual counsels. They manifest their wisdom and their value for the amendment of our life and the attainment of perfection by those who obey them when they receive the strong confirmation of results produced. In Proverbs we read the explicit declaration: 'Wrath destroyeth even the prudent,'[1] and the Apostle admonishes us as follows: 'Let all anger and indignation and clamour be put away from you with all malice.'[2] The Lord, likewise, says that whoever gives way lightly to anger against his brother is in danger of the judgment.[3] Now, when we have had experience with the vice of anger, not as arising within ourselves, but attacking us from without, like a sudden tempest, then, especially, do we perceive the excellence of the divine precept. If we have ever yielded before such anger, as if giving passage to a strongly flowing stream, and have studied calmly the shameful paroxysms which commonly afflict persons who are in the grip of this passion, we have also recognized in actual fact the validity of the saying: 'A wrathful man is not seemly.'[4] Indeed, this vice, when it has once succeeded in banishing reason, itself usurps the dominion over

---

1 Prov. 15.1 (Septuagint).
2 Eph. 4.31.
3 Matt. 5.22.
4 Prov. 11.25 (Septuagint).

447

the soul. It makes a man wholly bestial and, in fact, it does not even allow him to be a man, since he no longer has the aid of his reason. The effect of anger upon persons aroused by this passion is like that of the poison in animals who carry venom. They become rabid, like mad dogs; they dart about, like scorpions; they bite, like serpents. The Scripture also recognizes the truth of this and applies the names of wild animals to those who are under the power of any vice; for, by their wickedness, they acquire an affinity with them. Isaias calls them dumb dogs,[5] serpents, a generation of vipers,[6] etc. Certainly, they who are bent upon mutual destruction and upon doing harm to their fellow men, would be appropriately numbered with wild and poisonous beasts who by nature bear an implacable enmity toward mankind. Anger causes tongues to become unbridled,[7] and speech, unguarded. Physical violence, acts of contumely, reviling, accusations, blows, and other bad effects too numerous to recount are born of anger and indignation. By indignation, also, the sword is sharpened; a human hand dares to take a human life. For this cause, brothers have lost sight of their brotherhood; parents and children have forgotten their natural bond. Angry men become strangers first to themselves, then to all their friends as well. Like mountain torrents which converge their streams in the valleys and sweep along with them everything in their path, the violent and uncontrolled onset of an angry man carries all before it. The wrathful have no respect for old age, nor for a virtuous life, nor ties of kinship, nor favors received in the past, nor for anything else worthy of honor. Anger is a kind of temporary madness. Its victims often plunge headlong into open peril, so careless of themselves are they

5 Isa. 56.10.
6 Matt. 23.33.
7 James 1.26.

in their eagerness for revenge. Stung on all sides, as by a gad-
fly, by the recollection of the authors of their wrongs, their
wrath struggling and bounding within them, they do not rest
until they have inflicted some hurt upon their tormenter, or,
perhaps, as sometimes happens, until they themselves receive
an injury. For, very often, objects which are broken through
violent usage, in as much as they are shattered against resisting
bodies, suffer greater injury than they inflict.

Who could adequately describe the evil—how vehement
natures, fired with indignation for some trivial cause, shout
and rage and leap upon their prey more ruthlessly than a
venomous beast? Nor do they leave off until the flame has
spent itself and the wrath within them has burst like a bubble
in working great and even irremediable harm. Neither the
point of the sword, nor fire, nor any means of inspiring fear
is able to restrain the spirit frenzied with wrath, any more than
such threats subdue persons possessed by the Devil (from
whom angry men differ not at all, either in appearance or
state of soul). In those who are thirsting for revenge, the
blood boils around the heart as if it were seething and bub-
bling over a high fire. Bursting forth to the surface, his passion
reveals the angry man under a different aspect from his habitual one that is well known to all. It is as if a theatrical mask
altered his appearance. His friends do not discern in his eyes
their characteristic and wonted expression. His glance is wild
and presently darts fire. He gnashes his teeth like a charging
boar. His face is livid and suffused with blood, his body swells,
his veins burst, his breathing is labored because of the tempest raging within. His voice is hoarse and strained, his utterance thick, his words without logic, sequence, order, or meaning. When his anger has, by aggravation, reached the point
of uncontrollable fury, like a flame abundantly fed, then,
indeed, is the spectacle indescribable and unbearable to wit-

ness. His hands are lifted even against his kinsmen. No part of the body is safe. His feet trample ruthlessly upon the most vital organs and every object in sight becomes a weapon for his fury. And if such persons find arrayed against them an adversary who threatens them equally—that is, with another fit of anger and a like frenzy—they close with them, and both sides inflict and suffer as many injuries as the henchmen of so fierce a demon deserve. The combatants then carry off mutilated members as prizes for their wrath; not infrequently, even death results. It had begun with one of the pair unjustly laying violent hands upon the other. The latter then returns the blow and refuses to give way. Their bodies get well pummeled but anger deadens the pain. They have not time to become aware of their injuries, since their whole attention is taken up with wreaking vengeance.

Do not, therefore, endeavor to cure one evil with another and do not try to outdo one another in inflicting harm. The victor in unrighteous combats is the more unhappy, for he bears away the greater share of guilt. Do not, then, return evil for evil and do not increase your debt of wickedness by paying it. If someone in a fit of anger has treated you despitefully, bear the wrong in silence. But you, contrariwise, receive into your own heart your adversary's gust of wrath and then you imitate the winds which return by a counter-blast whatever is flung against the direction in which they are blowing. Let not your enemy be your teacher and model. Do not imitate what you hate. Do not become a mirror, as it were, for an angry man by reflecting his image. His face is flushed. Why has not yours turned red? His eyes are suffused with blood. Do you mean to say that yours keep their placid expression? His voice is hoarse. Surely, yours is not gentle! An echo in the desert is not so perfectly returned to the speaker as insults are turned back upon the reviler. Nay, the sound of an echo comes back the same, but the insult is answered with increase. Now, what sort of taunts are they which revilers utter back and forth? One calls the other a common fellow of ignoble stock. He, in turn, calls the first a slave of slaves. One says, 'pauper'; the other answers, 'vagabond.' One cries, 'fool'; the other shouts, 'madman'; until, like arrows, their armory of insults is exhausted. Then, when they have used up their stock of verbal abuse, they proceed to fighting it out with blows. Thus, anger stirs up strife, strife begets railing, railing leads to blows, blows to wounds, and from wounds, often enough, death results. Let us, however, check the evil at its source, by making use of every device for expelling anger from our souls. By so doing, we could exterminate most of our vices along with this one, which serves as their root and source. Has someone insulted you? Bless him. Has he struck you? Suffer it. Has he despised you and set you at naught? Reflect that you are made of earth and that you will return to the earth.[8] Whoever arms himself beforehand with these considerations will find that every insult falls short of the truth. Thus will you make it impossible for your enemy to avenge himself, since you show yourself impervious to his taunts. Further, you will secure for yourself the great crown of patience by making the insane fury of another the occasion for practicing your own philosophy. If you listen to me, therefore, you also will add force to the insults cast at you. If he calls you common, ignoble, a nobody, then call yourself earth and ashes. You are not more worthy of honor than our father, Abraham, and he used to refer to himself in this way.[9] If your enemy says you are an ignoramus, a beggar, a worthless fellow, call yourself in the words of David, 'a worm,'[10]

---

8 Gen. 3.19.
9 Gen. 18.27.
10 Ps. 21.7.

born of a dunghill. To these responses, add also Moses' noble conduct. When he was reviled by Aaron and Mary, he did not make accusations against them to God, but prayed for them.[11] Of whose disciples would you rather be—the saints, the friends of God, or men filled with the spirit of iniquity? Whenever the temptation to revile another assails you, consider that you are being put to the test: whether you will practice patience and go over to God's side or give way to anger and run off to His Adversary. Give your reason the opportunity of choosing the best part. For, either you will confer a kind of favor upon your enemy by giving him an example of mildness, or, by your disdaining to bandy insults with him, you will exact a crueler vengeance. What could be more painful to a hostile man than to see an enemy showing contempt for his insults? Retain your self-possession; be invulnerable to affronts. Let your enemy bark at you to no avail and let his rage burst upon himself. A man who strikes a person who has no feeling takes vengeance upon himself (for he did not succeed in exacting it from his enemy and he found no outlet for his wrath). In the same way, a person who showers abuse upon one who is insensible to his taunts finds himelf powerless to relieve his feelings, and, as I have said, he quite tears himself asunder. Moreover, what are the epithets that are applied to each of you under such circumstances? He is called an abusive fellow; you, a magnanimous one. He is dubbed irritable and rude; you, long-suffering and mild. He will suffer remorse for his words; you will never regret practicing virtue.

But, why should I go on at great length? [The main consideration is that] his railing keeps your enemy from entering the kingdom of heaven, for, railers shall not possess the

---

11 Num. 12.1ff.

kingdom of God.[12] Your silent endurance, on the other hand, entitles you to the kingdom, for 'he that shall persevere unto the end, he shall be saved.'[13] But, if you defend yourself and bandy insults with him, what excuse will you offer? That he provoked you? How do you deserve pardon on this ground? An adulterer who passes on the blame to his mistress, alleging that she led him into sin, is not regarded as less deserving of condemnation. There are no crowns where there are no antagonists; nor defeats without adversaries. Hear the words of David: 'When the sinner stood against me.' He does not say: 'I was provoked to anger,' but: 'I have set a guard to my mouth and I was humbled and kept silence from good things.'[14] You are angered by reviling because you consider such an action wicked, yet you, in turn, imitate it as if it were something good. You are entertaining that which you consider reprehensible. Or do you scrupulously analyze the wrongdoing of another and regard your own shameful action as of no consequence? Contumely is an evil, is it not? Do not imitate it, then. The fact that another provoked you does not constitute an excuse. Nay, you thereby become more justly an object of displeasure, in my opinion, because your enemy was not given an example of self-control. Upon beholding your angry foe behaving in a disgraceful manner, you did not refrain from reproducing his image in yourself, but you took offense; you became annoyed and, in turn, gave way to anger. Your passionate reaction really excuses the one who took the initiative in the quarrel, for by your response you release him from blame and you condemn yourself. If anger is wicked, why did you not 'decline from evil'?[15] If it deserves pardon,

12 1 Cor. 6.10.
13 Matt. 10.22.
14 Ps. 38.2.3.
15 Ps. 36.27.

why were you offended with your opponent for losing his temper? You are, therefore, in no better situation for having responded to provocation instead of initiating it. In the contests where crowns are the prize, the victor is crowned—not the first entrant. Consequently, not only is the inaugurator of a wicked action worthy of condemnation, but also the one who follows a wicked leader into sin. If he calls you a poor man and this is true, accept the truth. If he lies, what does it matter? You should not be angered by insults that do not apply to you any more than you should exult in praise which oversteps the limits of truth. Do you not observe how arrows are wont to pierce hard, resistant substances and how their force is weakened by a soft, yielding surface? Reflect that the same thing is true of reviling. He who resists it is pierced by it, but he who yields and gives way dissipates the evil directed against him by the gentleness of his manner. And why does the appellation, 'poor man,' disturb you? Remember your nature—that you came into the world naked and naked will leave it again.[16] What is more destitute than a naked man? You have been called nothing that is derogatory, unless you make the terms used really applicable to yourself. Who was ever haled to prison because he was poor? It is not being poor that is reprehensible, but failing to bear poverty with nobility. Recall that the Lord, 'being rich, became poor for our sakes.'[17] If you are called foolish and ignorant, think of the insults with which the Jews reviled the true Wisdom: 'Thou art a Samaritan and hast a devil.'[18] If you are moved to anger, you make good the opprobrious names. What is more foolish than anger? If you remain unruffled, you silence your insolent assailant by giving him a practical illustration of self-control.

16 Job 1.21.
17 2 Cor. 8.9.
18 John 8.48.

Were you struck? So also was the Lord. Were you spit upon? The Lord also suffered this, for 'He did not turn his face from the shame of the spittle.'[19] Were you falsely accused? So also was your Judge. Did they tear your garment? They stripped my Lord of His and parted His vesture among them.[20] You have not been condemned to death nor crucified. Much is being taken from you that you may the sooner be like Him.

Let each of these considerations find entrance into your mind and check the tumid growth of wrath. By such preparations and by acquiring such dispositions, we quiet the leaping and throbbing of the heart, and restore it to tranquil steadiness. This, indeed, is the implication in the words of David: 'I am ready and am not troubled.'[21] You must, therefore, repress the violent and frenzied movement of the soul by recalling the example of holy men. How gently, for instance, the mighty David bore the fury of Semei. He did not allow himself to grow angry, but turned his thoughts to God, saying: 'The Lord hath bid him curse David.'[22] Therefore, when he was called a man of blood and a wicked man, he did not become angry, but humbled himself as if he had met with deserved reproach. Rid yourself, then, of these two faults: that you should judge yourself as meriting great rewards or think that any man is below you in worth. Thus, anger will never be aroused in us, even when we are suffering indignities. It is indeed shameful for a man upon whom benefits have been conferred and who is under obligation for the greatest favors that, besides being guilty of ingratitude, he should be the first to resort to abuse and vituperation. This is a shameful act, but more so for the person who is guilty of it than for him

---

19 Isa. 50.6.
20 Matt. 27.31,35.
21 Ps. 118.60.
22 2 Sam. 16.10.

who suffers it. Let that foe of yours upbraid you, but do you
not upbraid him. Regard his words as a training ground in
which to exercise philosophy. If you have not been pierced,
you are still unwounded, and, if your spirit suffers some injury, confine the hurt within yourself; for the Psalmist says,
'my heart within me is troubled,'[23] that is, he gave no outward
expression of his feelings but repressed them, as a wave that
breaks within the confines of the shore and subsides. Quiet
your heart, I beg you, when it howls and rages. Make your
passions honor the appearance on the scene of your reason, as
an unruly boy respects the presence of a venerable man.
How might we avoid the harm that comes from yielding to
anger?—by persuading our wrath to await the guidance of our
reason; nay, by concentrating our efforts above all upon not
allowing it to outstrip our reason. We should keep it curbed,
as we would a horse, and obedient to our reason, which may
be compared to a bridle, so that it may never leave its
proper place, but allow itself to be led by the reason whither-
soever it may direct it. The irascible part of the soul,
however, is serviceable to us in many acts of virtue. When,
for example, like a soldier who has left his arms in the
keeping of his general, it promptly brings aid wherever it is
ordered to go and is an ally for the reason against sin, anger
is the sinew of the soul, which provides it with vigor for the
accomplishment of good works. If the soul should become enervated from pleasure, anger hardens it as with a tincture
of iron and restores it from a most weak and flaccid state
to strictness and vigor. Unless your anger has been aroused
against the Evil One, it is impossible for you to hate him as
fiercely as he deserves. For, our hatred of sin should be as
intense, I believe, as our love of virtue; and anger is very

23 Ps. 142.4.

useful for bringing this about, if, as a dog the shepherd, it follows closely the guidance of the reason and remains quiet and docile to those who are helping it and readily obedient to the call of reason. It should be aroused to savagery by a strange face and voice, although the stranger may seem to be offering a service, but it should become servile and subdued at the summons of a friend and familiar. This co-operation between the irascible and the rational part of the soul is most excellent and appropriate. A person who lives in this manner will never compromise with treachery nor ever ally himself with anything harmful, but he always will raise the cry and fall upon the deceitful pleasure as if he were attacking a wolf. Such, then, is the advantage to be derived from anger if one knows how to handle it. In the case of other powers also, each becomes a good or an evil for its possessoor according to the use made of it. For example, a man who abuses the concupiscible part of the soul by making it subservient to carnal enjoyment and impure pleasure becomes licentious and abominable, but one who directs this faculty toward the love of God and the desire for eternal goods is blessed and worthy of emulation. Again, he who administers well his rational faculty is reasonable and intelligent, but he who has sharpened his wits for the purpose of wronging his neighbor is a mischief maker and a villain.

Let us not, therefore, make the faculties which were given us by the Creator for our salvation an occasion of sin for ourselves. To illustrate again: anger, aroused at the proper time and in the proper manner, produces courage, endurance, and continency; acting contrary to right reason, however, it becomes a madness. The Psalmist admonishes us: 'Be ye angry and sin not.'[24] The Lord, moreover, threatens with condem-

---

24 Ps. 4.5.

nation one who lightly gives way to anger, but He does not
forbid that anger be directed against its proper objects, as
a medicinal device, so to speak. His words, 'I will put enmity
between thee and the serpent'[25] and 'Let the Madianites find
you their enemies,'[26] teach us to use anger as a weapon. Therefore did Moses, the meekest of all men,[27] demand retribution
for the practice of idolatry and arm the Levites for the slaying of their brethren. 'Put, every man,' he said, 'his sword
upon his thigh; go from gate to gate and return through
the midst of the camp and let every man kill his brother and
neighbor and friend.'[28] Then, a little farther on: 'and Moses
said: You have consecrated your hands this day to the Lord,
every man in his son and in his brother, that a blessing may
be given to you.'[29] What justified Phinees? Was not his a just
anger against the fornicators? He, otherwise a mild and gentle
man, upon beholding the public and shameless fornication of
Zambri and the Madianite woman, who did not even veil with
secrecy the disgraceful spectacle of their shameful act, refused
to tolerate it and, making a right use of anger, pierced both
of them through with his lance.[30] Again, did not Samuel, in
just wrath, publicly slay Agag, the king of Amalec, after his
life had been spared by Saul against the divine decree?[31] In
this way, anger frequently ministers to good actions. As still
another instance, it was in deliberate and reasonable anger, for
the good of all Israel, that the zealot, Elias, put to death the
four hundred and fifty men, priests of shame, and the four
hundred men, priests of the groves, who ate at Jezabel's

25 Gen. 3.15.
26 Num. 25.17.
27 Num. 12.3.
28 Exod. 32.27.
29 Exod. 32.29.
30 Num. 25.8.
31 1 Sam. 15.33.

table.[32] But you for trivial reasons become angry with your brother. Surely, it is on slight grounds indeed that you become angry when you lose your temper with someone merely because he prods you to it. By acting thus, you imitate the behavior of dogs which bite the stones when they cannot get hold of the person who is throwing them. The object of the provocation is deserving of pity, but the one who is the author of it merits hatred. Transfer your anger to him, the murderer of men, the father of lies,[33] the worker of sin, and sympathize rather with your brother, because, if he remains in sin, he will be consigned to everlasting fire along with the Devil. Now, as the words for indignation (*thumós*) and anger (*orgé*) are different, so also are the significations which they bear very different. Indignation is a kind of flaring and sudden ebullition of passion. Anger, on the other hand, nurses a grievance; the soul, itching, so to speak, for vengeance, constantly urges us to repay those who have wronged us. Accordingly, it is important to bear in mind that men err in both directions— either by becoming furiously and swiftly aroused against those who provoke them to anger or by craftily and treacherously laying snares for their enemies. Both of these errors we are obliged to shun.

How, then, could it be brought about that our passions would not be aroused against improper objects? How? First, by being grounded in the humility which the Lord taught in word and illustrated in act; when, on one occasion, He said: 'If any among you desire to be first he shall be the last of all,'[34] and when, at another time, He gently and calmly bore with the man who struck Him.[35] The Maker and Lord of

---

32 1 Kings 18.19ff.
33 John 8.44.
34 Mark 9.34.
35 John 18.22,23.

heaven and earth, He who is adored by every creature having sensation and reason, He, 'upholding all things by the
word of his power,'[36] did not cast that man living into hell—
the earth would have opened of itself to receive the impious
wretch—but He admonished and instructed him: 'If I have
spoken evil, give testimony of the evil; but if well, why
strikest thou me?'[37] If, according to the Lord's command, you
have formed the practice of making yourself the last of all,
then, under what circumstances would you ever experience
displeasure on the ground of suffering an affront to your dignity? If a little child revile you, you make his taunts a subject
for jest, and, if you are insulted by an insane person, you regard him as more worthy of pity than hatred. It is not, therefore, the words themselves that are wont to arouse vexation,
but it is our pride, stung by the person who reviled us, which
causes this and also the unrealistic opinion every man has
about himself. If you banish both of these from your mind,
you will consider the insults cast at you as having no more significance than the hollow ring of an echo. 'Cease from anger
and leave rage,'[38] therefore, that you may escape the trial of
wrath which 'is revealed from heaven against all ungodliness
and injustice of men.'[39] If, by the prudent use of reason, you
could cut away the bitter root of indignation, you would remove many other vices along with this, their source. Deceit,
suspicion, faithlessness, malice, treachery, rashness, and a
whole thicket of evils like these are offshoots of this vice. Let us
not, then, bring upon ourselves a misfortune so great. It is a
malady upon the soul, a dark mist over the reason. It brings
estrangement from God, forgetfulness of the ties of kindred,

36 Heb. 1.3.
37 John 18.23.
38 Ps. 36.8.
39 Rom. 1.18.

cause for strife, a full measure of disaster. It is a wicked demon coming to birth in our very souls, taking prior possession of our interior, like a shameless tenant, and barring entrance to the Holy Spirit. Whenever there are enmities, strifes, bursts of anger, intrigues, rivalries, causing restless agitation in the soul, there the Spirit of Meekness does not take His rest. Accordingly, in obedience to the admonition of the blessed Paul, let us put away from ourselves all anger and indignation and clamor, with all malice,[40] and let us be kind and compassionate to one another, awaiting the blessed hope promised to the meek (for, 'Blessed are the meek; for they shall possess the land'[41]) in Christ Jesus our Lord, to whom be glory and empire for ever and ever. Amen.

40 Eph. 4.31.
41 Matt. 5.4.

HOMILY 11

Concerning Envy

OD IS GOOD and He is the Giver of blessings to the deserving. The Devil is wicked and the deviser of every form of iniquity. And as freedom from envy is consistent with the good, so envy relates to the Devil. Therefore, brethren, let us shun the vice of envy. Let us not be sharers in the works of our Adversary and so be found condemned together with him by the same sentence of doom. If the proud man is subject to the judgment pronounced upon the Devil, how will the envious man escape the punishment that was prepared for the Devil? No vice more pernicious than envy is implanted in the souls of men. This passion is first and foremost a personal detriment to the one guilty of it and does not harm others in the least. As rust wears away iron, so envy corrodes the soul it inhabits. More than this, it consumes the soul that gives it birth, like the vipers which are said to be born by eating their way through the womb that conceived them. Now, envy is pain caused by our neighbor's prosperity. Hence, an envious man is never without cause for grief and despondency. If his neighbor's land is fertile, if his house abounds with all the goods of this life, if he, its master, enjoys continual gladness of heart—all these things aggravate the sickness and add to the pain of the envious man. He is exactly like a person who, stripped of his clothing, is being pierced with wounds from all quarters. Is anyone brave and vigorous? This is a blow to the envious man. Is someone else handsomer than he? Another blow. Does so-and-so

463

possess superior mental endowment? Is he looked up to and emulated because of his wisdom and eloquence? Is someone else rich and eager to lavish his wealth in alms to the poor and charitable contributions, and does he receive great praise from the beneficiaries of his charity? All these blessings are like so many blows and wounds piercing the envious man to his heart's core. The worst feature of this malady, however, is that its victim cannot reveal it to anyone, but he hangs his head and is mute. He is troubled and he laments and is utterly undone by this vice. When he is questioned about his state, he is ashamed to make known his sad condition and say: 'I am envious and bitter and the good fortune of my friend distresses me. I am grieving over my brother's joy and I cannot endure the sight of others' blessings. The happiness of my neighbors I make my own misfortune.' This would he say if he were willing to tell the truth. But, not choosing to reveal these sentiments, he confines in the depths of his soul this disease which is gnawing at his vitals and consuming them.

As a consequence, he does not call in a doctor for his malady and he is unable to discover a healing remedy, although the Scriptures are filled with such medicines. The sick man awaits only one alleviation of his distress—that, perchance, he may see one of the persons whom he envies fall into misfortune. This is the goal of his hatred—to behold the victim of his envy pass from happiness to misery, that he who is admired and emulated might become an object of pity. Then when he sees him weeping and beholds him deep in grief, he makes peace and becomes his friend. He does not rejoice with him when he is glad, but he weeps with him when he is in sorrow.[1] The reversal in the condition of the envied one,

---

1 Rom. 12.15.

his fall from such great prosperity to such bitter misfortune, he pities, and he speaks in glowing terms of his former state. This he does, not animated by humane sentiments or from sympathy, but that the misfortune may appear in a more calamitous light. He praises the envied man's son after he is dead and extols him with a thousand ecomiums—How fair he was to look upon! How quick to learn! How versatile! Yet, while the boy was living, he did not favor him with even a word of praise. If, however, he sees many persons joining in a chorus of eulogy, he reverses his attitude and envies the corpse. Wealth he admires after it has been lost. Beauty of body or strength and health he lauds and extols when illness comes. In a word, he is an enemy of present good fortune but its friend when it is no longer possessed.

What could be more fatal than this disease? It ruins our life, perverts our nature, arouses hatred of the goods bestowed on us by God, and places us in a hostile relation toward Him. What drove the Devil, that author of evils, to wage furious war upon mankind? Was it not envy? Because of envy, too, he was guilty even of open conflict with God. Filled with bitterness against God because of His liberality toward man, he wreaked vengeance upon man, since he was unable to avenge himself upon God. Cain also attempted this maneuver—Cain, that first disciple of the Devil, who learned from him envy and murder, crimes of brother against brother. This combination of vices Paul also presents to us when he says, 'full of envy, murder.'[2] What, then, did Cain do? He saw the honor conferred by God and was inflamed with jealousy. He slew the recipient of the honor in an effort to reach Him who had bestowed it. Since he could not contend with God, he followed the next best course and slew his brother.[3] Let us

2 Rom. 1.29.
3 Gen. 4.8.

flee, brethren, from this disease that would teach us to wage war upon God. It is mother to homicide, does violence to nature, causes us to disregard the closest ties of kinship, and brings upon us an unhappiness based upon irrational motives. Why do you grieve, my friend, when you yourself have suffered no misfortune? Why are you hostile to someone who is enjoying prosperity, when he has in no way caused your own possessions to decrease? If you are vexed even upon receiving a kindness [from the object of your spite], are you not quite clearly envious of your own good? Saul is an example of this. He made David's great favors to himself a motive for enmity with him. First, after he had been cured of insanity by the divine and melodious strains of David's harp, he attempted to run his benefactor through with a spear. Then, on another occasion, it happened that he and his army were delivered from the hands of the enemy and saved from embarrassment before Goliath. In singing the triumphal songs commemorating this victory, however, the dancers attributed to David a tenfold greater share in the achievement, saying: 'Saul slew his thousands and David his ten thousands.'[4] For this one utterance and because truth itself was witness to it, Saul first attempted murder and tried to slay David by treachery, then forced him to flee. But he still did not desist from his hatred, for he arrayed against him three thousand chosen men and combed the desert in search of him. If Saul had been asked the reason for his hostility, he would have been compelled to admit that it was the favors received from David's hand. Moreover, even though Saul had been found asleep by David during the very time that the latter was being pursued, and although Saul lay, an easy victim, before his enemy, his life was again spared by that just man, for he refrained from doing

---

4 1 Sam. 18.7.

him violence. Not even this act of benevolence moved Saul, however. Again he gathered an army and again he set out in pursuit, until he was a second time apprehended by David in the cave where he more clearly revealed his own iniquity and made the virtue of David even more resplendent.[5] Envy is the most savage form of hatred. Favors render those who are hostile to us for any other reason more tractable, but kind treatment shown to an envious and spiteful person only aggravates his dislike. The greater the favors he receives, the more displeased and vexed and ill-disposed he becomes. He is more distressed by the resources of his benefactor than he is thankful for the benefits received. Envious persons surpass every species of animal in brutality of behavior. Wild beasts do not possess a ferocity equal to theirs. When dogs are fed, they become gentle; lions become tractable when their wounds are dressed; but the envious are rendered more savage by kind offices.

What reduced the high-born Joseph to slavery?[6] Was it not the envy of his brethren? And here it is worth while noting the stupidity which this malady induces. Fearful that his dream would come true, they made their brother a slave, as if his being a slave would permanently exempt them from having to offer him homage. If dreams are true, what ruse will prevent the events foretold from coming to pass exactly as predicted? If the visions seen in dreams are false, why be envious of one who is under a delusion? As it turned out, indeed, the ingenuity of Joseph's brethren was foiled by the providence of God. The device by which they thought to forestall the prophecy proved to be the means of clearing the way toward its fulfillment. If Joseph had not been sold and had not gone to Egypt, he would not, for chastity's sake, have

5 1 Sam. 24.3ff; 26.7ff.
6 Gen. 37.28.

fallen victim to the intrigues of an unchaste woman. He would not have been cast into prison and become an intimate of Pharoah's ministers, nor would he have interpreted the dream whereby he obtained the rule of Egypt and was accorded the homage of his brethren who had recourse to him because of the famine.[7]

Let your thoughts turn now to that very bitter envy, touching upon matters of the very highest importance, which the madness of the Jews caused to break out against the Saviour. Why did they envy Him?—because of His miracles. And what were these miraculous works?—the salvation of the needy. The poor were fed and war was declared against Him who fed them. The dead were restored to life and He who gave them life was the object of envy. Devils were driven out and He who commanded them to depart was the victim of treachery. Lepers were cleansed, the lame walked, the deaf heard, the blind saw[8] and their Benefactor was cast out. Finally, they awarded death to the generous Giver of Life as His recompense. They scourged the Liberator of mankind and pronounced a sentence of doom upon the Judge of the world. So all-pervading is the malice of envy. With this weapon alone, the Devil, the destroyer of our life, has been inflicting wounds upon all men and striking them down from the foundation of the world, and he will continue to do so until its consummation. He who rejoices in our ruin and who fell because of envy, brings about our destruction also through the same vice. Wise, therefore, was he, who forbids us even to dine in company with an envious man,[9] and in mentioning this companionship at table, he implies a reference to all other social contacts as well. Just

7 Gen. 39-43.
8 Luke 7.22.
9 Prov. 23.6.

as we are careful to keep material which is easily inflammable as far away as possible from fire, so we must refrain insofar as we can from contracting friendships in circles of which envious persons are members. By so doing, we place ourselves beyond the range of their shafts. We can be caught in the toils of envy only by establishing intimacy with it. In the words of Solomon: 'A man is exposed to envy from his neighbor.[10] And so it is. The Scythian is not envious of the Egyptian, but each of them envies a fellow countryman. Among members of the same nation, the closest acquaintances and not strangers are objects of envy. Among acquaintances, neighbors and fellow workmen, or those who are otherwise brought into close contact, are envied and among these again, those of the same age and kinsmen and brothers. In short, as the red blight is a common pest to corn, so envy is the plague of friendship. One feature of this vice, however, calls for our approval—the more vigorously it has been aroused, the more troublesome it is to the person afflicted. As arrows shot with great force come back upon the archer when they strike a hard and unyielding surface, so also do the movements of envy strike the envious person himself and they harm the object of his spite not at all. Who, by his feelings of annoyance, ever caused a neighbor's goods to be diminished? But the envious person himself is consumed and pines away with grief. Even so, however, persons who suffer from this malady of envy are supposed to be even more dangerous than poisonous animals, since these inject their venom by piercing their victim; then, gradually, putrefaction spreads over the infected area, but some think that envious persons bring bad luck merely by a glance, so that healthy persons in the full flower and vigor of their prime are made to pine away under their

10 Eccle. 4.4.

spell, suddenly losing all their plumpness, which dwindles and wastes away under the gaze of the envious, as if washed away by a destructive flood. For my part, I reject these tales as popular fancies and old wives' gossip. But this I do say: the devils, who are enemies of all that is good, use for their own ends such free acts as they find congenial to their wishes. In this way, they make even the eyes of envious persons serviceable to their own purposes. Do you not shrink, therefore, from making of yourself a tool for the dread demon and submitting to wickedness, whereby you become an enemy to persons who have not harmed you in any way and an enemy also of God who is good and in whom there is no envy?

Let us fly from so abominable a vice. It is a lesson taught by a serpent, an invention of demons, the seed of discord, a pledge of punishment, a barrier to holiness, a path to hell, and a cause of losing heaven. The envious can, somehow, be clearly recognized by their very faces. Their eyes are dry and lustreless; their cheeks, sunken; their brow, contracted; their mind, distorted and confused by their passion and incapable of making valid judgments in handling their affairs. In their view, no work of virtue is praiseworthy, nor any eloquence, even though it be adorned with dignity and grace, nor anything else that deserves emulation and esteem. As vultures are attracted to ill-smelling places and fly past meadow after meadow and pleasant, fragrant regions, as flies pass by healthy flesh and swarm eagerly to a wound, so the envious avert their gaze from the brightness in life and the loftiness of good actions and fix their attention upon rottenness. If anything should go amiss (as human affairs often do) they publish it abroad and desire that this mistake may become as a brand upon those who committed it. They are like incompetent painters who show the identity of the figures in their drawings by a twisted nose, or a scar, or some deformity due to nature or accident. Envious persons are skilled in making what is praiseworthy seem despicable by means of unflattering distortions and in slandering virtue through the vice that is neighbor to it. The courageous man they call reckless; the temperate man, callous; the just man, severe; the clever man, cunning. A person of lavish tastes they term vulgar and one who is bountiful they name a profligate; on the other hand, the thrifty man is called niggardly. In general, all forms of virtue they invariably supply with a name taken over from its opposite vice.

But, now, what course shall I take? Shall I limit my discourse to the denunciation of this vice? That would be a half-cure, as it were. To show a sick man the seriousness of his malady with a view to inculcating a proper concern for his condition is not useless, but to abandon him at this point and not guide him toward health is tantamount to giving the sick man over entirely to his infirmity. What, then, is to be done? How might we avoid becoming affected by this disease and how, after we have contracted it, might we be cured? First, by not regarding the goods of this world—human prosperity, renown, which fades like a flower, health of body—as either great or admirable. We do not define our highest good in terms of these transitory things, but we are called to share in possessions that are real and eternal. Thus, the rich man is not enviable merely because of his wealth, nor the ruler because of the grandeur of his exalted position, nor the strong man because of his physical vigor, nor yet the learned man because of his great power of eloquence. These are instruments for practicing virtue to those who use them well. They do not contain any intrinsic good. The man who makes bad use of them, therefore, is to be pitied as being like a person who voluntarily wounds himself with the sword which he had been given as a means of defense against his enemies. But the man

who administers his possessions well and according to right
reason, who acts as a steward of the goods received from God
and does not amass wealth for his own private enjoyment, he
is justly accorded praise and affection because of his charity
to his brethren and the benevolence of his character. Again,
a man may excel in mental acuteness and may win esteem
for his eloquence in discoursing about God and his interpretation of His sacred words. Be not envious of such a one nor
ever wish that an interpreter of the Sacred Scripture would
hold his peace because, by the grace of the Holy Spirit, he
wins some favor and praise thereby from his hearers. The
benefit is yours and through your brother the gift of doctrine
is sent to you, if only you are willing to accept it. Besides, no
one dams up a gushing spring, nor does anyone wear a
blindfold when the sun is shining or envy those who behold
the sun, but he prays that he, too, may enjoy this blessing.
And when the stream of doctrine is gushing forth in the
Church and a devout heart is welling up with the gifts of the
Holy Spirit, do you not gladly give your attention? Do you
not receive this favor with thanksgiving? Yet, the applause
of the audience stings you and you would prefer that there
would be neither benefit received nor praise given. What excuse will you have for this before the Judge of our hearts?
The good that is of the soul, therefore, we must regard as
good by nature. Nevertheless, if a man who has a superabundance of wealth and who takes pride in his position of
sovereignty or in his vigor of body makes the right use of these
goods, we ought to love and honor him as being supplied with
resources which are generally serviceable for carrying on life
in this world. He should, however, administer these possessions
rightly. He will be generous in giving of his abundance to the
needy and he will offer physical assistance to the infirm and
regard that part of his wealth which is superfluous as belong-

ing to any destitute person as much as it does to himself. On the other hand, the man who does not adopt this view toward these goods ought to be considered wretched rather than enviable, inasmuch as he meets with stronger inducements to evil. This represents a way of losing one's soul at the cost of great exertion and labor. If, then, wealth is an instrument for perpetrating injustice, pitiable is the rich man. If it serves as an aid to virtue, envy is out of place, since all may derive benefit from the wealth, unless, perhaps, by an excess of malice, one would begrudge good to himself.

To sum up, if, aided by your reason, your thinking is elevated above human considerations and is intent upon that which is truly noble and praiseworthy, you will by no means regard perishable earthly goods as objects for covetousness or envy. It is impossible, indeed, that envy should ever be present in a person so disposed, for he is not obsessed with the craving for worldly goods in the mistaken belief that they have great value. At all events, if you are desirous of glory and wish to outshine the crowd and if, for this reason, you cannot bear to hold second place (this, too, is likely to furnish occasion for envy), turn your aspirations, as one would change the course of a stream, toward the acquisition of virtue. Free yourself entirely from the desire for any kind of earthly riches or for the esteem to be gained from possessing worldly goods. Ownership of these things is not under your control. But, be just and temperate, wise and brave and patient in the sufferings you endure in the name of piety. In this way, you will win salvation for yourself and, the greater your good deeds, the greater will be the glory manifested in you. Virtue is within our power and can be acquired by one who labors earnestly for it. A large fortune, physical vigor or beauty, or a high rank of dignity are not at our command. But, if virtue is a greater and more lasting good and is universally acknowledged as preferable, virtue is what we should strive to acquire. It cannot be present in the soul, however, unless the soul is free from all vice, especially envy.

Surely, you are aware of how great an evil hypocrisy is, and it is the fruit of envy. This vice, above all others, causes double-dealing among men. Hypocrites maintain an outward semblance of charity, while keeping their hatred deeply hidden within, like rocks under the surface of the sea, which, being covered with shallow water, bring unforeseen disaster to the unwary. If, then, death flows toward us from that source, as from a fountain, and also a loss of blessings, estrangement from God, transgression of the law, and, at the same time, the ruin of earthly prosperity, let us obey the Apostle and 'Let us not be made desirous of vainglory, provoking one another, envying one another,'[11] but rather, 'kind, merciful, forgiving one another, even as God hath forgiven us in Christ Jesus our Lord,'[12] to whom be glory together with the Father and the Holy Spirit for ever and ever. Amen.

---

11 Gal. 5.26.
12 Eph. 4.32.

HOMILY 20

Of Humility

WOULD THAT MAN had abided in the glory which he
possessed with God—he would have genuine instead
of fictitious dignity. For he would be ennobled by the
power of God, illumined with divine wisdom, and made joyful in the possession of eternal life and its blessings. But, because he ceased to desire divine glory in expectation of a better prize, and strove for the unattainable, he lost the good
which it was in his power to possess. The surest salvation
for him, the remedy of his ills, and the means of restoration
to his original state is in practicing humility and not pretend-
ing that he may lay claim to any glory through his own
efforts but seeking it from God. Thus will he make amends
for his error, thus will he be cured of his malady, thus will he
return to the observance of the holy precept which he has
abandoned. For the Devil, having caused man's ruin by holding out to him the hope of false glory, ceases not to tempt
him still by the same allurements and he devises innumerable
schemes to this end. For instance, he represents a large fortune to him as a great good, so that man will regard it as a
cause for boasting and expend effort to obtain it. Wealth,
however, leads not to glory but to great peril. To build a
fortune is to lay the foundation for avarice and the acquisition of money bears no relation to excellence of character.
Rather, it blinds a man to no purpose, arouses vain conceit,
and produces in his soul an effect something like an inflamed
swelling. Now, a tumor combined with inflammation is neither

475

healthful nor beneficial to the body, but unwholesome, injurious, a source of danger, and a cause of death. Such an effect does pride engender in the soul.

But money is not by any means the only instigator of arrogance. Men do not take pride only in the costly food and clothing which money buys, nor in setting luxurious tables with unnecessary extravagance, wearing superfluous ornaments, building and furnishing immense piles for their homes and adorning them with all sorts of finery, and attaching to their person great throngs of slaves as attendants and innumerables hordes of flatterers. [Not only by reason of wealth,] but also because of political honors, do men exalt themselves beyond what is due their nature. If the populace confer upon them a distinction, if it honor them with some office of authority, if an exceptional mark of dignity be voted in their favor by the people, thereupon, as though they had risen above human nature, they look upon themselves as well-nigh seated on the very clouds and regard the men beneath them as their footstool. They lord it over those who raised them to such honor and exalt themselves over the very ones at whose hands they received their sham distinctions. The position they occupy is entirely out of keeping with reason, for they possess a glory more unsubstantial than a dream. They are surrounded with a splendor more unreal than the phantoms of the night, since it comes into being or is swept away at the nod of the populace. A fool of this sort was that famous son of Solomon, youthful in years and younger still in wisdom, who threatened his people desiring a milder rule with an even harsher one and thereby destroyed his kingdom.[1] By his threat, the very expedient whereby he hoped to be elevated to a more royal state, he was bereft of the dignity already his. Strength of arm, swiftness of foot, and comeliness of body—

---

1 1 Kings 12.4,14.

the spoils of sickness and the plunder of time—also awaken
pride in man, unaware as he is that 'All flesh is grass and all
the glory of man as the flower of the field. The grass is
withered and the flower is fallen.'[2] Such was the arrogance
of the giants because of their strength.[3] Such also was the
God-defying pride of the witless Goliath.[4] Such a one was
Adonias, exulting in his beauty[5] and Absalom, glorying in
his luxuriant hair.[6]

Again, the goods which, of all man's possessions, appear
to be the greatest and most enduring—wisdom and sagacity
—these also are the causes of idle boasting and nourish false
pride. For, if the wisdom which is from God be lacking, these
acquistions are worthless. Even the Devil's plots against man
worked against himself and unwittingly he contrived his own
undoing by his schemes for the ruin of mankind. He did not
so much injure him whom he hoped to alienate from God and
eternal life as he betrayed himself, becoming as he did a rebel
against God, doomed to death forever. He was himself caught
in the snare he laid for the Lord. He was nailed to the cross
upon which he hoped to crucify Him. He died the death
wherewith he intended the Lord to be destroyed. But, if the
Prince of this world, the supreme, consummate, and invisible
master of worldly wisdom, is caught in his own traps and
ends finally in ultimate folly, far more will his followers and
supporters be thus ensnared, even though they devise a thousand wiles; 'professing themselves to be wise, they became
fools.'[7] Pharoah resorted to trickery for the ruin of Israel,
but his clever scheme was suddenly foiled from a quarter he

---

2 Isa. 40.6,7.
3 Gen. 6.4; Wisd. 14.6.
4 1 Sam. 17.4ff.
5 1 Kings 1.5ff.
6 2 Sam. 14.26.
7 Rom. 1.22.

least suspected. The babe condemned to be exposed at his order was secretly reared in the royal household, destroyed his power and that of his whole nation, and led Israel to safety.[8] The homicide Abimelech, bastard son of Gedeon, slew the seventy legitimate sons, and, thinking he had hit upon a ruse for securing his grasp on the royal power, he destroyed his accomplices in the crime. He, however, was in turned destroyed by them, and in the end was slain with a stone cast by a woman's hand.[9] Again, all the Jews devised a deadly plot against the Lord, saying to themselves: 'If we let him alone so, all will believe in him and the Romans will come and take away our place and nation.'[10] Passing from the conspiracy to the actual slaying of Christ with the intention of saving their place and nation, they suffered the loss of both through their intrigue, for they were not only cast out of their place, but were also made strangers to the laws and worship of God. In short, countless examples teach us that the profit of human wisdom is illusory, for it is a meagre and lowly thing and not a great and pre-eminent good.

No sensible man, then, will be proud of his wisdom or of possessing the other goods I have mentioned, but will follow the excellent advice of blessed Anna and of the Prophet Jeremias: 'Let not the wise man glory in his wisdom and let not the strong man glory in his strength and let not the rich man glory in his riches.'[11] But what is true glory and what makes a man great? 'In this,' says the Prophet, 'let him that glorieth, glory, that he understandeth and knoweth that I am the Lord.'[12] This constitutes the highest dignity of man, this is his glory and greatness: truly to know what is great

8 Exod. 1-3.
9 Judges 9.1ff.
10 John 11.48.
11 1 Sam. 2.3; Jer. 9.23.
12 Jer. 9.24.

and to cleave to it, and to seek after glory from the Lord of glory. The Apostle tells us: 'He that glorieth may glory in the Lord,' saying: 'Christ was made for us wisdom of God, justice and sanctification and redemption; that, as it is written: He that glorieth may glory in the Lord.'[13] Now, this is the perfect and consummate glory in God: not to exult in one's own justice, but, recognizing oneself as lacking true justice, to be justified by faith in Christ alone. Paul gloried in despising his own justice and in seeking after the justice by faith which is of God through Christ, that he might know Him and the power of His resurrection and the fellowship of His sufferings, being made conformable to His death,[14] so as to attain to the resurrection from the dead. Herewith topples the whole lofty pinnacle of arrogant pride. Naught, O man, remains for you to boast of, inasmuch as your glory and your hope consist in mortifying yourself in all things and in striving toward the life to come in Christ. The foretaste of this life we now enjoy, and we are already in possession of its goods, living as we do entirely by the grace and gift of God. God it is 'who worketh in us both to will and to accomplish according to his good will.'[15] God also reveals through His own Spirit His wisdom which is ordained unto our glory.[16] It is God who grants efficacy to our labors. 'I have labored more abundantly than all they,' says Paul, 'yet not I but the grace of God with me.'[17] God delivers from dangers which are beyond all human recourse. 'We had in ourselves,' says the Apostle, 'the answer of death that we should not trust in ourselves but in God who raiseth the dead. Who hath delivered and doth deliver us out

---

13 1 Cor. 1.30,31.
14 Phil. 3.9,10.
15 Phil. 2.13.
16 1 Cor. 2.7,10.
17 1 Cor. 15.10.

of so great dangers, in whom we trust that he will yet also deliver us.'[18]

Why, then, pray, do you glory in your goods as if they were your own instead of giving thanks to the Giver for His gifts? 'For what hast thou that thou hast not received? And if thou hast received, why dost thou glory as if thou hadst not received it?'[19] You have not known God by reason of your justice, but God has known you by reason of His goodness. 'After that you have known God,' says the Apostle, 'or rather are known by God.'[20] You did not apprehend Christ because of your virtue, but Christ apprehended you by His coming. 'I follow after,' says the Apostle, 'if I also may comprehend wherein I am also apprehended by Christ.'[21] 'You have not chosen me,' says the Lord, 'but I have chosen you.'[22] Yet you, because honor is accorded you, exalt yourself and find an occasion for pride in the mercy that is granted you. Know yourself, at length, for what you are—Adam expelled from paradise,[23] Saul abandoned by the Spirit of God,[24] Israel cut off from the sacred root. 'But thou standest by faith,' says the Apostle 'be not high-minded but fear.'[25] Judgment will be in accordance with grace, and the Judge will make examination of how you have used the graces bestowed upon you. If you do not understand that you have received grace and by an excess of stupidity ascribe to yourself the success which is a gift of grace, you will fare no better than St. Peter. Indeed, you will not be able to surpass in love for the Lord him who loved Him so ardently that he desired to die for Him. Yet, be-

---

18 2 Cor. 1.9,10.
19 1 Cor. 4.7.
20 Gal. 4.9.
21 Phil. 3.12.
22 John 15.16.
23 Gen. 3.24.
24 1 Sam. 16.14.
25 Rom. 11.20.

cause he spoke boastfully, saying: 'Although all shall be scandalized in thee, I will never be scandalized,'[26] he fell a victim to human cowardice and committed the act of denial, gaining prudence and caution through his fall. Moreover, he learned by discovering his own weakness to be indulgent to the weak. And clearly did he come to understand that, just as he had been lifted up by the helping Hand of Christ when he was sinking into the sea,[27] so, when he was in mortal danger from the billow of scandal because of his incredulity, he was protected by the power of Christ who had foretold to him what was to be, saying: 'Simon, Simon, behold Satan hath desired that he may sift you as wheat; but I have prayed for thee that thy faith fail not; and thou, being once converted, confirm thy brethren.'[28] Peter, thus reproved, was deservedly given aid, for he had learned how to put away his pride and show forbearance toward the weak. Again, that stern Pharisee, who in his overweening pride not only boasted of himself but also discredited the publican in the presence of God, made his justice void by being guilty of pride. The publican went down justified in preference to him because he had given glory to God, the Holy One, and did not dare to lift his eyes, but sought only to win mercy, accusing himself by his posture, by striking his breast, and by entertaining no other motive except propitiation.[29] Be on your guard, therefore, and bear in mind this example of grievous loss sustained through arrogance. The one guilty of insolent behavior suffered the loss of his justice and forfeited his reward by his bold self-reliance. He was rendered inferior to a humble man and a sinner because in his self-exaltation he did not await the judgment of God, but pronounced it of himself. Never place yourself above

26 Matt. 26.33.
27 Matt. 14.30,31.
28 Luke 22.31,32.
29 Luke 18.11-14.

anyone, not even great sinners. Humility often saves a sinner who has committed many grievous transgressions. Do not, then, justify yourself as regards another and never condemn yourself on the verdict of God by justifying yourself on the basis of your own. 'I judge not my own self,' says Paul, 'for I am not conscious to myself of anything, yet I am not hereby justified; but he that judgeth me is the Lord.'[30]

Think you that you have done something good? Give thanks to God and do not exalt yourself above your neighbor. 'Let every one prove his own work,' says the Apostle, 'and so he shall have glory in himself only and not in another.'[31] How have you helped your neighbor by making a profession of faith or by suffering exile for the Name of Christ, or by enduring austerities with constancy? The gain is not another's, but yours. Take care not to repeat the fall of the Devil. He, in exalting himself above man, fell at the hands of man, and is delivered up to be trodden upon as a footstool to him who had been under his heel. Another example is the fall of the Israelites. Although they vaunted their superiority over the Gentiles whom they regarded as unclean, they themselves became, in reality, unclean, but the Gentiles were made clean. And the justice of the Israelites became as the rag of a menstruous woman,[22] but the wickedness and impiety of the Gentiles was passed over because of their faith. In short, bear in mind that true proverb: 'God resisteth the proud but to the humble he giveth grace.'[33] Keep as your familiar that word of the Lord: 'Everyone that humbleth himself shall be exalted and he that exalteth himself shall be humbled.'[34] Be not an unjust judge of yourself and do not weigh your case favorably to

30 1 Cor. 4.3,4.
31 Gal. 6.4.
32 Isa. 64.6.
33 1 Pet. 5.5; James 4.6.
34 Luke 14.11.

yourself. If you appear to have something in your favor, do not, counting this to your credit and readily forgetting your mistakes, boast of your good deeds of today and grant yourself pardon for what you had done badly yesterday and in the past. Whenever the present arouses pride in you, recall the past to mind and you will check the foolish swelling of conceit. If you see your neighbor committing sin, take care not to dwell exclusively on his sin, but think of the many things he has done and continues to do rightly. Many times, by examining the whole and not taking the part only into account, you will find that he is better than you. God does not examine man according to the part, for He says: 'I come to gather together their works and thoughts.'[35] Furthermore, when He rebuked Josaphat for a sin committed in an unguarded moment, He mentioned also the good he had done, saying: 'But good works are found in thee.'[36]

Such reminders as these regarding self-exaltation we should keep reciting constantly to ourselves, demeaning ourselves that we may be exalted, in imitation of the Lord who descended from heaven to utter lowliness and who was, in turn, raised to the height which befitted Him. In everything which concerns the Lord we find lessons in humility. As an infant, He was straightway laid in a cave, and not upon a couch but in a manger. In the house of a carpenter and of a mother who was poor, He was subject to His mother and her spouse. He was taught and He paid heed to what He needed not to be told. He asked questions, but even in the asking He won admiration for His wisdom. He submitted to John—the Lord received baptism at the hands of His servant. He did not make use of the marvelous power which He possessed to resist any of those who attacked Him, but, as if yielding to superior

35 Isa. 66.18.
36 2 Par. 19.3.

force, He allowed temporal authority to exercise the power proper to it. He was brought before the high priest as though a criminal and then led to the governor. He bore calumnies in silence and submitted to His sentence, although He could have refuted the false witnesses. He was spat upon by slaves and the vilest menials. He delivered Himself up to death, the most shameful death known to men. Thus, from His birth to the end of His life, He experienced all the exigencies which befall mankind and, after displaying humility to such a degree, He manifested His glory, associating with Himself in glory those who had shared His disgrace. Of this number, the blessed disciples are first, who, poor and destitute, passed through this world, not adorned with the knowledge of rhetoric, not accompanied by a throng of followers, but unattended, as wanderers and solitaries, traveling on land and sea, scourged, stoned, hunted, and, finally, slain. These are divine teachings inherited from our fathers. Let us follow them, so that out of our abasement may spring up eternal happiness, that true and perfect gift of Christ.

But how shall we, casting off the deadly weight of pride, descend to saving humility? If such an aim governed our conduct under all circumstances, we should not overlook the least detail on the ground that we would suffer no harm therefrom. The soul comes to take on a resemblance to its preoccupations and it is stamped and molded to the form of its activities. Let your aspect, your garb, your manner of walking and sitting, your diet, bed, house and its furnishings reflect a customary thrift. Your manner of speaking and singing, your conversation with your neighbor, also, should aim at modesty rather than pretentiousness. Do not strive, I beg you, for artificial embellishment in speech, for cloying sweetness in song, or for a sonorous and high-flown style in conversation. In all your actions, be free from pomposity. Be obliging to your

friends, gentle toward your slaves, forbearing with the fro-
ward, benign to the lowly, a source of comfort to the afflicted,
a friend to the distressed, a condemner of no one. Be pleasant
in your address, genial in your response, courteous, accessible
to all. Speak not in your own praise, nor contrive that others
do so. Do not listen to indecent talk, and conceal insofar as
you can your own superior gifts. On the other hand, where
sin is concerned, be your own accuser,[37] and do not wait for
others to make the accusation. Thus, you will be like a just
man who accuses himself in the first speech made in court,
or like Job who was not deterred by the crowd of people in
the city from declaring his personal guilt before all.[38] Be not
rash in rebuking, nor quick to do so. Do not make accusation
while your passions are aroused (for such action savors of
willfulness), nor condemn anyone in matters of slight consequence as if you yourself were perfectly just. Receive those
who have fallen away and give them spiritual instruction,
'considering thyself also lest thou be tempted,' as the Apostle
advises.[39] Take as much care not to be glorified among men
as others do to obtain this glory, as you remember the words
of Christ, that one forfeits a reward from God by voluntarily
seeking renown from men or doing good to be seen by men.
'They have received their reward,' He says.[40] Do not cheat
yourself by desiring to be seen by men, for God is the great
Witness. Strive for glory with God, for His is a glorious
recompense. Suppose you have been deemed worthy of the
episcopate and men throng about you and hold you in esteem. Come down to the level of your subordinates, 'not as
lording it over the clergy,'[41] and do not behave as worldly

37 Prov. 18.17.
38 Job 31.34.
39 Gal. 6.1.
40 Matt. 6.2.
41 1 Peter 5.3.

potentates do. The Lord bade him who wishes to be first to be the servant of all.[42] To sum up, strive after humility as becomes a lover of this virtue. Love it and it will glorify you. Thus you will travel to good purpose the road leading to that true glory which is to be found with the angels and with God. Christ will acknowledge you as His own disciple before the angels[43] and He will glorify you if you imitate His humility, for He says: 'Learn of me because I am meek and humble of heart and you shall find rest to your souls.'[44] To Him be glory and empire for ever and ever. Amen.

42 Mark 10.44.
43 Luke 12.8.
44 Matt. 11.29.

HOMILY 21

On Detachment from Worldly Goods and Concerning the Conflagration Which Occurred in the Environs of the Church

THOUGHT, well-beloved, that, inasmuch as I had so vigorously plied you with the goad of my words on every and all occasions, you regarded me as a troublesome fellow, overbold for a stranger and for a man who is himself guilty on similar charges. Yet, by my rebukes you were moved to kindliness and the blows of my tongue you transformed into incentives to greater zeal. This, of course, is not a matter for surprise, since you are wise in the things of the spirit. Solomon says somewhere in his writings: 'Rebuke a wise man and he will love thee.'[1] Therefore, my brethren, I now again employ the same kind of exhortation in my desire to rescue you, insofar as I am able, from the snares of the Devil. Dearly beloved, it is a long and varied warfare which the Enemy of truth daily wages against us. He attacks us, as you know, by turning our own desires as arrows against ourselves and ever draws from our own selves the power to do us harm. Since, however, the Lord greatly limited his power by inviolable laws and did not permit him to destroy our race at once by his attacks, the malicious demon, taking advantage of our folly, wins his victories by stealth. Wicked and avaricious men whose business and deliberate policy it is to become rich at others' expense, but who have not the power to make use of open violence, are wont to lie in wait along the highways, and, if they espy any region nearby that is either cleft by deep ravines or shaded by a thick growth of bushes, they

---

1 Prov. 9.8.

hide therein and, screened by such coverts from the traveler's
range of vision, they suddenly leap upon him. Thus, no one is
able to see the perilous traps before he falls into them. In the
same way, our Enemy, hostile to us from the beginning, sneaks
into the shadows of worldly pleasures which grow thickly
enough about the road of life to hide the Brigand while he
plots against us. There he lurks in secret and spreads his nets
for our destruction. If, then, we would safely traverse the road
of life lying before us, and offer to Christ our body and soul
alike free from the shame of wounds, and receive the crown
for this victory, we must always and everywhere keep the
eyes of our soul wide open, holding in suspicion everything
that gives pleasure. We must unhesitatingly pass by such
things, without allowing our thoughts to rest in them, even if
we think that we see gold lying before us in heaps, ready to
be picked up by any who so desire. ('If riches abound,' says
the Scripture, 'set not your heart upon them.'[2]) We must pay
no heed, even if the earth bud forth every kind of delicacy
and offer luxurious dwellings to our gaze (for 'our conversation is in heaven; from whence also we look for the Saviour,
our Lord Jesus Christ')[3]; nor should we take notice when
dancing and merry-making and reveling and banquets ringing
with the sound of the flute are offered for our enjoyment (for
the Scripture says: 'Vanity of vanities and all is vanity.'[4]).
Pay no attention, either, if there be placed before you beautiful bodies wherein dwell wicked souls ('Flee from the face of
a woman as from the face of a serpent,' says the Wise Man.[5])
Heed it not even if you are offered powers and sovereignties,
throngs of attendants and flatterers, or a high and splendid
throne which holds cities and nations in voluntary servitude

---

2 Ps. 61.11.
3 Phil. 3.20.
4 Eccle. 1.2.
5 Eccli. 21.2.

(for 'all flesh is grass and all the glory of man as the flower of the field. The grass is withered and the flower is fallen.'[6]). Beneath all these pleasures which are so delightful lurks our common Enemy, waiting to see whether we will swerve from the straight path and fall into his lair, captivated by the enticements our eyes behold. Indeed, it is greatly to be feared that, by running recklessly after these delights and regarding the pleasure derived from their enjoyment as not harmful in the least, we may swallow the hook of treachery concealed in the first taste. Then, drawn on by this first experience, half willing and half reluctant, we become attached to these pleasures and are dragged without our realizing it into the Brigand's awful den, that is, to death.

Therefore, brethren, it is necessary and beneficial for us all to gird ourselves up like wayfarers or runners and, by ensuring our souls complete ease and lightness for this journey, to push straight on to the road's end. Nor should anyone think that I am a coiner of words because I have been calling human life a road [or a way]; for David, the Prophet, also applied this word to life. He says in one place: 'Blessed are the undefiled in the way, who walk in the law of the Lord,'[7] and in another passage, he cries out to his Lord: 'Remove from me the way of iniquity; and out of thy law have mercy on me.'[8] Again, praising to the sweet accompaniment of his lyre the swift aid of God afforded him against those who treated him despitefully, he said: 'And who is God but our God? God who hath girt me with strength, and made my way blameless.'[9] Rightly he considered that the sojourn of men on earth, whether illustrious or ignoble, should in all instances be so named. As they who are hastening to complete a

---

6 Isa. 40.6,7.
7 Ps. 118.1.
8 Ps. 118.29.
9 Ps. 17.32,33.

strenuous journey easily reach the end of the road by taking
one step forward and then another, one foot being placed
upon the ground in rapid alternation with the other, as if
their feet were vying with each other to complete the course,
so they who have been introduced into this life by the Creator,
advancing from the very beginning by moments of time in
perpetual succession, arrive at the end of their life. Does not
our life in this world seem to you also to stretch before us like
a long road, a journey broken at intervals by the periods of
life as by stages in a journey? It has its beginning for each of
us in the travail of our mothers and the end of its course in
the shelter of the grave. All men it conducts thither, some
rapidly, others more slowly; the latter passing through all
the intervals of time, the former not even tarrying for the
first stages of life. Now, in the case of other roads, those
leading from city to city, it is possible if one so desires to turn
aside and not travel at all. This road, however, draws those
who travel it by main force toward the end which has been
appointed by the Lord, even if we should prefer to prolong
our course. And it is not possible, dearly beloved, for one who
has once passed through the gate which leads toward this
life and has set out upon this road not to arrive at the end
of it. Each of us, after leaving the maternal womb, is straightway seized and borne along by the flow of time, ever leaving
behind the day already lived and never able to return to
yesterday, however much we may desire to do so. Yet, we
rejoice in being borne onward and, as if we were receiving
some gain, we are glad to pass from one period of life to the
next. We consider it a happy event when manhood succeeds
boyhood and when old age follows upon man's estate. We
do not think of the fact that as much of time as we have used
up at each stage of our life is so much of life already lived;
nor do we realize that our life time is being spent, although

we always measure it according to what has passed by and flowed away. Moreover, we do not reflect how uncertain is the length of time He who has sent us on this journey wills we should have to finish our course. We know not when He will unbar the gates of entrance to each runner, nor do we bear in mind that we must prepare ourselves daily for our departure hence and keep our eyes fixed upon the Lord awaiting His nod. For He says: 'Let your loins be girt and lamps burning in your hands; and you yourselves like to men who wait for their lord when he shall return from the wedding; that when he cometh and knocketh they may open to him immediately.'[10]

Furthermore, we are unwilling to take into careful consideration which kind of burdens will be light for the course we must run, which can help on their way those who have gathered them together, and what sort will make the life hereafter very happy for us by reason of their being adapted to the nature of those who carried them. Neither are we willing to ascertain which are the heavy, uncomfortable ones that drag on the ground and that are by their nature absolutely unsuited to men and do not allow their bearers to pass through that narrow gate. But we leave behind what we ought to pick up and take along and we add to our collection what we ought to pass over. That which can be naturally assimilated by us, and which can constitute a true adornment of body and soul alike, we do not even advert to, but possessions which will ever be alien to us and only brand us with shame—these we try to acquire, toiling fruitlessly and laboring like a man who would delude himself with the hope that he could fill a sieve with water. This truth I think every child even is aware of: that none of the pleasures of this life, the pursuit of which has caused madness in so many, are or can be truly

10 Luke 12.35,36.

possessed by us. They are, indeed, foreign to all alike—to those who appear to be enjoying them as well as to those who have not yet obtained them. Even if certain individuals should gather together an immense store of gold in this life, it would not remain permanently in their possession. Although they would have left nothing undone for its secure protection in every way, it would either escape them while they were yet alive, passing into the hands of persons stronger than they, or it would presently be lost to them at their death, its nature not being such that it could accompany them at their departure hence. But some who are drawn along the inevitable road by that power which forcibly separates our souls from this miserable flesh, turning back many times to their riches, bewail the hard labor which they had endured from their youth to amass it. The wealth, however, which had only inflicted upon them the toil of acquisition and the guilt of avarice, passes on into the hands of others. Even if a man would own countless acres of land, magnificent houses, and herds of every kind of animal, if he should be endowed, also, with absolute sovereignty among men, he will not possess these things forever. After enjoying the brief prestige they bring, he will, in his turn, give up his abundance to others, while he himself will be placed under a bit of earth. In many cases, even before a man is buried, even prior to his departure form this world, he sees his goods pass on to others —perhaps his enemies. Do we not know of many fields, houses, cities, and nations that have taken the name of other masters while they who had previously possessed them are still alive? Have we not also observed how those who were once slaves ascend the throne of sovereignty and how they who used to be called lords and masters are wont to take their place in the ranks of their subjects and bow down to their own slaves when their fortunes suffer a sudden reversal, as by a throw of the dice?

As for the concoctions we devise as food and drink and all the superfluities which arrogant wealth provides for the satisfaction of the capricious and undisciplined appetite, could they ever really belong to us, even if we were continually being surfeited with them? Edibles which produce some slight pleasure for the palate when they are only casually tasted we find offensive as soon as they are eaten in excess and we eagerly cast them out as if life were to be seriously endangered by their remaining in our intestines for any length of time. At any rate, overeating has been the cause of death for many and the reasons for their not having any further enjoyment. Again, are not wanton chamberings, impure embraces, and all such acts of a maddened and frenzied mind manifestly and in every respect detrimental to nature and notoriously harmful? Do they not represent the loss or diminution of powers which are in a very real sense proper and personal to the individual, since by such unions the body is weakened and depleted of aliment that is in the highest degree congruent with it and preservative of its members? So, it is the experience of everyone who engages in such wanton acts that, immediately after the deed, when the sting of the flesh is quieted and the mind, coming finally to abhor that which it has initiated, recollects itself as if from a fit of drunkenness or any such turbulent experience, and takes time to advert to its condition—[it generally happens to such a person, I say,] that a strong remorse for his intemperate conduct sweeps over him. He perceives that his body has been very much enfeebled and that it has been rendered torpid and quite without strength for the accomplishment of his duties. Even the masters of the gymnastic schools are aware of this and have laid down a rule of continence for the palaestra which protects the bodies of the youths against the danger of such pleasure. The contestants themselves are not permitted even so much as to gaze

upon the fair and glistening forms of their antagonists, if,
indeed, they would have their head adorned with the crown;
for incontinency in a wrestling match gives rise to laughter,
but does not win a crown.

All these pleasures, then, it is well for us to pass by with
our eyes closed, for they are absolutely foreign to our nature,
superfluous, and not capable of being really possessed by
anyone. On the other hand, we should be at great pains for
those possessions which can truly be ours. What, then, really
belongs to us? A soul, whereby we live, a light and spiritual
being which has no need of anything weighty, and a body,
which was provided for the soul by the Creator as a vehicle
for carrying on life. This, therefore, is man: a mind united
with a fitting and serviceable body. This mode of existence
was prepared by the all-wise Artificer of the universe in our
mothers' wombs. This, the time of travail brought to the light
out of the darkness of their marriage chambers. This being
it is which was appointed to rule over the earth. For him,
creation lies outspread, an exercise-ground for virtue. For
him, the law was made, commanding the imitation of the
Creator in accordance with his powers and a reproducing upon earth, as if in rough outline, of the good order of heaven.
This is the being which departs from this world at the summons. This it is which will be placed before the tribunal of
God who sent it forth, this it is which will be called to account.
This being will receive the recompense for the deeds performed during this life. Moreover, it is evident that virtues
become our possession when they are, through practice,
woven into our nature. They do not abandon us while we
labor on this earth, unless we voluntarily and forcibly cast
them out by giving entrance to vice. They eagerly run ahead
of us as we hasten toward the next world. They place their
possessor in the ranks of the angels and shine for all eternity

under the gaze of the Creator, Riches, power, renown, pleasure, and the whole throng of such follies which increase daily by reason of our stupidity do not enter into this life with us, nor do they accompany anyone in leaving this world. For every man, this saying of the just man of old is unalterably and sovereignly true: 'Naked came I out of my mother's womb and naked shall I return thither.'[11]

A man who has his own best interests at heart will therefore be especially concerned for his soul and will spare no pains to keep it stainless and true to itself. If his body is wasted by hunger or by its struggles with heat and cold, if it is afflicted by illness or suffers violence from anyone, he will make small account of it, and, echoing the words of Paul, he will say in each of his adversities: 'but though our outward man is corrupted, yet the inward man is renewed day by day.'[12] When he sees mortal danger approaching, he will not show fear, but he will say courageously to himself: 'We know, if our earthly house of this habitation be dissolved, that we have a building of God, a house not made with hands, eternal in heaven.'[13] But, if a man would also have mercy upon his body as being a possession necessary to the soul and its cooperator in carrying on the life on earth, he will occupy himself with its needs only so far as is required to preserve it and keep it vigorous by moderate care in the service of the soul. He will by no means allow it to become unmanageable through satiety. If ever he observe that it is inflamed by desires more than is good, he will address to it the precept of Paul: 'We brought nothing into this world, and certainly we can carry nothing out. But having food and wherewith to be covered, with these we are content.'[14] By continually reciting these words to his

---

11 Job 1.21.
12 2 Cor. 4.16.
13 2 Cor. 5.1.
14 1 Tim. 6.7,8.

body, he will render it tractable and nimble for its journey to heaven and he will have a stronger helpmate in the tasks that lie ahead. But, if he should permit it to become overbearing and to be surfeited with food of all sorts every day, it will, at length, like a wild beast, drag him forcibly to the earth along with itself, and there he will lie, groaning to no avail. And, when he is brought before the Lord and asked for the fruits of the journey on earth which was granted him, he will make long lament, since he has none to present, and he will dwell in everlasting darkness, uttering loud reproaches against luxury and its deceits, by which he was robbed of the time of his salvation. Yet, he will have no profit any more of of his laments; for 'who,' says David, 'shall confess to thee in hell?'[15]

Let us, then, flee with all speed the possibility of committing voluntary suicide. And if anyone has fallen victim in the past to deception and has amassed riches for himself through acts of injustice, fettering his mind to the protection of this wealth, or if anyone has contracted the ineffaceable defilement of fornication, or sated himself with other crimes, let him, while there is still time, before he has gone down to final destruction, cast off the greater part of his burden; before his ship goes under, let him get rid of his ill-gotten wares, as mariners do. When a billow surges foaming out of the sea, threatening to engulf the ship weighed down with cargo, the sailors drastically reduce the load with all speed; even though they may be carrying necessities on the ship, they throw the cargo indiscriminately into the sea, in order to raise the ship above the waves and, if possible, save only their bodies and souls from the peril. Surely it befits us far more than sailors to think and act in this way. They lose on the spot whatever they throw overboard and, perforce, suffer poverty afterward.

---

15 Ps. 6.6.

We however, in proportion as we cast off our burden of iniquity, will store up ever greater and more precious riches for our souls. Fornication and other vices of this sort are utterly destroyed when they are repudiated and they are entirely wiped out by repentant tears. Holiness and justice thereafter take their place, and, like buoyant objects, they cannot be submerged by the waves. Furthermore, money, when it is cast off to good purpose, is not lost to those who have flung it away and cast it from them. As if deposited in other, safer ships—the stomachs of the poor—it is preserved and, reaching the harbor in advance, is kept for those who have rid themselves of it, not to their peril but unto glory.

Let us, then, dearly beloved, determine upon a more benevolent course toward ourselves and distribute among many the weight of riches, if we would in reality possess our gains. These needy ones will joyfully bear it away and will lay up our wealth in the bosom of the Lord as in a safe treasury, 'where the moth doth not consume and thieves do not break through nor steal.'[16] Let us permit our wealth, which is meant for this purpose, to be poured out upon the needy. Let us not pass by the Lazaruses who continue even today to lie before our eyes, nor begrudge them the crumbs from our tables which suffice to still their hunger. By thus refusing to imitate the cruel Dives, we shall escape the fire of hell which was his portion.[17] Otherwise, we shall pray loudly to Abraham, loudly also to those who have led righteous lives, but our cries will be of no avail; 'No brother can redeem, shall man redeem?'[18] Every one of them will cry out to us and say: Do not seek mercy which you yourself failed to show to others. Desire not to receive such great favors, since you were so parsimonious in

16 Matt. 6.20.
17 Luke 16.19ff.
18 Ps. 48.8.

bestowing lesser ones. Enjoy the goods you gathered together in your lifetime. Weep now, since then you had no pity upon beholding your brothers' tears. These things they will say to us, and justly. And I am afraid that they will accuse us with sharper words than these, since, as you well know, our wickedness is greater than that of the rich man in the Gospel. Not wholly in the interest of thriftiness do we ignore our brethren lying prostrate upon the ground, and not in order to save our wealth for children or other relatives do we close our ears to the needy. We spend our money in pursuit of baser aims and make our extravagence an incentive to evil for those who pander to this lavish spending. How many men and women some rich men keep in attendance upon their table! Of these, some there are who beguile their host with vile jests; some enkindle the flame of incontinency by indecent glances and movements; some, in their efforts to amuse their host, engage in ribald repartee, and others mislead him by false flattery. Not only are these persons rewarded with a sumptuous dinner, but they leave with their hands filled with costly gifts and so learn under our tutelage that to participate in such revelry and to perform such actions are more gainful than the practice of virtue. If, however, a poor man, scarcely able to speak from hunger, present himself to us, we turn away from him, a fellow man. We are revolted and we hasten to get away, as if we feared that by walking more slowly we might become involved in his misfortune. If he bow down to the ground in shame for his unfortunate condition, we say that he is practicing hypocrisy. If, goaded by the last stages of hunger, he look us boldly in the face, we call him a shameless bully, and if, perchance, he be clothed in garments that are not torn (someone having given them to him), we drive him away as a greedy fellow and swear he is feigning poverty. If he be covered with rags that are falling to pieces, again we drive him away as ill-smelling. Although he may invoke in his pleading the Name of the Creator and, although he solemnly and unremittingly pray that a like misfortune may not befall us, he is unable to change our pitiless decision. For this reason I am inclined to think that the fire of hell will be more intense for us than for the rich man in the Gospel. If time allowed and if my strength were equal to the task, I should fulfill my obligation to preach by recounting all the evidence contained in the Scripture on this point; but it is time for your dismissal, and you are weary. Yet, if I have omitted something through weakness of mind and tongue alike, do you formulate it for yourselves and apply it as an unguent to the wounds of your soul. 'Give an occasion to a wise man,' says the Scripture, 'and wisdom shall be added unto him.'[19] 'And God is able to make all grace abound in you; that ye always, having all sufficiency in all things, may abound to every good work.'[20]

But, now that our discourse has, as you see, come already into port, certain of the brethren are urging me back again to my course of advice and exhortation. They bid me not to pass over the marvel wrought yesterday by the Lord and not to keep silence respecting the memorial erected by the Saviour to His victory over the fury of the Devil, so that I may afford you an occasion for hymns of joyful exultation. As you know, the Devil has again manifested his savage hostility toward us. With flames of fire for weapons, he laid siege to the sacred enclosure of the church. Once more, however, our common mother won the victory and turned back upon the Foe his engines of war. He accomplished nothing except to make a public avowal of his hatred. Grace, like an opposing gust of wind, checked the hostile fall of the scales. The church re-

19 Prov. 9.9.
20 2 Cor. 9.8.

mained unharmed. The tempest raised by our Adversary had not power to shake the rock upon which Christ had built the fold for His flock.[21] He is at His post even now, in our midst, who of old cooled the fiery furnace in Babylon.[22] How the Devil must be groaning today, since he did not reap the enjoyment he had planned to gain from his project. The villain had enkindled a pyre near the church in order to spoil our good work. From all quarters the fire fanned by his violent blasts was consuming whatever lay in its path, and feeding upon the surrounding air. Relentlessly, it approached the church, drawing us toward a participation in the disaster. But our Saviour caused this catastrophe to fall back upon the one who enkindled the blaze and bade him gather in his mad fury and take it to himself again. The Enemy made ready the bow of treachery, but he was forbidden to let fly the shaft—rather, he let it fly, but it was turned back again on his own head. He had for his own portion the bitter tears he had meant us to shed.

And now, brethren, let us make his wound still more unbearable for our malicious Foe. Let us intensify his pain. How this can be done I will tell you, and do you, on your part, accomplish it. There are some who were rescued from the power of the fire by the Creator, but they escaped the peril with their lives only and there remain to them no resources for their future livelihood. Those of us, therefore, who have not suffered this adversity should place at their disposal our own goods. Let us embrace as brothers those who have barely escaped with their lives. Let us say of them, each with regard to each, 'He was dead and is come to life again, was lost and is found,'[23] And let us clothe the body that is like our own. Let

---

21 Matt. 16.18. The circumstances of the fire referred to in this paragraph are unknown to me.
22 Dan. 3.49.
23 Luke 15.24.

us answer the contumely of the Evil One with our compassion, so that, even though he inflict injury, he may appear to do no great harm and may have no conquest to show for all his battling; so that, although he has stripped our brethren of their goods, he himself may be openly defeated by our liberality.

And you, my brethren, who have barely escaped this disaster, must not be greatly cast down by the evils which have occurred, nor even be disturbed in mind. Dispel the mist of grief and give renewed vigor to your soul by entertaining more courageous thoughts. Make this even an occasion for winning your crown. If you remain undisturbed and, like true gold, all-gleaming from the fire,[24] more strongly confirmed in the faith, you will increase the confusion of the Enemy, who will have failed to elicit even a tear from you by his plots. Recall to your minds the patience of Job. Say to yourselves as he did: 'the Lord gave and the Lord hath taken away; as it hath pleased the Lord, so also is it done.'[25] No one should be led by his sufferings to think or to say that no Providence rules our affairs, nor should any man cast aspersion upon the government and decree of the Lord. Let him contemplate the athlete just mentioned and provide himself with an adviser of wiser counsel. Let him review in his mind all the trials, one after another, in which Job distinguished himself and reflect that, for all the many shafts aimed at him by the Devil, he did not receive a mortal blow. The Devil took from him his domestic prosperity and planned to overwhelm him with reports of disasters, following closely upon one another. While the first messenger was announcing a heavy misfortune, another came, bringing news of more serious calamities. Evils were linked, one with another, and

24 Prov. 17.3.
25 Job 1.21.

the catastrophes were like onrushing waves. Before the first lamentation had ceased, cause for another was at hand. That just man, however, stood firm as a rock, receiving the blasts of the tempest and reducing to foam the dash of the waves. He sent forth to the Lord a loving cry: 'The Lord gave, the Lord hath taken away; as it hath pleased the Lord, so also is it done'; for he deemed worthy of tears none of the evils which were befalling him. But, when one came to report that, while his sons and daughters were feasting, a violent wind had blown down the chamber where the merry-making was going on, he rent his garments, showing his natural sympathy and proving by the action that he was a father who loved his children. But even at that moment he set a limit and measure to his grief and graced with words of piety the misfortune that had occurred: 'the Lord gave, the Lord hath taken away; as it hath pleased the Lord, so also is it done.' It was as if he were crying out: I was called a father for as long a time as He who made me wished it. He willed, in turn, to take from me the crown of offspring. I do not resist Him in what belongs to Him. May that which seems good to the Lord prevail. He is the Maker of my children; I am His instrument. Why should I, a servant, give way to useless mourning and bitter complaints against a decree which I am powerless to avoid? With such words did this just man shoot down the Devil.

But, when the Enemy saw that Job was winning the victory and that he could not be shaken by any of these disasters, he brought up another siege machine, temptations of the flesh. He flayed his body with unspeakable afflictions and made it exude streams of worms. From a kingly throne, he brought him down to a seat on a dunghill. Yet, although he was buffeted there by the woes I have just mentioned, he remained steadfast. His body was lacerated, but he kept inviolate in the depths of his soul the treasure of piety. The Enemy, having now no further recourse and bethinking himself of an ancient device of treachery, seduced the mind of Job's wife with an impious and blasphemous notion whereby she hoped to shake the athlete's resolution. She stood beside that just man, haranguing him at great length. She prostrated herself and struck her hands together at what she saw, casting revilings at him for the rewards his piety had brought, recounting the ancient prosperity of their house, calling attention to his present misfortunes, the state to which he was reduced, and the fine reward he had received from the Lord for his many sacrifices. On and on she spoke, expressing sentiments worthy of a woman's cowardly heart, yet such sentiments as are capable of disturbing any man and of subverting even a noble mind. 'I go about,' said she, 'like a vagrant and a hired servant. From a queen, I am become a slave. I am forced to keep my eyes on the hands of my servants;[26] I, who once supported many, now consider myself fortunate to be fed at the expense of strangers.' She added that it would be a better and more beneficial thing for him to destroy himself utterly and to blaspheme, thus sharpening the sword of the Creator's wrath, rather than that he prolong the labor of the struggle for himself and for her by persevering in the patient endurance of his misfortunes. Grieved by her words as by none of the evils that had previously afflicted him, he turned to his wife a countenance full of wrath. And what are his words? 'Why hast thou spoken like one of the foolish women?'[27] 'Repudiate, woman,' he says [in effect], 'this counsel How long wilt thou desecrate our life together by thy words! Thou didst speak falsely (may God avert the evil!) of the way of life which was mine and thou didst plot against my

---

26 Ps. 122.2.
27 Job 2.10.

life. Now, I think that half of myself has committed an impious act, since marriage has made us twain one body and thou hast committed blasphemy. If we have received good things at the hand of the Lord, shall we not receive evil?[28] Recall to your mind our past blessings. Weigh our prosperity in the balance with these adversities. For no man is life altogether happy. To prosper in all things belongs to God alone. But, if you are made sorrowful by our present circumstances, console yourself by remembering the past. Now you weep, but in former days you laughed. Now you are poor, but you have been rich. You used to quaff a limpid stream of life. Drink with patient endurance this turbid draught. The waters of a river do not look perfectly clear. Our life, as you know, is a river, flowing ceaselessly and covered with waves flowing, one upon the other. Part of the stream has already flowed away; part still follows its course. A portion has just now gushed out of its spring; another is about to do so. All of us are hurrying toward the common sea of death. If we have received good things at the hand of the Lord, should we not receive evil? Do we compel our Judge to provide us always with the same abundance? Do we teach the Lord how He ought to arrange our life? He Himself holds the authority over His own decrees. He directs our affairs as He wills. But He is wise, and He metes out that which is profitable to His servants. Do not curiously examine the Lord's decrees; only love the dispensations of His wisdom. Whatever He may bestow upon you, receive it with gladness. In adversity prove that you are worthy of the joy that was previously yours.'

Thus Job repulsed the Devil's attack and brought upon him the disgrace of total defeat. What happened then? His malady left him as if it had visited him to no avail and had gained no advantage. His flesh regained the health of a second youth.

---

28 *Ibid.*

His life prospered again with all good things and doubled riches flowed in from all sides upon his house. One half consisted of his former wealth, as if he had lost nothing, and the other half represented the reward of patience which is bestowed upon a just man. But why did he receive in double measure houses, mules, camels, sheep, fields, and all the accoutrements of wealth while the number of children born to him remained equal to those who had died? It was because brute beasts and riches of all kinds are completely destroyed when they perish. Children, on the other hand, even if they are dead, live on in the best part of their nature. Therefore, when he was favored by the Creator with other sons and daughters, he possessed this portion of his goods also in double measure—one family abiding with him to give joy to their parents, the other children gone before to await their father.

All of them will stand about Job when the Judge of human life will gather together the universal Church, when the trumpet which is to announce the coming of the King calls loudly to the tombs and demands the bodies which have been entrusted to their charge. Then, they who now appear to be dead will take their place before the Maker of the whole world more quickly than will the living. For this reason, I think, the Lord allotted to Job a double portion of his other wealth, but judged that he would be satisfied with the same number of children as before. Do you see how many blessings the just Job reaped from his patience? You, also, should therefore, bear patiently any harm which may have come to you from yesterday's fire enkindled by a demon's treachery, and alleviate your feelings of distress over your misfortune with more courageous thoughts, in accordance with the words of the Scripture: 'Cast thy care upon the Lord and he shall sustain thee.'[29] To Him is owing glory everlasting. Amen.

29 Ps. 54.23.

ON MERCY AND JUSTICE

BLESS ME, FATHER: Because the world is forgetting God, my brethren, injustice to neighbor and inhumanity to the weak prevail, confirming the words of the holy Apostle: 'As they liked not to have God in their knowledge, God delivered them up to a reprobate sense, to do those things which are not convenient. Being filled with all iniquity, malice, avarice, wickedness, full of envy, murder, contention, deceit, malignity, whisperers, detractors, hateful to God, contumelious, proud, haughty, inventors of evil things, disobedient to parents, foolish, without affection, without mercy.'[1] These sinners God is calling back to His service and He is instructing them to refrain from vice and to be diligent in showing compassion toward their neighbor, as the Prophet Isaias taught, speaking in God's stead: 'Cease to do perversely; learn to do well.'[2] The law contains many injunctions forbidding us to wrong our neighbor and many precepts directing us to be merciful and compassionate. If either of these admonitions be neglected, the other does not by itself justify a man. Benefactions to the needy, financed by unjust gains, are not acceptable with God; yet, a man who refrains from committing injustices, but does not share the goods he possesses with anyone, is not deserving of praise. With reference to the unjust who dare to offer gifts to God, it is written: 'The victims of the wicked are abominable to the Lord';[3] and, regarding the unmerciful: 'He that stoppeth his ear against the cry of the poor, shall also cry himself and shall not

---

1 Rom. 1.28-31.
2 Isa. 1.16-17.
3 Prov. 15.8.

507

be heard.'⁴ Proverbs, therefore, gives us also the admonition: 'Honor the Lord with thy just labors and give him of the first fruits of thy justice.'⁵ If you will make an offering to God from the fruits of injustice and rapine, it would be better not to possess such wealth and not to make an offering. An undefiled gift will carry our prayer to heaven, as it is written: 'the vows of the just are acceptable with him.'⁶ On the other hand, if you have acquired gains from honest toil and do not make offerings to God, whereby the poor may be fed, robbery will be alleged against you, as He says through Malachy: 'First fruits and tithes are in your possession and there will be plunder in your houses.'⁷ You must, therefore, combine justice with mercy, spending in mercy what you possess with justice, as it is written: 'Keep mercy and justice and draw near to thy God always.'⁸ Because God loves mercy and justice, he who takes care to do mercy and justice draws near to God. It remains, then, for each to examine himself and for the rich man to take careful inventory of the private resources from which he is to offer gifts to God, to make sure that he has not oppressed a poor man, or used force against one weaker than himself, or cheated one dependent upon him, thus exercising license rather than justice. We are bidden to practice fairness and justice also toward our slaves. Do not employ force because you are in command and do not take advantage because it is within your power to do so. On the contrary, show forth the deeds of justice because you are able to perform the deeds of power. Your fear of God and your obedience to Him are not exhibited in abstaining from acts which are beyond your competence, but in that, being able

---

4 Prov. 21.13.
5 Prov. 3.9.
6 Prov. 15.8.
7 Mal. 3.8,10 (Septuagint).
8 Osee 12.6.

to transgress the law, you do not transgress it.[9] If you give
alms to the poor after you have despoiled them of their goods,
it were better for you neither to have taken nor given. Why do
you defile the wealth that is rightfully yours by adding unjust
gains to it? Why do you make the gift from injustice which
you are daring to offer an abomination by forming the intention of showing mercy to some other poor man? Be merciful
to the one whom you have wronged. Exercise benevolence
toward him. Show him kindness and you will fulfill the duty
of mercy with justice. God will have no part in avarice nor
will the Lord be a comrade to thieves and robbers. He has
not left us the poor to feed because He is unable to do this,
but He asks from us, for our own good, the fruit of justice
and mercy. Mercy does not spring from injustice, nor blessing
from a curse, nor benefits from tears. God says to those who
draw forth tears from the victims of their injustice: 'that
which I have hated you did; you covered my altar with tears,
with weeping and groaning.'[10] Take pity on the goods you
have acquired by your labors and do not commit injustice
on the pretext of offering your mercy to God—mercy which
was made possible by injustice. This is vainglory and aspiring
to the praises of men, not to the praise which is from God.
Well does the Lord admonish us not to be seen by men.[11] If
you show mercy with God as Witness, you will be sure of not
doing it for selfish gain, since you are aware that this would
not be pleasing to God your Witness. Let us, then, show
mercy that we may receive it from God. But God bestows His
mercy upon those only whom He commends—and He does
not commend an avaricious man. You are not entitled to offer
gifts to God if you offend your brother. 'If thou offer thy gift

9 Eccli. 31.10.
10 Mal. 2.13.
11 Matt. 6.1.

at the altar,' says the Lord, 'and there thou remember that
thy brother hath anything against thee, go first to be reconciled to thy brother; and then, coming thou shalt offer thy
gift.'[12] Remember the publican, Zacheus, who asserted that
he restored fourfold if he committed any fraud and distributed
half of the remainder to the poor.[13] He wished to receive
Christ into his house, you see, and he knew that Christ would
approve of lavish alms to the poor only on condition that
restitution be made for gains unjustly acquired. The Lord,
therefore, commended the uprightness of Zacheus and said:
'This day is salvation come to this house.'[14] So much for those
who fulfill the precept insofar as showing mercy is concerned
but are careless of justice. To the man who refrains from committing injustice, but is negligent in showing mercy, we say:
'every tree that doth not yield fruit shall be cut down and
cast into the fire.'[15] Never will such a tree be pleasing to the
divine Husbandman who declared that He came seeking fruit
on the fig tree and found none and who ordered it to be cut
down that it might not cumber the ground.[16] It appears, also,
that one who does not give back his pledge to a poor man
stands condemned with God, for the following threat is directed against such a one: 'He who does not receive back his
pledge will cry to me,' says the Lord, 'and I will hear him
because I am compassionate.'[17] [Of old,] it was wicked and
unlawful to gather the sheaves left after the harvest, or to
glean the vines after the vintage, or to gather up the olives
that remain after the trees were picked, because these things
were to be left for the poor.[18] Now, if this was commanded

12 Matt. 5.23.24.
13 Luke 19.8.
14 Luke 19.9.
15 Matt. 3.10.
16 Luke 13.7.
17 Exod. 22.27.
22 Luke 6.38.
18 Deut. 24.19-21.

those who were under the Law, what shall we say of those who are in Christ? To them the Lord says: 'Unless your justice abound more than that of the scribes and Pharisees, you shall not enter into the kingdom of heaven.'[19] For this reason does the Apostle exhort us to share with the needy, not only the produce of our fields, and our profits, but also the work of our hands. 'Working with your hands,' he says, 'the thing which is good, that you may have something to give to him that suffereth need.'[20] And the Lord bids whoever would come after Him to sell all his possessions on behalf of the poor and then to follow Him.[21] Upon those who are already His followers and upon the perfect, however, He enjoins the accomplishment of the duty of charity in a perfect and unrestricted manner, so that, having fulfilled the ministry as regards worldly goods, they may pass on to the ministry of the reason and the spirit. From others, moreover, He requires a continual sharing and communicating of that which they possess, that, by showing mercy, sharing their goods, and conferring benefits, they may reproduce in themselves the benevolence of God. 'Give,' He says, 'and it shall be given to you.'[22] Furthermore, He has promised that if they practice these virtues, they will be united with Him. These, indeed, are they who will stand at the right hand of the Lord. To them the King will say at His coming: 'Come, blessed of my Father, possess you the kingdom prepared for you from the foundation of the world. For I was hungry and you gave me to eat; I was thirsty and you gave me to drink. I was naked and you covered me, a stranger, and you took me in, sick and in prison and you came to me.' And when the just wonder and say: 'When did we do these things to you, Lord?' He will

---

19 Matt. 5.20.
20 Eph. 4.28.
21 Matt. 19.21.

answer: 'Amen, amen, I say to you, as long as you did it to one of these, my least brethren, you did it to me.'[23] Ready kindness shown to the saints is piety toward Christ and he who ministers zealously to the poor man becomes a comrade of Christ—not only if he be rich and shares great possessions, but even if he offers to the needy the little that he has, although it be merely a cup of cold water which he gives a disciple to drink in the name of a disciple.[24] The neediness of the disciples which to the worldling is poverty is a source of true riches to you, O man of wealth, for you become thereby a co-worker with Christ. You nourish the soldiers of Christ, and this, not under compulsion but willingly. The kingdom of heaven does not employ force, nor does it exact tribute, but it welcomes those who freely offer their goods, so that, in giving them away, they may receive and may be honored in bestowing honor, and that, in sharing their temporal possessions, they may become partakers in eternal blessings. These thoughts let us ever keep in mind and before the eyes of our soul, that, when an opportunity offers, we may not pass it by and lose the present occasion in awaiting another; for, while we are thus waiting and postponing, we might be overtaken by death. The Lord make us fruitful, vigilant, and mindful of His commandments and grant that at His glorious coming we may be found ready and free from all impediment, in Christ our God, to whom with the Father and the Holy Spirit be glory, empire, and honor now and always and forever and ever. Amen.

23 Matt. 25.34-40.
24 Matt. 10.42.

INDEX

INDEX